CONIECTANEA BIBLICA • New Testament Series 20

Lilian Portefaix

Sisters Rejoice

Paul's Letter to the Philippians and Luke-Acts as Seen by
First-century Philippian Women

ALMQVIST & WIKSELL INTERNATIONAL

BS
2705.2
.P6
1988

ABSTRACT

Portefaix, L., 1988. Sisters Rejoice. Paul's Letter to the Philippians and Luke-Acts as Seen by First-century Philippian women. **Coniectanea Biblica. New Testament Series 20.** 280 pp. Uppsala. ISBN 91-22-01201-X.

The purpose of the present study, based on the 'reception theory' of literary texts held by W. Iser and H.R. Jauss, is to achieve as valid as possible a reconstruction of first-century women's understanding of the Christian message. These women are thought to have had little knowledge or experience of Judaism.

To this end Philippi has been chosen as providing a suitable setting for a case study which aims at the recreation of the historical recipients of Paul's letter and Luke-Acts (particularly Acts 16: 11-40). Consequently, Philippian women's socio-cultural and religious backgrounds have been reconstructed from surviving archaeological, epigraphical and literary sources. While Philippian women shared the same socio-cultural background, their religious referential frameworks differed: the latter were formed either by their previous pagan worship or by their Christian education and experience.

By means of an audience-orientated reading of the New Testament texts as received by these women, the following general conclusions are reached:
(1) Paul's initial audience consisted of women who had been converted to Christianity within the first decade after his first visit to the town. These women shared a pagan referential framework. The concepts of 'celestial citizenship' and 'servitude' became key words for their understanding of the letter. Although they were acquainted with these concepts from their pagan background the connection between the two and the moral implications inherent in the idea that taking on the suffering of a deity would open the way to a blessed after-life were alien to them. The 'imitatio Christi' placed their lives in a cosmic setting and gave their sufferings a hitherto unknown meaning.
(2) Luke-Acts was received by two different audiences. One consisted of newly-converted and pagan women with little or no experience of Christian life and the other of women who had been born into Christianity.

For the first Luke's message was seen as referring to an earthly Utopia illustrated by his account of the early church in Jerusalem. They saw the Philippian episode (Acts 16: 11-40) as an introduction by Paul of a new Dionysus into the colony—a Dionysus who would prove himself to be stronger than all other deities and above the Roman Empire.

The second audience saw Luke-Acts as a 'picture-book' illustrating their Christian upbringing. To them Luke's account of the early church pointed to their coming participation in the citizenship of Heaven and his female characters became models for Christian behaviour: of these Lydia was the most important to Christian women.

This book throws light on the manifold interpretations of the New Testament which were attributable to the variety of the religious referential frameworks of the audiences. Where a knowledge of Judaism was lacking and the leavening influence of that tradition was absent, the disparity of interpretation was greatest.

Lilian Portefaix. Department of Theology, Uppsala University, Box 1604, S-751 46 Uppsala, Sweden.

© 1988 Lilian Portefaix
Distributor: Almqvist & Wiksell International, Stockholm
ISBN 91-22-01201-X
Printed by Tryckkontakt, Uppsala

**Dedicated
to all the brethren**

CONTENTS

Part I
Philippian Women's Social and Religious backgrounds

0 GENERAL INTRODUCTION	3
0.1 The Problem and the Task	3
0.2 Method and Course of the Study	5
1 FEMALE EXISTENCE	9
1.1 Introduction	9
1.2 Woman's Chance of Survival	10
1.2.1 Exposure of Children	10
1.2.2 Infant Mortality	11
1.2.3 Adult Mortality	13
1.3 Family Relationships	15
1.3.1 The Ideal Roman Family	15
1.3.2 'Broken Homes'	17
1.3.2.1 Nurses and Stepmothers	19
1.3.2.2 The Status of Children	21
1.4 Summary	22
1.5 Excursus	23
1.5.1 Woman's Means of Support	23
1.5.1.1 Wives	23
1.5.1.2 Concubines	26
1.5.1.3 Courtezans	27
1.5.2 Attitudes towards Marriage	28
1.5.3 Summary	31
2 RELIGION AND FEMALE EXISTENCE	33
2.1 Introduction	33
2.2 Religious Practices Associated with Childhood	33
2.2.1 Learning Religion	33
2.2.1.1 By Listening	34
2.2.1.2 By Observing	36
2.2.1.3 By Acting	40
2.3 Religious Roles of Adult Women	43
2.3.1 'Sacra Privata'	43
2.3.1.1 Worship of the Household Deities	44
2.3.1.2 Family Celebrations	46
2.3.1.2.1 Weddings	46
2.3.1.2.2 Death and Burial	47
2.3.2 'Sacra Publica'	48
2.3.2.1 The Role of Worshipper	48

	2.3.2.2 The Role of Priestess	50
	2.3.3 Woman and Mystery Religions	50
	2.3.3.1 The Attraction of Mystery Religions	51
	2.3.3.2 Husbands' Attitudes	53
	2.3.4 Woman and 'Folk-Religion'	55
	2.3.4.1 The role of Priestess	56
	2.3.4.2 The role of Sorceress	56
2.4	Summary	58
3	**PHILIPPI AT THE TIME OF THE RISE OF CHRISTIANITY**	**59**
3.1	Introduction	59
3.2	History	59
3.3	Physical Features	61
3.4	Town and Countryside	62
	3.4.1 The town	62
	3.4.1.1 Buildings	62
	3.4.1.2 Burial places	64
	3.4.1.3 Adminstration	64
	3.4.2 The Countryside	65
	3.4.3 Communications	66
3.5	Population	67
3.6	Language and Culture	68
	3.6.1 Latin	68
	3.6.2 Greek	68
3.7	Religious Features	70
	3.7.1 The Town	71
	3.7.1.1 South of the Via Egnatia	71
	3.7.1.2 North of the Via Egnatia	71
	3.7.1.3 Outside the Town Wall	73
	3.7.2 The Countryside	73
3.8	Summary	74
4	**DEITIES OF IMPORTANCE TO WOMEN IN PHILIPPI**	**75**
4.1	Introduction	75
4.2	DIANA	75
	4.2.1 Historical Background	75
	4.2.2 The Importance of the Hunting Goddess	78
	4.2.2.1 Hecate as Pictured by Hesiod	80
	4.2.2.2 Diana in the Philippian Inscriptions	81
	4.2.2.2.1 Goddess of Healing	81
	4.2.2.2.2 Goddess of the Underworld	82
	4.2.2.3 Diana in the Philippian Rock Carvings	84
	4.2.2.3.1 Julia's Stele in Mesembria	88
	4.2.2.3.2 Aelia Procula's Altar in Rome	91
	4.2.2.3.3 Ariste's Epitaph in Podmol	93

4.2.2.4 Diana–the 'Ideal Woman'	94
4.2.3 Summary	95
4.2.4 Excursus: Archaeological Evidence of Woman Piety	96
4.3 DIONYSUS	98
4.3.1 Historical Background	98
4.3.2 The Importance of Dionysus	99
4.3.2.1 Women in the Dionysiac Ecstatic Cult	100
4.3.2.1.1 The Philippian Inscriptions	100
4.3.2.1.2 Ecstatic Women in Literature	101
4.3.2.2 Philippian Women in Dionysiac Mysteries	104
4.3.2.3 Identification with Mythical Figures	104
4.3.2.3.1 Ariadne	107
4.3.2.3.2 Semele	109
4.3.2.3.3 Eurydice	110
4.3.2.3.4 Alcestis	110
4.3.2.3.5 The Infant Dionysus	112
4.3.3 Summary	113
4.4 ISIS	114
4.4.1 Historical Background	114
4.4.2 The Importance of Isis	116
4.4.2.1 A Healing Goddess	117
4.4.2.2 A Protectress of Married Women	119
4.4.2.3 The Myth: Ideal Wife and Mother	121
4.4.2.3.1 The Ideal Wife	122
4.4.2.3.2 The Ideal mother	123
4.4.2.3.3 Identification with the Mourning Goddess	124
4.4.3 Summary	126
4.5 Concluding Remarks	127

Part II
The New Testament Texts as Received by Philippian Women

5 METHODOLOGICAL REMARKS	131
6 PAUL'S LETTER FROM A FIRST-CENTURY PHILIPPIAN FEMALE POINT OF VIEW	135
6.1 Introduction	135
6.2 The Audience	137
6.3 The Philippian Church–a Celestial Colony	138
6.3.1 The Battle for Christianity	140
6.4 The Ruler of the Celestial Colony	141
6.4.1 Christ as the Model Figure of Servitude	143
6.4.1.1 Joy in Suffering	145
6.4.2 Christ –the Absolute Ruler of the Cosmos	147

6.5 The Celestial Citizenship Ultimately Realized	149
6.6 Summary	152
6.7 Excursus: Uranopolis–a 'City of Heaven'	153

7 LUKE-ACTS AS RECEIVED BY FIRST-CENTURY PHILIPPIAN WOMEN — 155

7.1 Introduction	155
7.2 Luke's Philippian Audiences	157
7.3 Luke-Acts as Seen from a Social Point of View	158
7.3.1 Women of All Classes	158
7.3.2 Female Existence	160
7.4 Luke-Acts as Seen from a Religious Point of View	161
7.4.1 A Pagan and Newly-Converted Christian Audience	161
7.4.1.1 The Lukan Jesus	162
7.4.1.2 The Spirit and the Early Church in Jerusalem	164
7.4.2 A Second-Generation Christian Audience	165
7.4.2.1 Women's Roles in the Early Church	167
7.5 The Philippian Episode (Acts 16: 11-40)	169
7.5.1 A Pagan and Newly-Converted Philippian Audience	169
7.5.2 A Second-Generation Christian Audience	171
7.6 Summary	172

8 PAGAN PHILIPPIAN WOMEN AND CHRISTIANITY — 175

8.1 Introduction	175
8.2 The Appeal of the Pagan Cults and of Christianity	176
8.2.1 The Appeal of Pagan Philippian Cults	176
8.2.2 The Appeal of Christianity	177
8.2.2.1 The First-Generation	178
8.2.2.2 The Second-Generation	180
8.3 Christianity in the Life of a Philippian Wife	183
8.3.1 Congregational Christian Worship	185
8.3.2 Private Worship inside a Christian Household	185
8.3.2.1 Praying	186
8.3.2.2 Teaching	187
8.3.2.3 Charitable work	188
8.3.3 Reasons for Conflict with the Pagan Environment	189
8.3.3.1 The Imputed Immorality of Christians	189
8.3.3.2 Fear of the 'Name'	190
8.3.3.3 Fear of the 'Kingdom'	191
8.3.4 Private Christian Worship inside a Pagan Household	192
8.3.4.1 Reasons for Conflict in a 'Mixed Marriage'	193
8.3.4.1.1 Christian Education of Children	193
8.3.4.1.2 Money Spent on Charity	194
8.3.4.2 A Christian Wife's Endurance in a Pagan Family	195
8.3.4.2.1 Suffering as a Part of Christian Life	196

	8.3.4.2.2 The Transience of Suffering	197
	8.3.4.2.3 Converting the Family	197
	8.3.4.2.4 Share in the Fellowship of Christian Sisters	198
8.4	Summary	199

9 EPILOGUE 201

List of dates	203
Abbreviations	206
Bibliography – Texts and translations	209
Bibliography – Literature	221
Author index	243
Greek and Latin References	247

MAPS
Map 1 Macedonia and adjacent areas	XV
Map 2 Philippi–Colonia Augusta Julia Philippensis	XVII
Map 3 The town of Philippi	XIX

FIGURES
Fig. 1. The Philippian hunting goddess	79
Fig. 2. The Philippian hunting goddess and a female figure	83
Fig. 3. Stele from the eastern part of the archipelago	85
Fig. 4. Stele from Mesembria	87
Fig. 5. Grave altar from Rome	91
Fig. 6. Epitaph from Podmol	93

Map 1. Macedonia and Adjacent Areas

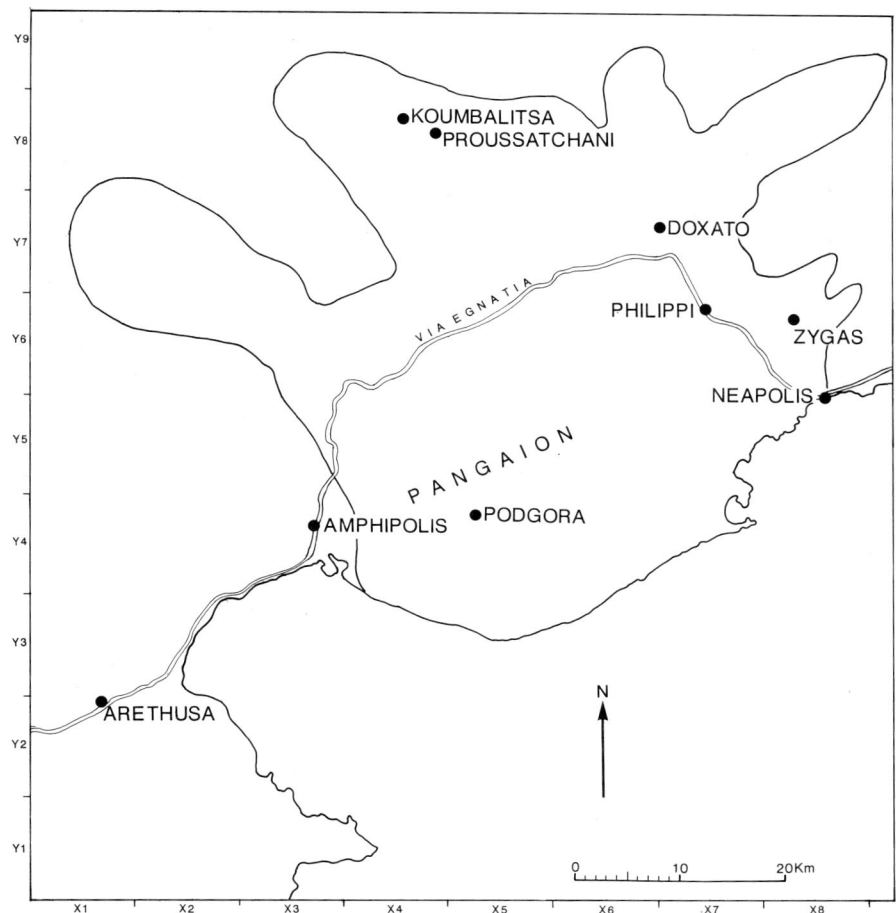

Map 2 Philippi–Colonia Augusta Iulia Philippensis (42 B.C. - A.D. 330)
(Based on Lazarides 1973, Fig. 8)

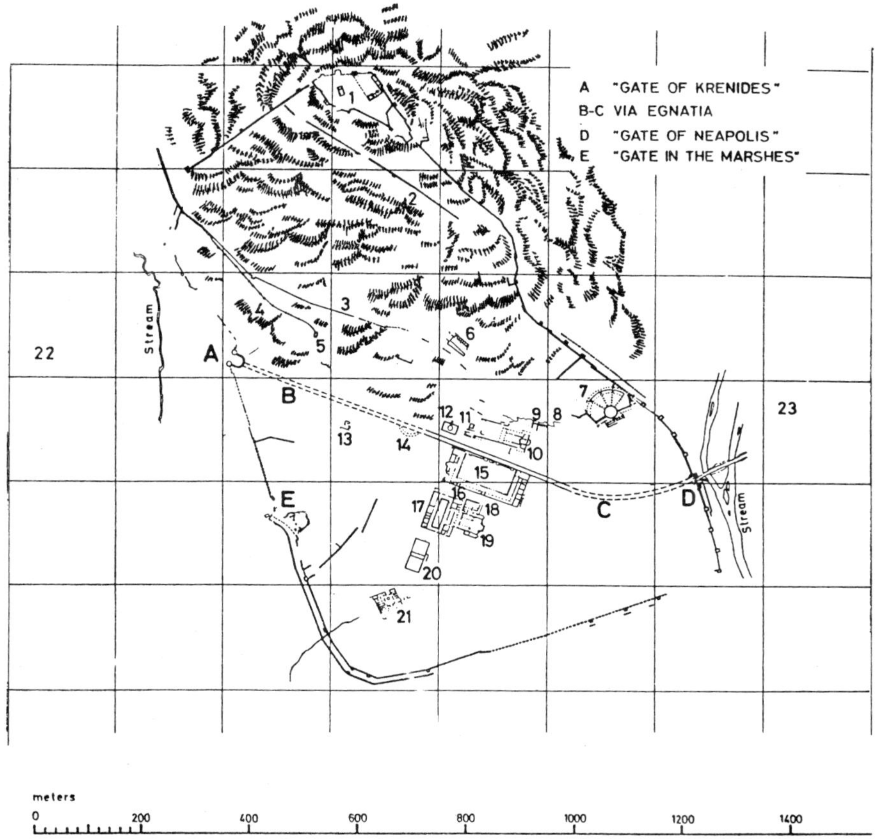

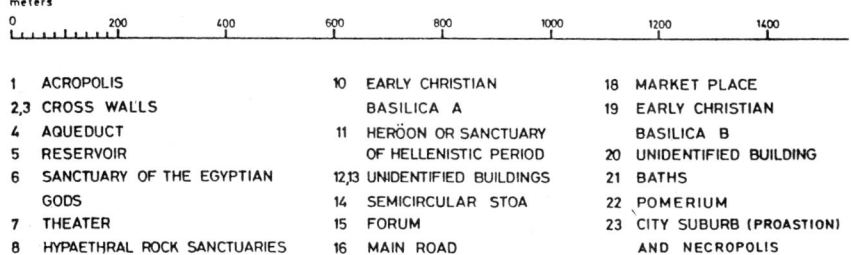

1	ACROPOLIS	10	EARLY CHRISTIAN	18	MARKET PLACE
2,3	CROSS WALLS		BASILICA A	19	EARLY CHRISTIAN
4	AQUEDUCT	11	HERÖON OR SANCTUARY		BASILICA B
5	RESERVOIR		OF HELLENISTIC PERIOD	20	UNIDENTIFIED BUILDING
6	SANCTUARY OF THE EGYPTIAN	12,13	UNIDENTIFIED BUILDINGS	21	BATHS
	GODS	14	SEMICIRCULAR STOA	22	POMERIUM
7	THEATER	15	FORUM	23	CITY SUBURB (PROASTION)
8	HYPAETHRAL ROCK SANCTUARIES	16	MAIN ROAD		AND NECROPOLIS
9	SANCTUARY OF SILVANUS	17	PALAISTRA		

Map 3 The Town of Philippi (356 B.C. - 10th Cent. A.D.) (Based on Lazarides 1973, Fig. 9)

PART I

PHILIPPIAN WOMEN'S SOCIAL AND RELIGIOUS BACKGROUNDS

0 GENERAL INTRODUCTION

0.1 THE PROBLEM AND THE TASK

The main purpose of this study is to elucidate how first-century Philippian women, converted or born into Christianity with no direct personal knowledge and experience of Judaism, received the gospel according to their differing socio-cultural and religious backgrounds. To the reader this approach to the New Testament text may appear as a revival of the long-buried corpse of the 'history-of-religions school' currently favoured by the flourishing spirit of the feminist movement and by the trend towards audience-orientated literary criticism. These three methods of research have indeed been my sources of inspiration even if my modus operandi differs from those usually applied by scholars who adopt these alternative perspectives.

As is well known, the 'history-of-religions school' took upon itself the task of reconstructing the religious environment of early Christianity in order to identify the part played by the pagan cults as well as the influence of Judaism.[1] At the same time the search for the roots of Christianity brought the authors of the *New Testament* under close scrutiny; it also brought in its train a male perspective since no part of the *New Testament* was written by women and biblical scholarship has been predominantly undertaken by men.[2]

Focusing on the author of a document has traditionally been the common view point in analyzing literary texts,[3] but within the last twenty years scholarly literary criticism has became directed more and more towards the receivers of a text.[4] This audience-orientated approach has been applied to the *New Testament* during the last few years,[5] and has dealt particularly with various kinds of 'implied readers' safely contained within the text.[6] The literary convention in antiquity, however, was to address a male audience, though women could assuredly be said to be subsumed under this form of address.[7] (Paul is unusual in his

---

[1] Kümmel 1970, 206ff.

[2] E. Schüssler Fiorenza (1984) points to the strong dominance of the male perspective in biblical interpretation. Cf. n. 9 infra.

[3] B. C. Lategan (1974) gives a useful survey of current issues in the hermeneutical debate.

[4] Lategan 1984, 4.

[5] *Semeia* (31, 1985) discusses different reader response approaches to biblical and secular texts.

[6] Lategan 1984, 4; Fowler 1985, 5-23.

[7] Cf. 7.1, p. 155 n. 4.

letters, when he explicitly directs his words towards women.[8]) The convention of addressing the male section of a community encourages promotion of the male perspective on the part of those who prefer to ignore the female element of an audience. My brief goes beyond that of determining the nature of the overall intended audience: it focuses attention upon contemporary women who were possibly brought into contact with the contents of the *New Testament*. A recreation of these women is, however, impossible without recourse to historical sources of various kinds outside biblical texts, but by consulting these sources and adding the information they provide to the slender information to be gleaned from the *New Testament* itself a broader understanding of the Christian message as received by these women is obtained. In taking this course I may well be charged with idiosyncratic behaviour, and I am fully aware of the problems of subjectivity inherent in my method, but an explanation of my apparently arbitrary choice of methodology should convince potential critics of the necessity for it.

First of all, the question why women converted to Christianity and the roles they played in the early church have never—as far as I know—been closely examined against a pagan background; women's position in the community has hitherto been treated in general terms from a theological and philosophical perspective derived strictly from textual sources and seen within the context of a Jewish conceptual framework.[9] However, the starting-point for women's religious needs must be seen as rooted in their living conditions, and it is only by comparing the pagan cults with Christianity[10] that the superior ability of the latter to satisfy these needs becomes evident and explains why women were converted.

Secondly, Judaism has for a long time been regarded as the main source for an understanding of the background of early Christianity.[11] Although Judaism was widespread and well known throughout the Roman Empire,[12] and New Testament authors suggest some knowledge

---

[8] For instance, Phil. 4: 2.

[9] A number of reliable studies of this kind have been made in the last few years of which only a few can be mentioned. *'Freunde in Christus werden . . .'* (Scharffenorth1977) has a section by K. Thraede dealing with the relationship between male and female in the early church. D. Balch (1981) traces particularly the philosophical background to the recommended submissiveness of females in the domestic code in 1 Peter. *'Die Frau im Urchristentum'* (Dautzenberg 1983), a collection of exegetical essays from a feminist perspective, can further be mentioned. The latter, however, has been criticised by E. Schüssler Fiorenza (1984, 94f) as having been written from a male point of view and of being in reality 'an attack on a feminist critical hermeneutics' [- - -] locating 'women's historical role [. . .] at the margin of socio-ecclesial relations'. Her own writings, stressing the feminist perspective, exemplifies this kind of New Testament woman studied from the macro-perspective. For references on the subject, see the bibliography edited by R. S. Kraemer (1983, 127-139).

[10] Such a comparison in a broad perspective has been made by A. D. Nock (1933) between the pagan cults and Christianity.

[11] Kümmel 1970, 245ff.

[12] Köster 1980, 227ff.

of Judaism among Christian converts,[13] there must have been groups confronted with Christianity who had a pagan background and who had no acquaintance with Judaism.

Thirdly, as emphasized above, the New Testament text has, up to now, been examined chiefly from the view point of its authors, and questions about the circumstances of these authors and what audiences they addressed have been of primary interest to scholars. I, on the contrary, intend to concentrate upon the female members of that audience and to throw light upon their understanding of the text rather than upon the intention of the writers.

0.2 METHOD AND COURSE OF THE STUDY

An understanding of the New Testament text as seen through the eyes of the recipients necessitates a reconstruction of their various backgrounds from surviving archaeological, epigraphical and literary sources. Although this approach seems to revive the methods of the 'history-of-religions school', I am going to the work from other perspectives than those taken by my forerunners. My reconstruction of the same environment has the purpose not to trace the roots of Christianity but to investigate how it was understood by a pagan audience. Furthermore, instead of studying the confrontation of Christianity with the Graeco-Roman cults from a bird's eye view—an angle adopted by the 'history-of-religions school'[14] and by feminist scholars[15]—I confine my investigation to one place only. A close-up picture of events seen obliquely from underneath emerges and is made up from all available sources. The resulting construct can safely be regarded as faithful to the lives of the women examined and avoids the sweeping generalizations which so often result from research covering too wide a field for want of adequate sources.

For my investigation I have chosen Philippi as a suitable subject for a case study for the following reasons:

(a) The town has been excavated since the middle of the nineteenth century.

(b) Two New Testament texts of various genres (Paul's letter to the Philippians and Acts 16: 11-40) as well as Polycarp's letter are connected with the early Philippian church and all call attention to women.

---

[13] This is evident inter alia from the many references to Old Testament scriptures in Paul's letters (Vielhauer 1978, 68f). Cf. n. 17 infra.

[14] Kümmel 1970, 206ff.

[15] Cf. n. 9 supra. Except for a brief study about the women in the Philippian church (Abrahamsen 1987), a purely feminist'perspective, dealing with women in the early church, has hitherto, as far as I know, never been attached to a case study located to an appointed place, based on all kinds of available sources. Neither G. Theissen's (1977 and 1979) nor P. Lampe's (1987) sociological studies stresses particularly the female aspect.

(c) In Philippi I am brought face to face with women characterized by an almost unmixed pagan religious background since no archaeological or epigraphical traces of Judaism have been found within the colony. On the other hand, Paul's attack on the Jews (or at any rate on some sort of Judaizing tendencies) in his letter to the Philippians (3: 2-3) points at least to the presence of Jewish influence within the colony;[16] the lack of epigraphical and archaeological traces, however, indicates that such factors might have been on a small scale,[17] and, accordingly, have been of slight importance to the religious conceptual framework of Philippian women.

However, even when focusing on one place only, it is difficult to give a satisfying account of women's lives at a certain period because of the lack of continuity in the excavated material. Therefore, Philippian sources from earlier and later periods as well as from other places within the same area are used to make up the picture of the women converting to the first and second-generation Philippian church.

As for the religious aspects, mythical stories relating to the cults which were of importance to those women, and particularly those myths which, even though not mentioned in the Philippian sources, were thought to have had their origin in the area, are suggested to have been well known to them as a part of their religious setting. For the same reason, the cults in question are treated separately even if, in reality, some sort of syncretism, impossible to trace in the sources, made up the religious features of individuals. In the inscriptions the deities are mentioned singly but the religious world of the individual was characterized by the worship of several deities at the same time.[18]

Furthermore, Philippian women's living conditions cannot be reconstructed solely from the sparse Philippian evidence. To supplement this deficiency I have consulted other sources which throw light upon woman's chance of survival. These include family relationships of females in the Roman Empire and have implications which shed light on female life in Philippi. Medical and legal sources, however, produce a reliable but one-sided negative picture of women's conditions (irrespective of class) and are based on enumerations of law-suits and accounts of diseases. This information does not tell us to what extent these calamities affected their lives in reality. I therefore include surviving inscriptions from various areas in order to give information on the life span of females and also to illustrate the daily life of the average woman. Sometimes these facts are corroborated by statements given in literature.

The first part of this book concentrates on the socio-cultural (Chapter 1 and 3) and religious (Chapter 2 and 4) backgrounds of Philippian women. The second part, which is opened by some methodological remarks on the perspective of audience (Chapter 5), confronts the New

---

[16] Gnilka 1980a, 211ff.

[17] In this respect, it is remarkable that Paul's letter to the Philippian lacks any scriptural citations (Johnson 1986, 340).

[18] This fact may be exemplified for instance by the Greek magical papyri where a countless number of deities is enumerated at the same time.

Testament texts in question with these backgrounds, and the texts are read through the filter which is thus provided. The impact of Paul's letter upon the Philippian women he addressed will be considered in the light of the pagan beliefs they had so recently held (Chapter 6). In respect of Luke, his double-work—and particularly the passage on Philippi in Acts (16: 11-40)—will initially be treated in the same way. It will further be re-examined through the consciousness of women of the next generation, whose pagan referential framework had crumbled and to whom Christianity had become familiar through repeated public readings of Paul's letter as a part of their Christian education and whose roles within the Philippian church are defined by Polycarp's letter (Chapter 7). In the concluding Chapter 8, not only the reasons for Philippian women's conversion to Christianity, but also the problems associated with their change of religion will be considered against their socio-cultural and religious backgrounds. Finally, my excursuses deal with a few topics which in some way or other are related to the main subject but which do not bear directly upon it.

1 FEMALE EXISTENCE

1.1 INTRODUCTION

In antiquity, rites and worship were fundamental to women's living conditions, and there are reasons to assume that women were the chief exponents of religion.[1] Regardless of her social position, the length of a woman's life was to a great extent determined by the high mortality rate associated with childbirth.[2] The paradox inherent in the female role, where the bringing forth of new life often resulted in death,[3] may well have accounted for woman's interest in, and her need for, religion. Furthermore, both as a child and as an adult she was often the victim of a social structure which gave the male legal power over the family unit[4]–a fact which affected woman's fate in various ways. The role of woman in these aspects, therefore, provides the basis of the discussion of this investigation, with medical, legal and social matters being brought into close focus.

In this chapter woman's chance of survival (1.2) and the changes in the family pattern taking place in the Augustan age (1.3) will be

---

[1] Cf. Strab. 297, quoted in p. 55.

[2] According to Finley (1968, 137f), early death was inevitable in all strata of society: 'In all classes there was one inescapable condition, and that was the high probability of early death. On a rough calculation, of the population of the Roman Empire which succeeded in reaching the age of fifteen (that is, which survived the heavy mortality of infancy and childhood), more than half of the women were dead before forty, and in some classes and areas, even before thirty-five. Women were very much worse off than men in this respect, partly because of the perils of childbirth, partly, in the lower classes, because of the risk of sheer exhaustion. Thus, in one family tomb in regular use in the 2nd and 3rd cent., sixty-eight wives were buried by their husbands and only forty-one husbands by their wives'.

[3] The idea of a close connection between marriage and death is expressed by Artemidorus (2, 49): 'For both marriage and death are considered to be critical points in a man's life, and one is always represented by the other.' (Transl. R. J. White).

[4] Except for the Vestal Virgins, all Roman women were originally legally dependent on a male tutor; authority to act had to be obtained from a father, a husband or from a male relative in the paternal line (Gardner 1986, 14). Augustus' social legislation, however, released some women from the necessity of having a tutor ('ius liberorum'): freeborn women who had three children and freedwomen who had four (after manumission) could apply through an official to get permission to act in their own right ('sui iuris') (Gardner 1986, 20). In this respect it must be remembered that in reality the legal freedom of a married woman was dependent on her relationship with her husband. It can be assumed that a wife in a good marriage had no real need to apply for this legal privilege.

discussed, and, finally, women's means of support and attitudes towards marriage will be elucidated in an excursus (1.5). In dealing with these topics it would have been desirable to give a specific picture of Philippian life in the 1st cent. A.D., but information on everyday life in the colony is unfortunately too incomplete for an investigation of that kind. Instead, I am going to concentrate on the living conditions of women throughout the Roman Empire, paying particular attention to their legal status and the availability of medical help for them. In this general survey I assume the women of Philippi to be included. Since Philippi became a Roman colony in 42 B.C. and to a great extent was dominated by Roman culture at that time (3.6.1), I give preference to Roman sources. In cases where it can be suggested that circumstances remained unchanged, sources from other periods and areas are referred to.

1.2 WOMAN'S CHANCE OF SURVIVAL

1.2.1 Exposure of Children

At the birth of a girl her coming fate was determined by the midwife and by the paterfamilias, both of whom had in different ways the authority to decide upon life or death for a newborn child. It was the task of the midwife to examine the child to assess its physical condition.[5] In those cases where she discovered deformity or obvious weakness the law ordained that the child, whatever its sex, should immediately be killed.[6] If the midwife found a girl capable of survival it was left to the father to determine whether she should be kept in the family or not.[7] When a girl

---

[5] Soran. Gyn. 2, 6, 10.

[6] XII Tabl. 4; Cic.Leg. 3, 19. According to Seneca weak and deformed children ('debiles monstrosique') were usually drowned (Sen. De ir. 1, 15, 2) (Delcourt 1938, 36). However, medical writings mention that Greek and Roman surgeons carried out operations on deformed children (Peiper 1951, 12f), which indicates that rich fathers might have sought medical advice in order to save a condemned child. The reason for a child to be misshapen was attributed to the mental condition of the mother at the child's conception. According to Soranus (Gyn. 1, 10, 38), the prominent gynaecologist, she should not be under the influence of wine when having sexual intercourse, as the alcohol might have a detrimental effect by inducing fantasies which could cause pathological changes in the foetus. As a warning example Soranus says (Gyn. 1, 10, 39) that women who had seen monkeys in their fantasies during intercourse might produce babies similar in appearance to those creatures.

[7] Gai. Inst. 1, 55. According to the old Royal Law all sons had to be brought up, but only the first-born daughter (Dion. Hal. Ant.Rom. 2, 15). Remarkably enough, this law was not revised by the Augustan matrimonial laws, which aimed at an overall increase in the population. Cf. n. 64 infra.

was rejected,[8] it was not, however, a matter of killing her,[9] as was the fate of deformed children.[10] The fact is that the unwanted girls were sold or exposed[11] in much-frequented places in the hope of their being rescued, either for mercy[12] or greed.[13] A girl might prove a financial asset as a servant to an innkeeper or the hostess of a brothel,[14] for instance.

1.2.2 Infant Mortality

The first days were looked upon as particularly crucial in regard to the survival of a child,[15] since infant mortality was high and many children died before they were a year old.[16] This fact was reflected in the law governing the mourning of relatives; ritual mourning of a child less than a year old was prohibited.[17] This suggests that the death of a baby

---

[8] Economic considerations were of vital importance when a decision had to be made. Poor families had to limit the numbers of daughters (Plut. Mor. 497E), bearing in mind that the dowry was a severe financial charge on the family (cf. Dion. Hal. Ant.Rom. 9, 51, 6). Rich fathers, however, often decided against bringing up several daughters, since they did not like to divide up the property of the family (Mus. Ruf. XV B, 119). Suspicions about illegitimate birth could also cause the exposure of a child (Suet. Claud.27).

[9] According to D. Engels (1980, 112ff), infant mortality was so great that the practice of female infanticide in antiquity rarely needed to be put into operation.

[10] See n. 6 supra.

[11] Diocletian forbade the exposure and sale of unwanted children in A.D. 374 (Watts 1973, 91 n. 14).

[12] These children could be taken care of by rich and childless couples (Juv.6, 602ff.; Suet. Gram. 7, 21) and from inscriptions we learn of the gratitude and affection such children felt towards their foster-parents (Balsdon 1969, 87).

[13] Seneca the Elder (Controv. 10, 4, 17), in one of his rhetorical exercises, accuses a man of having rescued a couple of children whom he subsequently mutilated in order to use them as beggars. Even if this is a fictitious example it reflects the dangers inherent in the position of the foundlings.

[14] Plautus gives us examples of such servants in the characters he portrays in *Casina* and *Cistellaria*. The complications implicit in the exposed child's situation provided material for other comedy writers of the day. Terentius exploits the same theme in *Hautontimorumenos*. Such preoccupations with this theme were peculiarly Greek and Roman authors, as the practice of disposing of unwanted children seems to have been unknown in many parts of the world: the Egyptians and the Jews (Strab. 824; Tac. Hist. 5, 5) are said to have retained all children born to their peoples. D. Redford (1967) gives a survey of 'the exposed child' as a motif in literature.

[15] It was not named until it was at least a week old (Arist. Hist. An. 588a, 3-10).

[16] Comparative evidence suggests that more than a quarter (28%) of all live-born Roman babies died within their first year of life, according to demographic assumptions based on an average expectation of life at birth of 25 years (Hopkins 1983, 225).

[17] FIRA, Vol. 3, 19 (=Plut.Vit.Num.12) (Hopkins 1983, 225 n. 32).

was too common an occurrence for it to be an object of the customary funeral rites.[18] As to illnesses which caused death to babies,[19] it was also recognized that defective hygienic condition[20] (particularly common in the tenement houses of the town[21]) contributed to infant mortality. Many babies must have died in consequence of infectious diseases, which medical science at that time had no hope of curing.[22]

Even after a child's first birthday life remained hazardous for it.[23] Recognition of this fact can be observed in that section of the above-mentioned law which prescribed that a child younger than three years must not be mourned more than 'by halves'.[24] The high death-rate of children is further mirrored in the Augustan matrimonial laws, which enacted that married couples must produce three children. If, however, two of the three failed to survive (as was often the case), the parents were considered to have fulfilled their legal obligations.[25]

Probably girls were more liable to diseases of malnutrition than boys, since the latter were given better food and in larger quantities than their sisters.[26] According to the author of the Hippocratic treatise *De octimestri partu*,[27] girls reached puberty more quickly than boys but they became prematurely old since their bodies were weakened by inadequate diet. Finally, archaeologists have noticed that the bones from women and infants are often difficult to identify in osteological remains, a fact which can be directly attributed to defiencies in the diet of young females.[28]

---

[18] Only 1.3% of 279 tombstones commemorate infants. The proportion of the sexes is 179 boys to 100 girls (Hopkins 1983, 225). According to the elder Pliny, children who had not yet got their teeth were not cremated (Pliny HN. 7, 16, 72).

[19] Hack 1913.

[20] Soranus (Gyn. 2, 10, 16) prescribed that babies should be kept clean. He advocated frequent changing of the bottom sheets on their beds, and in addition, advised that mosquito nets should be put up.

[21] It might not have been possible to nurse a baby properly if one had a long journey to the well and in addition had to carry water to the top floor of an apartment house. See 3.4.1.1, p. 64 n. 48.

[22] Finley 1981, 157.

[23] Hippocrates (Aph. 3, 24-28) enumerates diseases common to children at different ages.

[24] FIRA, Vol. 2, 321. According to another law children over three years of age should be mourned one month for each year of life until their tenth year; then the prescribed period for adults (10 months) should be observed (FIRA, Vol. 3, 19 = Plut.Vit.Num.12).

[25] FIRA, Vol. 2, XV.

[26] According to Soranus (Gyn. 2, 21, 48) girl babies were tougher than boys (cf. Arist. Hist.An. 608b, 15). Xenophon (Lac.1, 3) mentions that the Greeks, with the exception of the Spartans, used to grudge the girls meat and drink (Golden 1981, 326). Furthermore, of 300 children supported by Trajan at Velleia in Italy, only 36 were girls (Clark 1981, 195).

[27] 450, 20-4 (Golden 1981, 326).

[28] Engels 1980, 112f. It is difficult to establish the causes of death. Inscriptions on graves and epigraphs provide pathological information in exceptional cases only

1.2.3 Adult Mortality

However, the continuous want of nourishment had fatal implications for the adult lives of females, since girls were unsatisfactorily prepared for marriage[29] with regard to the physical strains of pregnancy. They were often scarcely sexually mature[30] and were usually physically weak, factors which frequently contributed to their early death in childbirth.[31] From a passage in Soranus we can conjecture that efforts were made to induce early sexual maturity in young girls, presumably in order to get them married as soon as possible:[32]

> For the sake of proper care one should try from the thirteenth year on, before the menstrual flux is secreted, to assist the discharge to take place spontaneously and before defloration.[33]

Further, Soranus emphasized the risks to child brides in early marriages:

> It is good to preserve the state of virginity until menstruation begins by itself.[34] [- - -] [For] danger arises when fertilization takes place while the uterus is still small in size.[35]

Other complications relating to pregnancy may be attributed to general ignorance on the part of the pregnant woman of her body's special needs.[36] In cases where the foetus died and could not achieve birth spontaneously it had to be removed by means of an operation[37] and in an advanced pregnancy such an operation was regarded as complicated and very dangerous.[38]

(Goetze 1974) and the osteological material also is elusive (Engels 1980, 112ff.). An inscription on an undated tomb (Kaibel 314 =CIG 3272) tells us of a four-year-old boy who died of tuberculosis (Zingerle 1928, 440ff). Further, examination of a mumified seven or eight-year-old girl from the 1st cent. A.D., found in Rome, reveals that she suffered from rachitis and died of tuberculosis (Toynbee 1971, 41f).

[29] Marriage is discussed in 1.5.1.1 and 1.5.2.

[30] Concerning the age of marriage, the medical and legal sources are of divergent opinion. According to the physicians, sexual maturity in girls was reached on average at the age of 13 or 14, while the legal minimum age for marriage was 12 (Amundsen 1969, 127ff). As males often remarried (1.3.2) the difference of age between the young wife and her husband could be considerable.

[31] Cf. n. 2 supra.

[32] Cf. Soph. fr. 583, quoted in p. 28f. See also n. 30 supra.

[33] Soran. 1, 5, 25. Translat. O.Temkin. Cf. n. 30 supra.

[34] Soran. 1, 8, 33. Transl. O. Temkin.

[35] Soran. 1, 8, 33. Transl. O.Temkin.

[36] Pliny Ep. 8, 10, 1-2.; Soranus (Gyn. 1, 14, 46) issued detailed instructions to pregnant women for the avoidance of miscarriage.

[37] Celsus Med. 7, 29.

[38] Celsus Med. 7, 29.

Along with exposure of unwanted children, various contraceptives and abortives were used in order to limit the number of children: this often jeopardized the life and health of the women.[39] As regards abortion, it was not considered a crime[40] since the foetus was not perceived as human life in embryonic form,[41] and a great number of methods to bring about a termination of pregnancy are described in medical writings.[42] Of the risks to women we are told by a physician of the Hippocratic school:

> A women who miscarries is exposed to great danger, since a miscarriage is more difficult than a normal delivery. The fact is that a miscarriage cannot occur without forcible means such as laxatives, potions, foodstuffs, insertions or baths. If such remedies fail, more violent methods might result in inflammation which would imperil the woman's life.[43]

The possibility that the woman might become pregnant again before she had recovered from the previous birth[44] reduced her chances of survival, as, in her weakened state, she was more susceptible to, say, malaria and tuberculosis, both of which diseases were widespread at that time.[45] This applied particularly to women of the lower classes who often lacked financial means for medical treatment. Further, inconvenient houses[46] and hard work in combination with undernourishment and poor medical facilities lessened their resistance to physical ills and imposed psychical strain.

---

[39] Krenkel 1971. (The author gives a comprehensive and methodical report of evidence on abortion in antiquity.) Contraception was presumably the task of the female. Aetios of Amida (6th cent. A.D.) enumerates 24 methods for avoiding pregnancy, only one of which has reference to the male, and medical writings do not mention 'coitus interruptus' (Noonan 1969, 13). Scientific and medical writings devote much space to describing various contraceptives, while there are extremely few references to them outside specialist literature (Noonan 1969, 14). However, references to potions with contraceptive and abortive properties are to be found in legal documents of the time, and the effect of such specifics is known to have been fatal in some cases (Dig. 48, 19, 38, 5) (Noonan 1969, 26).

[40] Romans of distinguished families seem to have been critical of abortion (Cic. Clu. 32) and disappointed at miscarriages in their wives (Cic. Att. 14, 20, 2; Pliny Ep. 8, 1). However, the reason for that was principally the continued existence of the family and not concern for the woman's life (Watts 1973, 98).

[41] Dig. 35, 2, 9; 25, 4, 1 (Clark 1981, 211 n. 13).

[42] Krenkel 1971. See n. 39 supra.

[43] Hippoc. De morb.mul. 72, 6-7. (The English translation, based on the Greek text, has been guided by the German one performed by H. Grensemann.) Here, it can be assumed, the writer is referring to induced, rather than natural, miscarriages.

[44] Medical writers seem not to have known that breast-feading prevents conception (Salskov-Roberts 1977, 30f).

[45] In addition, fevers, tetanus, diabetes, renal calculus and liver and skin diseases were common (Patrick 1967, 238ff).

[46] See 3.4.1.1, p. 64 n. 48. Cf. n. 2 supra.

1.3 FAMILY RELATIONSHIPS

1.3.1 The Ideal Roman Family

During the Republic the Roman family was entirely dominated by the paterfamilias who had an extraordinary power ('potestas') over his family;[47] not only could he expose a newborn child (1.2.1), but also dismiss an erring son to servile labour, order him to be flogged, imprisoned and even put to death.[48] The family under his control consisted of his wife 'in manus',[49] all his children (not only those living with him) including the children of his son, and, finally, his slaves.[50] Consequently, the potestas of an elderly paterfamilias with many sons and grandchildren could be far-reaching. The materfamilias, on the other hand, had no legal power over her children, even if she was widowed or divorced; in such cases the children required a male tutor.[51] The power of the paterfamilias over his family, however, brought a great responsibility, since he was legally liable for the actions of its members.[52]

However, from literature we know that in the Augustan era radical changes took place in the family life which affected the position of the paterfamilias. The expressive writings on the subject by Columella and Tacitus, contrasting their own time with the 'good old days', are worthy of quoting, even if we are given an idealized picture of the latter.[53] Columella has given the following account of family life in ancient times from the aspect of the relationship between husband and wife:

> For both among the Greeks and afterwards amongst the Romans down to the time which our fathers can remember domestic labour was practically the sphere of the married woman, the fathers of the families betaking themselves to the family fireside,

---

[47] Gardner 1986, 5 ff.

[48] Dion. Hal .Ant.Rom. 2, 26, 4.

[49] Cf. n. 66 infra. The wife 'in manus' was regarded in the situation of a daughter ('filia loco') in relation to her husband. His power over his wife, however, was more restricted than over a daughter since he had not the right of life and death over her. Still, she was not allowed to possess any property of her own since everything was absorbed into her husband's property (Pomeroy 1976, 221ff; Gardner 1986, 11).

[50] Gardner 1986, 5. The power of the Roman paterfamilias over his wife, his children and his slaves corresponded to ideas found in Greek philosophy. For instance, a passage in Aristotle (Pol. 1260a, 9-14) dealing with these relationships inside the household, runs in the following way:'Hence there are by nature various classes of rulers and ruled. For the free rules the slave, the male the female, and the man the child in a different way. And all possess the various parts of the soul, but possess them in different ways; for the slave has not got the deliberative part at all, and the female has it, but without full authority, while the child has it, but in an undeveloped form' (Transl. H. Rackham).

[51] Gardner 1986, 147. A woman could not found a family (Gardner 1986, 8).

[52] Gardner 1986, 7.

[53] The conception of the 'ideal wife' is also to be found in Artemidorus; in dreams she is characterized by phenomena located to the domestic sphere: the table, the hearth, the bed (1, 74) and the loom (3, 36).

all care laid aside, only to rest from their public activities. For the utmost reverence for them ruled in the home in an atmosphere of harmony and diligence, and the most beauteous of women was fired with emulation, being zealous by her care to increase and improve her husband's business. No separate ownership was to be seen in the house, nothing which either the husband or the wife claimed by right as one's own, but both conspired for the common advantage, so that the wife's diligence at home vied with the husband's public activities.[54]

The relationship between parents and children is described by Tacitus as follows:

In the good old days, every man's son, born in wedlock, was brought up not in the chamber of some hireling nurse, but in his mother's lap, and at her knee. And that mother could have no higher praise than that she managed the house and gave herself to her children. Again, some elderly relative would be selected in order that to her, as a person who had been tried and never found wanting, might be entrusted the care of all the youthful scions of the same house; in the presence of such an one no base word could be uttered without grave offence, and no wrong deed done. Religiously and with the utmost delicacy she regulated not only the serious tasks of her youthful charges, but their recreations also and their games.[55]

Further, Plutarch gives in his biography of Cato the Elder a picture of family life during the late Republic. A close relationship between the members is typical of the family as he saw it. For instance, the father does not fail to be present when his infant boy is nursed and at the appropriate time he does not entrust the education of his son to a stranger. Similarly, the mother breast-feeds her baby herself and, in addition, suckles some of the slave children with a view to providing her son with affectionate foster-brothers and sisters while he is growing up.[56]

These accounts of family life in ancient times depict the ideal wife, expressed in the term of 'univira' (a woman who married only once).[57] The univira was expected to be supportive and submissive to her husband, his children and his family[58] and further not to have intercourse with anybody other than her husband; Plutarch characterized this ideal wife in the picture of a tortoise, carrying her house on her back and communicating with other males only through her husband:

Pheidias made the Aphrodite of the Eleans with one foot on a tortoise, to typify for womankind keeping at home and keeping silence. For a woman ought to do her talking either to her husband or through her husband, and she should not feel aggrieved if, like the flute-player, she makes a more impressive sound through a tongue not her own.[59]

---

[54] Columella, Rust. 12, pref. 7-8. Transl. E.S. Forster & E.H. Heffner.
[55] Tac. Dial. 28, 4-5. Transl. W. Peterson. Rev. M. Winterbottom.
[56] Plut. Vit.Cat.Mai. 20.
[57] Lightman-Zeisel 1977, 19.
[58] Cf. also Livy 34, 7, 11-15 and Prop. 4, 11.
[59] Plut. Mor. 142D. Transl. F. C. Babbitt.

1.3.2 'Broken Homes'

However, this matrimonial ideal was shattered: the power of the paterfamilias over his wife was weakened while he gained influence over the marriage of his daughter.[60] Columella goes on to describe the careless women of his own time:

> Nowadays, however, when most women so abandon themselves to luxury and idleness that they do not deign to undertake even the superintendence of wool-making and there is a distaste for home-made garments and their perverse desire can only be satisfied by clothing purchased for large sums and almost the whole of their husband's income, one cannot be surprised that these same ladies are bored by a country estate and the implements of husbandry, and regard a few days' stay at a country house as a most sordid business.[61]

Similarly, Tacitus gives the following view of failed parental responsibility during the 1st cent. A.D:

> Nowadays, on the other hand, our children are handed over at their birth to some silly little Greek serving-maid, with a male slave, who may be anyone, to help her—quite frequently the most worthless member of the whole establishment, incompetent for any serious service. It is from the foolish tittle-tattle of such persons that the children receive their earliest impressions, while their minds are still green and unformed; and there is not a soul in the whole house who cares a jot what he says or does in the presence of his baby master. Yes, and the parents themselves make no effort to train their little ones in goodness and self-control; they grow up in an atmosphere of laxity and pertness, in which they come gradually to lose all sense of shame, and all respect both for themselves and for other people.[62]

As distinguished from the dutiful univirae, contemporary females are accused of luxury, idleness, taste for town life and indifference to their children who were entrusted to unconcerned servants.

These characteristics, however, attributable to women of Tacitus' own time, were signs of changes in woman's position. Such changes were brought about by legal and economic proceedings which resulted in a new family pattern, and the old signification of 'univira' declined and became to mean merely a 'good wife'.[63] These changes stemmed from several sources. For instance, the Augustan marriage laws[64] contradicted the ideal of the wife as belonging to only one husband, since a widow, between 20-50 years old, had to remarry within two years of the

---

[60] See n. 66 infra.

[61] Columella, Rust. 12, pref. 9-10. Transl. E. S. Forster & E. H. Heffner.

[62] Tac. Dial. 29, 1-3. Transl. W. Peterson. Rev. M. Winterbottom.

[63] Lightman-Zeisel 1977, 24.

[64] This enacted a system of provisions which aimed at furthering the population growth. For instance, unmarried people were not allowed to inherit from their next of kin, and couples without children had to give up half their legacy to other heirs or to the state. (Csillag 1976, 146ff). The Augustan marriage laws are further discussed by L. R. Raditsa (1980) and A. Wallace-Hadrill (1981).

death of her husband.⁶⁵ Furthermore, at that time the matrimonial form 'sine manu' was generally practised, and this facilitated divorce.⁶⁶ According to the funerary eulogy for 'Turia', dated to 10 or 9 B.C. a divorce must have been quite a common occurrence:

> In our day, marriages of such long duration, not dissolved by divorce, but terminated by death alone, are indeed rare. For our union was prolonged in unclouded happiness for forty-one years.⁶⁷

Finally, the instability of the family was also increased by the father's remarrying, sometimes more than once, owing to both the high death rate of his wives in childbirth⁶⁸ and to the ease of divorce.⁶⁹ In consequence, a complicated pattern of family relationships sometimes resulted, with the father representing the only thread of continuity, and, consequently, an important role was imposed on him in support of the children who were exposed to emotional rootlessness. This might have created a deeper relationship between fathers and daughters of such families.⁷⁰ An epitaph from the 1st cent. B.C., mentioning no mother,⁷¹ may illustrate such a relationship:

> [The grave] of Eucharis, freedwoman of Licinia, an unmarried girl, who was educated and learned in every skill. She lived fourteen years.
> 'Ah, as you look with wandering eye at the house of death, stay your foot and read what is inscribed here. This is what a father's love gave his daughter, where the remains of her body lie gathered. Just as my life with its young skills and growing years brought me fame, the sad hour of death rushed on me and forbade me to draw another breath in life. I was educated and taught as if by the muses' hands. I adorned

---

[65] Weiler 1980, 185ff. Csillag 1976, 77ff.

[66] Within a so-called 'manus-marriage' a daughter was no longer subject to the supremacy ('manus') of her father but entered into that of her husband, which gave him control over her possessions and inheritance (Pomeroy 1976, 221ff). From the 1st cent. B.C. marriages 'sine manu' became usual and in this case the daughter remained in the manus of her father and was obliged to get his permission where major financial transactions were concerned (Clark 1981, 203f). Within a marriage 'sine manu' it was easy to divorce and it was not even necessary to prove the breakdown of a union (Clark 1981, 203f). In addition, the wife's father could separate the couple, even against the wishes of his daughter (Clark 1981, 203f; Pomeroy 1976, 224ff).

[67] CIL 6, 1527, 27-28 (= ILS 8393). Transl. from WGR, 107. The identity of the woman is uncertain.

[68] Cf. n. 2 supra.

[69] 'A consequence, intensified by the ease of divorce, was the frequency of second and third marriages for both sexes, especially among men. This in turn complicated both personal and family relationships, economically as well as psychologically, and the prospect, even before the event, must have introduced a considerable element of tension in many women' (Finley 1968, 138).

[70] The relationship between Roman fathers and their daughters has been elucidated in a study by J. Hallett (1984).

[71] Lucian (Hermot. 11; Gallus 9) mentions fathers giving birthday parties for their daughters.

the nobility's festivals with my dancing, and first appeared before the common people in a Greek play. But now here in this tomb my enemies the Fates have placed my body's ashes. The patrons of learning—devotion, passion, praise, honor, fall silent before my burnt corpse and are made silent by my death. His child, I left lamentation to my father, though born after him, I preceded him in the day of my death. Now I observe my fourteenth birthday here among the shadows in Death's ageless home. I beg you when you leave, ask that the earth lie light upon me'.[72]

However, it will be remembered that a father, as the children grew up, could be absent from home for long periods, either on military service in those cases where he was enrolled in the Roman army[73] or travelling on business. On such occasions the responsibility for the girl was left to an elder sister[74] or to an elderly relative[75] who replaced both parents.

1.3.2.1 Nurses and Stepmothers

No matter how warm the relationship between father and daughter might have been, the remarriage of the father denied the daughter the experience of a developing relationship with her own mother, a deprivation indeed in view of the early marriage she herself would have to face.[76] However, even if the biological mother was alive, the relationship between the girl and her mother was often disturbed in consequence of the child's having been entrusted to a nurse. Gellius has described such an estrangement between mother and child:

> For when the child is given to another and removed from its mother's sight, the strength of maternal ardour is gradually and little by little extinguished, every call of impatient anxiety is silenced, and a child which has been given over to another to nurse is almost as completely forgotten as if it had been lost by death. Moreover, the child's own feelings of affection, fondness, and intimacy are centred wholly in the one by whom it is nursed, and therefore, just as happens in the case of those who are exposed at birth, it has no feeling for the mother, who bore it and no regret for her loss.[77]

---

[72] ILS 5213. Transl. from WGR, 104f.

[73] Cf. 3.2, p. 60 n. 12. Livy (42, 34) gives an account of the life of a legionar and his service to the army.

[74] Artem. 1, 78.

[75] Cf. Tac. Dial. 28, 4-5, quoted in p. 16.

[76] Cf. n. 30 supra. J. Phillips (1978) has shown that Roman mothers, as described in literature, often had a supportive role in the lives of their adult daughters.

[77] Gell. NA 12, 1, 22-23. Transl.J.C.Rolfe

However, if the nurse had been chosen with care[78] and had stayed with the family[79] she provided the necessary emotional stability for the children and particularly for the girls. This fact is evident from many epitaphs which mention nurses with gratitude and affection.[80] One of these inscriptions (on an Athenian grave relief[81]) reads as follows:

> Melitta, daughter of Apollodorus. Here lies beneath the earth Hippostrate's good nurse. And how Hippostrate now longs for you! I loved you so, dear nurse. And now, for all my life, I'll honor you, though you lie below. If the good receive a prize in the underworld, you now, I know, enjoy first place with Pluto and Persephone.[82]

A nurse must have been particularly important in those cases where the father had remarried and provided a stepmother; this was something that many children must have experienced through divorce[83] and death[84] and was regarded as a misfortune. The 'evil stepmother' was a common theme in the theatre,[85] and in rhetorical exercises she is sometimes presented as a poisoner[86] whose wickedness is an integral part of her.[87] These negative expectations must have presented great obstacles for the new wife who wished to be accepted by the children of the family. In one of his letters Jerome tells a young lady not to marry a widowed or divorced man and become a stepmother:

> If he, for his part, has issue by a former wife, when he brings you into his house, then, even though you have a heart of gold, you will be the cruel stepmother, against whom every comedy, every mime-writer, and every dealer in rhetorical commonplaces raises his voice. If your stepson falls sick or has headache, you will be maligned as a poisoner. If you refuse him food you will be cruel; if you give it, you will be said to have bewitched him. What benefit, I pray you, can a second marriage confer sufficient to compensate for these disadvantages?[88]

---

[78] The nurse needed to be chosen carefully, since it was thought that she transmitted her qualities be means of her milk. Soranus (Gyn. 2, 12, 19) recommended Greek nurses in order to transfuse Greek physical and psychical qualities to the baby.

[79] According to Soranus (Gyn. 2, 21, 47) the child ought to be totally weaned at the age of two.

[80] Himmelmann 1971, 44. It could happen that the nurse and the mother became rivals for the affection of the child (Pers. 2, 31-40).

[81] In contrast to the Philippians (cf. Chapt. 4), the Athenians seem to have had little belief in an afterlife (Mikalson 1983, 74ff), which is also reflected in the Athenian episode in Acts (17: 32).

[82] IG 2 (2) 7873 (=GV 747). Transl. from Mikalson 1983, 79.

[83] Cf. n. 69 supra.

[84] Cf. n. 2 supra.

[85] Diod. Sic. 12, 14, 3-15.

[86] Sen. Controv. 9, 5; 9, 6.; Quint. Inst. 2, 10, 5. Cf. Verg. G. 2, 128.

[87] S.v. 'metruia' in Liddell-Scott, 1131, and 'noverca' in Georges, Vol. 2, 1199.

[88] Jerome Ep. 54, 15. Transl. F. A. Wright.

The tensions in the relationship must have been trying for the stepmother as well as for the children, and might even have involved the father in family disputes.[89] Such conflict was often simulated in the exercises of elocution, where it would be recognized as true to life for many people.[90]

1.3.2.2 The Status of Children

In consequence of the changes in the family pattern there might have been several categories of children in the household. The fact that the father remarried several times would mean that the offspring of different wives grew up together, since by law the paterfamilias retained the children (and also the right to keep them with him) in the event of divorce as well as being left with the progeny of a dead wife.[91]

Besides the children of the family there could have been various kinds of foster-children. One category consisted of freeborn children who belonged to relatives and had been taken care of by them for some reason or other,[92] such as the death of a mother. In those cases it was felt that the father might not be able to take charge of his children.

In many families there might also have been foundlings.[93] Their position was intermediate between that of the children of the family and that of the slaves,[94] and consequently they were not able to feel a real kinship with either of these groups. In addition, their biological parents could for a variety of reasons reclaim them,[95] and this fact might have had an unsettling effect on these children. The ambiguity of their position and the uncertainty over their future may well have resulted in psychological damage to them.

---

[89] However, there is also evidence of wicked stepfathers who tried to murder their stepchildren. For instance, Livy (39, 9) mentions a stepfather who tried to get rid of his stepson by inducing him to become initiated into the Dionysiac mysteries in Rome. Another case is mentioned by Cicero (Clu. 9, 27).

[90] See Tac.Dial. 28, 4, quoted above in p. 16.

[91] Gardner 1986, 146. Consequently, even a child born after divorce belonged to the father.

[92] Literature tells of many cases where children were brought up by near relatives; for instance, in the family of an uncle (Pliny Ep. 4, 19, 1; Plut.Vit .Cat. Min.1) or in the house of their grandparents (Suet.Aug. 64, 2-3; Suet.Vesp. 2, 1) (Bonner 1977, 16ff).

[93] Cf. 1.2.1.

[94] The legal position of foundlings was obscure, since they were looked upon neither as slaves nor as freeborn (Corbett 1980, 310ff).

[95] Pliny Ep.10, 65. Corbett 1980, 310ff; Balsdon 1969, 87. Owing to the high death rate of children, parents sometimes wished to take back a child which had been exposed by them and had subsequently been rescued by another family. We find this theme in Plautus' comedies (for instance, Cist. 660ff).

Finally, most households contained slave children[96] who were brought up together with those of the family.[97] These children could either have been born in a 'slave marriage'[98] or to a slave woman and a freeborn man.[99] Slave girls in particular ran the risk of being sold away from their families,[100] even at an early age,[101] since there were often insufficient tasks for a female slave in an average family to warrant her being retained in it.[102]

1.4 SUMMARY

From medical and legal writings, in combination with other sources of the time, it is possible to draw some conclusions about women's living conditions irrespective of their social position.

Infant as well as adult mortality rate was high. Thus, even when a girl survived her childhood and attained marriageable age her chances of becoming a grandmother were small. In the Augustan age the old marriage pattern began to disintegrate and many girls, because of death or divorce, enjoyed but short relationships with their biological mothers; similarly, girls belonging to the categories of slaves and foundlings (whose legal position in the family was uncertain), could quite unexpectedly be separated from their foster-parents. Although contemporary writings give the impression of a nurse being the cornerstone of many families poor people could not afford such assistance; in these cases all domestic tasks were naturally performed by the women of

---

[96] It was regarded as a sign of prosperity if a family had several slave children (Tib. 2, 1, 21-24; Mart. 3, 58, 22) (Bonner 1977, 36).

[97] The wife of the elderly Cato is said to have nursed slave children together with her own child (Plut. Vit.Cat.Mai.20).The custom of bringing up the slave children together with the freeborn children survived throughout the period of the Roman Empire (cf. Quint. Inst. 1, 1, 7; Jerome Ep. 14, 3) (Bonner 1977, 36).

[98] Slaves could not marry legally and have legal children, but in the larger households they could live in paired relationships and have children (Gardner 1986, 213). Freed slaves could get legally married since manumission conferred Roman citizenship (Balsdon 1979, 89).

[99] The paterfamilias had often sexual relations with his own female slaves; for him sex with slave girls did not account. For his wife, on the other hand, sex with a slave was regarded as adultery (Gardner 1986, 221).

[100] The stability of the relationships of a slave couple was entirely dependent on the owner who could separate them from each other or from their children by sale or bequest, and, furthermore, family members were often manumitted separately (Gardner 1986, 213).

[101] There are cases recorded in Egypt where four to eight-year-old slave girls were sold (Bradley 1978, 243, Tabl. 1, Nos. 1-4). From literature we know that the Romans and the Greeks kept small slave children in their households, using them either as nurse-maids or for providing amusement and company (Slater 1974, 133).

[102] Female slaves did the same work as freeborn women (Clark 1981, 197ff).

the house, and daughters would be left to the care of younger sisters and brothers in those families where either the mother had died or the parents had separated.

1.5 EXCURSUS: WOMEN'S MEANS OF SUPPORT AND ATTITUDES TOWARDS MARRIAGE

1.5.1 Women's Means of Support

1.5.1.1 Wives

When girls (other than slaves[103]) became sexually mature[104] they had to quit their homes as soon as possible in order not to become a financial burden on the family.[105] Where there was enough money for a dowry, the girl was given away in marriage;[106] an unmarried daughter brought dishonour on a family and a woman remained single only in those cases where a man refused to accept her.[107] The dowry was of importance to a married woman not only in case of divorce or her husband's death. Her money, invested in the business of her husband,[108] would not only make a divorce more difficult[109] but at the same time it would give the wife some influence in family affairs and in some cases also in public life.[110]

---

[103] When a slave girl was not needed in the household she was sold. See n. 100 and 101 supra.

[104] Cf. n. 30 supra.

[105] Cf. n. 8 supra.

[106] There were three conditions to be fulfilled for a legally valid marriage: if both parties were free and citizens, had reached marriageable age and consented to the marriage (Gardner 1986, 31). By law the father's consent was necessary; there are examples, however, that children were able to take the initiative in choosing their partners (Gardner 1986, 41f).

[107] Cf. Ath. 13, 555C. Even if a girl desired to live alone she had presumably no chance of realising her wish without becoming a prostitute. She might stay unmarried for some time in the service of a deity who demanded total chastity, but it seems unlikely that this state of affairs could have been permanent. The most well-known chaste priestesses were the Pythia at Delphi, those of the cult of Artemis (Fehrle 1910, 98ff) and the Vestal Virgins; the latter were free to marry after their retirement at 35-40 years of age (Plut. Vit.Num. 10, 2) (Fehrle 1910, 210ff).

[108] By Roman (unlike Greek) law the dowry became the legal property of the husband (Gardner 1986, 102).

[109] In case of divorce the dowry was reclaimed by the wife or her family (Gardner 1986, 102).

[110] Wealth, combined with appropriate family relationships, could render a woman eligible for a public office of priestess. (See 2.3.2.2). It has been suggested that women, although they were not allowed to vote, had the opportunity to express their opinion by participating in public meals and games (Mohler 1932, 113). From phrases (on surviving pedestals belonging to statues) such as 'postulante populo',

From a male point of view, the problem of female financial influence is illustrated by the following quotation from Gellius:

> Marcus Cato, when recommending the Voconian law, spoke as follows: 'In the beginning the woman brought you a great dowry; then she holds back a large sum of money, which she does not entrust to the control of her husband, but lends it to her husband. Later, becoming angry with him, she orders a 'servus recepticius' or 'slave of her own' to hound him and demand the money'.[111]

However, a wife, particularly of the lower classes, had influence not through her dowry only, but often through her earning capacity[112] either by working on her own[113] or by sharing her husband's work. Surviving inscriptions tell us of wives working in the business of their husbands;[114] particularly in the case of purple trade business was carried on as a family concern.[115] A marriage built on fellowship of common profession is portrayed in an epitaph from the 2nd cent. A.D:

> Farewell, lady Panthia, from your husband. After your departure, I keep up my lasting grief for your cruel death. Hera, goddess of marriage, never saw such a wife: your beauty, your wisdom, your chastity. You bore me children completely like myself; you cared for your bridegroom and your children; you guided straight the rudder of life in our home and raised high our common fame in healing–though you were a woman you were not behind me in skill. [116]

This woman apparently shared her husband's profession as a physician, and in this respect he judges her equal to himself. She is, however, praised first for being a good housewife.

    'succlamante populo', 'ex consensu et postulatione populi' it is assumed that the people were consulted at more informal gatherings and that the women present voiced their opinion (Mohler 1932, 113f). In addition, the Pompeian graffiti show that women (rarely matrons) spread active propaganda through electoral recommendations among the citizens of the town (D'Avino 1967, 25).

[111] Gell. NA 17, 6, 1. Transl. J. C. Rolfe.

[112] In case of divorce a woman could reclaim her dowry only; she had no share in the money she had contributed to the household (Gardner 1986, 259f). However, in a small-scale family business the wife's labour, not being easily replaced, might have discouraged divorce (Gardner 1986, 260).

[113] Latin tomb inscriptions show lower-class women working in professions (midwives, female doctors) in crafts (clothes-production), as dealers (in perfumes and purple) and in personal services (wet-nurses, nurses, masseuses, dressers, hairdressers, brothel-keepers, inn-keepers, cookshop-owners, waitresses, prostitutes) (Treggiari 1979, 65ff).

[114] If there were no sons old enough a woman could carry on the business of a dead husband (Treggiari 1979, 77).

[115] Female purple dealers are recorded from Rome (CIL 6, 9846; 6, 9848; 2, 1743) (Treggiari 1979, 72, n. 27). Cf. Lydia in Acts 16: 14. Probably these women had a traditional skill in selling expensive cloth and perfumes (Treggiari 1979, 76).

[116] Pleket, 20. Transl. from WGR, 111.

Similarly, the majority of surviving inscriptions on tombstones glorify women for their service to family and home alone,[117] as is exemplified by the following one from the 2nd cent. B.C.:

> Friend, I have not much to say; stop and read it. This tomb, which is not fair, is for a fair woman. Her parents gave her the name Claudia. She loved her husband in her heart. She bore two sons, one of whom she left on earth, the other beneath it. She was pleasant to talk with, and she walked with grace. She kept the house and worked in wool. That is all. You may go.[118]

From our modern point of view housework is often considered as an inferior necessity when compared with professional work outside the home. In antiquity, on the other hand, the division of labour between husband and wife[119] conferred great importance on the woman. The production of provisions and clothes was vital to the survival of the family and the financial prosperity of the paterfamilias was to a great extent dependent on the woman's ability to economize.[120] In this respect the wife had a crucial task in her role as organizer of the work[121] which gave her absolute authority over those members of the household performing indoor domestic duties.[122] In spite of her financial importance to her husband, however, a wife had no legal share in his property but was totally dependent on his testamentary generosity.[123] In those cases, therefore, where a married woman was neither a practitioner of a trade nor had sufficient financial assets of her own a husband's death could precipitate a catastrophe for the family.[124]

---

[117] In Philippi rock carvings depicting women in their role of housewives seem to have replaced tomb inscriptions praising female duties (Cf. Schmaltz 1983, 238f).

[118] ILLRP 973. 2nd cent. B.C. Transl. from WGR, 104.

[119] In this connection, I call attention to the reliefs on a large sarcophagus (Inv. No. 7188) in the garden of the Archaeological Museum in Istanbul, picturing the male and female roles of husband and wife by symbols relating to their duties of everyday life. As for the wife, her role is symbolized by comb, jewel case, perfume bottle, distaff and wool basket–all those objects are to be found associated with female figures on Philippian rock carvings (4.2.2.3).

[120] The importance of a good housewife, being able to increase the fortune of her husband, is stressed by Xenophon (Oec. 7, 35-36). Cf. Columella, Rust. 12, pref. 9-10, quoted in p. 17.

[121] Columella has given a detailed description of the domestic tasks of the housewife (Rust. 12, pref. 1-8) and also of the bailiff's wife (Rust. 12, 1, 1-3). (Treggiari 1976, 77).

[122] According to XII Tables (4, 3), the keeping of the keys of the household designated the housewife, and her authority is symbolized on tomb reliefs by keys and locks of different sizes. Tombstones of this kind (Nos. K 1068, K 1069, K 1071) are to be seen in the Archaeological Museum in Istanbul. T. Pearce (1974) deals with the wife in the role of mistress of the house.

[123] Gardner 1986, 260

[124] Families of humble position could of course afford only a small amount of money for a daughter's dowry. Cf. Lucian Dial. Court. 6, quoted in p. 27.

1.5.1.2 Concubines

A girl who could not get a husband for economic reasons[125] would either become a concubine,[126] or, at worst, earn her living as a prostitute.[127] The difference between a marriage 'sine manu'[128] and a concubinage was the wedding ceremony itself and the evidence of dowry.[129] Concubinage was regular and accepted though it lacked the social prestige of a legal marriage[130] since one of the partners was usually socially inferior.[131] A married man could not at the same time cohabit with a concubine;[132] on the other hand, two unmarried men could share a concubine. The latter is illustrated by a tomb inscription (dated to the 3rd cent. A.D.) dedicated to Allia Potestas who was a freedwoman and who cohabitated with two men:

> She was courageous, chaste, resolute, honest, a trustworthy guardian. Clean at home, sufficiently clean when she went out, famous among the populace. She alone could confront whatever happened. She would speak briefly and so was never reproached. She was first to rise from her bed and last to return to her bed to rest after she had put each thing in its place. Her yarn never left her hands without good reason. Out of respect she yielded place to all; her habits were healthy. She was never self-satisfied and never took liberties. Her skin was white, she had beautiful eyes, and her hair was gold. An ivory glow always shone from her face—no mortal (so they say) ever possessed a face like it. The curve of her breasts was small on her snow-white bosom. And her legs? Atalanta's figure is comic beside hers. In her anxiety she did not stay still but moved her smooth limbs, beautiful with her generous body; she sought out every hair. Perhaps one might find fault with her hard hands; she was content with nothing but what she had done for herself. There was never a topic which she thought she knew well enough. She remained virtuous because she never committed any crime. While she lived she so guided her two young lovers that they became like the examples of Pylades and Orestes:

---

[125] There could also be other bars to marriage between people: (a) men and women of senatorial rank could not marry persons of undignified condition, for instance liberated slaves and actresses (including prostitutes) (Dig. 23.2.44) (Crook 1967, 99) (b) ordinary soldiers were not allowed (until the time of Septimius Severus) to marry during their service (FIRA, Vol. 3, 19) (Crook 1967, 100f) (c) officials of the provinces could not marry women of their province (Crook 1967, 100). There must have been many cases of concubinage in Philippi; the military colony had a mixed population, consisting of Thracians, Greeks and Romans (3.5).

[126] A concubine was a free woman who cohabited with a man, without being married to him (Gardner 1986, 56).

[127] Prostitutes could be slaves, freedwomen or even freeborn Roman women (Gardner 1986, 132). Prostitution was not regarded as a criminal offence; the women in question were recorded in a register, and sometimes they had to pay taxes (Gardner 1986, 132).

[128] See n. 66 supra.

[129] Crook 1967, 103.

[130] According to Plutarch (Mor. 1A-B ; 753D) a concubine did not have the status of a wife and her children were regarded as illegitimate.

[131] Dig. 32, 49, 4 (Crook 1967, 101).

[132] Gardner 1986, 56. However, the husband had right to sexual intercourse out of wedlock (Plut. Mor. 144D). Cf. n. 99 supra.

one house would hold them both and one spirit. But now that she is dead they will separate, and each is growing old by himself. [133]

This text gives the life of a concubine in a nutshell. Behind the flattering praises of her beauty a hard life of household duties and love-making is dimly seen; her future economic security was based on her lasting ability to answer her young lovers' expectations in these matters. Furthermore, the fate of this woman is typical for many liberated single female slaves[134] who had belonged to families of moderate wealth and had never learned a trade[135] and consequently were totally dependent on serving men in various ways to gain their living.

1.5.1.3 Courtezans

Many of these women, exposed to the arbitrariness of the male and never able to obtain a concubinage, had to depend on casual love affairs with different men. They fell into two categories: prostitutes (presumably being slaves) associated with a brothel[136] and women (often freeborn) who sold their services on their own account;[137] the price was different for these two kinds of prostitutes.[138]

Offering herself for sale was the last course open to a woman, and even a married women could in an emergency be forced to try this last resort. Lucian has pictured the exposed position of a poor widow left with her daughter, whom she proposes as a prostitute:

> Let me give you the rest of my instructions about what to do and how to behave with the men; for we have no other means of livelihood, daughter, and you must realise what a miserable life we've had these two years since your father died, God rest his soul. But, while he lived, we had plenty of everything; for he was a smith with a great name in the Piraeus, and you can hear anyone swear there never will be another smith to follow Philinus. After his death, first of all I sold his tongs, his anvil and his hammer for two minae, and that kept us for seven months; since then I've barely provided a starvation diet, now by weaving, now by spinning thread for woof or warp I've fed you and waited for my hopes to be realised.[139]

---

[133] CIL 6, 37 965, 8-31. Transl. from Lefkowitz 1981, 27ff.

[134] A slave could be liberated at the age of 30 (Treggiari 1976, 96).

[135] Big households had specialized female slaves who were personal servants and trained in several skills, such as hairdressing and massage. Treggiari (1976) lists titles of female occupations, found on inscriptions.

[136] Plut. Vit.Demetr. 24, 1.; Cf. Vit.Ant. 4, 2. Gardner 1986, 250ff.

[137] Plut. Vit.Alex. 41, 5. Gardner 1986, 250ff.

[138] Plut. Mor. 133B; 64F; Gardner 1986, 253. There were also high-class courtezans who received large sums of money for their services to rich lovers (Gardner 1986, 253).

[139] Lucian Dial. Court.6. Translat. M.D.Macleod. Cf. Apul. Met. 3, 8.

It goes without saying that a concubine, and also a prostitute, lacked the security which the dowry often rendered a married woman in case of divorce or the death of her husband. However, there must have been many widowed and divorced women lacking means of support. The poor widow described by Lucian exemplifies this group of women. She seems to have lacked sufficient financial means provided by a dowry, and since she was not able to go on with her husband's craft she had no other way out of her poverty than that of persuading her daughter to become a prostitute.[140]

1.5.2 Attitudes towards Marriage

As far we can conclude from the sources, marriage brought a comparatively favourable life to women—at least with reference to social reputation.[141] However, since females hardly ever had an opportunity of expressing themselves in writing we do not know how married women looked upon their lives. We are given the opportunity to see women only through the eyes of men, who have portrayed them in terms favourable to the male sex. Occasionally, however, a different picture is dimly visible through their writings. For instance, girls' fears, not only of scolding mothers-in-law[142] but also of childbearing and of adapting themselves to a new family, are reflected in literature from various periods. A passage from Sophocles illustrates the feelings of young girls when moving away from home:

> But now, outside of my father's home, I am nothing. Young women, in my opinion, have the sweetest existence known to mortals in their father's homes. For their innocence always keeps children safe and happy. But when we reach puberty and can understand, we are thrust out and sold away from our ancestral gods and from our parents. Some go to strange men's homes, other to foreigners', some to joyless houses,

---

140 We are also told of widowed women who were model mothers for their children—but they were wealthy and belonged to distinguished families. Tacitus (Dial. 28, 5) mentions Cornelia, the mother of the Gracchi, Aurelia, the mother of Caesar and Atia, the mother of Augustus.

141 The story (told by Livy in connection with the Bacchanalian scandal in 186 B.C.) about the courtezan Hispala Faecenia may illustrate the difficulties experienced by these women in their attempts to secure married status for themselves. Hispala Faecenia was now a freedwoman but have had the same occupation as a prostitute still as a slave (Livy 39, 9, 5). This woman loved a young man, Aebutius, whom she rescued from being murdered at the instigation of his stepfather; Aebutius was proposed to become initiated into the Dionysiac mysteries—a sure way of getting rid of him (Livy 39, 10) . However, his mistress, knowing that murder was going on in the mysteries, revealed her secret to the consul and was rewarded by being permitted to marry a man of free birth and was promised that no fraud or disgrace on this account would attach to the man who would marry her (Livy 39, 19, 5-6).

142 A bad relationship between a wife and her mother-in-law is mentioned in, for instance, Plut. Mor. 143AB; Ter. Hec. 220, 623; Ov. Fast. 2, 626; Apul. Met. 6, 9f (Dassmann 1986, 838).

some to hostile. And all this once the first night he yoked us to our husband, we are forced to praise and to say that all is well.[143]

Literary sources tell us that marriage was sometimes considered as a frightening prospect by the young bride. A young girl's terror of the wedding night is expressed in an epigraph by Antiphanes of Macedonia who lived during the Augustan era:

> By the unhappy marriage-bed of Petale at her bitter bridal stood Hades, not Hymen. For, as she fled alone through the darkness, dreading the first taste of the yoke of Cypris–a terror common to all maidens–the cruel watch-dogs killed her. We had hoped to see her a wife and suddenly we could hardly find her corpse.[144]

The most well-known example regarding the estrangement felt by a young woman in her new home, and her fear of bearing children, is given by Euripides in his drama *Medea*:

> Then, coming to new customs, habits new
> One need be a seer, to know the thing unlearnt
> At home, what manner of man her mate shall be.
> And if we learn our lesson, if our lord
> Dwell with us, plunging not against the yoke,
> Happy our lot is; else–no help but death.
> For the man, when the home-yoke galls his neck,
> Goes forth, to ease a weary sickened heart.
> By turning to some friend, some kindred soul:
> We to one heart alone can look for comfort.[145]

A little later Medea says:

> Thrice would I under shield,
> Stand, rather than bear childbirth-peril once.[146]

Marriage and childbearing, however, meant a fulfilled life for a female, and it was looked upon as a personal tragedy for a woman not to be able to bear children for her husband, who had to secure the continuity of the domestic worship of his family by providing an heir.(cf. 2.2.1.2).[147] The female dilemma of barrenness is illustrated by the eulogy

---

[143] Soph. fr. 583. Transl. from Lefkowitz 1981, 20.
[144] Anth. Gr. 9, 245. Transl. W. R. Paton
[145] Eur. Med. 238-248. Transl. A. S.Way.
[146] Eur. Med. 250-251. Transl. A. S.Way. It may be worth noting that in 1982 a survey of 139 pregnant women in Sweden revealed that 23% feared the birth. This fear derived from stories of the birth pangs experienced by their mothers and other females. Moreover, it was found that women who suffered in this way frequently had difficulty in establishing satisfactory emotional bonds with their babies in the early days of motherhood (Areskog 1982).
[147] Gardner 1986, 8. Barrenness of a wife was a typical cause of divorce (Gardner 1986, 81).Having children secured grave offerings and, consequently, a tolerable after-life in Hades (cf. Lucian De Luct. 2- 9).

for 'Turia' (see also 1.3.2). In this extract a childless woman's feeling of inferiority is reflected:

> When all the world was again at peace and the Republic re-established, peaceful and happy days followed. We longed for children, which an envious fate denied us. Had Fortune smiled on us in this, what had been lacking to complete our happiness? But an adverse destiny put an end to our hopes [- - -] Disconsolate to see me without children [- - -] you wished to put an end to my chagrin by proposing to me a divorce, offering to yield the place to another spouse more fertile, with the only intention of searching for and providing for me a spouse worthy of our mutual affection, whose children you assured me you would have treated as your own.[- - -] Nothing would have been changed, only you would had rendered to me henceforth the services of a devoted sister or mother-in-law. I will admit that I was so irritated and shocked by such a proposition that I had difficulty in restraining my anger and remaining master of myself. You spoke of divorce before the decree of fate had forced us to separate, and I could not comprehend how you could conceive of any reason why you, still living, should not be my wife, you who during my exile had always remained most faithful and loyal.[148]

These lines bear witness to an exceptionally happy relationship between husband and wife. To women in antiquity, however, matrimony was first of all the socially accepted frame of their work both inside and outside the household. As previously stated, the former was not without prestige, as it offered a creative outlet for a woman and gave her status within the family, as well, presumably, as providing her with personal satisfaction (1.5.1.1). According to the following epitaphs marital love is defined as mutual respect between husband and wife:

> For Lollia Victorina his sweetest wife Lollianus Porresimus the Procurator bought this monument, because she deserved it. With her he lived 20 years without any fault finding, on either side. That is having loved.[149]

Further, a woman, who had erected a tombstone to her late husband ('who was most generous and dutiful') and characterizes his relationship to herself in the following way:

> [- - -] while I lived with him, he never said a cruel word to me, never gave offence to me or anyone else. [150]

These words, which sum up a wife's lasting feelings towards her husband and define marital love as absence of quarrel, show the difference between present-day romantic expectations of a happy marriage and those of the average woman in antiquity. Still, we must be wary of judging the fate of such a woman from our perspective, since we accept woman's right to earn her own living and to determine the number of children she wants; such freedom of choice was, of course, undreamed of by the women of ancient Rome. However unacceptable a woman's male-dominated position may seem to us today we must keep

---

[148] CIL 6, 1527, 25-62 (= ILS 8393). Transl. from WGR, 109. See n. 67 supra.
[149] CIL 10, 1951. Transl. from Lefkowitz 1983, 44.
[150] CIL 8, 12 881. Transl. from Lefkowitz 1983, 44.

in mind that a female of that time had no option but to depend on a man for her maintenance, or at least for her social reputation. She knew of no alternative life with which to compare her own and, consequently, she estimated her existence within the limits set by males. Therefore, the majority of women, knowing nothing of a better earthly existence from our modern point of view and presumably very little about philosophical ideas of equality between the sexes,[151] may well have been happy and at one with their world.[152]

1.5.3 Summary

In concluding this section we notice that girls, in contrast to boys, were looked upon as economic burdens and had to forgo their adolescence by moving directly from childhood to the world of adults, either as wives or concubines or as prostitutes. No matter which fate a young girl met she had to leave home while still almost a child and become absorbed into an unfamiliar milieu. Such a move involved establishing new relationships in existing groups where it could not automatically be assumed that a welcome would be extended to her—one possible relationship, let it be remembered, was that of stepmother to unknown children. With a few exceptions females were in economic matter legally dependent on males, be they fathers, husbands or other form of guardians. In practice, however, her dowry as well as her actual assistance to her husband in the sphere of the household maintenance ensured for a wife a certain amount of influence in family affairs. In contrast to concubines and prostitutes a married woman was socially respected; not only was she financially supported but she enjoyed complete authority in the management of her domestic affairs; in spite of the fact that the paterfamilias was head of the household his area of autonomy was principally outdoors. Consequently, most housewives, it is safe to

---

[151] For instance, Musonius Rufus (III and IV) held a view which granted to girls the same opportunity of intellectual and moral growth as was given to boys.

[152] However, there did exist young females who had further ambitions than to devote themselves to domestic work. This fact is illustrated through an epigraph, dated to the 2nd cent. B.C., about the young poetess Erinna: 'This is the Lesbian honeycomb of Erinna, and though it be small, it is all infused with honey by the Muses. Her three hundred lines are equal to Homer, though she was but a child of nineteen years. Either plying her spindle in fear of her mother, or at the loom, she stood occupied in the service of the Muses. As much as Sappho excels Erinna in lyrics, so much does Erinna excel Sappho in hexameters' (Anth. Gr. 9, 190. Translat. W. R. Paton). Erinna was one of the few known female poets in antiquity (Anth. Gr. 9, 26). She was unmarried—presumably a priestess of a chaste deity—and before she died at the age of 19 she wrote a poem of 300 lines in hexameters and was judged equal with Homer (Anth. Gr.9, 190). 54 lines of this poem have been found and dated to the 1st cent. B.C. (Scholz 1973, 29). It commemorates her dead playmate Baucis and tells of their play which was ended by Baucis' marriage. Erinna wrote also two epigraphs which were probably intended for Baucis' tombstone (Anth. Gr. 7, 710; 712).

assume, did not hanker after a different existence (at least not in this life), since they saw no better alternatives open to them; on the other hand, there are strong reasons to suspect that concubines and prostitutes felt envious of married women's position of esteem and their social security.

2 RELIGION AND FEMALE EXISTENCE

2.1 INTRODUCTION

As stated in Chapter 1, woman's religious framework was closely related to her socio-cultural environment. After having given an account of matters of relevance to woman's religious experiences, I now turn to those very experiences, associated not only with the domestic cult ('sacra privata') (2.3.1) and the official cult ('sacra publica') (2.3.2) but also with the mystery religions (2.3.3), and finally with the wide and obscure phenomenon of 'folk-religion' (2.3.4).[1] These four categories of Graeco-Roman worship will be considered in relation to women from two aspects. First I focus on religious practice as it related to childhood (2.2), paying particular attention to the means by which religion was passed on to the next generation, and then I discuss religious roles and worship performed by adult women (2.3).

2.2 RELIGIOUS PRACTICES ASSOCIATED WITH CHILDHOOD

2.2.1 Learning Religion

Since infants as well as older children ran the risk of succumbing to diseases of various kinds (1.2.2), a child was from the very beginning an object of religious beliefs and rituals.[2] At the family celebration at which the child was given its name,[3] a freeborn girl made her first contact with the domestic religion: a capsule containing an amulet was hung around

---

[1] Cults of particular significance specifically to Philippian women will be discussed in Chapt. 4.

[2] Pregnancy and birth were occasions of female existence which were particularly subject to purifying rituals. The pregnant woman was regarded as ritually polluted during the first forty days of pregnancy when she was excluded from the shrines (Censorinus, D.N. 11, 7). According to Greek medical writers this period was important, since miscarriage is a constant danger during the first forty days after conception (Parker 1983, 48). Complications relating to pregnancy are discussed in 1.2.3.

[3] Macrob. Sat. 1, 16, 36 (Blümner 1911, 304).

her neck[4] as a protection against sorcery during her childhood.[5] From an early age the girl, along with her brothers, was trained in religious matters by the women of the family; mythical stories were narrated to her and she learned the correct cultic procedures in the worship devoted to the household deities, and at a more advanced age she was instructed in the ceremonial of other cults. Thus, religious education, starting early in childhood and continuing until a girl's marriage, kept pace with the mental development of the child and passed in turn through the stages of listening, observing and acting in accordance with the child's ability to respond at any given age in these three areas of learning.

In dealing with children's religious training in this section I shall concentrate on these three aspects of the learning process, though sources dealing with the subject are sparse. Plato gives some information which can safely be applied to the 1st cent. A.D., as the religious education of pagan children is unlikely to have been changed in such a short period of time. Furthermore, confirmation that this assumption is correct is offered by Prudentius in the criticism he made of pagan religion.

2.2.1.1 By Listening

From Plato we deduce that children's earliest religious education started by their listening to cradle-songs and stories based on mythological motifs:

[- - -] in those stories which they used to hear, while infants and sucklings, from the lips of their nurses and mothers—stories chanted to them, as it were, in lullabies, whether in jest or in earnest; and the same stories they heard repeated also in prayers at sacrifices[- - -][6]

This information, attributable to classical Athens, is confirmed by the story of a nurse telling the myth of Ariadne to her wards, as given to us by the elder Philostratus.[7] In the sources nurses (1.3.2.1) are mentioned as passing on traditional stories of the gods, but in poor families which could not afford a nurse this task was taken over by the mother, a

---

[4] Plaut. Rud. 1171. In this instance a capsule of gold is mentioned, but poor people used to keep their amulets in plain leather purses (Juv. 5, 164). The capsule was the so-called 'bulla' which at the same time was a mark of free birth (Val. Max. 5, 6, 8).

[5] Pliny HN 33, 84. Simultaneously, the relatives, and perhaps also a nurse (1.3.2.1), commended the child to the gods and they strengthened their good wishes by means of spitting on the baby as a defence against the evil eye (Pliny HN 28, 39; Pers. 2, 31, 40).

[6] Pl. Leg. 887D. Transl. R. G. Bury.

[7] Philostr. Imag. 1, 15, quoted in p. 108.

grandmother[8] or an older sister. It was primarily the mother's responsibility that her children should become acquainted with the proper myths:

> Nor again must mothers under the influence of such poets terrify their children with harmful tales, how that there are certain gods whose apparitions haunt the night in the likeness of many strangers from all manner of lands, lest while they speak evil of the gods they at the same time make cowards of the children.[9]

Among those mythical stories narrated to little children there might also have been beast fables[10] since they were highly valued for their moral worth, according to the following introduction in the *Corpus Glossariorum Latinorum*:

> At this point, then, I will begin to write the fables of Aesop, and will provide an illustration, for it is from him that the pictures are drawn; these fables are very necessary for the practical conduct of our lives.[11]

As girls grew in years so the means by which they heard stories with mythical themes increased. It was the practice for educated slaves to read aloud[12] for the family's benefit,[13] while sons of the household recited lengthy passages from literature[14] which they had learned in

---

[8] The expression of 'old wives tales' had became a common phrase (Cic. Nat.D. 3, 5,12; Hor. Sat. 2, 6, 77) which indicates that women of the older generation used to tell stories to their grandchildren; this was equally applicable to old nurses.

[9] Pl. Resp. 381E. Transl. P. Shorey. Cf. Tac. Dial. 29, 1-3, quoted in p. 17. Cf. also Min. Fel. Oct. 24, 1.

[10] According to Quintilian (Inst. 1, 9, 2), Aesop's fables 'were the natural successors of the fairy stories of the nursery.' (Transl. H. E. Butler).

[11] Corp.Gloss.Lat. 3, 39, 49ff. Transl. from Bonner 1977, 178. The *Corpus Glossariorum Latinorum* is an explanatory collation of archaic words and also of words difficult to understand put together during the whole imperial era (Fuhrmann 1967, 818).

[12] In antiquity people always used to read aloud (cf. Acts 8: 28-30)–a fact of utmost importance in regard to those who were not able to read.

[13] Pliny Ep. 9, 36, 4; 5, 19, 3; 8, 1, 2.

[14] Homer was thoroughly studied and recited in Greek (Bonner 1977, 213), and a Latin translation by Livius Andronicus was used in the time of Horace (Hor. Epist. 2, 1, 69ff; 2, 1, 62) (Bonner 1977, 213). However, Virgil was the most important Latin school text throughout the centuries (Bonner 1977, 213). According to Ovid (Tr. 2, 533-536), the most widely read part of the *Aeneid* was the love-story of Dido and Aeneas. Juvenal (6, 434ff) tells us that women were familiar with Homer and Virgil. Though there is no evidence of the use of Euripides as school text it is reasonable to suggest that he was studied along with Roman dramatists since his tragedies provided models for the Roman drama (Bonner 1977, 214). Furthermore, Quintilian (Inst. 10, 1, 67-68) recommends the study of Euripides to those who are preparing themselves in order to plead in court.

school.[15] Public readings were given in the towns,[16] and, though the average woman had few opportunities to attend to such readings (cf. 1.5), she would certainly have heard the contents of them discussed by other members of the household. Thus, even if a girl happened to be more or less illiterate,[17] she could by way of listening become acquainted with the mythical stories of importance to her religious education.

2.2.1.2 By Observing

As well as by the oral tradition religion was assimilated by sight. According to Prudentius paganism was handed down from one generation to another by works of art, and he describes a young man assimilating the pagan religion through the statues of the Capitolium at Rome:

> And then when he went abroad. and saw the lofty Capitol. and so gave his faith to the images and believed that the figures standing in a row, which he shuddered to look at, were the lords of the heavens. In such wise has the observance grown; starting in an evil hour long ago from our forefathers it was then handed on to the generations that followed and carried further by their remote descendants. Their unthinking hearts dragged a lengthening chain, and the blind custom spread down to depraved ages.[18]

Although young girls most often stayed in their close environment the way of learning pagan religion by works of art, as is described in this text, was of course also available to them.

Mythological themes were present everywhere in works of art and were not confined to sanctuaries and temples. In the home household

---

[15] Bonner 1977, 212ff. Learning literature implied also learning mythology. According to Cicero (Verr. 2, 18, 47) every educated boy would know the story of Latona giving birth to Apollo and Diana at Delos. Consequently, teachers of literature were obliged to give lessons on pagan gods and explain their names, their genealogies and the tales about them.

[16] Pliny Ep. 2, 19, 1; 3, 19, 4; 5, 3, 8; 7, 17, 1.

[17] As for the upper classes, many literate girls are recorded (Bonner 1977, 27ff.) and girls reading scrolls are sometimes depicted in Greek and Roman art (Klein 1932, 29f). Martial (1, 35, 1-3; 3, 69; 8, 3, 13-16) is even thought to speak of girls as attending grammar school (Bonner 1977, 136). Though education for girls of the lower classes was not common to that extent it may be suggested that at least those from the towns were sent to primary school, if they could not receive their lessons at home (Bonner 1977, 165). Since the whole family was often engaged in making their living through business (cf. 1.5.1.1) girls might have been shop assistants; in that role they needed a rudimentary knowledge of reading, writing and calculation.

[18] Prudent. c.Symm.1, 215-244. Transl. H. J.Thomson.

utensils[19] and oil lamps were often decorated with such motifs[20] and a well-to-do family would have a tessellated floor[21] or a wall-painting depicting the adventures of various deities.[22] Outside the home, the public baths often had mosaics with subjects from Greek mythology,[23] and the many fountains, providing water to the households, were an important means of information on mythological themes since they were frequently decorated with reliefs and statues relating to the divine sphere.[24] When dealing with the influence of religion on art, we must not disregard coins as a source of religious knowledge since they often employ the themes of myth and sometimes provide evidence of folk traditions local to the place of coinage.[25]

Besides visual art, we are told by Plato that the theatre was another important visual medium for obtaining familiarity with Greek mythology:

[- - -] and they (the demagogues) saw spectacles which illustrated them (the stories), of the kind which the young delight to see and hear when performed at sacrifices. [26]

This means of acquiring religious knowledge became increasingly useful when, to a great extent, Greek drama was replaced by pantomime.[27] Presumably, pantomime made the subject more comprehensible and easier to assimilate than Greek drama in its original form, and especially so in the case of a child.[28] Even when children were not allowed to watch the plays it can be assumed that a

---

[19] For instance, glazed earthenware vessels with relief decor (Marquardt 1886, 656ff).

[20] Roman oil lamps were often decorated with scenes from the world of the gods and heroes, from beast fables or from Oriental religion (Marquardt 1886, 644f).

[21] The motifs of the mosaics were appropriate to the function of the room. For instance, the Dionysiac thiasus was a common subject in a dining-room (v.Lorentz 1933, 339).

[22] Marquardt 1886, 616, n.3.

[23] Here Poseidon together with the whole body of divine inhabitants of the sea used to be depicted (v.Lorentz 1933, 399).

[24] Kapossy 1969, 12ff. Cf. 3.4.1.1, p. 64 n. 48.

[25] Lanckoronski 1958.

[26] Pl. Leg. 887D. Transl. R. G. Bury. Cf. Pl. Leg. 658D; Paus. 1, 3, 3; Tert. Apol. 15, 1-3.

[27] The pantomime, which takes its subjects mainly from the Greek mythology (Wüst 1983, 840), was widespread, especially in the eastern parts of the Empire (Wüst 1983, 847), and it reached its height of popularity in the Augustan era (Wüst 1983, 842). In Philippi mimes were performed as well, according to an inscription (CIL 3, 6113) (Mommsen 1869, 461ff; 495ff). In contrast to the pantomime, the mime presented everyday life in caricature (Wüst 1983, 862f).

[28] Lucian (Salt. 39; 49; 51) enumerates a great number of mythical themes which were presented in pantomime; among them subjects relating to Dionysus are common. The Dionysiac cult had special significance to Philippian women and is discussed in 4.3.

theatrical performance was an event to be spoken of by the members of the family.

Furthermore, through observing the worship of their parents children first became aquainted with rituals and religious ceremonies. Plato continues his account of children's religious education in the following way:

> [- - -] and their own parents they saw showing the utmost zeal on behalf of themselves and their children in addressing the gods in prayers and supplications. and at the rising and setting of the sun and moon they heard and saw the prostrations and devotions of all the Greeks and barbarians. directed to these luminaries. [29]

Finally, the observation of rituals and ceremonies offered to deceased female relatives was an important part of the inculcation of mourning rituals.[30] It had the further effect of instilling a respect for the continuity of the family. A girl thus became aware of herself as a potential link in the chain of her future husband's family (cf. 1.5.1.1). The model figures of her ancestresses,[31] often made of wax or plaster,[32] would have been utilized to further her moral education—as would stories calculated to keep green the memory of departed forebears. Pliny the Elder expresses the exemplary value of such images of ancestors to a male descendant in the following words:

> Outside the houses and round the doorways there were other representations of those mighty spirits, with spoils taken from the enemy fastened to them, which even one who bought the house was not permitted to unfasten, and the mansions eternally celebrated a triumph even though they changed their masters. This acted as a mighty incentive, when every day the very walls[33] reproached an unwarlike owner with intruding upon the the triumph of another![34]

---

[29] Pl. Leg. 887D-E. Transl. R. G. Bury.

[30] In the role of hired mourners women preceded the bier singing dirges (Blümner 1911, 492f). When mourning their relatives women appeared in white clothes and with dishevelled hair, and presumably with bare breasts (Blümner 1911, 497). They expressed their grief by beating their breasts, tearing their cheeks with their nails, tearing out their hair, and by calling out the name of the deceased (Blümner 1911, 497).

[31] Presumably a bride of a distinguished family used to bring the images of her own ancestors into her new home (Cic. Vatin. 11, 28; Sen.Controv. 2, 1, 17) (Drerup 1980, 121). From Augustus onwards images of women were also in use (Juv. 11, 18) (Drerup 1980, 122). Shrines dedicated to ancestors (pictured on grave reliefs) contain images of women (Frenz 1977, 55, Figs. 1-3).

[32] During the imperial time the waxen images were to a great extent replaced by plaster casts (Drerup 1980, 122) and the custom was extended to the middle classes (Drerup 1980, 123).

[33] In this case the images seem to have been fastened to the wall. Usually they were placed on altars in small shrines (Plin. HN 35, 6). See also Polyb. 6, 53, 3-6, quoted in p. 48.

[34] Pliny HN 35, 2, 7-8. Transl. H. Rackham.

The spectacle of an upper-class funeral, with the ancestors' images present in the procession, must have strongly affected young spectators. Polybius vividly described the impression made by such a funeral in the Forum Romanum in Republican time:

> Whenever any illustrious man dies, he is carried at his funeral into the forum to the so-called rostra, sometimes conspicious in an upright posture and more rarely reclined. Here with all the people standing round, a grown-up son, if he has left one who happens to be present, or if not some other relative mounts the rostra and discourses on the virtues and successful achievements of the dead. As a consequence the multitude and not only those who had a part in these achievements, but those also who had none, when the facts are recalled to their minds and brought before their eyes, are moved to such sympathy that the loss seems to be not confined to the mourners, but a public one affecting the whole people.[35] [- - -] and when any distinguished member of the family dies they take them (i.e. the images) to the funeral, putting them on men who seem to them to bear the closest resemblance to the original in stature and carriage. These representatives wear togas, with a purple border if the deceased was a consul or pretor, whole purple if he was a censor, and embroidered with gold if he had celebrated a triumph or achieved anything similar. They all ride in chariots preceded by the fasces, axes, and other insignia by which the different magistrates are wont to be accompanied according to the respective dignity of the offices of state held by each during his life; and when they arrive at the rostra they all seat themselves in a row on ivory chairs. There could not easily be a more ennobling spectacle for a young man who aspires to fame and virtue. For who would not be inspired by the sight of the images of men renowned for their excellence, all together and as if alive and breathing? What spectacle could be more glorious than this? Besides, he who makes the oration over the man about to be buried, when he has finished speaking of him recounts the successes and exploits of the rest whose images are present, beginning from the most ancient. By this means, by this constant renewal of the good report of brave men, the celebrity of those who performed noble deeds is rendered immortal, while at the same time the fame of those who did good service to their country becomes known to the people and a heritage for future generations. But the most important result is that young men are thus inspired to endure every suffering for the public welfare in the hope of winning the glory that attends on brave men.[36]

This long and detailed account deals with the funeral of a male and is reported from a male point of view. However, in the literary and epigraphical sources there are references to funerals of women who were equally honoured by discourses on female virtues[37] in the presence of the images of their ancestors. Tacitus tells us about the funeral of Junia, a distinguished wealthy woman:

> Junia, too, born niece to Cato, wife of Caius Cassius, sister of Marcus Brutus, looked her last on life, sixty-three full years after the field of Philippi. Her will was busily discussed by the crowd; because in disposing of her great wealth she mentioned nearly every patrician of note in complimentary terms, but omitted the Caesar. The slur was

---

[35] Polyb. 6, 53, 1-10. Transl. W. R. Paton.

[36] Polyb. 54, 1-3. Transl. W. R. Paton

[37] Surviving funeral eulogies from inscriptions tell us the contents of such panegyrics; for instance, the funeral eulogy for 'Turia' (CIL 6, 1527 = ILS 8393), partly quoted in p. 18, and in p. 30, and for Murdia (CIL 6, 10 230 = ILS 8394).

taken in good part, and he offered no objection to the celebration of her funeral with a panegyric at the Rostra and the rest of the customary ceremonies. The effigies of twenty great houses preceded her to the tomb—members of the Manlian and Quinctian families, and names of equal splendour.[38]

From a female point of view it is easy to imagine young girls to have been strongly influenced and strengthened in their future role as wives and mothers by watching such a funebrial pantomime as the one described in this text.

2.2.1.3 By Acting

Mythical stories and rituals, assimilated by listening and observing, were finally brought into practice through the girl's own participation. In this respect it may be appropriate to quote Aristotle:

> From childhood men have an instinct for representation, and in this respect man differs from the other animals [in] that he is far more imitative and learns his first lessons by representing things.[39]

According to ancient historians, Romulus prescribed that some rituals ought to be performed by women and that children should assist in these rituals all the while they lived in their parents' home.[40] Therefore, it was necessary for the mother and the nurse to involve the girl in the family's religious rites at an early age in order that she might learn her part in the ceremonial.[41] However, only freeborn children with both their parents undivorced and alive were allowed to assist in religious ceremonies, and these children showed off by wearing the 'toga praetexta', which was a robe with purple borders.[42] Consequently, children bereaved of their parents through death or divorce, foster-children and those born to slaves would be onlookers only and could not participate actively in the rituals; this segregation might have served to emphasize divisions within the family group (cf. 1.3.2.2).

As regards religious education Prudentius gives us a vivid description of an infant boy's introduction to worship through observing and acting, and similar formality would have governed the role of the girl:

---

[38] Tac. Ann. 3, 76. Transl. J. Jackson.
[39] Arist. Poet. 1448b, 2. Transl. W. H. Fyfe.
[40] Dion. Hal. Ant.Rom. 2, 22. For instance, the cult of the Lar Familiaris is attended to by the daughter in one of Plautus' comedies (Aul. 23-8, quoted in p. 43).
[41] In Aristophanes' *Acharnians* (241ff) there is a description of a young girl acting as a basket-bearer at the celebration of the 'Rural Dionysia' under the supervision of her mother.
[42] Dion. Hal. Ant.Rom. 2, 22; Tac. Hist. 4, 53, Ann. 2, 86 (Marquardt 1886, 70, n.3; van der Leeuw 1939, 12f).

The young heir bowed shuddering before anything which his hoary ancestors had designated as worshipful in their eyes. Children in their infancy drank in the error with their first milk while still at the crying stage, they had tasted of the sacrificial meal, and had seen mere stones coated with wax and the grimy gods of the house dripping with unguent. The little one had looked at a figure in the shape of Fortune, with her wealthy horn, standing in the house, a hallowed stone, and watched his mother palefaced, in prayer before it. Then, raised on his nurse's shoulder, he too pressed his lips to the flint and rubbed it with them, pouring out his childish petitions, asking for riches from a sightless stone, and convinced that all one's wishes must be sought from thence.[43]

Although this account is coloured by the writer's hostile feelings towards the pagan cults it gives an idea of the way an infant child was taught to pray to the household deities by the housewife and the nurse.
   At a more advanced age mythical stories, and beast-fables as well, would be brought to life by the little girl herself in her play. For instance, most children had a domestic pet of some kind[44] and this animal could be placed in the role of one of the beasts as the child re-enacted the fables told to her. Further, some of these domestic animals played their part in many myths and were identified with certain deities; for instance, Aphrodite was connected with the duck, the goose, the pigeon and the tortoise,[45] all of which are depicted as children's playmates on Greek vases,[46] grave reliefs[47] and statues.[48]
   Dolls were also important in this respect since they could serve to illustrate mythical stories and rituals[49] in a little girl's imagination.[50] Dolls which have been excavated are always shaped as adult women,[51] and are sometimes furnished with a veil or other kind of head-dress.[52] They often have moving arms and legs[53] and could presumably be dressed in a variety of clothes. Thus they could easily be imagined to take

---

[43] Prudent. c.Symm. 1, 197-214. Transl. H. J.Thomson.

[44] Such pets, reproduced in terracotta and found in children's tombs, were drawn from a variety of birds, dogs, hares, and tortoises (Klein 1932, 10ff).

[45] Keller 1909, v. index s.v. 'Venus'.

[46] Klein 1932, 10ff; Schmidt 1977, 66ff.

[47] Rühfel 1984, 165ff.

[48] Rühfel 1984, 185ff.

[49] In an Athenian tomb of a young girl two sacrifial baskets in miniature (Buschor 1976, 19f) were found together with a doll with moving arms and legs (Buschor 1976, 21ff) which may indicate that the girl used to play 'offering sacrifice' by imagining the doll to be either in the role of goddess or priestess.

[50] In antiquity dolls might not only have been for the purpose of occupying and amusing children but might have been used in a religious context as well (Schmidt 1977, 12; Buschor 1976, 21).

[51] Schmidt 1977, 127. Infant girls are lacking in Greek and Roman mythology. The infant Dionysus represents both sexes. Androgynous characteristics attributable to Dionysus are discussed in 4.3.2.3.5.

[52] Schmidt 1977, 127

[53] Schmidt 1977, 128.

part in processions and mythical adventures, and be made to represent goddesses of all cults.

Girls' (and boys') main religious tasks in the domestic cult, however, were connected with the meals. According to an ancient tradition, the food and the drinking-vessels were to be handed only by sexually immature young persons, and consequently the privileged children of the family were obliged to do the waiting at table;[54] before the meal they offered sacrifices to the family gods, stauettes of whom were placed by the hearth.[55] Presumably they also placed the salt boxes[56] and images of the gods on the table, which was regarded as sacred.[57]

However, the rituals to be learned by the girl included not only ceremonies of the domestic but also of the official cult.[58] The privileged children assisted the local high priestess ('flaminica') in the sacrifices,[59] and the girls had the task of weaving her mantle.[60] In addition, these children acted as choristers in processions[61] at festivals.[62] However, their less favoured sisters, brothers and playmates, who were not permitted to take part in these activities, had to be content with watching the ceremonies.

Finally, parents' exemplary role of donor in connection with the 'sacra publica' must be mentioned. According to an inscription, dated to A.D. 242,[63] a young priestess of Venus at Peltusium was appointed 'patrona':

> She has begun to show such affection and kindly regard, as her parents have always done before, that she deserves to be made a patroness of our praefecture.

To a great extent the recorded generosity of the parents might have been a means of introducing their girl into public life (cf. 2.3.2.2); we may not, however, exclude other motives.

---

[54] Columella Rust. 12, 4, 3 (van der Leeuw 1939, 453).

[55] Schol. Serv. Aen. 1, 730.

[56] Salt was regarded as holy (Hor. Carm. 2, 16, 13ff; Arn. Adv.Nat. 2, 67) (Nilsson 1954, 77).

[57] Arn. Adv.Nat. 2, 67; Plut. Mor. 704B (Nilsson 1954, 78).

[58] The rules pertaining to children in the domestic situation were valid also for the official cult in the town. Cf. n. 41 supra.

[59] Schol. Aen. 11, 543; Ov. Fast. 2, 650; Liv. 37, 3, 6.

[60] Festus Gloss.Lat. 407, s.v. 'Rica'. All girls had to learn spinning and weaving, since the manufacture of clothes was undertaken by the females in the family (Clark 1981, 198f).

[61] Boys and girls were trained in choir-singing and dancing for ceremonial occasions (For instance, Cic.DeOr. 3, 23, 87; Prop. 1, 2, 27-28; 2, 1, 9-10; Stat. Silv. 3, 5, 64ff; Juv. 7, 175-7) (Bonner 1977, 44, n. 85).

[62] Suet. Calig.16; Catull. 34,1ff ; Macrob. Sat. 1, 6.14.

[63] CIL 9, 3429, 7-11. Transl. from Mohler 1932, 116.

2.3 RELIGIOUS ROLES OF ADULT WOMEN

2.3.1 'Sacra Privata'

In putting her childhood behind her the young girl relinquished those deities which had formed part of it. The day before her wedding there was a ceremony at which she took leave of her childhood by sacrificing her toys either to the household deities or to Venus.[64] In domestic religion, the family formed a private unit with the paterfamilias as the high priest and his wife as the priestess.[65] Marriage brought allegiance to the gods of her husband's family:

> For on the first day of the marriage the bride is in retirement, but on the next day she must begin to assume authority in her husband's house and offer sacrifice.[66]

By law she became not only the domestic manager of the household (1.5.1.1) but also supporter of her husband's religious rituals:

> The law was to this effect, that a woman joined to her husband by a holy marriage should share in all his possessions and sacred rites.[67]

In addition to the responsibility she had for the religious education of her children (2.2.1.1), the housewife had many other important tasks[68] in various domains as the priestess of the home.[69] At diverse celebrations she had practical as well as religious duties to fulfil, as the whole family (including the slaves) gathered to take part in a banquet.[70] Consequently, although women are seldom mentioned in the sources in this role there is good reason to assume that they played an important

---

[64] Harmon 1978, 1598. We are also told that the young girl offered her toys to Artemis before the wedding (Anth. Gr. 6, 280). On that occasion a freeborn girl abandoned her 'bulla' which she had worn since she was a baby (see n. 4 supra).

[65] van der Leeuw 1939, 453.

[66] Macrob. Sat. 1, 15, 22. Transl. P. V. Davies. As regards the images of her own ancestors, see n. 31 supra.

[67] Dion. Hal. Ant.Rom. 2, 25, 2. Transl. E. Cary. According to Cicero (Leg. 2, 21, 52) the order of the 'sacra' was given by the pontifices as 'edicta' or 'decreta' and did not have the status of law ('pontificum auctoritate, nulla lege') (Bruck 1954, 25).

[68] A woman's social status seems to have decided her part in the cult actions. In the comedies of Plautus the freeborn married woman ('uxor') performs most cult actions while the hetaira ('meretrix') only prepares a sacrifice in connection with a meal together with her lover. If freeborn girls ('virgo') are mentioned in connection with a cult they have similar tasks as married women. Slave girls ('ancilla'), on the other hand, are only useful helpers at the sacrifices (Schuhmann 1977, 140f).

[69] She had to perform the sacrifices and prayers to the household gods in the way her husband desired (Xen. Oec. 7, 7-8).

[70] Columella Rust. 11, 1, 19; Ov. Fast. 6, 305f; Hor. Epod. 2, 65f; Hor. Sat. 2,5, 12ff, 6, 64f. (Wissowa 1902, 149 n.11; Nilsson 1954, 83).

part in the household cult, particularly in connection with practical domestic tasks such as the preparing of offerings and communal meals.

2.3.1.1 Worship of the Household Deities

Of the principal deities being worshipped in the home, the Lar, the Genius (i.e. the generative power of the paterfamilias) and the Penates were the main gods of the household.[71] Their worship is described in the Theodosian edict of A.D. 392 prohibiting the domestic cult; the Lar was offered sacrifice of fire, the Genius of unmixed wine, and the Penates of incense.[72]

Among these deities the Lar Familiaris[73] and the Genius were specifically protectors of the family. In Plautus' *Aulularia*, the Lar Familiaris rewards the young daughter of the house by helping her to obtain a dowry in return for her cultic observance. The Lar himself speaks the prologue:

> He has one daughter. She prays to me constantly, with daily gifts of incense, or wine, or something: she gives me garlands. Out of regard for her I caused Euclio (the father) to discover the treasure here in order that he might the more easily find her a husband, if he wished. For she has been ravished by a young gentleman of very high rank.[74]

---

[71] Other deities of the household were Athena (Theophr.Char.16), Dionysus (Ar. Ach.241ff) and Hecate (Eur. Med. 397). Zeus was worshipped particularly as protector of the family (Plut. Mor. 679D). Among these deities Hecate-Artemis, under the name of Diana (4.2), and Dionysus (4.3) were worshipped by Philippian women.

[72] Nilsson 1954, 85.

[73] Every family had a Lararium: a cupboard containing a little shrine with small statuettes representing the Lares (Petron. Sat. 29). There were two kinds of Lares: Lar Familiaris and Lar Compitalis. The latter was the guardian of the cross-roads and was included in the domestic cult (Ogilvie 1979, 101). The Lares seem to have been held in close regard by the housewife. When a woman married she brought three coins to her new home: one for her husband, a second for the Lares of the hearth and a third for the Lares Compitales (Non. 852) (Harmon 1978, 1595).

[74] Plaut. Aul. 23-8. Transl. P. Nixon.

From this text we can get an idea of the way in which the household deities were honoured by prayers[75] and sacrifices;[76] it is reasonable to assume that the housewife in her role of priestess was ultimately responsible for the rituals being properly performed by her daughter (cf. 2.2.1.3). The worship of the Lar Familiaris was intimately related to a wide range of family affairs; consequently, besides the daily observances performed in his honour he was worshipped both on fixed days[77] and on special occasions. For instance, the housewife paid tribute to this deity through decorating the hearth[78] with garlands and flowers[79] at the setting out and returning home of a member of the family who journeyed abroad, and in the case of a death within the family sacrifice was offered to this guardian spirit to purify the house.[80]

The cult of the Genius[81] seems to have been of great importance: every family was obliged to have its Genius[82] and the members used to swear by it.[83] The Genius was worshipped on the birthday of the paterfamilias and on his wedding day,[84] mostly with offerings of wine and honey cakes, pigs and occasionally also of lambs.[85] The Genius had its female

---

[75] When offering a prayer the housewife was expected to be veiled and to have clean hands (Plaut. Amph. 1093f) (Schuhmann 1977, 142). The prayers seem to have had a set form. Plautus has an example of a prayer said by a housewife: 'Apollo, I beseech thee, graciously grant thy favour, and safety and sound health, to our family, and may'st thou spare my son with thy gracious favour' (Merc. 678-680. Transl. P. Nixon). Cf. the following prayer found in Cato (Agr. 141, 2): 'Father Mars, I pray and beseech thee that thou be gracious and merciful to me, my house and my household' (Transl.W. D.Hooper. Rev. H. Boyd).

[76] According to Plautus the gifts offered to the household gods consisted most often of wine, incense, cakes and flowers while offerings of animals were rare (Schuhmann 1977, 140).

[77] For instance, on the Calends, Nonae and Idus to the Lar Familiaris (Cato, Agr. 143, 2) (Nilsson 1954, 81). Worship on fixed days was valid also for other deities of the household, for instance on the fourth and seventh day of every month to Hermes and Apollo respectively (Theophr. Char. 16).

[78] From a religious point of view the house could be seen as a shrine devoted to the household deities. According to literary sources cult statues were placed inside (Artem. 2, 33) and outside the house (Artem. 4, 78; Ar. Ran. 366) and at the entrance (Eur. Med. 397). The hearth, in particular, was an important place of worship being the centre of the family (2.2.1.3). The images of the ancestors were placed in small wooden shrines (Polyb. 6, 53, 3-6, quoted in p. 48).

[79] Cato, Agr. 143, 2 (Nilsson 1954, 81).

[80] Nilsson 1954, 81. Cic. Leg. 2, 55 (Wissowa 1912, 169).

[81] On the wall paintings in Pompeii the Genius of the family is portrayed as a young man dressed in a toga carrying a cornucopia and accompanied by the household snakes (Orr 1978, 1572).

[82] The Roman Genius included a great variety of roles associated with individuals, households, the army and the guilds (Orr 1978, 1575).

[83] Orr 1978, 1571.

[84] Orr 1978, 1571.

[85] Orr 1978, 1571.

counterpart in the Juno, the creative power of the materfamilias, but the latter had no prescribed cult of her own.[86] However, there is reason to believe that in some cases the Genius and the Juno were worshipped together and possibly seen as a divine power representing both male and female. For instance, there might have been a link between the Genius and the Juno in the worship of the wedding bed.[87] Moreover, the Genius is mentioned in connection with a woman, according to a surviving inscription,[88] and even the Genius of 'Urbs Romae' is said to be either male or female ('genio urbis Romae, sive mas sive femina').[89]

2.3.1.2 Family Celebrations

Furthermore, family affairs such as weddings and funerals involved prescribed rituals to be performed by the priestess of the household. On other occasions–for instance when a boy assumed the toga worn by adults[90] and at betrothals[91]–the main task of the housewife seems to have been the preparing of a banquet; this task was closely related to her everyday domestic obligations.

2.3.1.2.1 Weddings

Besides being responsible for preparing the wedding feast,[92] the housewife had at this occasion a more prominent religious role, if she happened to be a 'univira' in the original sense of the word.[93] When a daughter was given away in marriage she supervised the rites connected with the dressing of the bride and those associated with her transference to the family of the bridegroom.[94] However, the most significant ritual performed by the priestess of the household was that

---

[86] Nilsson 1954, 85.

[87] Orr 1978, 1570. The Genius of the paterfamilias warranted the continued existence of the family (Harmon 1978, 1595).

[88] CIL 8, 22 770 ('Genio Tarquitiae Marcelli Matri Piissimae') (Orr 1978, 1571 n. 87).

[89] Schol. Aen. 2, 351 (Orr 1978, 1571 n. 93).

[90] Blümner 1911, 335ff.

[91] Blümner 1911, 345ff.

[92] Blümner 1911, 357.

[93] Blümner 1911, 355 n. 9. The general concept of 'univira' is discussed in 1.3.1 and 1.3.2. From a religious point of view 'univira' is a term related to women entitled to perform cult ceremonies. For instance, during the Principate the flamen of Jupiter had to have a wife who was univira (Lightman-Zeisel 1977, 19).

[94] Harmon 1978, 1599.

undertaken by her in her role of 'pronuba':[95] after having presented the bride and bridegroom to the guests,[96] she joined their right hands together[97]–the ceremony is depicted in art as the most important symbolic act of the wedding.[98]

2.3.1.2.2 *Death and Burial*

Deaths imposed further obligations on the housewife, since she was responsible for the corpse being washed and prepared for burial.[99] Lucian has described this task as follows:

> Then they bathe them (i.e. the corpses) and after anointing with the finest of perfume that body which is already hasting to corruption, and crowning it with pretty flowers, they lay them in state, clothed in splendid raiment. [100]

Together with other female relatives she then took part in the lamentations and dirges at the funeral,[101] though her manifestations of mourning were at all times expected to be accompanied by a dignified demeanour.[102]

At this occasion the housewife (at least of a well-off family) in her role as priestess of the household presumably had the practical obligation of supervising the taking of a cast of the features of the deceased and of making preparations for the ceremonials, although it was the paterfamilias who was ultimately responsible for the ancestral worship.[103] Again, Polybius has given us a description of this custom:

---

[95] Tertullian (De exhort.castit.13) deals with the magical aspect of the 'univira-pronuba' (the handmaiden to the bride) (Lightman-Zeisel 1977, 20 n. 2).

[96] Blümner 1911, 354f.

[97] Blümner 1911, 355 n. 10.

[98] Blümner 1911, 355, n. 11 and 12.

[99] Isae. 6, 40-41; Plut. Mor. 119 B.

[100] Lucian De Luct. 11 (Transl. A.M. Harmon). According to Propertius (4, 3, 51), rich and distinguished women were shrouded in purple-coloured winding-sheets (cf. 1.5.1.1, p. 24, n. 115).

[101] Hopkins 1983, 217ff.

[102] An old Roman law prohibited women from shouting and scratching their faces at funerals (XII Tabl. 10, 4.) and, according to later philosophical essays, this was made necessary because of the excessive behaviour of mourners who wailed too loudly and for too long (Sen. Ad Marc. 2, 3ff; 3, 1ff; Plut. Mor. 609B ; cf. Plut. Mor. 114F-115A).

[103] If the paterfamilias had died, his role was taken over by the next male heir (Gardner 1986, 8). Cf. Hor.Epist. 2, 2 : 'naturae deus humanae mortalis in unum quodque caput'. The Genius passes 'to another person on the death of the first one' (Transl. from Orr 1978, 1571).

Next after the interment and the performance of the usual ceremonies, they (i.e. the mourners) place the image of the departed in the most conspicuous position in the house, enclosed in a wooden shrine. This image is a mask reproducing with remarkable fidelity both the features and the complexion of the deceased. On the occasion of public sacrifices they display these images, and decorate them with much care.[104]

In addition, the funeral and the commemoration of the dead included the preparation of several banquets. On the day of the funeral a banquet was held at the site of the burial;[105] after a nine-day period of mourning another one was held,[106] and at the same time a ritual sweeping of the house was performed.[107] Thereafter, meals were held annually at the tomb on four occasions;[108] the preparations for these banquets, being incumbent upon the housewife, might have been on a large scale since kitchens were often built at the burial places.[109]

2.3.2 'Sacra Publica'

Besides her position as a priestess in relation to the family deities, the housewife could also take part in the official worship of deities who protected community and state. She was, however, obliged to join in the cult of the Emperor.[110]

2.3.2.1 The Role of Worshipper

According to literary sources religious observances associated with the official cult took place at stated intervals. Housewives used to offer sacrifice to Juno on the first day of every month, which day was dedicated to this goddess.[111] Further, on the 1st of March Roman women celebrated the Matronalia in honour of Juno Lucina, whom they invoked for continuance of their marriages and happy delivery at childbirth,[112] and on the 19th of March they started the celebration of a five-day long

---

[104] Polyb. 6, 53, 3-6. Transl. W. R. Paton. The shrine was opened on festive days and the images were crowned with wreaths (Blümner 1911, 494).

[105] Cic. Leg. 2, 24, 60 (Blümner 1911, 509ff).

[106] Harmon 1978, 1602.

[107] Harmon 1978, 1602.

[108] On the Parentalia, Rosalia, the birthday of the deceased and on the Dies Violae (Blümner 1911, 509 n. 18).

[109] According to inscriptions found on burial grounds (Blümner 1911, 508 n. 8; 510).

[110] Latte 1960, 312.

[111] Plaut. Mil. 691f.

[112] Ziegler 1969, 1085.

feast for Minerva,[113] the protectress of female handicrafts of various kinds.[114]

Literature has preserved two pictures of Republican women practising cultic observances, and these portraits might be valid for female worship at later periods also. Polybius describes a distinguished Roman lady on her way to the temple:

> This lady whose name was Aemilia, used to display great magnificence whenever she left her house to take part in the ceremonies that women attend, having participated in the fortune of Scipio when he was at the height of his prosperity. For apart from the richness of her own dress and of the decorations of her carriage, all the baskets, cups, and other utensils for the sacrifice were either of gold or silver, and were borne in her train on all such solemn occasions, while the number of maids and men-servants in attendance was correspondingly large.[115]

We are further told that these splendid equipments, which after Aemilia's death were inherited by Scipio's mother and displayed by her at public sacrifices,[116] were highly admired and spoken of by other women:

> [- - -] for women are fond of talking and once they have started a thing never have too much of it.[117]

The other text, found in the writings of Cicero, portrays Sicilian women bringing offerings to Diana:

> No story is better known throughout Sicily than that of how, when Diana was being borne out of the town, all the matrons and maidens of Segesta flocked to the spot, anointed her with perfumes, covered her with garlands and flowers, and burning incense and spices escorted her to the frontier of their land.[118]

It is easy to imagine that such colourful spectacles of female worship performed before the public were highly attractive to women and effectively promoted the pagan cults.[119]

Besides their usual visits to the temple for sacrifice and prayer women could take an active part in the official cult on certain occasions. Female choirs often participated in processions at great celebrations;[120] Horace

---

[113] Plaut. Mil. 692. Ov. Fast. 3, 809ff.
[114] Schuhmann 1977, 140 n. 13.
[115] Polyb. 31, 26, 3-5. Transl. W. R. Paton.
[116] Polyb. 31, 26, 7-8.
[117] Polyb. 31, 26, 10. Transl. W. R. Paton.
[118] Cic. Verr.4, 35, 77. Transl. L. H. G. Greenwood.
[119] As regards cultic performances attracting women, Theocritus (Id. 15) gives a vivid picture of a visit of two Alexandrian women to the festival of Adonis.
[120] Quasten 1930, 111f.

refers to rehearsals of hymn-singing when he reminds women of his feast-day hymn which they sang when they were young.[121]

2.3.2.2 The Role of Priestess

As well as in the 'sacra privata' women had the role of priestess in the 'sacra publica'. However, poor women could not afford this dignity in the official cult. Rich and distinguished women, on the other hand, aspired to attain the opportunity to purchase a priesthood.[122] The fact is that wealth, high social rank and family connections[123] could obtain for a woman a priestly office,[124] which gave her the opportunity to enter upon a career of philanthropy.[125] These offices were elective (the priestess was appointed 'designata'),[126] and the electors expected the priestess to defray the expense[127] of new official buildings or to finance repairs to older ones, as well as providing banquets and games on public holidays;[128] according to inscriptions on them, a large number of statues of priestesses were erected in public places as rewards for their contributions.[129]

Two inscriptions, however, indicate that women holding priestly office could use their property for the public good by attending to the more personal needs of their fellow-citizens:

> To Agusia Priscilla, priestess of the Hope and Safety of Augustus, the honour of a statue was given by the Decuriones of Gabii. because after the expenditures customarily made by women of distinction in return for the priesthood, she had promised to repair the porticos of the Temple of Spes, and had fulfilled her religious obligations for the welfare of the Emperor Antoninus Pius and his children, giving an exceptional

---

[121] Hor. Carm.Saec. 75-6.

[122] According to Artemidorus (1, 56), it was advantageous for freeborn rich women and maidens to dream of driving in a carriage through the town, since the dream meant respected priestly offices.

[123] Husband and wife could both hold priestly office; fathers and daughters of the same family are also recorded as having held such offices (Mohler1932, 115).

[124] Mohler 1932, 115. These offices could also be related to the imperial cult (Mohler 1932, 116). In Philippi inscriptions mention two priestesses in the cult of the empress (3.4.1.3).

[125] Mohler 1932, 115. Titles show that female priestly offices could be joined to secular posts, for instance the head of the gymnasium (Mac Mullen 1980, 215).

[126] Mohler 1932, 115.

[127] The phrase 'out of her own resources' (ἐκ τῶν ἰδίων) is often found in inscriptions (Mac Mullen 1980, 216).

[128] Mohler 1932, 115ff.

[129] Mohler 1932, 116. In Philippi a statue was erected to a woman in the temple of the Egyptian gods (4.4.1). According to surviving inscriptions a woman could hold priestly offices in several places at the same time (Mohler 1932, 116). (Cf. ILS 1259, quoted in p. 52).

exhibitions of games, at which articles of clothing were presented to all the spectators.¹³⁰

This lady is said to have furnished people with clothes, and, according to the following inscription from Corinth (dated to about A.D. 43), another woman opened her home and invited the poor to communal meals:

> The deme of Patareis has decreed: Whereas Junia Theodora, a Roman resident in Corinth, a woman held in highest honor [- - -] who copiously supplied from her own means many of our citizens with generosity, and received them in her home and in particular never ceased acting on behalf of our citizens in regard to any favour asked—the majority of citizens have gathered in assembly to offer testimony on her behalf. ¹³¹

From these inscriptions we may conclude that property given by women in return for priestly office could be used to finance public assistance for the poor and needy. In this way religion might have been associated with charitable work in people's mind. In reality, however, this kind of charity was to a great extent a social activity performed by wealthy women within a religious framework in order to further the reputation of their families and the success of their children.¹³²

2.3.3 Woman and Mystery Religions

In dealing with various categories of Graeco-Roman worship associated with women, it may be appropriate to discuss also their propensity to the mystery religions. These religions centered on the transition from death to life by means of rituals which dramatized the cycle of life and conveyed belief in the immortality and resurrection of the deity. Such ideas were inherent in the female role of bringing forth new life, and, consequently, such rituals became vital to women. The mystery religions will be discussed in Chapter 4;¹³³ in this context I confine myself to focusing on the attraction they had for women and the attitudes they evoked from the women's husbands.

2.3.3.1 The Attraction of Mystery Religions to Women

In discussing the attraction of the mystery religions to women I take as my starting point the famous grave inscription of Praetextatus and

---

¹³⁰ CIL 14, 2808. Transl. from Mohler 1932, 116.
¹³¹ Pleket, 8, 22-31. Transl. from WGR, 113.
¹³² Cf. CIL 9, 3429, 7-11, quoted in p. 42.
¹³³ In Philippi all cults had more or less the character of mysteries since they were related to funeral associations.

Paulina. Although it dates from the 4th cent. A.D.[134] it gives valuable information—which to a great extent is also valid for the time of the rise of Christianity—of relevance to the present subject and throws light on the relationship between husband and wife in matters of religion. In this respect the most important section runs as follows:

> You as pious initiate conceal in the secrecy of your mind what was revealed in the sacred mysteries, and you with knowledge worship the manifold divinity of the gods; you kindly include as colleague in the rites your wife, who is respectful of men and gods and is faithful to you.[- - -] My husband, by the gift of your learning you keep me from the fate of death pure and chaste; you take me into the temples and devote me as the servant of the gods. With you as my witness I am introduced to all the mysteries; you my pious consort, honour me as priestess of Dindymene and Attis with the sacrificial rites of the taurobolium; you instruct me as minister of Hecate in the triple secret and you make me worthy of the rites of the Greek Ceres.[- - -] Now men, now women approve the insignia that you as a teacher have given me.[135]

From this passage (where Paulina is thought to be speaking) we learn that Praetextatus himself taught his wife in religious matters. Apparently, in contrast to many other husbands (as will be shown in 2.3.3.2) he valued highly the mysteries, and Paulina is said to have been initiated into them all—she even participated in the role of priestess in the taurobolium[136] and in other mysteries. We are further told that through the rituals she was made a participant of the new life achieved by the deity and that happiness in the afterlife was ensured for her.

This inscription is an important document throwing light upon the importance of the mystery religions to women. In this respect it is striking that Paulina, who seems to have been a wealthy woman, became an adherent of them all; this decision (apparently approved by her husband) was presumably rooted in a feeling of uncertainty as to the most propitious cult to choose to make certain of a blessed life in the hereafter. Not all women, however, could afford to take such precautions in this way since initiation into a mystery cult could be an expensive affair.[137] In addition to the fact that the mystery religions seem to have provided a more intense religious experience than could be offered by the domestic or by the offical cult,[138] their attraction for women may be explained by the fact that the promise of a blessed after-life extended to

---

[134] Praetextatus was governor of Achaea in A.D. 362 under the Emperor Julian (Lefkowitz 1986, 78).

[135] ILS 1259, 13-37. Transl. from Lefkowitz 1986, 77f.

[136] The taurobolium, a kind of baptism in the blood of a bull slaughtered on a floor above the initiate, belonged to the cult of Magna Mater and Attis and first occurred in the 4th century A.D. (Vermaseren 1977, 101ff).

[137] According to Apuleius (Met. 11, 24), the initiate seems to have been expected to invite relatives and friends to a banquet celebrating the new life acquired through the initiation.

[138] The dramatization of mythical events in the mystery religons which offered women an emotional participation in the fate of a deity had no correspondence in other cults. As to the dramatization of the Isiac myth, see 4.4.2.3.3.

their children as well as to themselves. As has been stated before, children were threatened by an early death (1.2.2), and an untimely death–for child or adult alike–was thought to have an adverse effect on one's existence in the world to come.[139] Happily, this cruel fate could be averted by initiation into a mystery cult. These matters are further discussed in 4.3.2.2.

2.3.3.2 Husbands' Attitudes towards Mystery Religions

From literature we find that women who inclined towards the mystery cults could become figures of scorn to their husbands. A few texts serve to illustrate women's attachment to these cults as seen from the male point of view.

Plutarch has much to say on the subject. First, he states that women lack a critical attitude towards foreign worship, exemplified by the cults of Magna Mater and the Egyptian gods:

> However, the thing that most filled the poetic art with disrepute was the tribe of wandering soothsayers and rogues that practised their charlatanry about the shrines of the Great Mother and of Serapis, making up oracles, some using their own ingenuity, others taking by lot from certain treatises oracles for the benefit of servants and womenfolk, who are most enticed by verse and of a poetic vocabulary.[140]

According to another text, he explicitly declares that women have to be directed in matters of religion, and, therefore, it is appropriate for a husband to determine which deities are to be worshipped by his wife:

> A wife ought not to make friends of her own, but to enjoy her husband's friends in common with him. The gods are the first and most important friends. Wherefore it is becoming for a wife to worship and know only the gods that her husband believes in, and to shut the front door tight upon all queer rituals and outlandish superstitions. For with no god do stealthy and secret rites performed by a woman find any favour.[141]

---

139 Virgil (Aen. 6, 426-429) reports that dead infants had to share the fate of the damned in Hades. Further, it could be regarded as a disaster to die unmarried and childless, and for those who did consignment to Hades was thought of as a depressing experience (Rohde 1921, Part 1, 327 and Part 2, 392 n. 2). According to one of the magical papyri those untimely deceased were expected to join the dreadful company of Hecate, a company ever ready to respond to the curses of all who called upon them (GMP 4, 2708-84). An inscription on a tombstone from Krim (IPE 519), dated to the 2nd cent. A.D., describes the sorry fate of a young wife who died childless (Dölger 1930, 34 and n. 88b). In the Roman world those who died before their time (cf. Eur. Alc. 153-174, quoted in p. 111) were known by their funeral designations as 'funera acerba' ('untimely funerals') (Blümner 1911, 489f). Concurrently with this epithet ran the idea that the death of an unmarried girl resulted in marrige to Hades in the underworld (Rose 1925, 238ff; Szepessy 1972, 341ff).

140 Plut. Mor. 407C. Transl. F. C. Babbitt.
141 Plut. Mor. 140D. Transl. F. C.Babbitt.

Accordingly, the housewife should not be allowed to participate on her own in the secret and arcane rites of mystery religions which he characterizes as 'outlandish superstitions'.

Similarly, Cato the Elder points to the power of the paterfamilias to control the religious matters of the household; such power relating to the female slaves could apparently be delegated to the materfamilias (cf. 1.5.1.1):

> She must not engage in religious worship herself or get others to engage in it for her without the orders of the master or the mistress; let her remember that the master attends to the devotions for the whole household.[142]

According to this text, a slave woman should follow her master's or mistress's directions in practising religious observances, and, furthermore, she was not allowed to propagate a new cult within the household without their approval.[143]

As well as being accused of an uncritical attitude towards the mystery religions, women attending these ceremonies were said to be negligent of their domestic duties. (Pseudo-) Lucian in the early 4th cent. A.D. gives the following account from a male point of view:

> They (i.e. the wives) leave the house immediately and visit every god that plagues married men, though the wretched husbands do not even know the very names of some of these, be they Coliades and Genetyllides[144] or the Phrygian goddess and the rout that commemorates an unhappy love and honours the shepherd-boy. Then follow secret initiations and suspicious all-female mysteries and, to put things bluntly, the corruption of their souls.[145]

The author goes on to censure the women for having extravagant communal meals in their own homes: he further reprobates them for talking with disdain of men and male sexuality in the presence of their husbands:

> But when they've finished with these, the moment they're home they have long baths, and by heavens, sumptuous meals accompanied by much coyness towards the men. For when they are surfeited with gorging the dishes in front of them, and even their throats can now hold no more, they score each of the foods before them with their fingertips to taste them. Meanwhile they talk of their nights, their heterosexual

---

[142] Cato, Agr. 143, 1-2. Transl. W. D. Hooper. Rev. H. Boyd.
[143] Such propagation was most likely among newly- purchased slaves worshipping other deities than those of their new master. The Oriental cults were to a great extent spread by slaves, soldiers and merchants (Nock 1933, 48ff) Cf. 3.7.
[144] Coliades and Gentyllides were goddesses presiding over generation and birth and seem to have been worshipped by women by means of wanton rites (Transl.comm.).
[145] Lucian. Amor. 42. Transl. M. D. Macleod.

slumbers, and their beds fraught with femininity, on rising from which every man immediately needs a bath.[146]

Finally, women were critizised by their husbands for wasting money on sacrifices associated with the mystery cults.[147] This fact is mirrored in two fragmented texts of Menander (reproduced by Strabo) dealing with the religion of the Getae, a Thracian tribe living alongside the Lower Danube:[148]

> [- - -] for all agree in regarding the women as the chief founders of religion, and it is the women who provoke the men to the more attentive worship of the gods, to festivals, and to supplications, and it is a rare thing for a man who lives by himself to be found addicted to these things. See again what the same poet says when he introduces as speaker the man who is vexed by the money spent by the women in connection with the sacrifices: 'The gods are the undoing of us, especially us married men, for we must always be celebrating some festival'; and again when he introduces the 'Woman-hater', who complains about these very things: 'we used to sacrifice five times a day, and seven female attendants would beat the cymbals all round us, while others would cry out to the gods'.[149]

From these texts we may conclude that the negative attitudes held by men towards the mystery religions were ultimately rooted in the fear that their wives would join a fellowship of women and thus place themselves beyond the reach of their husbands' powers (1.3.1).[150] Such a membership would cause a wife to neglect her domestic duties and waste the housekeeping money and possibly might also encourage her to obstruct the conjugal rights of her husband.

2.3.4 Woman and 'Folk-Religion'

Under the vague heading of 'folk-religion' I include two different kinds of private worship—known to us through literature—which can hardly be associated with any of the categories of Graeco-Roman worship discussed above. Both are characterized by women serving their fellow human beings through the performance of rituals undertaken on their own initiative, either by acting in a traditional cult in the role of priestess or by assuming the role of sorceress and using the powers of magic.

---

146 Lucian. Amor. 42. Transl. M. D. Macleod.

147 Women's need of money for the purpose of religious observances of various kinds is to be found in the comedies of Plautus (For instance, Mil. 690ff. Cf. Cic. Div. 1, 6, 12) (Schuhmann 1977, 143).

148 Meyer 1965, 1082.

149 Strab. 297. Transl. H. L. Jones. Cf. 3.7, p. 70 n. 121.

150 In the wide perspective of the state the mystery cults were seen as a danger to society. The Dionysiac cult was persecuted in Rome in 186 B.C. (see 1.5.2, p. 28 n. 141), and, similarly, the Isiac cult was persecuted and regarded with suspicion (Latte 1960, 282ff).

Consequently, a distinction will be made, on the one hand, between a priestess assigned to a temple (2.3.4.1), and, on the other, a sorceress acting on her own (2.3.4.2). It can be assumed that the latter category consisted to a great extent of poor women who had to contribute to the maintenance of the family or of slaves earning money for their owners.

2.3.4.1 The Role of Priestess

From Pausanias' writings we know of the existence of a great number of priestesses attached to temples devoted principally to female deities, and Plautus makes us further acquainted with such a priestess in one of his comedies.[151] He portrays a woman in the service of Venus, whom she is serving at her own expense.[152] She is an old woman[153] living in extreme poverty;[154] she even has to borrow from a neighbour living close to the temple the utensils to be used for the sacrifices.[155] In spite of these straitened circumstances she shares her few possessions with two slave girls who are escaping from a procurer and taking refuge in the temple.[156]

The picture of this poor priestess, characterized by acts of charity, is a remarkable antithesis to the luxurious conditions and ceremonious lives of the Vestals serving the state;[157] in this respect Plautus' priestess might have appealed to his audience of poor women. Although she is a fictitious figure, it may be suggested that he portrayed a category of priestess well known to his audience, and it is therefore reasonable to believe that such humble women, benefiting their fellow creatures in the service of a deity, were frequently to be found throughout the Roman Empire.

2.3.4.2 The Role of Sorceress

Besides priestesses attached to a temple, we are told about women performing religious rites without serving any particular cult. They used to wander from place to place, even in the company of their

---

151 *Rudens ('The Rope')*.
152 Plaut. Rud. 283f.
153 Plaut. Rud. 406.
154 Plaut. Rud. 282.
155 Plaut. Rud. 131ff. This indicates that poor people did not need to bring their own utensils to the temple. Cf. Polyb. 31, 26, 3-5, quoted in p. 49.
156 Plaut. Rud. 270ff.
157 Plut. Num. 9-11; Dion. Hal. Ant.Rom. 2, 64-69.

children,[158] offering their services to people who needed their assistance. Their religious task was associated with magic, and in this respect Circe[159] and Medea[160] might have been a source of inspiration to women of this kind. They could either be freeborn, in which case they collected alms in return for their services,[161] or slaves who earned money for their owners. The Philippian slave girl telling fortunes, portrayed by Luke in Acts (16: 16-18), exemplifies the latter category.

The titles attributed to these women reveal the kaleidoscopic nature of their activities. Plautus tells of a housewife asking her husband for money to give to a sorceress ('praecantrix') at the festival of Minerva; in addition, she needs money to pay a dream-interpreter ('coniectrix'), a clairvoyant ('hariola'), a soothsayer ('haruspica') and a woman who tells the fortune from the eyebrows ('quae supercilio spicit').[162] From Theophrastus we further conclude that an important task of these women consisted of the performing of purifying rites;[163] such rites were necessary on occasions of birth[164] and death (2.3.1.2.2). As regards the magic rites performed by these women, Theocritus gives a detailed picture of the activities of a sorceress in her efforts to persuade a false lover to return to his previous mistress;[165] Hecate-Artemis,[166] associated with the moon and the Underworld,[167] is assigned a central role in the ritual, and the sorceress tries by means of a variety of charms and incantations to induce the goddess to act in accordance with her desire.

Besides the passages quoted from Plautus' comedy, Roman literature is rich in material on the subject. The recurrence of the theme suggests that women employing supernatural powers were far from uncommon

---

[158] From Greek literature we know of two eminent men, Epicurus and Aeschines, whose mothers are said to have been women of this kind and to have been assisted by their sons in their work: Epicurus in reading charms (Diog. Laert. 10, 4) and Aeschines in assisting his mother in her initiating people into some Dionysiac rites (Dem. De Cor. 259-60).

[159] Circe was a sorceress who gave the companions of Odysseus evil drugs which turned them into swine (Hom. Od. 10, 235-43).

[160] Medea is portrayed principally in the role of sorceress by Euripides in his drama.

[161] Dem. De Cor. 260. In this respect their model figure might have been no less than Hera in the role of priestess collecting alms (Pl. Resp. 381D).

[162] Plaut. Mil. 693f.

[163] Theophr. Char.16, 14.

[164] Birth was thought to pollute not only the mother but the household itself (Parker 1983, 50), and both mother and child (Suet. Ner. 6) (Blümner 1911, 304) as well as those who had assisted at the delivery were ritually purified (Samter 1901, 59ff). A special ritual for purification of the house is not recorded (Parker 1983, 51).

[165] Theoc. Id. 2. Apuleius (Met. 3, 17-18) also tells us of the performance of a sorceress.

[166] In the Greek magical papyri Hecate is invoked together with Hermes as psychopomp (evidence in Heckenbach 1912, 2774). Artemis-Hecate, under her Roman name of Diana, was of particular importance to Philippian women. Her worship in Philippi is discussed in 4.2.

[167] Theoc. Id. 2, 10ff.

in the Augustan age.[168] Unfortunately, Roman authors were principally interested in sorcery in connection with love affairs,[169] which is why their pictures of women performing magic rites are scarcely representative of this heterogeneous group whose services were sought across a wide spectrum of activity.[170]

2.4 SUMMARY

According to the sources, woman's life was permeated by the influence of myth and religious observances. At an early age girls were introduced to mythical stories and trained in the performance of cult ceremonies. As for the latter, however, changes in the old family pattern affecting religious matters (defined by the ideal of the univira) brought about a segregation of those children who were highly qualified to perform rituals and those who were less privileged. When a young girl was given away in marriage she left not only her parental home but also the parental deities. The young bride would therefore face a double adjustment in her new life: the unfamiliar environment with its new sets of relationships was partnered by the need to adjust to fresh ceremonies appropriate to different gods. A married woman was powerful in the worship of her husband's deities who protected the house, and, furthermore, the possibility of achieving priestly office in the official cult existed for those who were of high social position and owned property. In spite of their favourable position in the 'sacra privata', and sometimes also in the 'sacra publica', women were attracted to mystery religions which dealt more fully with the questions of life and death. In addition, they were also serving others outside the family by performing rituals of various kinds, either in the role of priestess attached to a temple or by operating on their own through the power of magic.

---

[168] Luck 1962, 5.
[169] Luck 1962.
[170] Their activities are reflected in the spells of the Greek magical papyri.

3 PHILIPPI AT THE TIME OF THE RISE OF CHRISTIANITY

3.1 INTRODUCTION

At first glance the description of Philippi in Acts (16: 11-40)[1] gives a picture of a typical Roman town with Roman government and administration of justice. According to Luke, however, the first convert to Christianity was a female immigrant from Asia Minor (16: 14), and a slave girl understood Paul (16:17) even though he was speaking Greek. In fact, the Philippian episode reflects to a great extent the character of the town, which was a meeting-place for influences from east and west as a result both of its situation near Asia Minor and its position as a Roman colony.

In this chapter I am going to give an outline of its history (3.2), natural resources (3.3), habitation (3.4), population (3.5), language and culture (3.6) and religious features (3.7) as a necessary background for my reconstruction of Philippian women's socio-cultural and religious conceptual frameworks.

3.2 HISTORY

The area covered by the colony of Philippi (Map 2) was originally inhabited by Thracian tribes and they are mentioned in the sources for the first time in connection with the Persian invasion in 490 B.C. Herodotus lets us know that Xerxes during his march to Hellas passed Mount Pangaion (Map 1; Map 2: Y5-X5), where Thracian tribes had in their possession gold and silver mines.[2] These mines tempted not only the Athenians[3] but also the Greek colonists from the nearby island of

---

[1] The scholarly exploration of ancient Philippi began in the year 1861 by Leon Heuzey at the request of Napoleon III. The excavations have been continued by French and Greek archaeologists and are still going on. A survey of the excavations and a bibliography are given by D. Lazarides (1976, 704-705).

[2] Hdt. 7, 112.

[3] The mines were unimportant (Diod. Sic. 16, 8, 6-7), but in spite of that the Athenians in 436 B.C. founded the colony Amphipolis (Map 1; Map 2: Y4-X3) (Diod. Sic. 11, 70, 5) (Collart 1937, 68ff) quite near Mount Pangaion in order to look after their financial interests in the area. The Athenian colonization caused hostility between the Greeks and the Thracian tribes (Diod. Sic. 11, 70,5; 12, 68, 1-3), and this antagonism between the Thracians and the intruding colonists lasted until A.D. 44

Thasos (Map 1) into looking after their financial interests in this area.[4] In 360 B.C. the Thasians founded a colony, named Crenides or Datus (the future town of Philippi)[5] close to Mount Pangaion.[6] The colonists were soon harassed by the Thracian tribes in the area and the Greeks sought the assistance of the Macedonian king Philip II against the Thracians.[7] At that time, however, Philip had begun to expand his power eastwards, and now he took the opportunity to invade Crenides for his own use in 356 B.C. and to name the town after himself.[8] Further, he increased the population of the town to a considerable extent and enlarged the mines in order to exploit them intensively.[9]

The heyday of Philippi was, however, short, since Philip had to a great extent emptied the mines of their gold. The town declined and became an unimportant provincial town until 42 B.C, when it came into the limelight, thanks to the battle between Octavian and Antony on the one hand and the assassins of Julius Caesar on the other.[10] After the battle Philippi became a Roman colony[11] with a permanent settlement of discharged veteran soldiers.[12] The presence of these men and their families[13] ensured that stable colonization would result and that the interests of the Empire would be protected. After the battle at Actium in 30 B.C. Augustus renamed the town Colonia Augusta Julia Philippensis[14] when its population was increased by another contingent of Roman colonists.[15] This group consisted of a cohort from the praetorian guard[16] and a number of landowners, who, as adherents to Antony, had lost their land in Italy and now were compensated by Augustus with land in the Macedonian province.[17]

---

when Thrace became a Roman province and the Thracian population was pacified (Collart 1937, 256).

[4] Thasos was colonized from Paros during the seventh cent. B.C. (Collart 1937, 93f).

[5] App. BCiv. 4, 105, quoted in p. 62.

[6] Hdt. 7, 112; Diod. Sic. 16, 3, 7 (Collart 1937, 134).

[7] Diod. Sic. 16, 3, 7 (Collart 1937, 154).

[8] Diod.Sic.16, 8, 6-7; App. BCiv. 4, 105, quoted in p. 62. Collart 1937, 155.

[9] Diodorus Siculus (16, 8, 6-7) reports that Philip succeeded in extracting 1000 talents of gold from these mines and with this fortune he was able to secure his position on the Balkan Peninsula (Collart 1937, 155).

[10] Strab.7, Frg.41; Collart 1937, 190.

[11] Collart 1937, 224f.

[12] App. BCiv.5, 3; Dio Cass.48, 2, 3 (Collart 1937, 228f). Soldiers could be either legionaries, auxiliaries or praetorians (Clauss 1986, 1080ff).

[13] Cf. 1.5.1.2, p. 26 n. 125.

[14] Collart 1937, 236. Octavian was honoured by the title Augustus in 27 B.C. (Cagnat 1964, 177).

[15] Dio Cass. 51-56 (Collart 1937, 235).

[16] Collart 1937, 235. A cohort consisted of 500 soldiers at that time (Clauss 1986, 1080).

[17] Dio Cass. 51-56 (Collart 1937, 228f). Cf. 3.4.2.

3.3 PHYSICAL FEATURES

Philippi was situated in the eastern part of Macedonia near the border of Thrace. The colony covered an area of 730 square miles (Map 2), and in broad outline it extended from the river Strymon in the west to the river Nestos in the east (Map 1).[18] To the north and to the south it was bordered by mountains[19] which also included Mount Pangaion (Map 2: Y5-X5), and to the south it touched upon the sea at the place where its seaport Neapolis was situated (Map 2: Y5-X8). It was intersected by the Via Egnatia (Map 3: B-C), which was the only line of communication on land between Rome and the East (Map 1).

According to the description of Philippi, given by Appian,[20] we can understand that Philippi was situated in a rich area, and its fertility is mentioned by Theophrastus, who seems to have taken an interest in this district. He reports that the soil in Philippi had such growing power that seeds from some weeds even gave rise to cultivated plants,[21] and the wild roses of Mount Pangaion were well known for their large many-petalled flowers.[22]

In addition to a rich vegetation Philippi also had a supply of minerals. The nearby Mount Pangaion had both gold and silver[23] and we are told that these deposits had formed the basis for the expansion of the Macedonian power.[24] According to Diodorus Siculus, the mines were exhausted by Philip II,[25] and actually we do not hear about them at the time of the rise of Christianity, though there must have been some mining still going on,[26] since the Philippians could afford to build no less than four huge Christian basilicas in the fourth and fifth centuries.[27]

---

[18] Collart 1937, 276ff, Pl. 2; Levick 1967, 45 n. 5; Papazouglou 1982, 90ff.

[19] This information is only approximate. Opinions are divided about the exact border line of the colony (Papazouglou 1982, 90ff).

[20] App. BCiv. 4, 102, quoted in p. 62.

[21] Theophr. Hist.Pl. 2, 2, 7.

[22] Theophr. Hist.Pl. 6, 6,4.

[23] Hdt.7,112; Strab.7, Frg.34; App. BCiv.4, 106.

[24] See n. 9 supra.

[25] Diod.Sic.16, 8, 6-7.

[26] Livy (39, 24) reports that the Macedonian king Philip V (221-179 B.C.) reopened old mines long since disused and started new ones at many places. After the battle of Pydna in 168 B.C. the Romans reopened the Macedonian mines of gold and silver (Préaux 1978, 174). There are reasons to believe that the mines of Pangaion were included in this revival of Macedonian mining.

[27] Lazarides 1976, 705.

3.4 TOWN AND COUNTRYSIDE

3.4.1 The Town

The town of Philippi was situated near Mount Pangaion on a hill, surrounded by marshes (Map 2: Y6-X7), at a distance of about 20 km from the seaport of Neapolis (Map 2: Y5-X8), from which the maritime route led across to Alexandria Troas on the coast of Asia Minor (Map 1). Appian gives us a description of the situation and surroundings of Philippi in connection with his account of the famous battle in 42 B.C.:

> Philippi is a city that was formely called Datus, and before that Crenides, because there are many springs bubbling around a hill there. Philip fortified it because he considered it an excellent stronghold against the Thracians, and named it from himself, Philippi. It is situated on a precipitous hill and its size is exactly that of the summit of the hill.[28] There are woods on the north through which Rhascupolis led the army of Brutus and Cassius. On the south is a marsh extending to the sea. On the east are the gorges of the Sapaeans and Corpileans, and on the west a very fertile and beautiful plain extending to the towns of Murcinus and Drabiscus and the river Strymon, about 350 stades.[29]

Appian tells us that Philip fortified the town and excavations have confirmed this information. Its strategic situation close to the mines of Mount Pangaion led him to build a fortified town wall for protection against the Thracians.[30] The town of Philippi was surrounded by the wall with three gates in it (Map 3: A, D, E). Two of these (Map 3: A, D) faced the Via Egnatia which ran through the town.[31] Outside the wall the town was surrounded by an area of uncultivated land without houses (Map 3: 22), according to Roman custom. This area was the so-called pomerium.[32] and in Philippi its outer line was marked by an arch,[33] situated about 2 km from the western gate.[34]

3.4.1.1 Buildings

Of the buildings in Philippi dating back to the 1st cent. A.D. there are only a few remnants to be found today, namely, the wall with the eastern

---

[28] The town is in fact situated on the plain at the foot of the hill, which was practically uninhabited (Map 3). Cf. 3.4.1.1 and 3.7.1.2.
[29] App. BCiv. 4, 105. Transl. H. White.
[30] Diod. Sic.16, 3, 7 (Collart 1937, 168).
[31] It constituted the 'decumanus' (i.e. the main street of the town) (Collart 1937, 319).
[32] Krause 1965*b*, 2893; Collart 1937, 322.
[33] This kind of arch has for a long time been confused with triumphal arches (Frothingham 1905, 216). It was the first Roman official building in the colony and the style was that of the 1st cent. A.D. (Collart 1937, 322).
[34] The area of the Philippian pomerium was remarkably large (Collart 1937, 322f).

gate (Map 3: D), the theatre (Map 3: 7) and a small sanctuary of Dionysus. The theatre is fairly well preserved although it is the oldest remaining building in Philippi.[35] It was built by Philip II (3.2) and is situated in close proximity to the wall on the slope of the acropolis and opens up towards the plain with mountains in the background.[36] The sanctuary was found during the excavations of the public baths (Map 3: 21), dating back to the 2nd cent. A.D.[37] In this place there were also found some Latin inscriptions dedicated to Liber, Libera and Hercules, which identifies the building as a sanctuary, and its situation dates it back to the first period of the Roman colony.[38]

Besides remnants of official buildings there are also traces of dwelling-houses, presumably from this period. On the slope of the acropolis (Map 3), to the south-east of the temple dedicated to the Egyptian gods (Map 3: 6), the remains of a block of Greek and Roman houses have been discovered.[39] The centre of the town, however, was situated on the other side of the Via Egnatia and here the archaeologists have traced a few remains both of private houses and tenements. In connection with the excavations of the forum (Map 3:15), dating to the 2nd cent. A.D., two rooms with mosaic-floors were discovered beneath the level of the forum.[40] One room was furnished with an outlet, which indicates that it had been used as an atrium.[41] The rooms are thought to have belonged to a private house, and the style of the mosaics suggests that it goes back to the Augustan era.[42]

Beside the palaestra (Map 3: 17) there were found traces of a block of flats dated to the 2nd cent. A.D.,[43] but there are good reasons to assume that there were such flats in Philippi in an earlier period. The fact is that the habitable area of the town was small and limited by the surrounding marshes[44] and the inaccessibility of the acropolis.[45] This might have necessitated multi-storey houses being built in Philippi, as in Rome[46] and Ostia,[47] the top floors of which provided quarters for poor people and

---

[35] Collart 1937, 175.
[36] Collart 1937, 175; 371ff.
[37] Collart 1937, 367
[38] Underneath the public baths there are remains of a small building, the walls of which had been used as foundations in the north-western corner of the baths (Collart 1937, 367f). The inscriptions are discussed in 4.3.2.1.1.
[39] Collart 1937, 368.
[40] Excavation report 1922, 530; Collart 1937, 357.
[41] Excavation report 1935, 287.
[42] Excavation report 1935, 287; Collart 1937, 357f.
[43] Lazarides 1973, Fig. 15:8.
[44] App. BCiv. 4, 105, quoted in p. 62.
[45] Collart 1937, 369. The slopes are still steep. Cf. Map 3.
[46] Wotschitzky 1955, 155ff. According to Livy (21, 62) there were already three-storeyed houses in Rome during the 3rd cent.B.C.
[47] Packer 1971, 65ff. As regards urban living conditions in Ostia see Packer 1971, 72ff.

slaves.[48] Martial has described life in a Roman tenement house: endless stairs to the top floors,[49] buildings so close that neighbours could shake hands from their respective windows[50] and cramped uncomfortable houses without running water.[51]

3.4.1.2   Burial Places

Since the ground was holy for the Romans it was prohibited to bury the dead inside the town walls and inside the outer line of the pomerium.[52] In Philippi, therefore, the burial places were situated far outside the town where the tombstones bordered the Via Egnatia.[53]

3.4.1.3   Administration

Although it had a mixed population (cf. 3.2) Philippi seems to have had an entirely Roman stamp at that time.[54] Latin was the official language[55] and its chronology dated from 148 B.C., the year when Macedonia became a Roman province.[56] Finally, Philippi got the benefit

---

[48] The remains of a house of this kind, situated on the Capitolium in Rome, still exist (Wotschitzky 1955, 156ff). Archaeologists suggest that the top floors contained a long passage with rooms on either side where slaves and other poor people were accommodated (Blanck 1976, 35). The floor below them provided quarters for the wealthy, while lower still came another level also occupied by slaves and poor people. This was a low-pitched area offering little comfort. The ground floor was devoted to shop premises. Entrance to the first floor was by means of a ladder placed outside the building, while interior stairways are thought to have provided access to upper floors (Blanck 1976, 35). In the apartment houses there was no running water since the the hydraulic pressure was not strong enough in the mains. The tenants had to fetch water from a well situated in the street or in an inner backyard. A privy, common to the whole house, was sometimes provided. The alternative was the public latrine, and the thermae offered the only bathing facility for all who lived in the house (Blanck 1976, 40). In addition, the apartment houses had no separate kitchens (Packer 1971, 72).

[49] Mart. 1, 117, 7; 7, 20, 20.

[50] Mart. 1, 86, 12.

[51] Mart. 9, 18.

[52] XII Tabl. 10, 1.

[53] Collart 1937, 499. Cf. n. 34 supra.

[54] It belonged to the tribe Voltinia (Collart 1937, 258), which was one of Rome's oldest tribes (Radke 1975, 1326).

[55] Collart 1937, 301.

[56] This is now commonly accepted. Against it Perdrizet gives the year 30 B.C. as the starting-point (Collart 1937, 306ff).

of Italic law and justice,[57] which meant a privileged judicial and economic position for a colony situated in a province.[58]

The colony was governed centrally from the town,[59] and, according to the inscriptions, there were the usual Roman officials such as the quaestors, the aediles and the duumviri.[60] Furthermore there were official priests: an augur, two pontifices and a number of flamines in the imperial cult, including two priestesses in the cult of the empress, are referred to.[61] (Besides this office of priestess in the imperial cult the inscriptions mention priestesses in the cult of Diana.[62])

3.4.2 The Countryside

Most of the population, however, did not live in the town but in villages in the countryside since Philippi was principally an agricultural colony,[63] but there is no excavated evidence of those estates where the landowners of the time lived together with their slaves.[64] Even if there is only slight evidence for the organization of these estates there are no reasons to believe that they were managed any differently from estates in other places.[65] Each estate used to be an independent economic unit, employing a great number of slaves to carry out the wide variety of tasks

---

[57] Collart 1937, 230f.

[58] In a colony with Italic law and justice estates could be sold, and they were also tax-free. A province, however, was usually looked upon as the property of the Roman state and land could not be bought (Simon, D. 1969, 14). That an exception was made in the case of Philippi may be seen as an attempt by Augustus to compensate those adherents of Antony who had lost their land in Italy (cf. 3.2) (Collart 1937, 230).

[59] Collart 1937, 288; 499.

[60] Collart 1937, 262.

[61] CIL 3, 651 (Collart 1937, 265); Collart 1933, 347, No. 13.

[62] The inscriptions are discussed in 4.2.2.2. Furthermore, a statue dedicated to a woman and placed in the temple of the Egyptian gods (4.4.1) may refer to a priestess.

[63] Cf. 3.2 and 3.3.

[64] There have not been any methodical excavations in the countryside of the ancient colony. In a few cases the larger villages in the countryside show traces of burial places (Collart 1937, 285).

[65] The farm usually consisted of a villa with subsidiary buildings such as storehouses, stables and wine-cellars, along with space in which the relevant forms of husbandry could take place. The multiple provision of buildings offered a degree of segregation for those occupying the dwelling-house (Blanck 1976, 36). The urban counterpart of the farm villa had a narrow and inconvenient kitchen while that on the farm served both as a living-room and a work area (Paoli 1961, 92).

to be done;[66] the bondswomen were principally occupied in cooking or manufacturing clothes both for their owners and their fellow slaves.[67]

In the countryside the largest villages[68] had a certain amount of self-government and provided provincial centres for the region. These villages had officials who attended to some local affairs but for more important matters they were subordinated to the central government in the town.[69]

3.4.3 Communications

At first glance the colony seemed to enjoy good communications, both within its own area and with the world outside, as Philippi was situated near the sea and on the Via Egnatia, the main military road and commercial route joining Rome to the East (Map 1). The Via Egnatia was built by the Romans in the 2nd cent. B.C.,[70] but according to a pair of inscriptions found in Philippi it deteriorated for a long time until it was repaired by Trajan in the 2nd cent. A.D. as he expanded the Empire eastwards.[71] When Paul arrived at Philippi (c. A.D. 50), however, it was still a remote provincial town on the old Via Egnatia and was almost totally dependent on the sea for its communications with the outer world.[72]

In addition to the Via Egnatia which connected Philippi with the seaport Neapolis there were some local roads from Philippi to various places in Macedonia and Thrace. These roads also crossed the colony and facilitated communications between the town and the countryside.[73]

---

[66] Columella gives (particularly in Rust. Chapt. 12). a picture of the life and occupations on an estate.

[67] Columella Rust. 12, 3, 3ff.

[68] These villages have been identified by visible remains of burial places (Collart 1937, 285f). Cf. n. 64 supra. The inhabitants are named 'vicanus' (villager) in the inscriptions (Collart 1937, 286f).

[69] Collart 1937, 288.

[70] When building the Via Egnatia the Romans followed an ancient route used by the Persians (cf. 3.2), Greeks and Macedonians (Collart 1937, 487).

[71] Gren 1941, 32. Owing to its situation, the Roman armies had to pass Philippi on their way to and from Rome and the East (Gren 1941, 33) which brought about prosperity in the colony and resulted in building activity in the 2nd cent. A.D. (Collart 1937, 358ff). Cf. 3.4.1.1.

[72] The sea line between Neapolis and Alexandria Troas (Map 1) was of importance for communications between Philippi and Asia Minor (Collart 1937, 493ff.). Cf. Acts 16:11.

[73] It is still possible to follow stretches of these local roads, though parts of them have completely disappeared (Collart 1937, 506ff).

3.5 POPULATION

When the Romans arrived in Philippi the town was unimportant. It was inhabited by Thracians, by descendants of the first Greek colonists who founded Crenides and by the descendants of those Macedonians who had been brought to the town by Philip II (3.2).[74] Both the Greeks and the Thracians in Philippi lived remote lives during the Roman era[75] and they managed to maintain their cultural individuality. For the Greeks it was their language that survived,[76] while the Thracians succeeded in preserving their religion.[77]

Economically, Philippi was dominated by the Romans. They were to a great extent owners[78] of large landed estates in the countryside.[79] However, the Romans did not command in the countryside alone as they also had a ruling position in the town where the veterans often held high office,[80] and inscriptions show that the town of Philippi owned a number of slaves who seem to have had inferior posts in the administration.[81]

The Greeks in Philippi consisted of two different groups at that time, namely, the original Greek population (cf. 3.2) and Greek immigrants who came principally from Asia Minor.[82] Judging from the inscriptions, the native Greeks had a subordinate position[83] and might have earned their living as shopkeepers and workmen,[84] while the Greek immigrants, as in other places in the area, were presumably businessmen[85] who imported materials of different kinds, including expensive textiles.[86]

---

[74] The Greeks had once ousted the Thracians who took refuge in hidden valleys; the Thracian proper names of the inscriptions show the places where they lived (Collart 1937, 296ff).

[75] Collart 1937, 301.

[76] Collart 1937, 302.

[77] Collart 1937, 296. See also 3.7.2.

[78] Collart 1937, 289.

[79] Collart 1937, 288. Cf. 3.4.2.

[80] Collart 1937, 293. Soldiers and veterans belonged to 'honestiores' who were accorded privileged legal treatment: for instance, exile rather than death for capital crimes and greater credibility and more lenient treatment before the courts (Garnsey 1970, 221f; 267).

[81] Collart 1937, 274; 403ff.

[82] Gren 1941, 72.

[83] Collart 1937, 301f.

[84] Collart 1937, 305. An inscription mentions a Greek stone-cutter (Collart-Ducrey 1975, 51, No. 20).

[85] Gren 1941, 72. This group is reflected in Acts (16: 14) by the figure of Lydia who is said to have made her living by trading in purple.

[86] Gren 1941, 71.

Finally, the Thracians were to be found in remote parts of the colony[87] where they cultivated the land, sometimes as well-off landowners, if the evidence provided by their tombstones is to be believed.[88]

3.6 LANGUAGE AND CULTURE

3.6.1 Latin

As mentioned above Latin was the official language of Philippi after 42 B.C. (3.2) and it maintained an unusually strong position in the colony until the beginning of the 4th cent. A.D.[89] The surviving Latin inscriptions are principally from this period; they are found both in the town and in the countryside[90] and relate to official and private matters.[91] The superiority of the Latin language in Philippi[92] can partly be explained by the fact that Philippi was colonized by Rome in two stages in 42 B.C. and 30 B.C. (3.2). Further, Latin was the language of the Roman army[93] and Philippi was to a great extent a colony consisting of veterans (3.2). Finally, Latin inscriptions with Greek or Thracian proper names[94] were possibly calculated to flatter the government in the hope that Roman citizenship might be achieved in course of time.[95]

3.6.2 Greek

In spite of the predominance of Latin, the Greek language—earlier the official language in Philippi for about three hundred years[96]—survived in several areas. The Greek alphabet was sometimes used in Latin inscriptions[97] and for markings on the stones of the second-century

---

[87] Cf. 3.2 and 3.4.2, and also 3.7.2.

[88] Collart 1937, 296ff; 413ff.

[89] Compared with the Roman colonies in Anatolia in Asia Minor Latin had a remarkably strong position in Philippi (Levick 1967, 161). From 42 B.C.- A.D. 330 there are 421 Latin and only 60 Greek inscriptions in Philippi (Levick 1967, 161).

[90] Collart 1937, 300ff.

[91] Collart 1937, 300ff.

[92] Cf. n. 143 infra.

[93] Balsdon 1979, 118ff.

[94] See n. 110 infra.

[95] The Emperor Claudius expected that a Roman citizen should speak Latin (Dio Cass. 60, 17, 4).

[96] Between 360-42 B.C. (Collart 1937, 300).

[97] Collart 1937, 304ff.

Roman buildings,[98] and Greek units of measurements were used in the countryside.[99] Furthermore, Greek seems to have survived particularly in regard to the Oriental cults, according to the existing epigraphical material.[100] This survival of the Greek language in Philippi was due partly to influences from the nearby Greek Amphipolis (Map 2: Y4-X3)[101] and from Asia Minor.[102]

Furthermore, there was little cause for the Greek population (3.5) to learn Latin since educated Romans usually spoke Greek,[103] and Greek translators were used for official documents.[104] Only slaves in Roman households,[105] soldiers in the Roman army[106] or those who strove for employment in the administration had to learn Latin.[107] Greek finally took over from Latin in the 4th cent. A.D., and consequently the whole body of Christian inscriptions is in that language.[108]

The Thracians in Philippi had been hellenized, first through the influence of the Greek colonies at the coast and then from Amphipolis and Crenides (the former name of the town of Philippi).[109] They had no written language of their own and they used Greek and (at a later date) also Latin for their writings, according to inscriptions with Thracian proper names.[110] The presence of a Greek theatre within the colony

---

[98] Collart 1937, 305.

[99] Collart 1937, 305f.

[100] In the cult of Isis (4.4) there are 10 surviving inscriptions, 6 of which are in Greek (Collart 1937, 303).

[101] See n. 3 supra.

[102] Collart 1937, 315. Cf. 3.4.3 and 3.5.

[103] Balsdon 1979,125f. The Romans studied Greek as their main language at school (Pliny Ep. 2, 14, 2; Quint.Inst. 1, 8, 5ff), and educated Romans endeavoured to aquire Greek culture (Dio Chrys. 37, 25). Half-educated people as well boasted of their Greek education (Petron. Sat. 48, 3), and Roman women are said to have scattered their talk with Greek words (Mart. 10, 68; Juv. 6, 184-199).

[104] Balsdon 1979, 123f.

[105] Balsdon 1979, 124f.

[106] It is uncertain to what degree soldiers who were not Romans actually mastered Latin. They might have been conditioned to respond to the words of command and the names of the weapons rather than to understand the language used. For instance, soldiers were commanded to 'form the turtle' by holding their shields together to create an enormous tortoise-shell, and a catapult was called 'the scorpion' (Gell.NA 10, 9; Amm.Marc. 23, 4) (Balsdon 1979, 119f).

[107] Balsdon 1979, 125.

[108] Collart 1937, 313. In the 4th cent. A.D. the rhetor Himerius (6, 2, 3) praised the Philippians for their pure Attic–a purity which he attributed to Callistratus, the founder of Crenides (Collart 1937, 313 n. 5) Cf. 3.2.

[109] Collart 1937, 313. See also 3.2.

[110] There are 24 Greek inscriptions and 26 in Latin with Thracian proper names (Collart 1937, 301 n. 5).

(3.4.1.1)[111] might have contributed to their adoption of Greek culture and language.

3.7 RELIGIOUS FEATURES

When the Romans arrived (3.2) they brought their own religion to Philippi.[112] There existed already the cults of the Thracians[113] and of the Greek colonists,[114] and in addition some Oriental cults[115] had been brought into Macedonia in the 3rd cent. B.C., presumably by businessmen from Alexandria[116] and Asia Minor.[117] The Roman religion, however, was leavened with Greek myths and ideas[118] and soon it absorbed the old Greek cults in Philippi.[119] On the other hand, the Thracian religion (found particularly in the countryside [cf. 3.5]) survived. It had maintained its distinctive character during the Greek and Macedonian colonisations[120] and now it influenced the Roman cults in various ways.[121]

---

[111] The theatre was rebuilt on the Roman model during the 2nd cent. A.D. It was reconstructed once more during the 3rd cent. A.D. and was made fit for hunting and gladiatorial fights. This alteration removed the stage and the building could not thereafter be used for plays (Collart 1937, 381f).

[112] Collart 1937, 392.

[113] The Thracian cult at Philippi concerned especially the Thracian Bacchus (Collart 1937, 413ff and 4.3.1), the Thracian horseman (Collart 1937, 423ff) and Bendis, who was the Thracian equivalent of the Greek Artemis (Collart 1937, 430ff and 4.2.1). According to Herodotus (5, 7) the Thracians worshipped Dionysus, Artemis and Ares.

[114] Collart 1937, 392. These Greek cults referred to Zeus, Artemis (Collart-Ducrey 1975, 222), Apollo, Heracles, Parthenos and Dionysus (Collart 1937, 182f). As to Artemis and Dionysus, see 4.2 and 4.3.

[115] The Oriental cults at Philippi were dedicated to the Egyptian gods (Collart 1937, 444ff) and Magna Mater; the latter has left hardly any traces of female worship within the colony. Only one fragmented inscription in the countryside mentions a woman (Collart 1937, 454ff).

[116] Collart 1937, 453f.

[117] Collart 1937, 454. Cf. 3.5.

[118] The Roman religion at that time had been restored by Augustus and it was already open to Oriental cults (Collart 1937, 393).

[119] Collart 1937, 392. See also 4. 2. 1 and 4. 3. 1.

[120] Collart 1937, 392. Cf. 3.2.

[121] Collart 1937, 392. According to Pausanias (9, 29, 3) the Thracians were known as being more religious than the Macedonians.

3.7.1 The Town

Viewed from a religious standpoint the town of Philippi could be divided into three different districts (Map 3). Two of these were separated from each other by the Via Egnatia; they developed individual characteristics, one retaining earlier religious practices (3.7.1.2) and the other adopting those imported by the Romans (3.7.1.1). Of the third one, however, which is thought to have been located somewhere outside the town wall (3.7.1.3), there is only slight evidence.

3.7.1.1 South of the Via Egnatia

The area to the south of the Via Egnatia (Map 3: B-C), where the town centre was situated, was dominated by the Roman state religion.[122] The archaeologists have found traces of the Roman gods Jupiter,[123] Juno,[124] Minerva,[125] Diana,[126] and Mercury[127] and also of the imperial cult which was prominent in Philippi.[128] In this region, as mentioned above, a small sanctuary also was situated, where Dionysus was worshipped under his Roman name Liber Pater (3.4.1.1); originally it may have belonged to the Thracian Bacchus.[129] Finally, the Oriental cults were represented in this area by traces of associations with the Egyptian gods[130] and with the cult of Magna Mater.[131]

3.7.1.2 North of the Via Egnatia

The acropolis (Map 3: 1), situated to the north of the Via Egnatia, was uninhabited except for a block if dwelling-houses (3.4.1.1). This area was the seat of the 'folk religion'[132] and here are to be found remains of Greek-Roman, Thracian and Oriental cults.

---

[122] Collart 1937, 393ff.
[123] Collart, 393.
[124] Collart 1937, 395.
[125] Collart 1937, 395f.
[126] A votive inscription dedicated to Diana Lucifera (Collart 1937, 398; 442f). This inscription is dicussed in 4.2.3, p. 82 n. 48.
[127] Collart 1937, 398.
[128] Collart 1937, 412. Cf. 3.4.1.3.
[129] Collart 1937, 401; 413.
[130] Collart 1937, 452f.
[131] Collart 1937, 413.
[132] As regards the term 'folk-religion' see 2.3.4. This folk piety in Philippi may be visible in the expression 'ex imperio' of the inscriptions dedicated to Isis (Collart 1937, 447), Liber Pater (Collart 1937, 414) and the Thracian horseman (Collart 1937,

A number of religious groups had their sanctuaries (Map 3: 8) in an abandoned quarry where the plain-cut rock face was utilized to form the walls of these rough buildings.[133] According to inscriptions they were constructed by worshippers of Silvanus,[134] Magna Mater[135] and Diana.[136] The only real temple of the acropolis belonged to the Egyptian gods (Map 3: 6) and is dated to the Augustan era.[137] The remains of the temple show that at least some adherents of this cult might have been well off;[138] presumably there were some rich businessmen among the worshippers (cf. 3. 5).

Besides the rock sanctuaries there are in this area a great number of reliefs cut in the rock, and many are still preserved.[139] These stone carvings, spread all over the acropolis, are of varied artistic quality.[140] Many of them seem to have been made by stone-cutters without any artistic pretentions which indicates that they may have been dedicated by the lower strata of the population. Some of them have Latin inscriptions and are dedicated to deities with Latinized names, which indicates that these reliefs originate from the Roman colonists.[141] The deities named in these inscriptions are the Thracian horseman, Jupiter, Minerva and Magna Mater.[142] However, the majority of these stone carvings are dedicated to a hunting goddess named Diana,[143] and several are situated near other carvings which depict women.[144]

---

426). The phrase seems to indicate some idea of personal relationship between these deities and their worshippers.

[133] Collart-Ducrey 1975, 14ff.

[134] The rock sanctuaries are difficult to date as marble has been quarried there since the 2nd cent. B.C. when Philip II built the town wall and the theatre (Collart-Ducrey 1975, 14ff). Cf. 3.2 and 3.4.1.1.

[135] Collart-Ducrey 1975, 17.

[136] This 'sanctuary' consists of three rock carvings picturing Diana killing a stag (Collart-Ducrey 1975, Nos. 80, 81, 82); in connection with the carvings is a pit for sacrifices (Collart-Ducrey 1975, 18, Fig. 6).

[137] Salditt-Trappmann 1970, 52f. The cult of Isis is discussed in 4.4.

[138] Beside marble quarried on the spot more expensive marble was imported and used for the outside walls and for the flooring of the terrace (Collart 1937, 72; 74).

[139] The latest inventory of the rock carvings was made in 1969 and the result includes 187 reliefs (Collart-Ducrey 1975, 28). Many carvings which earlier would have been capable of interpretation have been eroded, and several inscriptions are now illegible (Collart-Ducrey 1975, passim).

[140] Collart 1937, 390.

[141] Collart 1937, 391. The carvings are difficult to date and belong presumably to the 1st and 2nd cent. A.D. (Collart 1937, 391).

[142] The Thracian horseman (Collart-Ducrey 1975, Nos. 1-7), Jupiter (Nos. 138-142), Minerva (Nos. 143-144) and Magna Mater (Nos. 145-147).

[143] Ninety carvings show the hunting goddess (Collart-Ducrey 1975, Nos. 8-97) and 8 of these have inscriptions: 7 are in Latin and one has the signature of a Greek artist (Collart-Ducrey 1975, 221). See 4.2.2.3 and also Abrahamsen 1986.

[144] Forty carvings depict women. 6 of these have female attributes and are situated quite near reliefs representing the hunting goddess (Collart-Ducrey 1975, 31).

3.7.1.3 Outside the Town Wall

Among the Oriental cults in Philippi there was, according to Luke (Acts 16: 13), a Jewish congregation which is said to have had its meetingplace outside the town wall.[145] Furthermore, we are told that Paul and his companions found women only at this place. There are, however, no archaelogical traces of Judaism within the colony, nor are there remains of any synagogue or inscriptions. Luke's reference to Judaism in Philippi may hint at some Jewish missionary work, particularly among the women, but this proselytizing seems to have met with little success, as could be expected in a Roman military colony (3.2) where the Jews might have been in a minority.[146]

3.7.2 The Countryside

Regarding the cults in the countryside the Thracian influence is remarkable. A large number of surviving tombstones represent the Thracian horseman,[147] and the Thracian Bacchus (named Dionysus or Liber Pater) is mentioned in several Greek and Latin inscriptions along with Thracian proper names.[148] Followers of Dionysus were particularly strong among the Thracians and small groups of adherents to that cult worshipped in rural areas throughout the colony.[149] Finally, on Mount Pangaion they possessed an oracle, dedicated to Dionysus, where they retained a priesthood for a long time.[150]

As regards religious traces outside the town the story of the rape of Persephone must not be forgotten. Appian tells us that in Philippi people were of the opinion that this event occurred at the river Zygactes (about

---

These carvings are dealt with in 4.2.2.3. Besides women there were two more groups in Philippi who might have dedicated carvings to the hunting goddess. Diana was worshipped by the praetorians (cf. 3.2) (Domaszewski 1895, 52ff), and the venatores at the amphitheatre (cf. n. 111 supra) worshipped Nemesis (Collart 1937, 410f) whom they might have identified with Diana (Cook 1914, 275f).

[145] Today, a likely site in close connection with a little river outside the wall of the ancient Philippi is commemorated by a church devoted to Lydia.

[146] For several reasons the Jews were excused from serving in the Roman army. They were forbidden by the Law to participate in a battle or to march on the Sabbath. Further, being in the field they had difficulty in keeping the diet rules, and, finally, their aversion to images made it impossible for them to follow the Roman Eagle and other symbols relating to the legions (Clauss 1986, 1094).

[147] Collart 1937, 423ff.

[148] Collart 1937, 413ff. The Thracian Dionysus is discussed in 4.3.1.

[149] Collart 1937, 415ff.

[150] Perdrizet 1910, 36ff. The oracle is mentioned by Herodotus (7, 111) and by Plutarch (Vit.Crass. 8, 3). See also 4.3.2.1.2.

10 km outside the town) and it was further told that at this occasion Hades' wagon was damaged.[151]

3.8 SUMMARY

According to ancient sources Philippi was known both for its rich vegetation and its deposits of gold and silver. This fact, and the situation of the town near the sea, made it attractive for conquerors at different periods and thus determined its history; consequently it was captured in turn by the Greeks, the Macedonians and the Romans. The existent archaeological and epigraphical material gives roughly the following picture of Colonia Julia Augusta Philippensis at the time of the rise of Christianity.

Philippi was a veteran colony and had principally an agricultural character. The town of Philippi was the main centre for government and trade; it was favourably situated on the Via Egnatia but at that time the road had deteriorated and the sea was the main connecting link with the outer world. The colony had a mixed population consisting of Romans, Greeks and Thracians and was a meeting-place for influences both from the East and the West. The Romans were the principal employers of peasants as well as being the largest body of slave owners in Philippi. They occupied all the senior official posts while the Greeks and the Thracians held the more subsidiary positions. There were many slaves in the colony, chiefly on the estates in the countryside. In the town the population lived in private houses as well as in apartment houses where the poor had to live on the top floors in straitened circumstances. Besides the Roman state religion there was a folk piety in Philippi which found expression in a number of devotional groups dedicated to various deities. In spite of the fact that Latin was the official language of the colony Greek lived on and was used alongside Latin. The Thracians used it as their principal written language and it survived also in connection with the Oriental cults.

---

[151] App. BCiv. 4, 105-6. Today there is a village named Zygas (Map 2: Y6-X8).

4 DEITIES OF IMPORTANCE TO WOMEN IN PHILIPPI

4.1 INTRODUCTION

I have already touched upon this subject in a brief sketch of the deities of the colony (3.7) and in some degree also in Chapter 2, which surveys the religious observances undertaken by women. In this chapter I concentrate on those deities who seemed to meet the special needs of Philippian women; their conditions of living in a society organized by men for the advantage of the male sex is described in Chapter 1. In this context there are three divinities in particular in Philippi to be mentioned, two of whom, Diana and Dionysus, were indigenous while Isis were brought to the colony, presumably by merchants from Egypt.

In the following pages I shall focus on these three. I begin with a brief outline of their historical backgrounds before looking at the aspects of their myths which had particular significance for Philippian women. This examination will highlight those episodes with which women could identify by virtue of the cord of recognition being struck for them. Furthermore, archeological and epigraphical remains relating to rituals will be examined–these being considered particularly from a feminine point of view.

As already mentioned in the General Introduction (0.2), this picture will be a simplified one since our sources give the impression that these deities were worshipped independently. Although we are not able to reveal the pattern of intertwining we ought to keep in mind that in reality they were often identified with each other, and their followers did not always confine themselves to one cult only.

4.2 DIANA

4.2.1 Historical Background

According to inscriptions the hunting goddess was venerated in Philippi under various names, which can be explained by the fact that the town was colonized in stages by different ethnic groups (3.2). According to Herodotus the Thracians, who originally inhabited the area covered by the colony, worshipped Artemis, who is said to be an 'interpretatio graeca' of the Thracian goddess Bendis;[1] this is confirmed by Hesychius,[2] who related them both to the moon.[3] Moreover, he identifies Bendis with Hecate[4] as well as with Persephone,[5] which links her to Hades. Bendis, a figure of Thracian worship, has left only a few epigraphical traces in Philippi[6]—one of which is an altar with an inscription in Latin, found in the village of Proussotchani (Map 2: Y8-X4),[7] which indicates the continued existence of her cult in the countryside during the Roman era (cf. 3.7.2).[8] In addition, Bendis was also used as a personal name within the colony, according to three further Latin inscriptions.[9]

However, the Thracian Bendis had to give way to the Greek Artemis, who was brought by the first colonists from Thasos (cf. 3.2). Artemis, like Bendis, was associated with the lower regions, for, as well as being a protectress of women during childbirth,[10] she was both a goddess of death and of the nether world.[11] Although the Greeks had Philippi in

---

[1] Hdt. 5, 7 (Kraus 1960, 75 and n. 373). Herodotus (4, 33) further tells us that Thracian women were furnished with wheat-straw in offering sacrifice to Bendis.

[2] Hsch. s.v. Βενδῖς· ἡ ˮΑρτεμις. Θρᾳκιστί. (Kraus 1960, 75 n. 373).

[3] Hsch. s.v. δίλογχον· τὴν γὰρ σελήνην Βενδῖν καὶ ˮΑρτεμιν νομίζουσιν. (Kraus 1960, 76 n. 375).

[4] The origin of Hecate is regarded as crucial. Most scholars are of the opinion that she derived from Asia Minor (Kraus 1960, 24ff), but she has also been located to Thrace, particularly by R. Farnell (1896, 507) and Th. Kraus (1960, 57ff).

[5] Hsch s.v. ᾽Αδμήτου κόρη· ῾Εκατη, τινὲς δὲ τὴν Βενδῖν (Kraus 1960, 75 and n. 374).

[6] As to the position of the Thracians within the colony see 3.2 and 3.5.

[7] Perdrizet 1900, 307

[8] According to G. Kazarow (1936, 507) the goddess who is reproduced on the stone carvings (3.7.1.2) is none other than the Thracian Bendis. In view of the fact that the use of Latin for the inscriptions suggests that they date from the Roman period it would seem that this goddess is a mixture of the Thracian, the Greek and the Roman hunting goddess. Furthermore, the huntress portrayed is not furnished with the cap made of fox skin (see n. 13 infra).

[9] Collart 1937, 442 n. 1; Lemerle 1937, 416, No. 10. Bendis used as a name for females is rare (Kazarow 1936, 505).

[10] Nilsson 1967, 494.

[11] According to Homer (Il. 21, 483f) Artemis was especially associated with the death of women (Nilsson 1967, 482). Presumably the Thasian Artemis had traits of Hecate since this goddess was of great importance on the island (Kraus 1960, 69f), and Artemis was identified with Hecate in 450 B.C., according to an inscription (Kraus 1960, 69 and n. 340). Furthermore, Artemis and Hecate were identified with each other as goddesses both protecting childbirth; the first evidence is to be found in Aeschylus (Supp. 676; Heckenbach 1912, 2770). In an article (*Religio-ecological Aspects of Ancient Greek Religion from the Point of View of Woman: a Tentative Approach*) I discuss the historical background to the fact that Artemis, although a virgin, had the function of protecting childbirth (Portefaix 1985, 144ff). According to Virgil (Aen. 4, 511), Hecate is identified with Artemis in those aspects of her which relate to magic.

their possession for about three hundred years[12] there are scarcely any epigraphical vestiges of the Greek hunting goddess, though her external appearance as regards dress and equipment is visible in the stone carvings (3.7.1.2).[13] One inscription only, found by the archeologists in the forum (Map 3: 15) and dated to the middle of the 4th century B.C., mentions Artemis together with Apollon Kômaios,[14] who was worshipped on Thasos.[15]

The reason for the Thracian Bendis and the Greek Artemis receiving scant mention in the epigraphical material may be that Diana, who was transferred to Philippi by the Roman colonists (3.7), had traits in common with both these goddesses; therefore they were easily identified with their Roman counterpart. Diana was originally a Latin goddess of nature and light, and, like Bendis and Artemis, was associated with the moon:[16] she was also a goddess of childbirth.[17] As were Bendis and Artemis, she too was linked to the nether world; in this connection Diana was identified with Hecate under the name of Trivia.[18] Diana and Artemis were early identified with each other in Rome[19] and throughout Latium[20] where Diana assumed the appearance of the Greek huntress in her dress and equipment.[21] Consequently, sharing as they did the same connections with the moon and the Underworld, it was reasonable for Artemis in Philippi and the Thracian Bendis to be identified with the Roman goddess and to adopt her name.

---

[12] 360 B.C.-42 B.C. (3.2).

[13] A characteristic of the Thracian goddess in works of art is a cap made of fox skin furnished with ear flaps (Knaack 1903, 247).

[14] Daux 1962, 826 (Excavation report 1961); 1965, 832 (Excavation report 1964).

[15] The worship of Apollo played an important part on Thasos, where there was a rich temple dedicated to Apollo Pythios (Salviat 1958, 263) and where the feast of Apollo Kômaios was celebrated (Salviat 1958, 261f).

[16] Latte 1960, 169. Cf. n. 3 supra.

[17] In this role she was invoked as Lucina (Carter 1902, 30). Cf. n. 48 infra.

[18] Verg. Aen. 4, 511. As Trivia Diana-Hecate was portrayed with three faces (Kraus 1960, 153ff).

[19] Apollo and Artemis reached Rome in 399 B.C. (Wissowa 1912, 251).

[20] 'Diana triformis' had an important sanctuary at Aricia, which was situated on the lake of Nemi (Latte 1960, 169). According to Propertius (2, 32, 8ff), Roman women used to carry torches in pigrimage to Diana of Aricia. Diana Nemorensis in Aricia was identical to Artemis Tauropolos, who was worshipped in Amphipolis (Map 1; Map 2: Y4-X3) (Strab. 239). Cf. 3.2.

[21] In the *Homeric hymn to Demeter* (59-61) Hecate is said to be holding flaming torches in her hands when looking for Persephone. Hecate is also pictured in works of art holding one or two torches (Kraus 1960, 30f), and she is often portrayed carrying torches on Thracian coins during the Hellenistic and imperial periods (Collart-Ducrey 1975, 211f). Furthermore, Diana Nemorensis was portrayed in the guise of a huntress carrying a torch (Wissowa 1912, 251).

4.2.2 The Importance of the Hunting Goddess to Philippian Women

From this historical survey dealing with the existence of the hunting goddess in Philippi we can conclude that the goddess who is pictured on the rock carvings and named Diana in the inscriptions was the result of an amalgamation of the Thracian Bendis, the Greek Artemis and the Roman Diana; the function of this goddess was primarily related to the figure of Hecate although her external appearance was that of the Greek Artemis;[22] she is principally pictured on the carvings in a short dress and carrying a bow.[23] Sometimes she is armed with a spear, but she is always accompanied by a stag and one or two hounds (Fig. 2 A).[24]

As regards the remnants of the cult we can state that no temple or sanctuary connected with this goddess has been found in Philippi. The only trace of a place of worship in connection with Diana is an altar on the acropolis situated close to carvings picturing the hunting goddess; it has a pit cut out of the rock for sacrificial offerings[25]–a characteristic peculiar to offerings to chthonic deities.[26] This not only underlines her close connection with Hecate but, in my opinion, also indicates that the mound was regarded as an open-air sanctuary dedicated to the hunting goddess and took the place of an ordinary temple.[27] Only a few inscriptions relating to her exist.[28] On the acropolis of the town, however, many of the surviving carvings already mentioned depict Diana and tell us that she was worshipped there.[29] Evidence for her particular importance to the women of Philippi is given in the juxtaposition of the goddess and a female figure in these carvings.[30]

Before I concentrate upon these sources it may be appropriate to begin with the picture of Hecate given by Hesiod since it provides literary corroboration for the archaeological and epigraphical information on the goddess to be found in Philippi.

---

[22] Contrary to G. Kazarow (see n. 8 supra) Th. Kraus (1960, 75 and n. 372) is of the opinion that the goddess pictured on the Philippian carvings represents Hecate.

[23] Collart-Ducrey 1975, 28, Nos. 8-58.

[24] Collart-Ducrey 1975, 28, Nos. 59-65.

[25] Excavation report 1922, 529.

[26] Nilsson 1967, 78.

[27] Cf. n. 83 infra. The associating of Diana with the open air of the acropolis is in accord with the Roman tradition; Diana Nemorensis was called 'Diana apud lucem' ('in the grove') (Tac. Ann. 12, 8). (Cf. n. 20 supra). The practice of worshiping Diana in the open air was preserved for a long period in Italy (Latte 1960, 170 n. 1). Cf. Abrahamsen 1987, 21.

[28] The epigraphical material includes in all 12 inscriptions, 8 of which mention women. Except for 2 Greek inscriptions all of them are in Latin (Collart 1937, 442f; Collart-Ducrey 1975, 29).

[29] Collart-Ducrey 1975, 28, Nos. 8-97.

[30] Collart-Ducrey 1975, Nos. 9, 44, 48, 57, 60, 65, 73, 93. Cf. n. 54 and 57 infra.

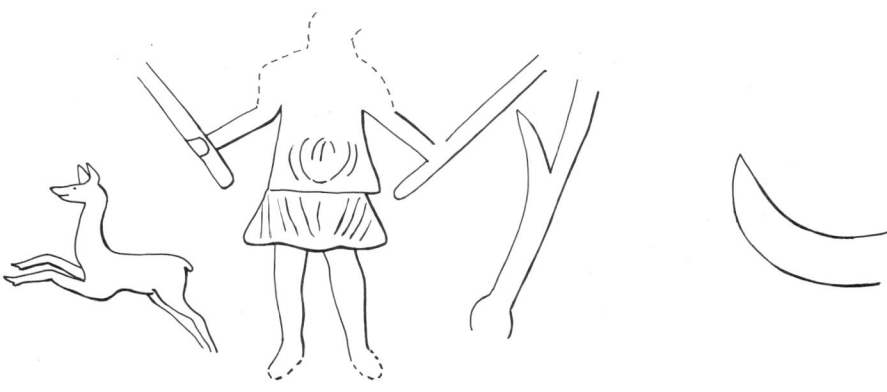

Fig. 1. The hunting goddess pictured on a Philippian stone carving (Collart-Ducrey 1975, Relief 83, Fig. 106)

4.2.2.1 Hecate as Pictured by Hesiod

In the Theogony we find an exhaustive description praising the goddess Hecate,[31] although she is not even mentioned by Homer. According to Hesiod she is next to almighty, since she is entrusted with the ruling of the cosmos in co-operation with her father Zeus:

> And she (i.e. Phoebe) conceived and bare Hecate whom Zeus the son of Cronos honoured above all. He gave her splendid gifts, to have a share of the earth[32] and the unfruitful sea. She received honour also in starry heaven, and is honoured exceedingly by the deathless gods.[33]

However, Hecate is also said to care for human beings in their temporal anxieties:

> For to this day, whenever any one of men on earth offers rich sacrifices and prays for favour according to custom, he calls upon Hecate. Great honour comes full easily to him whose prayers the goddess receives favourably, and she bestows wealth upon him; for the power surely is with her.[34] [- - -]. Whom she will she greatly aids and advances: she sits by worshipful kings in judgement, and in the assembly whom she will is distinguished among the people. And when men arm themselves for the battle that destroys men, then the goddess is at hand to give victory and grant glory readily to whom she will.[35]

In addition, she was also made a protectress of children:

> And the son of Cronos made her a nurse of the young who after that day saw with their eyes the light of all-seeing Dawn. So from the beginning she is a nurse of the young,

---

[31] Hes. Theog. 411-52. This long and detailed description of the power of Hecate has been regarded by some scholars as a later interpolation influenced by Orphic ideas. Th. Kraus (1960, 58ff) accounts for the different opinions held by scholars. Among other difficulties it has been regarded as a problem that the omnipotent figure of Hecate, portrayed in the Theogony, differs highly from the usual picture of the goddess as a deity of ghosts and being invoked particularly by women in connection with all kinds of magic (Nilsson 1967, 725). As regards the latter argument, in my opinion, these two ideas of the goddess do not necessarily exclude the one from the other. On the contrary, the universal power of Hecate, as described by Hesiod, can be seen as the prerequisite condition for her ability to answer to various magic rituals–i.e. rituals privately performed for a specific purpose (Burkert 1977, 100)–demanding all kinds of demons to be subordinated to her wishes, as is shown in the Greek magical papyri from the 4th cent. A.D. (For instance, GMP 4, 1390-1495 and 2708-84).

[32] There is reason to assume that Hecate's power over the earth included also the underworld, since she was thought to be keeping the keys to the gate of Hades (Hymn. Orph. 1, 7) (Kraus 1960, 49 and n. 235).Furthermore, Artemidorus (2, 34) characterizes Hecate as a terrestrial as well as a chthonic deity. Cf. n. 41 infra.

[33] Hes. Theog. 411-415. Transl. H. G. Evelyn-White.

[34] Hes. Theog. 416-420. Transl. H. G. Evelyn-White.

[35] Hes. Theog. 429-433. Transl. H. G. Evelyn-White.

and these are her honours.³⁶

These lines give the picture of a mighty deity sharing dominion over the heavens, the earth (presumably including the underworld) and the sea, and caring also for human beings and especially for children.

In my opinion, Hecate's responsibilities, as described by Hesiod, agree so closely with those of the Philippian hunting goddess that she may be entitled to the name of Diana-Hecate (for the sake of simplicity I name her Diana in the following). In only one surviving stone carving is she depicted in her Hecate aspect: she is shown carrying two upright torches³⁷ in the immediate vicinity of a crescent moon (Fig. 1)³⁸ In the ancient colony, however, it is likely that her three-faced image³⁹ was often to be seen outside the front doors of the dwelling-houses⁴⁰ as an indication that the goddess was near at hand to answer the prayers of the women of the household.⁴¹

In dealing with the surviving sources I shall first discuss the information provided by the inscriptions (4.2.2.2) and thereafter I shall examine the rock carvings (4.2.2.3)–focusing particularly on the religious meaning they held for Philippian women.

4.2.2.2 Diana in the Philippian Inscriptions

4.2.2.2.1 *Goddess of Healing*

There are hardly any epigraphical references in the colony to suggest that Diana was of particular importance to women—not even in her protective role at childbirth.⁴² One votive inscription only, located on the acropolis (cf. 3.7.1.2), makes a connection with female life:

Galgestia Primilla pro filia De[a]ne v[otum] s[olvit] l[ibens] m[erito].⁴³

---

36 Hes. Theog. 450-452. Transl. H.G. Evelyn-White. Hecate is further called Kourotrophos by Aristophanes (Schol. in Vesp. 804), and she is Kourotrophos in the late Orphic hymns (1, 8; 12, 8) (Price 1978, 192).

37 See n. 21 supra. Cf. the inscription from Doxato (quoted in p. 105) which mentions torches in connection with the Dionysiac festal procession in the after-life.

38 Collart-Ducrey 1975, 111 No. 83; 210ff. In this case Diana is pictured immobile and in full face posture (Fig. 1); she is usually depicted in profile and moving from left to right (from the view of the spectator) (Fig. 2 *B*).

39 Artemidorus (2, 37) mentions a three-faced Hecate standing on a pedestal. See n. 18 supra.

40 Nilsson 1967, 725.

41 Nilsson 1967, 724f. According to Artemidorus (2, 34), both Artemis, who is said to be an ethereal deity, and Hecate, in her role as a terrestrial goddess, can be perceived by the senses. Cf. n. 32 supra.

42 There are no surviving inscription whatsoever relating to childbirth in Philippi.

43 Collart-Ducrey 1975, 170, No. 149.

It tells of a woman invoking Diana (symbolized by a crescent moon[44]) to aid her daughter who was most likely suffering from an eye disease of some kind, since an eye is pictured in immediate connection with the inscription.[45] This one example does, however, indicate that the Philippian Diana was connected with the healing of children, and this role of patroness of the young associates her with Hecate[46]–an identification which is further supported by the reference to the crescent moon.[47]

4.2.2.2.2 Goddess of the Underworld

In Philippi the two surviving inscriptions dedicated to the hunting goddess which contain references to women focus on her connection with the Underworld.

An already mentioned Latin inscription from the village of Proussotchani (Map 2: Y8-X4)[48] tells of Diana as a protectress of a burial fund:[49]

> Cintis Polulae fil[ius] Scaporenus sibi et uxori suae Secu Bithi fil[iae] v[ivus] f[aciendum] c[uravit]. Dedu her[edibus] meis * LX ut [e]x usuris eius adaiant Rosal[ibus] sub curat[ione] Zipae Mesti fil[ii]. Ad arbiterio eius q[ui] s[upra] n[ominatus] e[st] Diane * CCL.

---

[44] The crescent moon was significant for Diana and was also attributed to Hecate (Kraus 1960, 103f). Cf. n. 3 supra. Furthermore, Selene was related to the sight. Artemidorus (2, 36) reports that 'Selene, the moon, [- - -] indicates the dreamer's eyes, since she herself is the cause of sight as well as its mistress' (Transl. R. J. White).

[45] Cf. Anth. Gr. 9, 46. Pictures of the different parts of the body were often dedicated to the deity in connection with votive offerings (Nilsson 1967, 138).

[46] See Hes. Theog. 450-52, quoted in p. 80f.

[47] See n. 21 supra. A crescent moon is also pictured in connection with the rock carving representing the hunting goddess carrying torches (Fig. 1).

[48] Perdrizet 1900, 310f. A damaged Latin inscription ('Deana[e Lu]ci[ferae] Q. S[t]ellius Q. [f. V]ol. Vopiscus testamento fieri iussit') dedicated by a male, found in the forum (Map.3:15), seems to belong to the same sphere and is most likely dedicated to Diana Lucifera (cf. Mart. 10, 70, 7) as the protectress of a burial fund (Collart 1933, No. 7, Fig. 7, 331ff). Because of the damage to the stone, however, only the letters -ci- from the epithet of the goddess remain, which is why the inscription has also been attributed to 'Lucina' (Collart 1933, 332f)–a name attributable to Diana as a protectress of childbirth (see n. 17 supra). The fact that the inscription is dedicated by a male and is situated in the forum points, in my opinion, to 'Lucifera'. Had it referred to Diana Lucina it would more likely have been dedicated by a female and have been located in a more remote place–for instance, the acropolis (cf. 4.2.2.2.1). The epithet of 'Lucifera' may further be supported by the existence of the above-mentioned rock carving portraying Diana carrying torches (Fig. 1) and identifying her with Hecate (Collart-Ducrey 1975, 212 and n. 3).

[49] Burial funds in Philippi are also to be found in connection with the worship of Dionysus and are further discussed in 4.3.2.2.

Fig. 2 *A-B*. Philippian stone carving showing a female figure in close connection with the hunting goddess. (Collart-Ducrey 1975, Reliefs No. 120 and 60, Fig. 75)

We learn of a married couple of Thracian origin who bequeathed a sum of money to the fund to secure a dignified funeral and to finance the annual celebration of the Rosalia at the tomb.[50]

The second inscription, also in Latin, located at Koumbaliste (Map 2: Y8-X4) and dedicated by Manta Zercedis, a priestess ('sacerdos') of Thracian origin,[51] to Diana Minervia, might also be related to the nether world:

> Deanae Minerviae quae a[....... re]stiterunt ho[c] loco vicani Sc....? Nicaenses et Coreni et Zcambu[.... tectum ae-]dis sub curatoribus: (here follows a row of Thracian proper names) Manta Zercedis sacerdos.[52]

In it a village ('vicus'), by the Greek name of Coreni, is mentioned. This name may refer to the myth of Hades' abduction of Core to the lower region, which event was thought to have taken place within the colony (3.7.2).

4.2.2.3 The Philippian Stone Carvings

Accordingly, from the inscriptions it can be presumed that Diana was principally worshipped in Philippi in her aspect of Hecate as a deity of the lower region—a fact which also seems to be confirmed by the rock carvings. As to the latter, however, the importance of Diana to women is made obvious by the inclusion of the female figure in the carvings to which reference has already been made (3.7.1.2). At the same time the exact significance of these carvings for women is extremely difficult to determine since adequate inscriptions are lacking.[53] The surviving reliefs, which can be associated with female religious feeling, give the following picture:

Eight surviving carvings featuring Diana are situated close to others depicting females.[54] One of the 8 carvings portrays a women within

---

[50] Rosalia was a commemoration at which the tombs were decorated with roses (Perdrizet 1900, 299ff; Radke 1972, 1457). Cf. also 3.3.

[51] Another priestess, by the Latin name of Valeria Severa, devoted to the cult of Diana Gazoria is mentioned in an inscription found in the village of Doxato (Map 2: Y7-X7) (Perdrizet 1898, 345ff).

[52] Salac 1923, No. 24, 64ff.

[53] Seven of the 8 inscriptions on rock carvings featuring Diana are dedicated by males (Collart-Ducrey 1975, 221). Cf. 3.7.1.2, p. 72f n. 144. For the carving dedicated by a woman, see n. 95 infra.

[54] I have included in my research only those carvings portraying Diana and those of female figures where the distance between them is 10 inches or less (Collart-Ducrey 1975, Nos. 103, 112, 114, 119, 120, 131, 132, 133). In my opinion, a space exceeding 10 inches renders the connection uncertain. There are in all 15 surviving female figures near to carvings picturing the hunting goddess (Collart-Ducrey 1975, 31).

Fig. 3. Stele from the eastern area of the Greek archipelago (Pfuhl-Möbius 1979, Tafelband I, Pl. 71: 427)

the same frame.⁵⁵ The uniqueness of this must be stressed, as in all other cases each figure is confined within its own frame. Even when the figures are shown separately their proximity to each other suggests a close connection between them. When, however, both share the same space the connection must surely be more than coincidental.

The females are all depicted full face and in a stiff posture. They wear long tunics with cloaks and veils (Fig. 2 A). Their constricting clothing reflects their restricted lives and they contrast sharply with the active deity who wears a short dress suitable for hunting and is armed with a quiver and bow or with a lance; she is seen moving to the right and is attended by a stag and a dog (Fig. 2 B).⁵⁶ Four of these carvings showing female figures⁵⁷ correspond in shape to eastern Greek tomb reliefs from the Hellenistic and Roman era.⁵⁸ Within the frames objects belonging to the world of females are reproduced: distaff, wool basket, a pair of sandals, jewel box and parfume bottle (today scarcely visible in Fig. 2 A). These items, which constituted the bride's wedding presents, symbolize the woman's responsibilities in the domestic sphere and her position as legalised courtezan to her husband.⁵⁹ In addition, the characters are usually carved in a niche, completed at the top by a 'tympanon' (Fig. 3) or an arch (cf. Fig. 5), thus forming a 'naiskos,' a common design for grave reliefs,⁶⁰ but owing to the absence of inscriptions the carvings in question cannot be identified as memorials. However, an almost identical free-standing relief from the same cultural area (Fig. 3) is furnished with an epitaph;⁶¹ with regard to form at least this encourages us to place the rock carvings in Philippi in the same category.

However, even if these carvings are of a shape appropriate to a tomb they could not have been intended to provide memorials to the dead in Philippi. As already mentioned Roman law prohibited burials inside the town walls (3.4.1.2) which is why the necropolises in Philippi were situated outside the eastern and western gates on the Via Egnatia (Map 3: A, D), which thoroughfare was lined with tombs to the boundaries of the burial areas.⁶² The carvings we are now considering must therefore be votive pictures which for some reason were dedicated to Diana on the acropolis.

---

55 Collart-Ducrey 1975, 82, No. 57 and No. 132, Fig. 71.

56 Diana is always portrayed as coming from the left and moving towards the right hand side. In this connection it may be noted that the actor, representing the countryside in drama, entered the stage from the same direction (Oehmichen 1890, 241).

57 Collart-Ducrey 1975, Nos. 112, 114, 119, 120.

58 Collart-Ducrey 1975, 233. The objects relating to the domestic sphere in these carvings are often difficult to discern since they are more or less eroded. Cf. Fig. 3. See also n. 68 infra.

59 Redfield 1982, 193; Schmaltz 1983, 238f.

60 Krause 1965, 2055.

61 Pfuhl-Möbius 1977, Tafelband 1, Fig. 71, No. 427.

62 Collart 1937, 499.

Fig. 4. Stele from Mesembria. (Kazarow 1930, Fig. 63)

Nevertheless, it may seem puzzling that these carvings are shaped as memorial stones without their having any connection with a tomb. However, parallel material from the same cultural area shows that their connection with the dead may have had a more profound religious dimension—a dimension which would not have necessitated their being placed in a burial ground but one which would indicate the closest possible unity between the dead who are celebrated and the goddess.

4.2.2.3.1 *Julia's Stele in Mesembria*

A striking parallel to these carvings in Philippi is a stele (Fig. 4), dated to the 1st cent. A.D. and situated at Mesembria on the western coast of the Black Sea (Map 1).[63]

This stone has four panels placed one above the other. Each panel is separated from the one beneath it by an inscription which reads continuously down the stone. There are two distinct subjects, one dealt with in the top and bottom sections and the other in the middle two. The top panel shows the goddess hunting,[64] while the bottom one continues the theme with two dogs[65] chasing a hare. Sandwiched between these scenes are the two panels devoted to the second subject. In the upper one the deceased woman commemorated by the stone is shown in the person of Hecate, while the lower one shows her in the same guise being conveyed to the other world on a horse-drawn chariot.

As Artemis is identified with Hecate[66] she is here seen in her dual capacity—that of a huntress and that of a protectress. Homer tells us of her care of women as a goddess of death.[67] In that role she 'protects' women by freeing them from intolerable pain and, in her role of Hecate, transports them to a new life. A detailed examination of the four panels reveals that this stone depicts the dual role of the goddess. The deceased woman, named Julia, is portrayed in two stages. The upper of the middle panels reveals her still in her home surrounded by her daughters or bondswomen, who are holding up objects[68] similar to those shown in the carvings in Philippi (4.2.2.3). She has the same dress[69] and

---

[63] Kazarow 1930, 111ff, Fig. 63.

[64] The hunting motif in connection with death is shown on Roman sarcophagi (Sichtermann-Koch 1975, index, s.v. 'Jagd').

[65] The dog was also associated with Hecate. She was supposed to be surrounded by howling dogs and this animal was sacrificed to her (Nilsson 1967, 724). In her role as door-keeper in Hades (cf. n. 32 supra) she had charge over Cerberus, with whom she is depicted on South Italic vases (Roscher 1886-90, 1895).

[66] See n. 11 supra.

[67] See n. 11 supra.

[68] The adult is assumed to be holding a wool basket and a distaff and the girl a mirror and a little jug (Kazarow 1930, 112).

[69] Hecate seems most often to have been portrayed wearing a long dress (Kraus 1960, Pl. 1-23).

carriage as the Philippian figures (Fig. 2 A) and similar to one of these carvings (Fig. 1) she holds a torch in either hand: the torches are turned downwards and symbolize death.[70] In the lower panel Julia has passed into another sphere; this is indicated by the upturned torches. These are attributed to Hecate[71] and reveal that Julia is identified with the goddess. She has, indeed, became immortal and is now seated in the carriage which takes her to the Underworld.[72] The deification, figuratively reproduced, is confirmed by the inscription on the stone:[73]

> Ἐνθάδε ἐγὼ κεῖμε Ἑκάτη
> θεὸς ὡς ἐσορᾷς ἤμην τὸ
> πάλαι βροτὸς νῦν δὲ ἀθάνα-
> τος καὶ ἀγήρως· Ἰουλία Νεικίου
> δυγάτηρ μεγαλήτορος ἀνδρὸς.
> Μεσεμβρία δέ μυ πατρὶς, ἀπὸ
> Μέλσα καὶ βρία. ζήσασα ἔτη ὅς
> μοι στήλη κατέχει τρὶς πέντε
> δὶς εἴκοσι καὶ δέκα πέντε.
> Εὐτυχεῖτε παροδῖται.

(I, the goddess Hecate, lie here, as you see. Earlier I was mortal, now, as a goddess, I am immortal and young for ever. I, Julia, daughter of the generous Nikias. My native city was Mesembria–the name comes from Melsa and 'bria'.[74] The stone commemorates the years I lived: in all, three times five, twice over twenty, and, in addition, ten and five.)

On this tombstone the goddess is shown both as the huntress whose instrument of death is the arrow and as the regenerative power whose symbol is the torch. Julia is identified with her in the latter aspect,[75] a fact which sheds light on the females of the carvings at Philippi. In conformity with the stele at Mesembria they can be interpreted as deified women identified with Diana-Hecate–in this case in her outward appearance of the hunting goddess. This is confirmed by the fact that one of the Philippian carvings shows Diana with the same objects (a jewel-case and a wool basket) (Fig. 2 B) relating to the domestic sphere as are

---

[70] Gage 1969, 161.

[71] See n. 21 supra.

[72] It is principally from Virgil that we learn of the Roman belief in an after-life (Norden 1957, 295). According to the *Aeneid* (6, 637-638) Elysium is located in the underworld.

[73] Kazarow 1930, 112f. There are the following remarks: κεῖμε, ε = αι. θεός is feminine. ἀθανατος καὶ ἀγήρως and μεγαλήτορος are reminiscences from Homer. μυ = μοι. Ε in Μέλσα is partly retained on the stone. ὸς = ὡς.

[74] Mesembria is a derivation of the town name Melsa and 'bria' is the word for 'city' in the Thracian language (cf. Strab. 319) (Kazarow 1930, 113).

[75] Literature mentions a similar deification: Agamemnon's daughter Iphigeneia is said never to have been killed but to have been transformed into Hecate by the order of Artemis (Hes. Catal.of wom. 71; Paus. 1, 43, 1).

Fig. 5. Grave altar from Rome. (Wrede 1971, Pl. 78:1)

attributed to the female figure in an adjacent carving (Fig. 2 A).[76] This identification with the hunting goddess, expressed in a simple and straightforward way, indicates that either this Philippian woman herself or her relatives hoped for her share in the free existence of the hunting goddess after death.

4.2.2.3.2 Aelia Procula's Grave Altar in Rome

The same idea of deification after death in the guise of the hunting goddess is to be found on a grave altar originating from a Roman mausoleum, dated to the second century A.D. (Fig. 5).[77] The inscription runs as follows:

D. M. / SACRUM / DEANAE ET / MEMORIAE / AELIAE / PROCULAE / P. AELIUS ASCLEPIACUS / AUG. LIB. / ET ULPIA PRISCILLA FILIAE / DULCISSIME FECERUNT.

According to the inscription, the altar is dedicated to Diana and to the memory of Aelia Procula who seems to have been about five years old when she died. Diana was the protectress of children until their marriage,[78] and, consequently, Aelia Procula was identified with the goddess after death.

The relief on the altar shows the little girl portrayed as Diana in her usual role of huntress, and the child-like face contradicts the maturity of the female body. This discrepancy between face and body illustrates strikingly the hope of the parents for their daughter's share in the

---

[76] Collart-Ducrey 1975, No. 60, p. 84f and No.120, p. 143. Cf. Fig. 3. Among these objects, today almost eroded, the jewel-case, which is attributed also to the hunting goddess, is still distinct (Fig. 2 B). These objects, relating to the domestic sphere, have been seen as having only a decorative purpose in this carving picturing the hunting goddess (Collart-Ducrey 1975, 233).

[77] Wrede 1971, 138ff. Five more inscriptions dealing with deification in connection with Diana during the imperial period are mentioned by W. Altmann (1905, 282). Incidentally, human deification is mentioned no less than forty times in the comedies of Plautus, which shows that already the Romans of the Republican period were familiar with the idea (Hanson 1959, 69).

[78] Nilsson 1967, 493. This role is also valid for her aspect of Hecate (Hes. Theog. 450-452, quoted in p. 80f). Further evidence of deification of a young girl relating to Diana as a huntress is shown by a sarcophagus, furnished with an inscription (IG 10, 2, 1, 539), from Thessaloniki (dated to the 2nd cent. A.D.) on which a deceased young girl is depicted in the guise of the hunting goddess (Düll 1975, 121ff). In spite of the fact that the sarcophagus is located in the same cultural area I have chosen to publish the picture of the Roman altar because of its pedagogical qualities.

Fig. 6. Epitaph from Podmol. (Egger 1950, Pl. II: 2; Spomenik der kgl. serbischen Akademie 77, 1934, p. 34, No. 6)

existence of the hunting goddess in the afterlife,[79] expressed in a naive way by the girl's share in her bodily form. (It may be observed in passing that this gives ground for speculation as to whether the ill-matched figure demonstrated belief in the soul's preservation of its individual qualities after death.)

4.2.2.3.3 Ariste's Epitaph in Podmol

Although the tombstone from Mesembria as well as Aelia Procula's grave altar are instrumental in explaining the purpose of the rock carvings in Philippi they do not contribute to solving the problem of their apparent lack of connection with a burial place. However, a relief (Fig. 6) from Podmol in Yugoslavia (dated to the 3rd cent. A.D.) commemorates the deification after death of a woman, named Ariste, who was a priestess in the cult of Aphrodite.[80] The stone was found among the remnants of the temple devoted to the goddess where the woman herself was subsequently commemorated.

The relief, which is a primitive work of art, shows her full face holding a bowl and a jug (the usual attributes of a priestess); in the relief there is also a pine cone symbolizing immortality.[81] According to the inscription in hexameter[82] the carving was dedicated to the deceased priestess and put into the temple by order of Aphrodite:

ἄνθεσαν αἱ δμω | αἱ δῶρον | προτέραις | Ἀφροδῖ | της
ἐκ μερόπων μακάρεσσιν ἁ | ναρπαχθεῖσαν Ἀρίστην |
μήτηρ Ἀνάλημψις, κασι | γνήτη δ' Ἀφροδιτώ | .
αὐτὴ γὰρ σύνναον ἔ| μεν Κυθέρεια θέλη | σεν.

(The maidservants of Aphrodite, the mother Analempsis and her daughter-in-law Aphrodite, have dedicated (i.e. the stone) to the blessed Ariste who was earlier carried away from the human world; Cythereia herself wished her to share the temple.)

The fact that the deceased Ariste was invited to share the temple with the goddess indicates that the commemoration in this case took place within the shrine and not at the burial-ground. In my opinion, it would be reasonable to suggest that the carvings in Philippi are analogous to this relief in that they might be interpreted as votive carvings which were cut into the rock on the acropolis—and that the acropolis was considered as the temple of Diana (4.2.2). In that case the ceremonies which were carried out by the family or the members of the burial

---

[79] The same parental hope for a dead child is expressed by the inscription from Doxato (quoted in p. 105) relating to the Dionysiac cult .

[80] Egger 1950, 11.

[81] Egger 1950, 11.

[82] Egger 1950, 11. In the first two lines words belonging together are separated because of the meter. Furter, πρότεραι is proposed to be πρεσβύτεραι (Egger 1950, 11 n. 31). .

association (cf. 4.2.2.2.2) might have taken place on the acropolis and not at the tombs outside the town walls (3.4.1.2).[83]

4.2.2.4 Diana-the 'Ideal Woman'

The fact that Philippian women identified themselves with the divine huntress in the hope of their being identified with her after death, as presumably is shown by the rock carvings, can easily be explained by the way she was depicted in the literature as the 'ideal woman'. It would seem that there was little in the life of Diana, the epitome of freedom, with which the average woman could identify (cf. 1.5), but in her idealized form she was the model for all members of her sex.

For instance, Homer's account of her relationship with her stepmother Hera, as told in the Iliad, replicated the experience of many women and provided an episode in their life with which they could both identify and sympathize:

> Therewith she caught both the other's hands by the wrist with her left hand, and with her right took the bow and its gear from her shoulders, and with these self-same weapons, smiling the while, she beat her about the ears, as she turned this way and that; and her swift arrows fell out of from the quiver. Then weeping the goddess fled from before her even as a dove that from before a falcon flieth into a hollow rock, a cleft—nor is it her lot to be taken; even so fled Artemis weeping, and left her bow and arrows where they lay.[84]

This expressive behaviour should be seen in the context of the battle of which Homer writes, but there was much in it that women and girls with stepmothers (1.3.2.1) could easily recognize as relevant to their own situations. The awareness that a deity shared many of the hardships they themselves endured must have given consolation and help to this group of women.

Furthermore, Homer describes Artemis as an outstanding young woman, exceeding all other females in her beauty and stature.[85]

---

[83] As far as I know, I am the first to interpret these carvings picturing females in close connection with Diana as memorials. Hitherto all the female figures in the carvings have been seen as representing goddesses (in more than 20 cases picturing Isis [Picard 1922, 172ff; Collart 1937, 448]) or as living worshippers or priestesses (devoted particularly to Diana) in a huge open-air sanctuary (Collart-Ducrey 1975, 235; Abrahamsen 1986, 21-86). In my opinion, however, there could have been various groups of worshippers in different periods devoted to the hunting goddess who had different needs of divine support (see 3.7.1.2, p. 72f n. 144); therefore, a homogeneous interpretation of the female figures may be insufficent. Besides the female figures in question, which I interpret as memorials, I judge another group of 10 carvings picturing females (see n. 96 infra) as representing living worshippers or priestesses of some kind.

[84] Hom.Il. 21, 489-496. Transl. A. T. Murray.

[85] Hom. Od. 6, 102ff. Young girls might have prayed to Artemis to be blessed with her beauty of face and figure (Hom.Od. 20, 70-72). The goddess was close to young girls

Helen,[86] Penelope[87] and Nausikaa[88] are all likened to the stately hunting goddess, which indicates that she was viewed as the ideal for mature women and young girls alike.

Virgil, also, depicts Diana as a paragon. In the *Aeneid* the matron whom he compares with the goddess is Queen Dido who excited the admiration and love of the hero as she walked at the head of her retinue.[89] Further, the perfection of Diana as a young girl is embodied in Camilla, a Jeanne d' Arc in antiquity, who saved her people from the enemy:

> To crown the array comes Camilla, of Volscian race, leading her troop of horse, and squadrons gay with brass–a warrior-maid, never having trained her woman's hands to Minerva's distaff or basket of wool, but hardy to bear the battle-brunt and in speed of foot to outstrip the winds.[90] [- - -] All the youth, streaming from house and field, and thronging matrons marvel, and gaze at her as she goes; agape with wonder how the glory of royal purple drapes her smooth shoulders; how the clasp entwines her hair with gold; how her own hands bear a Lycian quiver and the pastoral myrtle tipped with steel.[91]

In these quotations from the *Aeneid* Virgil contrasts the ideal life of Diana with the everyday life of women. He represents the latter by describing matrons as pushing among the young people to catch a glimpse of the girl on horseback dressed as the hunting goddess. This incident described by Virgil reminds us of the Philippian rock carvings where the figure of Diana is also contrasted with those of the married women (Fig. 2 *A-B)*. The fact that the goddess is idealized in literature helps to explain why these women seem to have hoped for an after-life under her protection. Admiration for Diana as an unattainable ideal in this life was probably one reason why women in Philippi identified with the hunting goddess in order to share not only in her beauty and freedom but also in her powerful position relating to female existence and seemingly in her authority in the Underworld.

4.2.3 Summary

According to inscriptions Diana was worshipped in Philippi principally as a goddess of the Underworld in her aspect of Hecate, while there is scant epigraphical reference to her in her usual role as a protectress of

---

and kept watch over their virginity. We are told that she killed her friend, the nymph Callisto, when the girl did not keep her maidenhood (Apollod. Bibl. 3, 8, 2).

[86] Hom. Od. 4, 120-122.
[87] Hom. Od. 17, 36-44.
[88] Hom. Od. 6, 149-152.
[89] Verg. Aen. 1, 496-504.
[90] Verg. Aen. 7, 803-807. Transl. H. R. Fairclough.
[91] Verg. Aen. 7, 812-117. Transl. H. R. Fairclough.

women. Nevertheless, woman worshippers of Diana have left traces in the rock carvings on the acropolis, where the proximity of their figures to those of the hunting goddess raises problems of interpretation. However, from archaeological parallels we may assume that it was the subject of deification after death that was depicted in these rock carvings. Thus, they may show women identifying themselves with Diana in order to become sharers of her independent life–a way of living unattainable to them in this mortal life. In addition, support for this is given in literature which tells of women as identifying with the hunting goddess.

4.2.4 Excursus: Archaeological Evidence of Woman Piety in Philippi

Of the rock carvings on the acropolis in Philippi which are today discernible, 40 portray female figures.[92] I have hitherto discussed only those 8 carvings where a connection with Diana seems reasonable[93] and where comparative archaeological material and literary sources facilitate an interpretation.

The siting of the other 32 carvings depicting women, however, suggests that no connection with any deity is intended as they are not in the vicinity of a shrine or carved representation of a god. Six of them have objects relating to females[94] and one is furnished with an inscription telling us that it was dedicated by a woman.[95] It is extremely difficult to grasp the meaning of these carvings. Their comparative segregation and the absence of any context which might aid interpretation renders them virtually incomprehensible.

There are, however, 10 of these 32 carvings,[96] located just above the theatre (Map 3: 7), which might be seen as exceptions. They form a separate group and their site is relatively isolated. These latter carvings are all highly eroded and it is impossible to determine whether they ever had any inscriptions or objects within their frames.[97] Adjacent to this group there are three niches of about the same size as the carvings.[98] One of these has a depth of only about 2 inches and has a roughened surface,[99] a fact which may indicate an unfinished relief. The others

---

[92] Collart-Ducrey 1975, 28, Nos. 98-137.

[93] See n. 30 supra.

[94] Collart-Ducrey 1975, Nos. 113, 116, 117 , 121, 122, 125.

[95] Collart-Ducrey 1975, 157, No. 135 . Atena is a Roman proper name and has no connection with the Greek goddess Athena (Collart-Ducrey 1975, 230ff).

[96] Collart-Ducrey 1975, Nos. 102, 107, 109, 110, 111, 126, 127, 128, 129, 134. Cf. Fig. 125.

[97] I refer to the photographs in Collart-Ducrey 1975.

[98] Collart-Ducrey 1975, 189ff, Nos. 176, 177, and 178. The measurements of the reliefs average 12*8*1 inches.

[99] Collart-Ducrey 1975, 189, Nos. 176 (Fig. 164) The shallowness of the niche hardly gives any space for a statuette. Surfaces of rocks could be used also for paintings

(3.5[100] and 6 inches[101] deep respectively) are smooth; perhaps these were meant for stauettes or other votive offerings.

The sense of these carvings is hard to comprehend but their isolated location, their grouping, and the presence of niches may be of help in our attempts to assess their meaning. According to the epigraphical material these 10 female figures could represent a religious group of some kind and be associated with one or several deities, the images of whom may have been in the niches. Consequently, there are three possible interpretations. According to inscriptions, priestesses existed in the cult of Diana[102] as well as in that of the imperial cult;[103] the figures might therefore be those of members of an association of female officials.[104] Secondly, they could also be looked upon as representing members of some secret female group of worshippers. In this case it may be reasonable to adjudge such a group as belonging to the ecstatic cult of Dionysus, since there was a thiasus of maenads in the town (4.3.2.1.1). Finally, there is the third possibility of interpreting these female figures as being connected with the goddess Libera (4.3.1). This Latin name may hide the Greek goddesses Demeter and Persephone,[105] and Appian's mention of Persephone's abduction in connection with Philippi (3.7.2) might indicate a cult of Demeter within the colony.[106] In that case the figures in question would represent a religious group of women celebrating the Thesmophoria.[107] Like the rites of the maenads,[108] only females had admittance to this feast, which occurred in the open air and had a close connection with mountains.[109]

Even if it is only possible to present various theories about these carvings they do give evidence of a conscious piety relating to Philippian

---

(Collart-Ducrey 1975, 253), but there are no traces left of a painting since the niche has been highly exposed to damage by rain and wind.

[100] Collart-Ducrey 1975, 191, No. 177 (Fig. 207). The measurements are 9*8*3.5 inches. It is shaped as an arch and the depth would allow small statuettes to be placed within it.

[101] Collart-Ducrey 1975, 190f, No. 178 (Fig. 207). The niche is rectangular and its size (12.5*17*6 inches) clearly indicates that there is room for several statuettes.

[102] As to priestesses in the cult of Diana, see 4.2.2.2 and n. 51 supra.

[103] Two inscriptions mention priestesses in the cult of Livia (3.4.1.3).

[104] Poland (1909, 290ff) records Greek associations of priestesses.

[105] Latte 1960, 161f.

[106] This myth is connected with the mysteries in Eleusis but the Thesmophoria was celebrated by women in all Greek tribes; therefore the abduction of Core was located to various places (Nilsson 1967, 476f). The Thesmophoria was celebrated on Thasos (Paus. 10, 28, 3) (Nilsson 1906, 314, n. 6), which is why the Thasian colonists could have brought the celebration of this feast to Philippi (cf. 3.2).

[107] Nilsson 1967, 465f.

[108] Maenads presumably celebrated their feasts at Mount Pangaion every two years (Ov. Rem. Am. 593-594). Cf. 4.3.2.1.1.

[109] In Athens the Thesmophoria was held at the Pnyx where women passed the festival days seated on the earth in huts (Deubner 1966, 54f).

women expressing itself in a very visible way–presumably recording some kind of fellowship of female worshippers.

4.3 DIONYSUS

4.3.1 Historical Background

According to Herodotus Dionysus was worshipped by the Thracians,[110] which is why some scholars are convinced of the Thracian origin of this deity.[111] Dionysus as worshipped in that country had a chthonic trait which was signified by the ceremonies performed throughout the area.[112] According to inscriptions from the Roman era, the cult in the countryside among the Thracians was characterised by mystical rites which, incidentally, enabled its followers to benefit from burial funds.[113]

The Greek colonists brought a Dionysus with them, presumably from Thasos (cf. 3.2). This Thasian Dionysus had the same chthonic significance as his Thracian counterpart[114] and was worshipped together with Hercules, the most important deity of the island.[115] According to Herodotus this latter deity also was related to the Underworld.[116] There are no remaining inscriptions from the Greek era in Philippi which is why it is impossible to know if Hercules was linked with Dionysus at that time.[117]

Latin inscriptions, on the other hand, show the Roman colonists as worshipping Dionysus under the name of Liber together with Hercules

---

[110] Hdt. 5, 7.

[111] E. Rohde, U. Wilamowitz-Moellendorff and M. P. Nilsson hold this opinion, while K.Kerényi assumes that Dionysus originated in Crete (Kerényi 1956, 10ff).

[112] Nilsson 1957, 131f.

[113] Collart 1937, 416ff. The burial funds were utilized to a great extent by immigrants of the lower classes who lacked relatives to effect the necessary commemorative rituals. Besides providing funerals and annual ceremonies at the tombs they also had a social application through banquets held in commemoration with these rituals (Kornemann 1901, 386ff).The Greek burial funds date back to the 3rd cent. B.C. (Bruck 1954, 49), while the Romans did not institute such associations until about A.D. 100 (Bruck 1954, 48).

[114] Seyrig 1927, 201.

[115] According to an inscription (IG 12, 8, 356), dated to the late 6th or early 5th cent. B.C., Hercules and Dionysus were considered to be guardians of the town of Thasos (Bergquist 1973, 36).

[116] Hdt. 2, 44. This association was strong in Thrace (Bayet 1929, 36ff). At Hercules' temple on Thasos chthonic sacrifices were presumably made to him (Bergquist 1973, 57).

[117] Such a connection would be possible because the tradition regarding Alexander the Great was strong in Philippi (Collart 1937, 188 n. 1) and the king identified himself with Hercules as well as with Dionysus (Kern 1938, 39ff).

and a goddess named Libera.[118] This goddess might be either the Greek Persephone (of whom the abduction by Hades was said to have taken place within the colony[119]) or an Italic deity who was introduced by the colonists.[120] In Philippi Dionysus was worshipped also as Liber Pater, who originally was an indigenous Italic deity whose cult had an orgiastic quality.[121] However, it is impossible to determine whether the Latin names are only translations of the Greek or if they refer to deities of an Italic origin.

4.3.2 The Importance of Dionysus to Philippian Women

Regarding the worship of Dionysus the archaeological traces are few. Besides two rock carvings depicting a phallus and a centaur,[122] the archaeologists have found remnants of two small shrines only. One of these was in the acropolis (Map 3: 8) and belonged presumably to some Dionysian mystery group;[123] the other one, located in the town centre, was the meeting-place of a thiasus of maenads.[124]

However, the surviving inscriptions designate Dionysus as having been an important deity in Philippi, particularly for women.[125] Five of the inscriptions derive from the ecstatic cult in the town, while the others, relating to mysteries, were found in the countryside; in addition, literature mentions a priestess of Dionysus at an oracle on Mount

---

[118] See n. 129, 131, and 134 infra. This fact can be explained either by the Thasian Hercules' survival from the time of the Greek colonists or by the arrival of the Romans, since his cult was extensive in Italy, and in Rome he was worshipped at the Ara Maxima by Greek ritual (Latte 1960, 213ff).

[119] See n. 106 supra.

[120] Liber and Libera were a couple of Italic divinities of nature (Latte 1960, 60) who in course of time became identified with Dionysus and Persephone (Latte 1960, 60) ; Libera was also identified with Ariadne (Ov. Fast. 3, 512; Pliny HN 36, 29).

[121] Liber Pater was a god of fertility connected with phallic rites and was early identified with Dionysus (Latte 1960, 70).

[122] Collart-Ducrey 1975, 177ff, No. 158 and 156. These carvings are considered to belong to the Dionysian circle since the cult is attested by inscriptions and traces of a shrine (3.4.1.1). Dionysus was earlier identified on a carving near the theatre (Heuzey 1876, 79f) but this identification is uncertain since the carving has gradually been obliterated by erosion (Collart-Ducrey 1975, 174f, No. 153).

[123] Cf. 3.7.1.2. The finding of a Pan's pipe of silver and two clay lamps decorated with Dionysiac motifs indicates a meeting-place for followers of this god (Excavation report 1922, 530). However, the lamps do not necessarily indicate a connection with the Dionysiac cult since they lack inscriptions. Only those cases where a lamp has a mythological motif in connection with an inscription can we be sure of its use in a cult (Hug 1927, 1585).

[124] Collart 1937, 414. See also 3.4.1.1 and 3.7.1.1.

[125] The epigraphical material includes 17 inscriptions, 7 of which mention women (6 are in Latin, 1 in Greek) (Collart 1937, 414ff).

Pangaion.[126] Mythically, Dionysus was thoroughly at home in these surroundings since several of the stories about him were located on Mount Pangaion (Map 2: Y5-X5).[127]

Dealing first with the ecstatic cult I take the inscriptions as my starting point (4.3.2.1.1); the information they give will be examined and supported by references in literature (4.3.2.1.2). Thereafter I discuss women's roles in the Dionysiac mysteries (4.3.2.2), and, finally, I examine the opportunities for identification offered by the mythical figures of the Dionysiac circle who were particularly associated with the colony (4.3.2.3).

4.3.2.1 Women in the Dionysiac Ecstatic Cult

4.3.2.1.1 The Philippian Inscriptions

Five inscriptions relating to a Dionysiac ecstatic cult were found during the excavations of the public baths (Map 3: 21).[128] Three of them are dedicated to the triad Liber-Libera-Hercules and the others to Liber Pater. One of the inscriptions in question is dedicated by a thiasus of maenads,[129] three of them by separate women[130]–Pomponia Hilara,[131] Salvia Pisidia[132] and Pisidia Helpis[133]–and the last by Marronia Eutychia who is mentioned together with her husband.[134]

It is difficult to know the stratum of society to which these women belonged: Pomponia Hilara may have been either a noble female of the Pomponians[135] or a liberated bondswoman who had been given the name

---

[126] Hdt. 7, 111. The oracle is discussed in 4.3.2.1.2.

[127] Nysa, the mountain where the infant Dionysus was tended by his nurses, was identified with Mount Pangaion (Perdrizet 1910, 48ff), and stories about Orpheus (Perdrizet 1910, 29ff) and Cadmus, the father of Semele and grandfather of Dionysus, (Eur. Bacch. 1ff; Apollod. Bibl. 3, 1, 1; Plin. HN 4, 4) were also located there. See also Gruppe 1906, 213ff.

[128] Collart 1937, 367ff. See also 3.4.1.1, p.63 n. 38.

[129] Lib[ero] et Lib[era] et Her[culi], / thiasus Maenad[arum] / regianar[um] aq/[ua]m induxit [p. s.] (= pecunia sua) (Collart 1937, 414 n. 1).

[130] These women might well have belonged to the thiasus of maenads.

[131] ex imperio / Liberi et Liberae / et Herculis, / nequis nequ/eve velit faciem / tangere, nesi / siqui imperat/um fueret / ex imperio, / Pomponia / Hilara posuit (Collart 1937, 414 n. 1).

[132] Salvia / Pisidia / Lib[ero] Pat[ri] M N (Collart 1937, 415 n.4).

[133] Pisidia / Helpis / L[ibero] P[atri], v. s. / l. a. (=votum soluit animo libens) (Collart 1937, 415 n. 4; Cagnat 1914, 471).

[134] Lib[ero] et Lib[erae] / Herc[uli] sac[rum], / C. Valer. / Fortunatus cum Marroni/a Eutyci/[a] ux[ore] (Collart 1937, 414 n.1). Also males could be initiated into the ecstatic Dionysiac cult (Burkert 1977, 434).

[135] The Pomponians were a distinguished Roman family (Gundel 1952, 2323f).

of her mistress.¹³⁶ Furthermore, three of these women have names derived from geographical places, a fact which would suggest that they were liberated slaves.¹³⁷ Marronia Eutychia presumably originated from the nearby Maroneia,¹³⁸ while Salvia Pisidia and Pisidia Helpis would have had their roots in Asia Minor.

Three of these votive inscriptions give more than the names of the donors: Pomponia Hilara seems to dedicate a statue ('faciem')¹³⁹ and Salvia Pisidia offers a sestertia (=1000 denarii) to Liber Pater,¹⁴⁰ while the maenads bequeath a water conduit in honour of Liber, Libera and Hercules.¹⁴¹ As indicated by the inscriptions, these women had a remarkable degree of economic independence, which can be explained by the fact that they enjoyed complete control over their money, in case they had fulfilled the requirements of the Augustan marriage laws ('ius liberorum').¹⁴²

4.3.2.1.2 Ecstatic Women in Literature

According to Diodorus Siculus, the maenads re-enacted in their ceremonies the nymphs' care of the infant Dionysus at Mount Nysa.¹⁴³ As this mountain was identified with Mount Pangaion¹⁴⁴ the roles played by these nymphs were both physically and emotionally close to women in Philippi, which can explain the popularity of the ecstatic cult in the town. There is no information on their rituals in the Philippian material, and the literary sources present a picture referring more to myth and to rites of an archaic past¹⁴⁵ than to rituals practised by house-

---

[136] Rix 1965, 2268.

[137] Heubeck 1965, 2268.

[138] Maroneia was a town on the Via Egnatia, about 70 km to the east of the town of Philippi (Map 1).

[139] See n. 131 supra.

[140] See n. 132 supra.

[141] See n. 129 supra. It is remarkable that Hercules is found in connection with an extremely female cult. It may be explained by the fact that the story of his relationship with Queen Omphale seems to have been well known in Macedonia; a herm, illustrating Omphale changing her sex for that of the hero and showing her dressed in the lion skin and holding the club, is to be seen in the Archaeological Museum at Thessaloniki (Inv.No. 7). On the other hand, women were excluded from the sacrifices to Hercules both on Thasos (IG 12, Suppl.14, 3f) (Bergquist 1973, 85) and in Rome (Plut. Mor. 278E-F) (Latte 1960, 214).

[142] See 1.1, p.9 n. 4. Macedonian women were known for their readiness to make sacrifices in connection with religion, a fact which vexed their husbands (Strab. 297, quoted in p. 55.).

[143] Diod. Sic. 4, 3.

[144] See n. 127 supra.

[145] Plutarch (Vit.Alex. 2) tells us about the ecstatic worship of Dionysus in Thrace where Alexander's mother, Olympias, was an adherent of the cult. In the 4th cent.

wives of the Roman era. The cult seems to have been more or less institutionalized at that time[146] (for instance, the Philippian maenads took an interest in such practical things as the installation of water mains[147]) although it retained it ecstatic character.[148]

However, there are good reasons to assume that drama had familiarized Philippian women with the mythical story of Dionysus' arrival in Greece from Asia Minor and also with the archaic rituals of the ecstatic cult (cf. 2.2.1.2). Euripides' drama the *Bacchanals*, which might have been a potential source of inspiration to later maenadic cult,[149] was in all probability well known in Philippi, since the tomb of Euripides was said to be located in Arethusa,[150] a small place about 75 km from the town (Map 2: Y2-X1). The grave attracted various legends[151]and the historian Ammianus Marcellinus tells us that it was still visited in the late 4th cent. A.D.;[152] this suggests Arethusa as a resort of pilgrims, a fact which indicates that the tragedian and his Macedonian drama were known throughout Philippi.[153] In the theatre (3.4.1.1) the *Bacchanals* might have been performed both as a drama[154] and as a pantomime[155] (cf. 2.2.1.2), and adherents of the ecstatic cult in the town would have been interested spectators, even if they could not be said fully to recognize the forms of the worship described by Euripides. However, they might have recognized the all-embracing and pervading

---

    B.C., according to Plutarch's description, the worshippers seem to have been completely disordered and dispersed to the wilds, while snake-handling became a characteristic feature of their activities. The fact that the snakes are said to have been tame seems to indicate a civilizing of rites which derived from an earlier stage of their culture (cf. Portefaix 1983, 144-149).

146   Henrichs 1978, 147ff.

147   See n. 129 supra. Cf. also 2.3.2.2.

148   J. Bremmer (1984, 275ff) has reconstructed the maenadic ritual by a critical use of literary and epigraphical sources. With the help of neuro-psychological reserch he also pays attention to the effects of the rituals on the women.

149   Henrichs 1978, 122. The drama was written in Macedonia in the late 5th cent. B.C (Dodds 1944, XXXIV; Henrichs 1978, 122) and possibly Euripides was influenced by the Dionysiac cult in the area (Dieterich 1909, 1263).

150   Amm. Marc. 27, 4, 8.

151   For instance, two streams were said to have their sources at the tomb; the one had health-giving water while the other brought forth fatal poison (Vitr. De Arch. 8, 16.; Pliny NH 31) (Nestle, 1898, 145ff).

152   Amm. Marc. 27, 4, 8. Vitruvius (De Arch. 8, 16) tells us that travellers used to recline and take their lunch at the stream with the good water.

153   Euripides seems to have been still popular in Roman times. According to Artemidorus (4, 59) people could dream of slave women and poor people reciting passages from Euripides' dramas, as well as of Dionysiac figures belonging to the *Bacchanals* (Artem. 4, 39). In this connection it may be noted that ecstatic Dionysiac women seem to have been generally accepted (Plut. Mor. 249E-F).

154   In the Roman era Attius made a free translation of the drama and it was also performed in Latin at that time. Evidence is collated by E. Bruhns (1891, 30).

155   The *Bacchanals* became popular as a pantomime as well (Bruhns 1891, 30).

Dionysiac life force (represented by wine and the phallus) as breaking all boundaries.[156] The Dionysiac bliss was expressed in the drama by phenomena which were characteristic of the state of Paradise–the earth gives milk, honey and wine without toil,[157] the snakes do not sting the women who are handling them,[158] and the maenads give their milk to fawns and wolf cubs.[159] What must have been fascinating to women was that in the drama frenzied women behaved as men, since ecstatic union with the god resulted in reversed sex roles.[160] The ecstatic climax is described by Euripides as a union between the god and the woman (ὅταν γὰρ ὁ θεὸς εἰς τὸ σῶμ' ἔλθῃ πολύς, λέγειν τὸ μέλλον τοὺς μεμηνότας ποιεῖ),[161] a union which seems to have had a sexual character[162] and resulted in her predicting the future. This sexual relationship is still more accentuated by Philostratus when he describes a picture of the island of Dionysus where Silenus tries to seize a maenad:

> But you are bold enough, my boy, not to fear even the Seilenus here that guards the island, though he is both drunken and is trying to seize a Bacchante. She, however, does not deign to look at him, but since she loves Dionysus she fashions his image in her mind and pictures him and sees him, absent though he is; for though the look of the Bacchante's eyes is wavering (ὀφθαλμῶν [- -] μετέωρον), yet assuredly it is not free from dreams of love.[163]

According to the author, the artist had reproduced the woman in question with flickering eyes, or possibly as turning up her eyes to heaven–a criterion of ecstasy, according to representations of maenads on vases.[164]

Despite the fact that much of the enthusiastic behaviour described by Euripides in his drama was lacking in the Dionysiac ecstatic cult in real life, we must suggest that it presented the followers with a more profound religious experience than either domestic (2.3.1) or official

---

156 Dodds 1951, 270ff.
157 Eur. Bacch. 704-710.
158 Eur. Bacch. 101-103.
159 Eur. Bacch. 699-703.
160 Segal 1978, 195.
161 Eur. Bacch. 300f. In an article (*Concepts of Ecstasy in Euripides' 'Bacchanals' and their Interpretation*) I have discussed various interpretations of the concept of ecstasy in the *Bacchanals* (Portefaix 1981, 201-210).
162 In this connection it may be noted that only married women could be initiated Bacchanals ; the maidens merely carried the thyrsi (Diod. Sic. 4, 3, 3) (Burkert 1977, 436).
163 Philostr. Imag. 2,17. Transl. A. Fairbanks.
164 Rapp 1872, 565. The sexual union with the deity is further reflected in the mysteries by the fact that female officials used to carry the phallus in the processions. This function is evidenced by the well-known inscription from Torre Nova in Italy, describing a priestess as a carrier of the phallus (φαλλοφόρος) (Vogliano 1933, 239f). The existence of a rock carving on the acropolis depicting a phallus (see n. 122 supra) suggests that similar ceremonies were observed in Philippi.

worship (2.3.2) could provide. During the rites, which might have made them feel united with the life of Nature, they were liberated for a few days from their usual life and the tasks in the household, since the ceremonies took place in the open air on Mount Pangaion (presumably every two years[165]) and these occasions also provided an opportunity for women to meet in an environment outside that of their everyday existence.

Finally, history records instances of Dionysiac ecstasy within the colony. According to Herodotus the Thracians had an oracle belonging to Dionysus and situated on the highest peaks of Mount Pangaion.[166] In conformity with the Delphic oracle it possessed an ecstatic priestess as well as priests.[167] Plutarch tells us that the wife of Spartacus had been in charge at an oracle which answers the description of that on Mount Pangaion.[168] Furthermore, it is mentioned by contemporary Roman historians in connection with conflict between Thracian tribes.[169]

4.3.2.2 Philippian Women in Dionysiac Mysteries

Two inscriptions in the countryside make reference to Dionysiac mysteries. One of them is located in Podgora, a village on the southern slope of Mount Pangaion (Map 2: Y4-X5) inhabited by Thracians. Their presence is substantiated by the Thracian proper names in the Greek inscription (dated to the beginning of the third century A.D.[170]) constituting a will:[171]

Ζείπας ἑαυτῷ καὶ τῇ ἰδίᾳ [συνβίω] | Κλευδι καὶ τοῖς ἰδίοις τέκνοις πᾶσι [ν ἐποίησε]. | Καταλινπάν[ω] | δὲ μύσ[τ]αις | [Δι]ονύσου δηνάρια ˙ ρκ΄. | Παρακαύσουσίν μοι ῥόδοις κα[τ' ἔτος)

Zipas, the father of the family, bequeaths 120 denarii on behalf of himself, his wife Kleudis and their children to the mysteries of Dionysus for roses to be burnt annually by the cult members at the grave. Obviously, the worship of Dionysus at Podgora was organized around religious mysteries, but it also made provision for a burial fund. By donating a sum of money to the fund, Zipas ensured that the annual

---

[165] Ov. Rem. Am. 593-4. See n. 108 supra.
[166] Hdt. 7, 111. Cf. Eur. Rhes. 965.
[167] Hdt. 7, 111. The priestess (πρόμαντις) communicated the oracle's message to the priests (οἱ προφητεύοντες) who articulated it for the benefit of the visitor (Vollgraff 1903, 274).
[168] Plut. Vit.Crass.8.
[169] Dio Cass. 51, 25; 54, 34.
[170] The inscription is to be found on a tombstone where the whole family is depicted, and the female hair style gives a clue to its date (Perdrizet 1900, 304, Pl.12).
[171] Perdrizet 1894, 445; 1900, 304f; Collart 1937, 417 and n. 1.

celebration of Rosalia[172] would be held by the members in the form of a banquet at which roses (cf. 3.3) were to be sacrificed on his account. His wife, however, who is mentioned by name in the inscription, seems to have had no independent function in connection with the realization of the will.

The second inscription from the countryside was found in the church at Doxato, a village about 20 km from the town of Philippi (Map 2: Y7-X7). It consists of a flat piece of marble inscribed with a long poetic epitaph in Latin,[173] dated to the 3rd cent. A.D.[174] It is dedicated to a little boy who had been initiated into the mysteries of Dionysus; it expresses the feelings of loss on the part of the parents but at the same time their expectations of the child's survival in another world:

> [- - -] et reparatus item vivis in Elysiis.
> sic placitum est divis a[e]terna vivere for[ma],
> qui bene de supero lumine sit meritus.
> quae tibi castifico promisit munera cursu
> olim iussa deo simplicitas facilis.
> nunc seu te Bromio signatae mystides at se
> florilego in prato congreg[em uti] Satyrum
> sive canistriferae poscunt sibi Naides aequ[e],
> qui ducibus taedis agmina festa trahas,
> sis quo[d]cunque, puer, quo te tua protulit aetas,
> dummodo [- - -] [175]

(You are calm and restored ('reparatus') and living in the Elysian fields—we tormented and overcome with grief. The godhead had promised gifts to you for your chaste life once easy simplicity had been ordered by the god. Either the tattooed women initiated into the mysteries of Bromios ('signatae mystides') call you into the flower-bearing meadows of the Satyrs or the basket-bearing Naiads demand equally that you lead festive bands with flaming torches. Whatsoever you are, boy, whether your age has borne you, yet for your merit you dwell in the blessed fields.)[176]

This text is unique in its description of the Dionysiac paradise[177] which was a frequent motif on sarcophagi at that time.[178] The child is received by tattooed female initiates ('signatae mystides'), presumably the shades of deceased women, or by mythical naiads[179] who are dancing together in flowery meadows—it is remarkable that this paradisial dancing seems to take place in darkness, as can be deduced by the reference to torches ('taedes'). Consequently, followers of Dionysus imagined themselves to

---

[172] See n.50 supra.

[173] Heuzey 1876, 129.

[174] Dölger 1930, 107.

[175] CIL 3, 686, B 1233. Collart 1937, 419.

[176] Translation by T. M. Watson.

[177] Nilsson 1957, 130.

[178] Turcan 1966, 405ff

[179] Dionysus had a close connection with the element of water (Otto 1933, 148ff) and even with the sea (Hom. Il. 6, 130ff).

pass their after-lives in eternal bliss while participating in the Dionysiac festal procession. According to the inscription the maenads were thought to have been prominent in this procession, and they are described as having the mark of the deity on their bodies—a particular characteristic of Thracian maenads.[180]

While there is evidence of women participating in the Dionysiac ecstatic cult in Philippi they are mentioned only indirectly in the epigraphical material regarding the mysteries. However, since inscriptions in other places tell of women's involvement in the Dionysiac mysteries[181] it can be assumed that they also had an important position in such rites in Philippi. These mysteries were often organized on a family basis and were conducted by a male and a female named 'pater' and 'mater', who were reproduced in art in the mythical guise of a satyr and a maenad.[182] The above-mentioned inscription from Torre Nova, dated to the 3rd cent. A.D.,[183] gives us a picture of such a Dionysiac group. The priestess Pompeia Agrippinilla officiated as the leader of a host of male and female participants.[184] According to the epithets the women had a leading position in the group as well as the responsibility of carrying the holy objects.[185]

Children as well as adults were included in the Dionysiac family. The inscription from Doxato quoted above is one of many which show that children of different ages were initiated into the mysteries;[186] the mythical model was the initiation of the infant Dionysus.[187] The Orphic myth about the infant god who, under the name of Zagreus, was torn to pieces by the Titans and was reborn as Dionysus[188] also gave the hope that a child, initiated into the mysteries, would gain a happy after-life.[189] The knowledge that a child was so admitted in to the mysteries could be a comfort to its parents in the event of its death. (It certainly seems likely that this was so in the case of the Doxato inscription.) In this connection it is worth noting that the adherents of the Dionysiac mysteries did not

---

[180] According to Plutarch (Mor. 557D), Thracian women were tattooed as a punishment for their killing of Orpheus. Dölger is of the opinion that the Thracian custom of tattooing was a matter of tribal marking which had no religious significance (Dölger 1930, 115f , Pl. 9, 1).

[181] Nilsson 1957, Chapt. 5 and 6.

[182] Horn 1972, 88ff.

[183] Vogliano 1933, 216ff; 264f.

[184] Vogliano 1933, 222f; 264f.

[185] For priestesses there are the following titles: ἀρχιβασσάραι, δᾳδοῦχος, ἱέραιαι, κισταφόροι, λικναφόροι, φαλλοφόρος(Vogliano 1933, 227; 239 ff). Cf. n. 164 supra.

[186] Nilsson 1957, 106f.

[187] Nilsson 1957, 110.

[188] The myth is preserved by Nonnos, 10, 292f; 27, 341; 44, 213 (Hunger 1959, 374).

[189] Nilsson (1957, 130f) is of the opinion that the Orphic myth had little significance for the adherents of the Dionysiac mysteries.

believe in resurrection but in an after-life of eternal bliss and joy, as is described in this inscription.[190]

4.3.2.3 Identification with Mythical Figures of the Dionysiac Circle

The epigraphical material shows that the worship of Dionysus was particularly attractive to women.[191] It was principally W. F. Otto who called attention to the importance of the Dionysiac cult to them. Its myths offered stories which paralleled their own experiences and provided them with the emotional satisfaction of identifying with the god at many levels of their existence.[192] Contributing to its popularity at Philippi may have been the idea that several of the Dionysiac myths were thought to have originated in the colony. Nysa, the place where the child Dionysus was looked after by his nurses, was located on Mount Pangaion, as were some myths connected with Orpheus and Cadmus[193]–a fact that made the mythical figures belonging to the Dionysiac circle lifelike in a very special way. In addition, the identification with these mythical figures was facilitated by the artists, who often took their themes from Dionysiac myths,[194] a fact that must also have operated in Philippi, though there is no surviving art from that colony to support this theory. Thanks to these artistic representations even illiterate women could easily assimilate the mythical events (2.2.1.2). For that reason I am using iconography as well as literature[195] to illustrate my contention that these myths might have been recognised by women in Philippi as reflecting their living conditions.

4.3.2.3.1 *Ariadne*

In works of art one can say without hesitation that Ariadne was the female figure of the Dionysiac circle most frequently portrayed by the artists.[196] As the wife of Dionysus she was, according to Roman poets,

---

[190] Nilsson 1957, 130

[191] In Philippi there are 7 surviving inscriptions dedicated to Dionysus (see n. 125 supra), 5 to Diana (see n. 43, 49, 52, 54 and 96 supra) and one to Isis (see n. 255 infra), which mention women.

[192] Otto 1933, 159ff.

[193] The oracle is discussed in 4.3.2.1.2.

[194] Thraemer 1884-1886, 1089ff; Schwabacher 1941, 182-228.; Baur 1941, 229-248.

[195] Roscher's dictionary (1884-1937), being the hitherto most exhaustive source of ancient mythology, is used for references on the subject. For quotations of mythical stories, made up of several myths, I refer to Hunger (1959), who gives references to primary sources.

[196] Stoll 1884-1886, 544ff.

identified with Libera[197] and in this way she was linked with Philippi. The mythical events about her are briefly summarized:

> Ariadne was a daughter of Minos, king of Crete. She fell in love with Theseus when he arrived from Athens in a band of fourteen young people of both sexes who were destined to be sacrificed to Minotaur, the monster who lived within the famous labyrinth. Ariadne gave Theseus a ball of yarn to take with him into the maze. This enabled him to retrace his footsteps and make good his escape. Together with Ariadne, who abandoned her family, he set out for Athens. During the journey he seduced her and left her behind on the isle of Naxos. However, Dionysus found the forsaken girl and made her his wedded wife. As time went on Ariadne gave birth to four sons; after her death Dionysus rescued her from the Underworld and brought her to Olympus.[198]

There are several scenes in this myth which have been popular with artists and poets alike. In art the loving and helping girl forms a frequent motif[199] but most often she is portrayed asleep on a rock in Naxos.[200] Roman poets, however, found greater drama in the misery and the affliction of her awakening,[201] and this episode might have been well known and popular, particular among women. In the second century A.D., Philostratus begins his description of a picture employing this dramatic scene in the following way:

> That Theseus treated Ariadne unjustly–though some say not with unjust intent, but under the compulsion of Dionysus–when he abandoned her while asleep on the island of Dia, you must have heard from your nurse for those women are skilled in telling such tales and they weep over them whenever they will (cf. 2.2.1.1).[202]

Furthermore, Dionysus' matrimonial union with Ariadne is often depicted in art[203] and literature. A tale in Xenophon's *Symposium* is typical. The host had commissioned two actors to present the marriage of Dionysus and Ariadne as a pantomime in the presence of his guests. The players succeeded in expressing their sexual joy in their union so successfully that the married men in the audience left immediately and ran home to their wives.[204]

As regards works of art, the motif of Dionysus' and Ariadne's marriage often recurs on sarcophagi where it is a part of the eschatological festal procession.[205] In this connection Ariadne embodies

---

[197] See n. 120 supra. See also the inscriptions quoted in n. 129, 131 and 134 supra.
[198] Hunger 1959, 49ff.
[199] Stoll 1884-1886, 545.
[200] Stoll 1884-1886, 545.
[201] Catull. 64, 124 ff; Ov. Her. 10, Ars. Am. 1, 527ff, Met. 8, 175ff; Nonnus Dion. 47, 268ff.
[202] Philostrat. Imag. 1, 15. Transl. A. Fairbanks.
[203] Stoll 1884-1886, 546.
[204] Xen. Symp. 9, 2-7.
[205] Turcan 1966, 521 ff. Cf. the inscription from Doxato, quoted in p. 105.

the eternal bliss in which she was made to participate when Dionysus rendered her immortal.[206]

All these scenes describe situations more or less well known to women. Ariadne is the prototype for the 'abandoned girl' who sacrifices everything for her lover but at last becomes the 'happy wife' as the spouse of another man. She personifies the matrimonial bliss not only of this world but also the after-life, which the reliefs on sarcophagi often describe as a wedding in Hades between Dionysus and Ariadne.[207]

4.3.2.3.2 Semele

Semele, the mother of Dionysus, was, like Ariadne, important as a figure with whom women could identify.[208] Her myth has been expressed both in literature and in art.[209] It was of interest to the tragedians[210] and was also presented as pantomime[211] (cf. 2.2.1.2). Like Ariadne, Semele is to be found in the Dionysiac procession on sarcophagi.[212] Through her kinship with Cadmus she was included in those myths which were located on Mount Pangaion.[213] This geographical closeness may have made her particularly lifelike to women in Philippi who could visualize her as a near neighbour. About Semele we are told briefly:

> Semele was a daughter of Cadmus, king of Thebes. Zeus became her lover, which evoked the jealousy of Hera. Pretending to be Semele's old nurse Hera told her to ask Zeus to assume his usual guise, that of a flash of lightning. Unsuspecting, Semele took the advice but was consumed by Zeus' thunderbolt. She was pregnant but he rescued the foetus and sewed it into his own thigh, from which the infant was brought forth. Furthermore, it is told that Dionysus subsequently descended into Hades, collected his mother and brought her to Olympus.[214]

According to Hesiod Semele was originally a mortal woman who gained immortality by giving birth to Dionysus;[215] this idea emerged in the worship of the god in those areas from which the legend has it that he

---

[206] Hes.Theog. 947ff.
[207] Turcan 1966, 521ff.
[208] Semele seems to have had divine status in Macedonia and Thrace and to have been worshipped in these areas (Sittig 1911, 87).
[209] Jessen 1909-1915, 669ff.
[210] Diod. Sic. 1, 23, 8.
[211] Lucian Salt. 39; cf. 80.
[212] Turcan 1966, index, s.v. 'Semele'.
[213] See n. 127 supra.
[214] Hunger 1959, 323.
[215] Hes.Theog. 940ff.

descended into the Underworld.[216] Furthermore, the story of the pregnant Semele who was killed by lightning might have seemed for some women to be a metaphor for death in childbirth. This fate became a reality for many females at that time (1.2.3). It might, therefore, have been comforting for a dead woman's family to realize that even the mother of Dionysus met the same tragic end, and to know that, like Semele, she would form part of the Dionysiac procession.[217]

4.3.2.3.3 Eurydice

Another often depicted mythical figure of the Dionysiac circle connected with Philippi is Eurydice.[218] She was the wife of Orpheus, the Thracian singer who was killed by the maenads on Mount Pangaion.[219] It is told that Orpheus tried to get Eurydice back from Hades after death but she had to return there because he broke the agreement not to look round and face her during the journey from the Underworld.[220] (Human beings still alive were forbidden to face those who had passed away to Hades.[221])

However, from a feminine point of view Eurydice could be seen as a woman to be envied, as the love she evoked in her husband was so great that he ran the risk of losing his own life to bring her back to him. That his temptation to gaze upon her was stronger than his fear of losing her for ever testified to his love for her.

4.3.2.3.4 Alcestis

A counterpart to Eurydice is Alcestis who is often depicted in art and literature. Her figure is to be found on sarcophagi[222] and her myth was presented on the stage both in tragedy[223] and pantomime (cf. 2.2.1.2).[224] In literature[225] and art Alcestis is portrayed together with Hercules,[226]

---

[216] In Troizen (Paus. 2, 31, 2) and in Argos (Paus. 2, 37, 5).
[217] Cf. the inscription from Doxato, quoted in p. 105.
[218] Gruppe 1897-1902, 1194ff; Stoll 1884-1886, 1421ff.
[219] Perdrizet 1910, 29 ff. See n. 180 supra.
[220] Verg. G. 4, 453ff; Ov. Met. 10, 1ff; Apollod. Bibl. 1, 3, 2, 2 (Hunger 1959 255ff).
[221] Ziegler 1939, 1269 n. 1.
[222] Andrae 1963, index, s.v. 'Alkestis'.
[223] Euripides'*Alcestis*; cf. Juv.6, 652.
[224] Lucian Salt. 52.
[225] In Euripides' drama *Alcestis* (1008ff), Heracles rescues her from Hades.
[226] Hercules rescuing Alcestis from Hades is pictured in the catacomb in Via Latina in Rome (Bertelli 1965, Pl. 23; Simon, M. 1964, 327ff). Cf. also n. 222 supra.

and her fate must have been well known in Philippi where he was worshipped together with Dionysus.[227] About Alcestis we are told:

> Alcestis was the wife of Admetus in Thessaly. He failed to perform the necessary sacrifice to Artemis before his wedding, an omission which the goddess punished by sending snakes into the bridal chamber. Since further revenge from Artemis might succeed in bringing about his death, the Fates protected him with a promise that he might live if a substitute could be found to die in his place. However, when at an early age he lay on his death-bed it became evident that not even his old parents were prepared to rescue him. So great was Alcestis' love for her husband, however, that she begged to give her life for him in spite of leaving two small sons behind her. Immediately after her death Hercules happened to visit Admetus and was welcomed in the house of mourning. In acknowledgement of this hospitality Hercules descended into Hades and returned with Alcestis whom he presented to Admetus.[228]

Euripides describes the heroic self-sacrifice of Alcestis and presents her in the role of priestess of the household (2.3.1.1) before her death:

> What must the woman be who passeth her? / How could a wife give honour to her lord / More than by yielding her to die for him? / And this—yea, all the city knoweth this; / But what within she did, hear thou, and marvel. / For when she knew that the appointed day / Was come, in river-water her white skin / She bathed, and from the cedar-chests took forth / Vesture and jewels, and decked her gloriously, / And before Vesta's altar stood, and prayed: / 'Queen, for I pass beneath the earth, I fall / Before thee now, and nevermore, and pray: / Be mother to my orphans: mate with him / A loving wife, with her a noble husband. / Nor, as their mother dieth, so may they, / My children, die untimely, but with weal / In the home-land fill up a life of bliss.' / To all the altars through Admetus' halls / She went, with wreaths she hung them, and she prayed, / Plucking the while the tresses of the myrtle, / Tearless, unsighing, and the imminent fate / changed not the lovely rose-tint of her cheek.[229]

The only favour she asks of Admetus is not to marry again and give her children a stepmother (cf. 1.3.2.1),[230] and she takes leave of him with the following words:

> Admetus,—for thou seest all my plight,—/ Fain would I speak mine heart's wish ere I die. / I, honouring thee, and setting thee in place / Before mine own soul still to see this light, / Am dying, unconstrained to die for thee.[231]

These mythical tales of Eurydice and Alcestis could be seen not only as dealing with the ideal love between husband and wife but also as hiding a deeper meaning. According to Plato the figures of Alcestis and Orpheus contrast self-sacrificing love with egoism. True self-sacrificing love, represented by Alcestis, conquers death; Orpheus, on the other hand, is characterized as a coward who liked the magic power of his

---

227 See the inscriptions, quoted in n. 129, 131, and 134 supra.
228 Hunger 1959, 19ff.
229 Eur. Alc. 153-174. Transl. A. S. Way.
230 Eur. Alc. 305-307.
231 Eur. Alc. 280-284. Transl. A. S. Way.

music[232] more than he loved Eurydice, and this caused him to fail in his mission.[233] These tales also illustrate the previously mentioned attitudes of males and females towards religion.[234] Orpheus relied entirely upon his own power while Alcestis commended herself to the protection of the household deity.

To sum up, the myths of Ariadne, Semele and Alcestis all follow the same pattern: all three women are brought back from the Underworld. In this connection Persephone must not be forgotten; she was abducted by the god of the dead but was returned to the Olympus for two-thirds of the year.[235] This myth must have been of great interest to Philippian women because the abduction was believed to have taken place within the colony (3.7.2). Again, the geographical proximity was an important factor, but the most desirable aspect of the myths must have been the immortality achieved by their heroines.

4.3.2.3.5 The Infant Dionysus

Finally, the infant Dionysus was of importance to women in their living conditions. The divine child was often portrayed on sarcophagi,[236] and references to him in literature extend from Homer to Nonnos.[237] His story is as follows:

> After the death of Semele, Zeus carried the foetus of her child within his thigh and Hermes later helped to bring it forth. The latter entrusted the child to the care of the nymphs on Mount Nysa, one of whom, Ino (sister of Semele), took particular responsibility for the little boy. Further, it is told that the Thracian king Lycurgus once pursued the nymphs, on which occasion the terrified child plunged into the sea and, trembling, was rescued by the sea-goddess Thetis. At a later stage Dionysus left the care of the nymphs and was tended by the old satyr Silenus.[238]

In northern Greece Nysa (the holy mountain of Dionysus) was thought to be an alternative name for Mount Pangaion;[239] therefore these tales of Dionysus' childhood had local value within the colony. The story of the infant Dionysus can be seen as a prototype for all stories about children who were brought up by relatives or strangers (cf. 1.3.2.2). The Lycurgus

---

[232] It was Orpheus' power over the wild beasts, obtained by his music, which caused him to be depicted as representing Christ in the role of 'the good shepherd' in early Christian art (Ziegler 1939, 1314).

[233] Pl. Symp. 179C-D.

[234] See Strab. 297, quoted in p. 55.

[235] Hymn. Hom. Cer. 459-68; Diod. Sic. 5, 3, 2, 3; 5, 4, 3-6; Ov. Fast. 4, 419ff, Met. 5, 341ff (Hunger 1959, 84ff).

[236] Turcan 1966, 405ff.

[237] Laager 1957, 119.

[238] Hunger 1959, 92ff; 163f; 205.

[239] See n. 127 supra.

episode reflects the often harsh treatment of these children; such an upbringing was the fate of many girls owing to the practice of exposing unwanted female babies at birth (1.2.1).

As is often suggested in this chapter, the knowledge that a deity shared the hardships of human beings might have been consoling to women and have contributed to their being reconciled to the severe experiences of their childhood. However, in this connection it should be observed that the infant Dionysus represented the divine principle of childhood without regard to sex,[240] since baby girls are non-existent in Greek mythology.[241] As an adult he also had this twofold identity, though evidence of it is confined to epithets which reveal him as androgynous[242] and to art where he is often depicted wearing female dress.[243] It is not surprising, therefore, that women identified with those episodes in his childhood which related to their own youthful experiences, as, in adult life, the stories about him tell of his marriage to Ariadne and present him in all aspects as fully male.

4.3.3 Summary

The worship of Dionysus was significant within the colony. The location of several Dionysiac myths on Mount Pangaion can be assumed to have contributed to the penetration of the cult, and the oracle was presumably of importance for its success. Furthermore, Dionysiac worship was particularly attractive to Philippian women, both in regard to its rituals and to its mythical tales.

In the town it had the character of an ecstatic cult exclusively supported by women of Greek and Roman origin. As the ecstatic aspect was significant in Philippi, Euripides' *Bacchanals* must have been familiar to the women since the content of his myth touched upon their religious experiences. The ecstatic cult offered them intense religious consciousness in their encounter with the divine together with other women, while the joy of sex related to a deity found expression in the rapturous aspects of the ceremonies performed by the female worshippers.

---

[240] This can be assumed from the pictorial representations on the sarcophagi (Turcan 1966, 424ff, 570ff). In addition, Apollodorus (Bibl. 3, 4, 3) tells us that Dionysus was reared as a girl. See also Gruppe 1897-1902, 904 n. 3.

[241] Exceptionally the infant Artemis on the lap of Zeus is described in Callimachus' hymn (Dian. 1-40) dedicated to the goddess, though this tale is not part of mythical lore but is merely a private literary fiction (Cahen 1930, 89). Dolls seem always to have been shapen as adult women (2.2.1.3).

[242] For instance, ἀνδρόγυνος (Pl. Symp.189D), γυναικόμορφος (Eur. Bacch. 855), θηλύμορφος (Eur. Bacch. 353). For later evidence see Preller 1894, 664 n. 3.

[243] The feminine traits of the adult Dionysus appear most striking in the vase paintings depicting the ecstatic worship of the god. Here he is most often shown in female dress at the head of his worshippers (Thraemer 1884-1886, 1089ff).

In the countryside, on the other hand, the cult had a mystical basis and was organised to provide burial funds; the followers seem particularly to have been Thracians, and the epigraphical material suggests that women played subsidiary roles only, though in reality they might have had more prominent positions. In the mysteries women became members of an extended family. In this family group they were looked upon as equal to men in their roles as priestesses. Through the burial funds they could secure commemoration after death, and initation into the mysteries inspired hope of an after-life as participants in the Dionysiac procession—both for themselves and their children.

Finally, mythical figures belonging to the Dionysiac circle offered the women models of identification in various situations of their lives. They could recognize the roles of the 'abandoned woman' and the 'woman dying in childbirth'. Further, the child Dionysus became the model both for the 'orphan child' and the 'deceased and revived child' of both sexes. However, the Dionysiac myths reflected more than the troubles and ills of women's lives. The happiness of marriage and children was also represented in them, particularly in the figure of Ariadne as well as in the self-sacrificing marital love personified by Alcestis.

4.4 ISIS

4.4.1 Historical Background

The Egyptian gods played an important part in the religious life of Philippi, according to the archaeological and epigraphical findings.[244] Their cult was present in Philippi on the arrival of the Romans (3.7); it presumably spread from Egypt through the trade routes and it is evidenced on Thasos and in Amphipolis during the 3rd cent. B.C.[245] Of these deities Isis seems to have been particularly important to the colony and we are told by an inscription that she was regarded as its divine protectress.[246] In the town of Philippi she was worshipped together with Sarapis and Harpocrates,[247] while Anubis seems to have been absent from the traditional divine family.[248]

---

[244] The local popularity of the cult can possibly be explained by the fact that the Egyptian gods were regarded as the protectors of Antony and his followers in the battle for the authority over the Roman Empire (Verg. Aen. 8, 685ff; Prop. 3, 11, 39ff) and Philippi had to a great extent been colonized by the adherents of Antony who had lost their land in Italy (3.2).

[245] Collart 1937, 453f.

[246] The inscription is quoted in p. 118.

[247] Collart 1929, 87.

[248] Collart 1929, 88.

As to the surviving remnants of the cult there are traces both of a temple on the acropolis (Map 3: 6)[249] and of a meeting-place for a religious group in the town centre,[250] and several inscriptions have been revealed by excavations.[251] As regards the temple (dated to the Augustan era[252]) it should be noted that only two—or possibly three—temples dedicated to the Egyptian gods have been found on the mainland of Greece.[253]

Although Isis held such a predominant position in the colony there are hardly any traces of that Philippian women participated in her cult.[254] However, in connection with the excavations of the temple dedicated to the Egyptian gods the remaining base of a statue was found among the ruins furnished with the following inscription:[255]

Πρεῖσκαν Φον | τήιαν ὁ ἱερεὺς | τῆς Εἴσιδος | Καλλίνικος Καλλινεί | κου

It informs us that the missing statue depicted a woman named Preiska Fonteia and was dedicated to the temple by one of the priests belonging to the cult of Isis. The woman is assumed to have been a relative of L. Priscus, governor of Macedonia in A.D. 250-251,[256] which dates the

---

[249] The temple was excavated in 1921 and the results are published by P.Collart (1929, 70-100). See also 3.7.1.2.

[250] Collart 1937, 447.; Collart 1938, 428, No. 10 (cf. No. 13).

[251] Ten inscriptions have been found in connection with the Egyptian gods, 6 of which are in Greek and 4 in Latin (Collart 1937, 446ff).Cf. 3.6.

[252] Salditt-Trappmann 1970, 52f.

[253] The second identified temple has been excavated in Thessaloniki (Salditt-Trappmann 1970, 47). Apuleius' account (Met. Book 11) and Pausanias' description (2, 2, 3) of the harbour area indicates that there was also a temple of Isis in Kenchreai. American excavations have revealed a 'temple-like structure' associated with mosaics decorated with profane motifs referring to Egypt (Griffiths 1975, 18f, referring to preliminary reports). No inscriptions, however, have helped to identify the building beyond any possible doubt. See Smith (1977) and particularly the final reports (Scranton 1976 and 1978).

[254] Isis' importance to women has been discussed by S. K. Heyob (1975). Isis was the protectress of women during birth, marriage and death (Heyob 1975, 80) but she can hardly be characterized as a goddess of women. Of the 1099 inscriptions recorded by L. Vidman (1969) 200 mention women (Heyob 1975, 81). These 200 inscriptions are cover eight centuries, while the female element in the Isiac cult culminated between the 3rd cent. B.C. and the 3rd cent. A.D. (Heyob 1975, 86), and the female adherents of the goddess were located particularly to Athens and Rome (Heyob 1975, 110). In this respect it is worth noting that Clea (c. A.D. 120), to whom Plutarch (Mor. 364E) dedicated his essay, is the first known female initiate of the Isiac cult (Heyob 1975, 109). Isis' demand from her followers (known particularly for females) for sexual abstinence on certain 'holy' days could possibly have frightened women from her cult. Juvenal (6, 535-41) is complaining about the sacred days of chastity for female Isiac devotees (Heyob 1975, 64f; 120ff). Cf. n. 291 infra.

[255] Collart 1929, 76f, No. l, Fig. 6; Collart 1937, 446, No. 1.

[256] Collart 1929, 77.

inscription to the third century. The inscription indicates that there were female followers of Isis in Philippi and that they could occupy prominent positions within her cult. With few exceptions women could hold the same priestly offices as men,[257] so Preiska Fonteia can be assumed to have been a priestess. Alternatively, she might have been a follower who was honoured by means of a statue in the temple of the goddess because of particular contributions to the cult (cf. 2.3.2.2). Anyhow, the absence of any title of priestess or report of her contributions is remarkable and permits no other conclusion. Although this woman belonged to the upper classes there are reasons to assume that in Philippi poor females also were worshippers of Isis, as will be seen in the following pages.

4.4.2 The Importance of Isis to Philippian Women

Even if Isis cannot be characterized as a goddess exclusively protecting females[258] the absence of reference to Philippian women in appreciable numbers is surprising since her myth was deeply rooted in the everyday lives of married women. However, it must not be forgotten that Isis was thought to personify all the deities as she presented herself as 'deorum dearumque facies uniformis' ('the single form that fuses all gods and goddesses'[259]), and accordingly could be imagined to represent all the other deities.[260] Therefore, not only the female figures[261] but also the hunting goddess[262] pictured on the Philippian rock carvings (4.2.2.3) might well have been interpreted by her followers as portraying Isis.

To enable us to elucidate that aspect of Isis which it was desirable for women to emulate, and to understand her role as a protectress of them, epigraphical evidence from surrounding areas and from literature will be examined alongside the Philippian findings. Regarding the epigraphical sources, the aretalogies of Isis[263] found in Macedonia

---

[257] Heyob 1975, 10.

[258] See n. 254 supra.

[259] Apul. Met. 11, Transl. J. G. Griffiths.

[260] Apuleius (Met.11, 22) calls Isis 'dea multinominis', and he gives a list of goddesses who were identified with her (Met.11, 5). Among the enumerated female deities Diana-Hecate (4.2), Persephone (3.7.2) and presumably also Demeter (4.2.4) were familiar to Philippian women.

[261] These carvings have been interpreted as picturing Isis by Ch. Picard (1922, 117ff). See n. 83 supra and also 4.2.2.3.

[262] Apuleius (Met.11, 5) gives evidence for such an 'interpretatio Isiaca' of the hunting goddess armed with bow and arrows. As regards works of art, the identifying of Isis with Artemis is represented on a silver patera from the Boscoreale treasure (found in the vicinity of Pompeii), illustrating Isis as 'dea multinominis et multiformis'; along with emblems of other goddesses she is also furnished with the bow and quiver of Artemis (Witt 1971, 171, Fig. 36).

[263] The aretalogies of Isis are mostly worded in the first person singular as praises by the goddess herself and are written in Greek (Vidman 1981, 140). These

(which was an area with an established tradition of aretalogies[264]) will be used in combination with the mythical stories by Diodorus Siculus (the vulgata of the myths of the Egyptian gods[265]) and Apuleius' book on Isis[266] to illustrate her function as guardian. Her exemplary character for women will be discussed from Plutarch's essay *De Iside et Osiride* which was dedicated to Clea, a priestess of Dionysus and at the same time an initiate in the Isiac cult.[267] This essay can be considered to reflect the knowledge of the Egyptian gods prevailing in the learned Graeco-Roman world at that time,[268] and it was principally intended as a philosophical interpretation of the myth.[269] However, Plutarch's portrait of Isis remarkably touches upon problems of female everyday life,[270] as will be shown in the following (4.4.2.3), which is why it is reasonable to suggest that he also used ideas of the Egyptian gods current among ordinary people in the Graeco-Roman world.

4.4.2.1 Archaeological and Epigraphical Evidence: a Healing Goddess

In Philippi the Egyptian gods seem to have had a predominantly healing function. As shown by the excavations the temple had a portico,

---

aretalogies exist in many inscriptions and to a great extent are of the same tenor; they all represent a firmly tested and living tradition (Nilsson 1974, 626f).The Egyptian background to the aretalogies has been elucidated by J.Bergman in 'Ich bin Isis. Studien zum memphitischen Hintergrund der griechischen Isisaretalogien' (1968).

[264] Surviving Macedonian aretalogies have been found in Thessaloniki and Maroneia (Map 1) (see n. 288 and 290 infra); while on the Greek mainland there is one (dedicated to Karpokrates) extant in Chalcis in Euboia (Harder 1944). Since Philippi had favourable maritime connections (3.4.3) the tradition of aretalogies in the coastal part of Asia Minor (there are surviving aretalogies in the isles of Andros and Ios and in Cyme on the mainland [Grandjean 1975, 8f]) may also have influenced the ideas of Isis held by Philippian women.

[265] Since Diodorus draws on other sources for information the historical reliability of his writings from the Egyptological point of view has been differently valued by various scholars (Burton 1972, 1ff). However, the section of Diodorus' first book (25, 2-7), chosen for my purpose, is considered to represent 'almost entirely Egyptian thought of the Hellenistic era'(Burton 1972, 18).

[266] This part of Apuleius' 'Metamorphoses' (Book 11) may be regarded as reflecting his own experiences as an Isiac initiate and therefore is of great value as a source for the cult in a Greek centre (Kenchreai) (Griffiths 1975, 6) in the middle of the 2nd cent. A.D.(Griffiths 1975, 7ff).

[267] Cf. n. 254 supra.

[268] Griffiths 1970, 75ff.

[269] Griffiths 1970, 18ff.

[270] Cf. Griffiths 1970, 73.

assumed to be intended for incubation.²⁷¹ The archaeological findings in the temple show that the Egyptian deities in Philippi had some connection with Aesculapius, the god of medicine.²⁷² According to an inscription in connection with the Sarapiasts, one of the members defrayed the expenses of a game in honour of Aesculapius,²⁷³ and, further, in the temple a statuette has been found portraying Telesphorus, the god of recovery,²⁷⁴ who may have been worshipped together with Aesculapius.²⁷⁵ This corresponds to the information given by Diodorus Siculus that a healing function was attributed particularly to Isis; the passage also gives evidence for the practice of incubation:

> As for Isis, the Egyptians say that she was the discoverer of many health-giving drugs and was greatly versed in the science of healing; consequently, now that she has attained immortality, she finds her greatest delight in the healing of mankind and gives aid in their sleep to those who call upon her, plainly manifesting both her very presence and her beneficence towards men who ask her help [- - -] For standing above the sick in their sleep she gives them aid for their diseases and works remarkable cures upon such as submit themselves to her; and many who have been despaired of by their physicians because of the difficult nature of their malady are restored to health by her, while numbers who have altogether lost the use of their eyes or of some other part of their body, whenever they turn for help to this goddess, are restored to their previous condition.²⁷⁶

Besides the archaeological findings in the temple an inscription on an altar,²⁷⁷ found close by the eastern gate (Map 3: D) and dated to the late second century A.D.,²⁷⁸ may indicate that among the Egyptian gods in Philippi Isis in particular represented healing:

> Isidi Reg[inae] sac[rum], ob honor[em] divin[ae] / domus, pro salute/ colon[iae] Aug[ustae] Philippen[sis],/ Q. Mofius Euhemer[us], / medicus, ex imperio, / p[ecunia] s[ua] p[osuit]. Idem subsel[lia] IIII, loco adsig[nato], d[ecreto] d[ecurionem].

---

271   Collart 1929, 99. Cf. 3.7.1.2, p. 72   n. 138. Egyptian temples were known for medical cures and in this respect incubation played an important part in the healing (Burton 1972, 107).

272   A few fragmented terracotta objects, possibly representing parts of the body, were found in the temple (Collart 1929, 32), and a rock carving, depicting an ear, about 100 metres away (Collart-Ducrey 1975, No. 161) may indicate the healing function of the Egyptian deities in Philippi (Collart 1937, 452). However, an ear pictured in connection with the Egyptian gods may equally be interpreted as ἐπήκοος ('listening to prayers') (Collart 1929, 93) as is also expressed in the Karpokrates hymn (Harder 1944, 8, v. 1) mentioning ἀκοαῖς τῆς Ἴσιδος ('the hearing of Isis'). The latter statement has also been interpreted as 'the ears of Isis' (Harder 1944, 9).

273   Lemerle 1935, 140f. No. 40 and 41.

274   Collart 1929, 89

275   Schmidt 1916-1924, 309

276   Diod. Sic. 1, 25, 2-5. Transl. C. H. Oldfather.

277   Collart 1929, 83, No. 7.

278   Collart 1929, 84.

The inscription tells us that a physician ('medicus'), by name Q.Mofius[279] Euhemerus, dedicated the altar to Isis Regina by order of the goddess ('ex imperio') for the prosperity ('pro salute') of the colony. In this connection the title 'Regina' is of importance to the understanding of the inscription and of Isis' position in Philippi at that time. This title designated Isis as the heavenly queen in ancient Egypt and it corresponds also to the picture of the goddess conquering disease and death as given by Diodorus Siculus.[280] Finally, the epithet 'Regina' characterizes Isis principally as a goddess of Destiny,[281] as is triumphantly expressed in the Cymean aretalogy[282] and also in the writings of Apuleius.[283] Finally, Isis carrying a rudder was represented in works of art portraying the goddess as Isis Tyche in her role as mistress of Fate;[284] such representations might have been of particular importance to illiterate women in reminding them of the all-embracing power of the goddess (cf. 2.2.1.2). From this omnipotence attributed to Isis we can deduce that our inscription may refer also to the function of healing implied in her power although it does not directly address Isis in her role of healing goddess; the fact that the dedication was made by a physician suggests that healing formed a part of the success ('salus')[285] he besought for the inhabitants of the colony and it also fitted into the almighty power of the goddess. The aspect of healing in the character of Isis was of importance to women in view of their gynaecological needs (1.2.3)[286] and might have attracted particularly those who lacked the economic means to consult a doctor for themselves (1.2.3) and their children (1.2.2).

4.4.2.2 The Aretalogies: a Protectress of Married Women

Apart from her function of healing, Isis was a goddess who, to a greater extent than others, might have fascinated married women. This can be deduced from her myth and from rituals connected with her cult and

---

279 The family name Mofius, only mentioned in this inscription, could possibly be a Latinized Hebraic name (Picard 1922, 182).

280 Diod. Sic. 1, 25, 2-5, quoted above, and also 1, 25, 6, quoted in p. 126.

281 J. Bergman (1964, 35ff) deals particularly with this aspect of the power of Isis.

282 'I overcome Fate. Fate harkens to me' (vv.55, 56).

283 '[- - -] know thou that I alone may prolong thy days above the time that the fates have appointed and ordained' (Apul. Met. 11, 6. Transl. S. Gaselee). The title of 'Regina' is to be found in Apuleius' eulogy (Met. 11, 5) both as a part of the formula introducing the goddess to the receivers, where she is presented as the queen of the dead ('regina manium'), and as the final proclamation of her power ('vero nomine reginam Isidem').

284 Drexler 1890-1894, 545f; Nilsson 1974, 632.

285 The word 'salus' denotes 'health' as well as 'success' (Georges 1916, s.v. 'salus').

286 Isis was also thought to take action against the exposure of baby girls. See Ov. Met. 9, 666-76, quoted in p. 123f.

particularly from the aretalogies which depict her as a guardian of married women. There are good reasons to believe that women in Philippi were familiar with the ideas which formed the basis of these hymns written in praise of Isis, since Macedonia formed a part of an area which seems to have been particularly acquainted with this kind of Isiac praise.[287] Of special importance are two aretalogies which survive in fragmented form only and which have been found in Thessaloniki and Maroneia—towns on the Via Egnatia about 150 and 70 km respectively from Philippi (Map 1).[288] Another aretalogy, found in Cyme in Asia Minor, is well preserved[289] and corresponds to a great extent in both form and content to those in Macedonia.[290] It is thus ideally suited to represent the viewpoint of married women and will here be used as the basis of an account from that perspective. This aretalogy includes 57 statements, 7 of which describe Isis as a protectress of women and reads as follows:

(10) I am the one whom women call (evoke as) the goddess.
(17) I united female and male (γυναῖκα καὶ ἄνδρα συνήγαγον).
(18) I decided for the woman to bear a ten-month foetus.
(19) I prescribed that parents should be loved by their children.
(20) I inflicted punishment on those who are uncharitable to their parents.
(27) I made it essential for wives to be loved by their husbands (στέργεσθαι γυναῖκας ὑπὸ ἀνδρῶν ἠνάγκασα).
(30) I have invented the marriage contract.

According to these statements Isis first of all displays herself as a goddess caring particularly for women (10) and then she tells us in what way she gave them their mission and protected them. She instituted matrimony (17; 30), and in this respect it is worth noting that the female party is mentioned before the male. Further, she entrusted women with childbearing, prescribed the duration of pregnancy (18)[291] and ensured for the wife her husband's love (27). Finally, she ordained that unless children loved their parents (19) they should be punished (20) and by this means the unity of the family was secured.

Though her decrees provide a standard for family relationships, the emphasis on feminine rights is striking; the housewife is sure of the affection of her husband as well as of her children but the goddess does

---

[287] See n. 264 supra.

[288] That from Thessaloniki is dated to the 1st or 2nd cent. A.D. (Grandjean 1975, 9) while the other from Maroneia is dated from the 2nd or 1st cent. B.C. (Grandjean 1975, 113).

[289] Grandjean 1975, 122. It is dated to the 1st or 2nd cent. A.D. (Grandjean 1975, 8).

[290] As regards contents, Nos. 17, 18, 19 and 27 agree with the aretalogies of Thessaloniki and Maroneia ; No. 30 is found in the latter and No. 10 is absent in both of them.

[291] The time of ten months may correspond to the old Egyptian calender based on the moon phases (Bonnet 1952, 474f). J. Bergman (1972) deals with the subject in a study of the abstinence prescribed for initiation into the Isiac mysteries.

not expressis verbis require her to give her love in return. According to another aretalogy (where the goddess is addressed 'thee' and 'thou') preserved in fragments on a papyrus from Oxyrynchus,[292] Isis is said to go further in her care for women. She gives females the same power as males[293] and thus she regards the sexes as equal. Further than that, however, Isis' exemplary marital relationship to Osiris, according to Diodorus, encouraged the Egyptians to make a law which established women as superior to men:

> It is for these reasons, in fact, that, it was ordained that the queen should have greater power and honour than the king (καταδειχθῆναι μείζονος ἐξουσίας καὶ τιμῆς τυγχάνειν τὴν βασίλισσαν τοῦ βασιλέως) and that among private persons the wife should enjoy authority over her husband (κυριεύειν τὴν γυναῖκα τἀνδρός)–the husbands agreeing in the marriage contract that they will be obedient in all things to their wives.[294]

4.4.2.3 The Myth: Ideal Wife and Mother

The above-mentioned texts elucidate Isis' importance as a protectress of married women,[295] but several traits in her myth also brought her nearer to their everyday lives and made her a desirable model for them to emulate. In this respect Plutarch's essay is most useful; according to him the myth runs briefly thus:[296]

> Isis married her twin brother Osiris[297] already in the womb of their mother (356A). When the couple had grown up Osiris had to fulfil his predestined task of civilizing the world, and during his absence from Egypt Isis successfully ruled the country. On returning, however, Osiris was treacherously murdered by his brother Typhon. The latter enticed Osiris into lying down in a coffin, whereupon Typhon closed the lid and threw him into the river (356B). Isis dressed immediately in mourning (356D) and went to look for him. She consulted everybody she met and finally some children revealed where the coffin was to be found (356E). Isis discovered the coffin and hid it away but Typhon found it and tore the corpse of Osiris into fourteen pieces, which he scattered all over the country (358A). After a long search Isis managed to gather together all the pieces, except for his phallus. She reconstructed the body and gave him

---

[292] POxy 11, 1380,190-220. This aretalogy is considered to emanate from the end of the 1st or the beginning of the 2nd cent. A.D. (Grandjean 1975,10).

[293] σὺ γυναιξὶν ἴσην δύναμιν τῶν ἀνδρῶν ἐποίησας (POxy 11, 1380, 214-215).

[294] Diod.Sic. 1, 27, 1-2. Transl. C.H. Oldfather.

[295] See also Ov. Met. 9, 666-776, quoted in p. 123f.

[296] The related myth is a paraphrase of Plut.Mor. 356A- 361D. Transl. F.C.Babbitt.

[297] Plutarch locates the myth in Egypt and therefore deals with Osiris. In the Greek world this god was given the name of Sarapis (Fraser 1972, 252ff) but also of Dionysus (Hdt. 2, 42; Diod. Sic.1, 23, 1) (Griffiths 1972, 429ff). In respect of the latter connection it may be noticed that Clea is said to be a priestess of Dionysus (Plut. Mor. 364E) and at the same time initiated into the cult of Isis (Plut. Mor. 351E; 352C).

an artificial penis (358B), and so Osiris was restored and became ruler of the Underworld (361E). However, Horus, the son of Isis and Osiris, fought Typhon to avenge his father, and Horus succeeded in capturing his uncle whom he handed over to Isis. Instead of sentencing Typhon to death she set him free, which caused Horus to lay hands on his mother in disappointment at her behaviour. (Nevertheless, Horus managed to conquer Typhon later on) (358D). Regarding the children of Isis, Horus is said to have been conceived when his parents had intercourse in their mother's womb (356A), and Harpocrates was born as a result of Isis' associating with the dead Osiris. This second son, however, was crippled in his legs (358E). Finally, Osiris had a child out of wedlock with Isis' sister Nephthys, the wife of Typhon. By mistake Osiris had had intercourse with Nephthys who bore a son, whom she exposed to die for fear of the wrath of Typhon. When her sister Isis heard of this she went to look for the child with the help of bloodhounds. As soon as she found it she gave it the name of Anubis and adopted the boy, who later on became her faithful companion and guardian (356F).

4.4.2.3.1 The Ideal Wife

In Plutarch's reading of her myth Isis is portrayed principally as the Roman ideal wife (1.3.1), and from Apuleius' description of the goddess we learn that she was characterized by great beauty.[298] His description mirrors in words the model of female beauty made visual in the rock carvings of Philippi where the women's figures are furnished with perfume bottle, comb and jewel-case.[299] Isis was also an example of matrimonial fidelity; this was mythically expressed by the fact that she could not choose a husband since the couple were already united in the womb of their mother. As a widow she remained faithful (according to Diodorus she had taken a vow never to marry again[300]) and therefore she became dependent on her eldest son. Further, she is characterized as extremely loyal to her husband. When he was abroad she took responsibility for his activities and when she became aware of his extra-marital child she received it as her own.

Seen through the eyes of Philippian women Isis' mythical story could easily be related to their own experiences of life. Her associating with Osiris before the birth of the spouses would be seen as reflecting the compulsory situation that parents created by arranging marriages for their children, even if this mythical 'matrimony in the womb' was intended to characterize Isis as the ideal partner 'ex ovo'. Moreover, the dependence of a poor widow on her eldest son, or on her closest male relative, and a wife's responsibility for the maintenance of the family in the absence of her husband, were apparent.[301] Similarly, there was the expectation that a husband's sexual escapades should be tolerated without rancour (cf. 1.5.1.2).

---

[298] Apul. Met. 11, 3.
[299] 4.2.2.3. Cf. n. 261 supra.
[300] Diod. Sic. 1, 27, 1.
[301] Lucian Dial.Court. 6, quoted in p. 27. See also 1.3.1 and 1.5.1.1.

4.4.2.3.2 The Ideal Mother

Further, Isis' role as an affectionate mother is carefully described and includes different kinds of children: Horus represents the 'independent and determined son', Harpocrates[302] the 'disabled child' and, finally, Anubis portrays the 'exposed child' as well as the 'foster-child'. In this connection the children who revealed to Isis where the coffin was to be found would also be seen as expressing her intimate association with children.

Isis' close relationship to children of various kinds, as described in Plutarch's version of the myth, corresponded to the pattern of many families at that time (cf. 1.3.2.2), and therefore she could easily be taken as a model by mothers faced with problems in the upbringing of their children. The 'independent and determined son', although well behaved, could cause his widowed mother humiliation when she was economically dependent on him. The 'disabled child' was a reality for many women in consequence of malnutrition or sequelae of diseases (1.2.2) and such a child naturally called for her special care. Further, in her relationship to Anubis, Isis portrayed the 'ideal stepmother' and this model differed greatly from the usual one of the 'evil stepmother' (cf. 1.3.2.1). The thought of the 'exposed child' must have haunted all pregnant women with the fear that they might lose the child they carried—a risk that was particularly great if that child was a female (1.2.1). From one of the tales in Ovid's *Metamorphoses*[303] we not only know that pregnant women invoked Isis but we also learn how the goddess rescued a girl by changing her sex. Abridged, this long story runs as follows:

> In Crete a married couple, Ligidus and Telethusa by name, were expecting a child and before its birth Ligidus told his wife: ' There are two things which I would ask of Heaven, that you may be delivered with the least possible pain, and that your child may be a boy. Girls are more trouble, and Fortune has denied them strength. Therefore (and may Heaven save the mark !), if by chance your child should prove to be a girl (I hate to say it, and may I be pardoned for the impiety), let her be put to death' (675-679). However, in a vision Isis spoke to Telethusa: 'O, Telethusa, one of my own worshippers, put away your grievous cares, and think not to obey your husband's orders. And do not hesitate, when Lucina has delivered you, to save your child, whatever it shall be. I am the goddess who brings help and succour to those who call upon me; nor shall you have cause to complain that you have worshipped a thankless deity ' (696-701). When the birth was accomplished the child proved to be a girl and was saved by the goddess who made Telethusa assure Ligidus that it was a boy. The child was called Iphis—a name of common gender—and was dressed like a boy, so nobody suspected a fraud. However, when Iphis was thirteen years old Ligidus planned to get his son married to a young girl of great beauty, but Telethusa, making all kinds of excuses, tried to delay this marriage between the two girls as long as possible. However, when the unavoidable wedding-day was at hand, Telethusa and Iphis fled to the altar of Isis to invoke the goddess to help them: 'That this, my daughter, still looks on the light, that I have not been punished, behold, is all of thy counsel and thy gift. Pity us two, and help us with thy

---

302 Harpocrates was a popular motif in works of art. Many statuettes have been found portraying the child either sitting in the lap of Isis (Nilsson 1974, 631, Fig. 9, 2) or standing or sitting alone with a finger on his mouth (Nilsson 1974, 632).
303 Ov. Met. 9, 666-676. Transl. F. J.Miller.

aid' (779-781). The goddess answered the prayer through several signs of her presence and on the way home Iphis was changed into a male.

This text portrays Isis principally as a powerful protectress of women and children but she is also shown as the conqueror of Fate (4.4.2.1), as she managed to change the appointed lot of Iphis from that of being a female into that of being a male. From a social point of view Ovid's tale reflects the worry and suffering of a pregnant wife who might fear that delivery could bring a supernumerary daughter who would have to be furnished with a dowry. However, it also gives a picture of the inescapable responsibility incurred by a paterfamilias of limited financial resources not to jeopardize the security of his family by retaining too many girls.[304]

4.4.2.3.3 The Cult Drama: Identification with the Mourning Goddess

Isis' power over life and death, as presented in the literary sources, was expressed in her rituals, particularly at an annual festival in the autumn,[305] and this celebration can be assumed also for Philippi.[306] At this event Osiris' death and 'resurrection'[307] were commemorated through a dramatization of the mythical events related above (4.4.2.3). Minucius Felix gives a critical description of the rituals in the following way:

> Isis, with her Cynocephalus (i.e. Anubis)[308] and shaven priests, mourning, bewailing and searching for her lost son; her miserable votaries beating their breasts and mimicking the sorrows of the unhappy mother; then, when the stripling is found, Isis rejoices, her priests jump for joy, the Cynocephalus glories in his discovery [- - -][309]

From this text, complemented with information drawn from Plutarch and other writers, we are able to reconstruct at least some of the features of the ceremony. According to Minucius' account the cult drama consisted of two acts: the search for Osiris' body (Horus' body in

---

[304] See 1.2.1 and 1.3.1.

[305] This celebration seems to have lasted about four days (Wissowa 1912, 353f).

[306] The daily worship, the processions and celebrations could take place only where a temple with priests existed (Vidman 1981, 139).

[307] In this case the term 'resurrection' is incorrect. Osiris was revived only to become a ruler of the Underworld (Plut. Mor. 361E) (Bonnet 1953, 569f).

[308] The priest of Anubis used to appear wearing a mask in the shape of a dog. (App. BCiv. 4, 47).

[309] Min. Fel. Oct. 23, 1. Transl. G. H. Rendall. Information on this celebration is to be found only in late sources. The most exhaustive accounts are to be found in Minucius Felix (Oct. 23, 1, quoted above) and Firmicus Maternus (Err.prof.rel. 2, 1-3). Further evidence is to be found in Wissowa (1912, 354 n. 2).

Minucius' text) which is said to have been cut into pieces,[310] and the recovering and reforming of his body to raise him from the dead[311]—a proof of Isis' creative force (characterizing the aretalogies). In the first act Isis, attended by her son Anubis (in Minucius text called 'Cynocephalus') the roles of whom were played by the priests and possibly also by the participants, looked for the pieces of the body and cried out in grief and despair.[312] In the second act the cry of despair changes into a shout of joy εὑρήκαμεν, συγχαίρομεν ('We have found it! Together we rejoice!')[313] and signals the finding and uniting of the pieces of the body.[314]

From information on the Isiac cult given by Aelianus we can conclude that women bereft of male relatives were eager to identify with the mourning goddess,[315] and Plutarch confirms that Isis founded her cult to edify and comfort those who suffered the same troubles she herself had overcome:

> [- - -] the sister and wife of Osiris [- - -] was not indifferent to the contests and struggles which she had endured [- - -] nor would she accept oblivion and silence for them, but she intermingled in the most holy rites portrayals and suggestions and representations of her own experiences at that time, and sanctified them, both as a lesson in godliness and an encouragement for men and women who find themselves in the clutch of like calamities.[316]

According to the text the identification of human beings with the mourning goddess was intended by Isis herself. The participation of women in the rituals of the 'Inventio Osiridis' had a social as well as a religious aspect. Through the feeling of oneness in mourning, not only with the goddess but also with sisters similarly bereaved, women were able to express their grief in a way that was not only forbidden by the Roman law but was also regarded as unbecoming.[317] From a religious point of view the cult of the Egyptian gods opened up hopeful perspectives for the after-life. In their grief Philippian women might have found consolation in the assurance that their deceased male relatives were revived to a life in the Underworld under the protection of the Egyptian gods. In this respect, Isis Regina[318] in her role as mistress of Fate (implying the control of life and death) was predominant. According to Diodorus, Isis raised her son Horus from the dead and made him immortal:

---

[310] Plut. Mor. 356A.
[311] Plut. Mor. 358B.
[312] Cf. Prudent. c.Symm. 1, 629ff.
[313] Firm.Mat.Err.prof.rel. 2, 9; Sen. Apocol. 13, 4.
[314] Plut. Mor. 358B.
[315] According to Aelian (NA 10, 23), women in particular were adherents of Isis; above all, those who were mourning a husband, a son or a brother.
[316] Plut. Mor. 361D. Transl. F. C. Babbitt.
[317] See 2.3.1.2.2, p. 47 and n. 102.
[318] See the Philippian inscription, quoted in p. 118.

Furthermore, she discovered also the drug which gives immortality, by means of which she not only raised from the dead her son Horus, who had been the object of plots on the part of the Titans and had been found dead under the water, giving him his soul again, but also made him immortal.[319]

Isis' power over life and death brought hope and consolation to mothers who had lost their boys. This is shown by the final line of a grave inscription ('nomen tenebit Isidis nati puer') commemorating a sixteen-year-old boy who is identified with the son of Isis.[320]

With regard to females, on the other hand, their appointed fate in the after-life is hard to trace in the sources. In ancient Egypt women were 'osirianized' as well as men.[321] Thus, in the tomb inscriptions they have the Osiris title ('Osiris NN') and the Osiris status ('Justified') added to their ordinary proper names. However, that should not simply be taken as an indication of a change into the male sex, as their representations on tomb stelae and in tomb reliefs are female, as are their names in the inscriptions and their treatment in the texts (female endings, pronominas etc). (It is only in the Graeco-Roman period that some instances of the title Hathor NN–instead of Osiris NN–can be documented. How this change is to be explained and further interpreted is far from clear.) Thus, deceased females were given largely the same death ceremonial as men, which certainly gave them great prestige in ancient Egypt. To what extent these ceremonials and the status of women thus demonstrated spread to devotees of Isis abroad–to the Macedonian area and Philippi–we do not know. Generally speaking, the prestige of ancient Egyptian burial ceremonials and practices was very high in all the eastern parts of the Mediterranean. Therefore, it is reasonable to suppose that considerable esteem was attached to female Isiacae in the very active religious Isis-Serapis movement outside Egypt, where the first rank of Isis (above Sarapis/Osiris) was more and more accentuated through the centuries of Late antiquity.

4.4.3 Summary

According to the epigraphical and archaeological material the cult of the Egyptian gods was important in Philippi and its aspect of healing linked particularly with Isis who had the title of 'Regina'. Although evidence is

---

[319] Diod. Sic. 1, 25, 6. Transl. C. H. Oldfather.
[320] CIL 11, 6426, quoted in Heyob 1975, 64 n. 48.
[321] This state of affair seems to be so evident to Egyptologists that the ordinary manuals normally do not even mention it. My guide in these complicated matters is Professor J. Bergman, who is preparing a special study on the position of deceased women in Egypt particularly during the Graeco-Roman period. He points to the fact that the 'osirianization' of deceased women (indicated by the title of Osiris joined to a female name in the funeral texts) is well documented in Egypt through almost three millenia, with the pyramid texts of the queens Neith, Apouit and Oudebten (6th dynasty) as a significant point of departure.

scant, there were female followers of the goddess within the colony and it is reasonable to assume that Isis was popular among women. The idea of her as a protectress of them was represented in two surviving aretalogies found in Macedonia and there is no reason to believe that these two were the only ones of their kind in this area. Further, the myth and rituals of the goddess might have attracted women who were able to identify with her in various aspects of their lives. For the 'ideal wife' and the 'affectionate mother' in particular, Isis was an example to follow in everyday life. The opportunity of undertaking the same role as the mourning goddess enabled women to give vent fully to their grief, and the association of their dead male relatives with the revived Osiris gave them comfort in their loss. However, to what extent and in what way females were included in the sharing of Osiris' revival is unknown.

4.5 CONCLUDING REMARKS

According to surviving sources, female worship in Philippi was particularly connected with the cults of Diana, Dionysus and Isis. Women are mentioned in 13 inscriptions, dedicated as follows: 5 to Diana (of which 2 refer to priestesses), 7 to Dionysus and one to Isis. In addition, there are 8 rock carvings attributable to Diana, and literature tells us that there was a priestess in charge to Dionysus at his oracle on Mount Pangaion. This mountain was also considered to be the setting for some of the stories of the Dionysiac circle, a geographical proximity which brought the mythical figures correspondingly near to the lives of the women of the colony. Further, the myth of Demeter and Core was located to Philippi, since the latter was said to have been raped on a plain outside the town.

Examined from a female point of view these cults were important to women in different areas of their lives. They provided patterns for this life and the hereafter, gave emotional support in time of sickness, offered equal official positions for men and women, and enabled members of religious groups to communicate outside their families; the patterns they provided crossed all barriers of age and social condition.

As regards identification with mythical figures, young girls and mature women alike could look upon Diana as an ideal of beauty and freedom and she was also a model for a girl ill-treated by her stepmother. The marital experiences of Ariadne comforted females whose husbands deceived them and gave them hope for another partner—perhaps one similar to Orpheus. Married women, as well as concubines, could be drawn towards Isis in coping with their problems of everyday lives. From her own experience the goddess knew what the absence of the husband meant to a family. She also knew the problems and sorrow of bearing a disabled child and (like Ino, the 'model nurse') Isis was the 'ideal stepmother'. She represented particularly the relationship of mothers to sons, while Demeter portrayed the relationship of mothers to daughters lost through marriage. Finally, Isis epitomised the widowed woman both in her mourning and in her submissiveness to her eldest son.

With regard to the after-life, mythical figures offered women different possibilities of identification for themselves and for their relatives. Semele, the exemplary women dying in childbirth, was brought back from the Underworld, as was Alcestis who sacrificed herself for her husband even unto death. Further, women could imagine themselves in the after-life associating with Semele or Ariadne and participating as maenads in the Dionysiac festal procession. Alternatively, they saw themselves in the guise of Diana as a hunting goddess enjoying total independence. The restored infant Dionysus represented children of both sexes while Osiris in some way or other performed the same function for adults.

Besides their exemplary roles Diana and Isis, in their healing aspect, were expected to come to the rescue of women and children. Further, women in Philippi were able to seek advice from the Dionysiac oracle, and its unfavourable pronouncements, along with the unhappiness of love or life, could be submitted to Diana-Hecate for transformation by her magical powers.

Finally, the social function embodied in the worship of these deities was of great importance to Philippian women. In the rituals of the Dionysiac ecstatic cult, and also at the annual commemoration of Osiris, women had opportunities to associate outside the family. In the religious groups of the mysteries they were received as members of families beyond kinship, and as officials of such communities they could reach a position which they were not able to attain within their own families.

From this brief survey we can deduce that religious observance played an important part in the lives of Philippian women. However, it must not be forgotten that in return for the provision of emotional security the cults in question made demands on their adherents which could cause conflict within the family and particularly with their husbands. Periodically, followers of Isis had to observe total sexual abstinence, while priestesses of the cult of Diana and of the Dionysiac oracle were not allowed to marry while in office. Further, adherents of the ecstatic Dionysiac cult had to leave their homes and husbands for several days to participate in the rituals on Mount Pangaion. In addition, women had to make financial contributions in connection with the votive offerings.

Indeed, against this background we can understand the already quoted uttering of a Thracian husband complaining of the enthusiasm for religious worship of his wife (2.3.3.2):

[- - -] for all (i.e. the Getae) agree in regarding the women as the chief founders of religion, and it is the women who provoke the men to the more attentive worship of the gods, to festivals, and to supplications, and it is a rare thing for a man who lives by himself to be found addicted to these things.

This text reflects circumstances in the same cultural area about two centuries B.C. However, the archeological and epigraphical remains suggest that women in Philippi were characterized by the same susceptibility for religious worship at the time of Paul's arrival in the town, and this fact makes our further investigation still more exciting. Yet another religion had arrived in the colony.

PART II

THE NEW TESTAMENT TEXTS AS SEEN BY PHILIPPIAN WOMEN

5 METHODOLOGICAL REMARKS ON THE PERSPECTIVE OF AUDIENCE

After having reconstructed Philippian women's socio-cultural (Chapter 1 and 3) and religious (Chapter 2 and 4) backgrounds in the first part of this study, I am now, as already stated in the General Introduction (0.2), going to read Paul's letter to the Philippians (Chapter 6) and Luke-Acts (Chapter 7) through the eyes of the recreated Philippian female recipients, who represent the first two generations of women converting to the Philippian church. A comparison of the conjectured reactions to the Christian message between these two generations of Christian women, against their socio-cultural and religious conceptual frameworks, will throw light upon the motives of Philippian women for converting to Christianity (Chapter 8).

Before turning to a study of the New Testament text it seems appropriate to include a few methodological remarks on the perspective of audience. My interpretation of the text from the view point of contemporary Philippian women is based on the 'reception theory' of literary texts[1] held by members of the 'School of Constance', where Wolfgang Iser and Hans Robert Jauss are the predominant figures. The two main points of this theory applicable to my investigation run briefly as follows.

(*a*) A text is received in various ways owing to the diverse conceptual frameworks ('Erwartungshorizont'; 'horizon of expectations') of the receptors acquired through experiences of life in various ways,[2] and up to a point every receptor is said to 'produce' his own text.[3] Consequently, for pagan and newly- converted Philippian women, Euripides' *Bacchanals*, as well as their familiarity with the fate of mythical

---

[1] The 'reception theory' has been characterized in the following way: 'The attempt to account both for the dialectic of production and reception of literary works in a given culture at a given time, and for historical continuities and discontinuities in the reception of individual works or authors' (Suleiman 1980, 35). The main points of the theory are to be found in Jauss (1970-1971, 7-37).

[2] The conceptual framework of the receptors is thought to be of two kinds: an intrinsic ('innerliterarisch') and an extrinsic ('lebensweltlich') one. The former, related to the formal aspect of literature, is based on the receptors' familiarity with literary composition (Jauss 1970-1971, 11); the latter, on the other hand, depends on their cultural, political, social and religious experience of life in general (Jauss 1970-1971, 14). As regards illiterate Philippian women, however, it is difficult to separate the two horizons of expectations from each other since it is impossible to know to what extent they were able to comprehend literary forms by listening only; therefore, I take the intrinsic and the extrinsic horizons of expectations as a unit.

[3] '[- -] the literary text makes no objectively real demands on its readers, it opens up a freedom that everyone can interpret in his own way' (Iser 1971, 44).

characters and their own participation in rituals of various kinds, must have been important in forming the horizon of expectations against which they received the gospel. The contents of the drama can therefore be considered to have coloured their understanding–particularly of the Philippian episode in Acts. For second-generation Philippian Christian women, on the other hand, Paul's letter (and Christian teaching other than Paul's) and Christian experience formed their horizon of expectations and conditioned their reception of Luke-Acts. Their reaction to the Philippian episode might have resulted from hearing the word-of-mouth accounts of events relating to Paul's visit to the town and to the story of a local woman's role in the foundation of the Philippian church.[4]

(b) Recipients identify themselves with the suffering hero in the text,[5] and this identification may affect them in various ways.[6] This theory, based on Aristotle's conception of catharsis[7] and related to literary texts in a strict sense, may also by applied to tales orally transmitted from generation to generation;[8] thus mythical stories, known to Philippian women by this oral tradition and also by their participation in ceremonies dramatizing ritual stories, are thought to have offered them the possibility of identification in their everyday lives.[9] According to this theory pre-Christian receptors' identification with the suffering hero is said mainly to have been 'cathartic', that is, related to imagination only, and to have brought a 'purification' of their emotions of fear and compassion;[10] it might have involved a changed attitude to their own

---

[4] No traces of Lydia's house or of her name are to be found in Philippi; a highly fragmented Latin inscription with the surviving letters (pu)RPURARI (CIL 3, 664) (Wikenhauser 1921, 411) gives evidence only for the existence of a trade in purple within the colony. Therefore, it is safer to consider Lydia as a fictitious figure, hiding a germ of historical truth, rather than an entirely authentic person; Luke could scarcely have made up the story of Lydia altogether if he could claim to be considered as reliable in the eyes of recipients familiar with the Philippian church.

[5] Jauss 1974.

[6] Following Aristotle, Jauss recognizes five levels of identification with a suffering hero (Jauss 1974). For my purpose, however, the level of 'cathartic identification' (Jauss 1974, 310ff) in particular is applicable to pagan Philippian women.

[7] 'Since living persons (lit. 'men doing or experiencing something') are the objects of representation, these must necessarily be either good men or inferior–thus only are characters normally distinguished, since ethical differences depend on vice and virtue–that is to say either better than ourselves or worse or much what we are' (Arist. Poet. 1448a. Transl. W. Hamilton Fyfe).

[8] According to Aristotle, the theory of catharsis is applicable not only to performances in the theatre but also to identification with characters outside the stage. 'The plot should be so constructed that even without seeing the play, anyone hearing of the incidents happening thrills with fear and pity as a result of what occurs' (Arist. Poet. 1453b. Translat. W. Hamilton Fyfe).

[9] This is shown in Chapt. 4, particularly in 4.3.2.3 and 4.4.2.3.3.

[10] Jauss' definition runs :'By "cathartic identification" we mean the aesthetic disposition described by Aristotle in which the spectator is lifted out of the real interests and affective entanglements of his usual world and placed in the position

suffering in comparison with that of the hero, and resulted in acceptance of their appointed lot.[11] Consequently, pagan Philippian women gained strength to endure the hardships of their everyday lives by identifying themselves with various female mythical model characters; such an identification was provided for wives in a very tangible way in the cult of Isis (4.4.2.3). With the breakthrough of Christianity, however, the identification with the suffering hero was changed from a merely aesthetical into an ethical identification; that is, the receptors were expected not only to take part emotionally in the sufferings of the hero but also actively to imitate his actions,[12] as is clearly shown by Paul's letter. To Philippian women, who converted to Christianity, this changed religion from a mere carrying out of rituals into a way of life that emulated that lived by Christ and other Christians. The 'imitatio Christi' as presented by Luke was addressed principally to men, and such parts of it as related to women dealt with their activities in the service of the church. No possibility of identification with this male god was offered in any aspect of their matrimonial lives, as the hardships and rejoicings of motherhood and domesticity were peculiar to the female sex.

There is, however, one point in the 'reception theory' regarding the receptors' understanding of the text—already mentioned in the General Introduction (0.2)—which has to be further scrutinized. Although it is said that receptors give the text their own meaning[13] it is also said that they do not receive it uncontrolled.[14] In reality, the 'reception theory' does not refer to empirical receptors at all but to readers implied in the text.[15] My investigation, however, brings into focus empirical readers outside the text, while an examination of 'implied readers' is beyond my

---

of the suffering or hard-pressed hero in order to undergo, by way of tragic emotional upheaval or comic release, an inner liberation' (Jauss 1974, 312).

[11] '[- - -] to bring about for him an inner liberation which is supposed to facilitate the free use of his judgement rather than the adoption of specific patterns of activity' (Jauss 1974, 296).

[12] 'The authority of the Christian church and doctrine, to the extent it gained power over everyday life, not only made use of the Platonic tenet that poets lie, but also, in order to legitimize its own Christian poetry, gradually developed arguments which gave aesthetic experience a new framework. The exemplary was opposed to the imaginary, pity leading to action was opposed to purgation by catharsis, the hortatory principle of emulation was opposed to the aestethic pleasure derived from imitation' (Jauss 1974, 289). 'Of one who listens to religious poetry it is expected that he be shaken by 'compassio' and thus to undertake action in emulation of Christ' (Jauss 1974, 291).

[13] Cf. n. 3 supra.

[14] This is expressed by Iser in the following sophisticated way: 'Literary texts differ from those which formulate a concrete meaning of truth [- - -] The meaning is conditioned by the text itself, but only in a form that allows the reader himself to bring it out' (Iser 1971, 43). As regards the freedom of the reader Iser is inconsequent (cf. n. 3 supra) and his reader is in fact text-bound (Lategan 1984, 11).

[15] 'Implied reader' is a concept with many meanings; it can be defined briefly as the role of the reader which always, visibly or not, is implied in the text by the author (Iser 1978, 27ff.).

scope. This fact, however, presents a problem, since the limiting of an investigation to the empirical side of reception makes the exegesis idiosyncratic and dependent on the suggestion that a present-day scholar is able to look at life through the eyes of human beings in a remote past. However, this dilemma of subjectivity[16] is unavoidable in connection with an interpretation from the view point of empirical receptors who have to be reconstructed exclusively from historical sources. Such a tentative approach, based on a range of hypotheses, will offer results within a spectrum of probability only, but, nevertheless, it may be justified[17] since probability does reflect facts in some way or another, even if seen 'in a mirror dimly'. Hence it may open up new perspectives for the understanding of the New Testament text.

---

[16] At this point it may be appropriate to quote B. C. Lategan: 'By far the most serious challenge is to handle (methodologically speaking) the discovery of the creative dimensions of reception. If we allow for the creative input of the reader, how are we going to control it ? Have we not put our foot on the path of destabilizing the text which in the end must lead to its abolishment? Where does reading end and association begin?' (Lategan 1984, 14).

[17] In spite of his apprehensions Lategan agrees to this way of approaching New Testament text: 'Finally, theological hermeneutics does have the ability to deal with the creative dimensions of understanding. When the text is neither understood as an 'imitatio' of reality, nor as a fozzilization of the original situation, its instructions, its 'Leserangebot' can be seen as a re-description of reality, which opens up new possibilities of understanding for the reader'(Lategan 1984, 14). 'For the first time the completion of the act of understanding has become recognized (if not the dominant) part of the theoretical reflection on the communication process. [- -] The attempt to look at the process of understanding in its totality, opens up new perspectives, but also makes the consideration of old issues possible, be it on a different level'. (Lategan 1984, 13).

6. PAUL'S LETTER AS SEEN BY FIRST-CENTURY PHILIPPIAN WOMEN

6.1 INTRODUCTION

The letter to the Philippians is practically the only historical source for our knowledge of their church in its initial stage.[1] The Philippian episode in Acts (16: 11-40) can hardly be used as a reliable source, even if it contains a germ of historical truth, since the section must be seen as having been written with the predominant purpose of showing Paul's heroic role in the progress of Christianity.[2]

The letter is considered to have been written by Paul himself,[3] though the time and place of its origin are unknown.[4] It has a strongly personal stamp of spiritual guidance and admonition[5] and seems to have been written at a critical point of time in the existence of the Philippian church. Disagreement among the members is a pervading characteristic of the epistle and it gives the impression that the community risked dissolution under the external pressure of the pagan environment (cf. Phil. 1: 30; 1 Thess. 2: 2)[6] and the internal disruption of

---

[1] Ernst 1974, 24.

[2] Plümacher 1972, 95ff; 137.

[3] Gnilka 1980a, 5.

[4] Ernst 1974, 7f. Most scholars locate the origin of the letter to Ephesus and date it to A.D. 55/56 (Gnilka 1980a, 18ff), about five years later than Paul's first visit to Philippi (Gnilka 1980a, 3).

[5] Its lack of structure creates difficulties for interpretation (Ernst 1974, 21). There are hypotheses that the letter is a compound of two or three written at different times; an account of these hypotheses is to be found in Gnilka (1980a, 6 ff). For reasons of textual linguistics it has recently been suggested that it is an amalgamation of three different letters (Schenk 1984). Since these hypotheses are inconclusive I consider the letter as having been written on one occasion only. Indeed, the adoption of either of the alternative hypotheses would have been of little value for my method of approach.

[6] Ernst 1974, 24. The hostility of the pagan environment, where presumably apostates from Christianity were included, could easily be recognized in 'the enemies of the cross of Christ' (Phil. 3: 19), even if Paul referred specifically to heretical Jews (Phil. 3: 2) (Gnilka 1980a, 305f). The demands Christianity made for moral action were alien to Christians with a pagan background (see 6.4.1.1), and it might have caused them to consider Paul's moral claims as too pressing, which is why it is likely that apostates existed among the enemies of Christianity. The'enemies of the cross' could further be associated with members of pagan cults. Paul describes them as extremely interested in food, drink and sex and with their minds entirely set upon earthly things—they are even accused of considering the belly as a god (Phil.

some sections of Jewish traditionalists propagating for circumcision (Phil. 3: 2). Some of the propaganda opposed by Paul may have emanated from unconverted Jews but may equally have been the work of Christians who retained Jewish customs.[7] For my purpose, however, it is sufficient to state that Paul's rejection of circumcision was of particular importance to wives of 'mixed marriages'. Christian mothers who had their infant sons circumcised not only faced anxiety over the possible dangers of such surgery (cf. 1.2.2) but, according to the religious backgrounds of their own and their husbands' families, may well have faced antagonism from their relatives.

The purpose of this chapter is to examine Paul's letter in the light of contemporary Philippian women's social and religious setting and its message will be scrutinized against the background which has been reconstructed in previous chapters. For the purpose of my present argument I am concentrating on Paul's primary audience only.(It would of course have been possible to deal also with his second-generation audience in a similar way.) Consequently, I first give a brief survey of those to whom the letter was addressed (6.2), based chiefly on information given in Chapter 3. After that I focus on the two concepts of 'celestial citizenship' (πολίτευμα ἐν οὐρανοῖς) (Phil. 3: 20) and 'servitude' (expressed in δοῦλος) (Phil. 1: 1; 2: 7), and, taking πολίτευμα as the principal concept, I suggest them to have been the most important key words for Philippian women's interpretation of Paul's message. However, repetition of the letter (which may be assumed to have been applied to the whole of the Pauline corpus[8]) was necessary for the audience to grasp the notion of 'celestial citizenship' as its predominant topic, since the concept is found only at the end of it (Phil. 3: 20).[9]

In dealing with these concepts from the viewpoint of the audience I first treat of the Philippian church conceived as a celestial colony in opposition to the Roman colony of Philippi (6.3). After that the figure of the sovereign of the heavenly colony is scrutinized in his roles of the 'model figure of servitude' (6.4.1) and the 'absolute ruler' (6.4.2), and, finally, the conclusive realization of the celestial citizenship will be discussed. In an excursus I concludingly call attention to an effort to create a Utopian 'city of Heaven' on earth—a project which might have been known to the receivers of Paul's message, and which, consequently,

---

3: 19). Paul's picture of this group is in accordance with our knowledge of the customs of the Dionysiac mysteries, particularly in connection with commemoration of the dead (4.3.2.2).

[7] Different hypotheses of these kinds of propagandists are to be found in Gnilka (1980a, 211ff).

[8] Cf. 1Clem. 47, 1. L. Hartman (1986, 144f) is of the opinion that the addressees were expected to reread the letters several times, perhaps even in the service, and that the message of them was intended to reach other churches as well.

[9] Repeated readings of the text brought repetitions of this concept and thus the horizon of expectations of the audience was broadened (cf. Chapt. 5). Soon the concept was seen from a wider perspective and became a key for interpretation of the message of the letter (Iser 1974, 280f).

is likely to have contributed to the formation of their referential framework on the subject (6.7).

6.2 THE AUDIENCE

As stated above, our knowledge of the members and the structure of the early Philippian church in its first period is confined to what we learn from Paul's epistle. This literary source can in some degree be supplemented by archaeological data regarding population and financial circumstances within the colony which are accounted for in Chapter 3. However, since the archaeological material is often fragmentary and of a later period, and since there are no historical references in the letter, the following picture of Paul's audience is largely conjectural.

From the letter we can deduce that the members of the Philippian church at that time consisted principally of Greeks with a pagan religious background. Paul's branding of Jews as 'the dogs' indulging in malpractices (Phil. 3: 2) and the lack of Old Testament allusions in the letter[10] indicate there were no members with a Jewish referential framework. From the fact that the proper names in the letter are mainly Greek[11] it may further be deduced that the first Philippian Christians were principally of Greek origin. From the financial support Paul received (Phil. 2: 25; 4: 15-16) it seems further reasonable to suggest that some of them belonged to the group of Greek merchants who had migrated to Philippi chiefly from Asia Minor;[12] the original Greeks in Philippi would hardly have had the financial resources for that kind of charity (cf. 3.5).

Similarly, as regards the size of the Philippian community, we are also reduced to conjectures. However, Paul's reference to leaders of the church (ἐπίσκοποι) and also to assistants (διάκονοι) (Phil.1: 1) indicates the development of some organization. This implies that the size of the membership was so great that it had become necessary to create officials in order that the tasks could be delegated to them.

Dealing with the female part of the community, the fact that two women are directly addressed by Paul (Phil. 4: 2) shows not only that there was a number of Christian women in Philippi but also that they

---

[10] Johnson 1986, 340.

[11] Epaphroditus (Phil. 2: 25 ; 4: 18), Syntyche and Euodia (Phil. 4: 2). The proper names of the latter are not to be found in the epigraphical material in Philippi, but these names turn up in inscriptions in other places (Zahn 1906, 378f).

[12] Lydia (Acts 16: 14) belonged to this category, as (according to W. Meeks [1983, 57]) did Syntyche and Euodia. Meeks (1983, 73) assumes that there were probably many liberated slaves with high income but with low social status. However, from the proper names of the inscriptions it is often difficult to judge whether a person was a slave, liberated or freeborn (cf. 4.3.2.1.1). Therefore it is impossible to give an idea of the number of slaves and manumitted slaves among the Greeks in Philippi at that time. The ecstatic girl in Acts (16: 16-18) may reflect the bondage in this group of the population.

played an important role in the church.¹³ The picture Paul gives of Syntyche and Euodia as struggling in the cause of the gospel (Phil. 4: 3) accords with the one we already have of Philippian women's interest in religious matters—a fact well substantiated by the archaeological and epigraphical sources examined earlier.[14]

As has been shown in Chapter 4, in the town of Philippi there were at least three deities who attracted female worshippers. From this diversity of religious experience we may conclude that controversies existed among Christian Philippian women regarding the interpretation of the Christian message which could have resulted in such feuds as those actually referred to in Paul's letter. Paul's beseeching of Euodia and Syntyche 'to agree in the Lord' (Phil. 4: 2) suggests that women were susceptible to this form of hostility, and points to his awareness of the dangers inherent in it (cf. Phil. 4: 3). Furthermore, there might have been another cause of disagreement among the women of the community. From the letter we conclude that the members worked for the dissemination of the gospel on two levels. They were expected to support Paul's missionary work by financial means (Phil. 4: 14-16) and also to spread the Christian message themselves to their families and friends—not only by telling the joyful message but also by exemplifying it in their way of living (Phil. 2: 2-5; 4: 5) and expressing it in works of charity.[15] In view of married women's restricted position in religious matters relating to the domestic cult (2.3.1) it seems reasonable to suppose that in this respect Christian wives within 'mixed marriages' had little opportunity to make personal contributions to the work of the church in their homes. This could of course seem unjust to women belonging to Christian families who accordingly had to carry a heavier burden. Widows, on the other hand, can be suggested to have had more personal freedom to involve themselves[16] and to open their homes to the work of the church (cf. Acts 16: 15, 40).

6.3 THE PHILIPPIAN CHURCH–A CELESTIAL COLONY INSIDE THE COLONIA JULIA AUGUSTA PHILIPPENSIS

The fact that women were told that as Christians they would have the dignity of citizens—in this life inside the church and after it in the Kingdom of God—must have been appealing to them. Their social

---

[13] Syntyche and Euodia could have been among the διάκονοι (Phil. 1: 1) (Lohfink 1983, 326). Lay workers could be male or female, and the official positions they occupied required them to perform acts of charity as assistants inside the Christian community (Aalen 1984, 7ff; cf. Dibelius 1937, 414ff).

[14] For Diana see 4.2.2, for Dionysus 4.3.2, and for Isis 4.4.2. See also 4.2.4.

[15] Dibelius 1937, 414ff; Lohfink 1983, 326.

[16] Polycarp's letter (4: 3) points to this being the case at a later period in the Philippian church.

background being what it was, it is reasonable to assume that they interpreted 'citizenship' as the main theme of the letter, since for many Philippian women (if they were not citizens by birth) it might have been inconceivable within the Roman Empire.[17]

Initially, Paul's letter would appear to treat of the affairs of the Roman state, as it made reference to the praetorian guard (Phil. 1: 13), warfare (Phil. 1: 27), rulership (Phil. 2: 10-11) and Caesar's household (Phil. 4: 22). Soon, however, those addressed might have noticed that his main theme was not actually the Roman Empire but their membership of a colony which appeared to be located in the Roman colony of Philippi but was ultimately to be realized in a heavenly Kingdom. To his audience Paul's use of the word πολίτευμα (Phil. 3: 20) might easily have paralleled the relationship between the capital of Rome and Colonia Julia Augusta Philippensis with that of the distant capital of Christ and the Philippian church;[18] in this perspective the church could be seen as a microcosm of the celestial state.[19]

In Paul's letter the celestial and the secular colony are contrasted with each other in various ways. A unifying theme connected with the celestial colony is that of 'communion' (κοινωνία) (Phil. 1: 5; 2: 1; 3: 10) of like-minded people, designated as 'all the saints in Christ Jesus who are in Philippi' (οἵ ἅγιοι ἐν Χριστῷ 'Ιησοῦ ὄντες ἐν Φιλίπποις) (Phil. 1: 1; cf. 4: 22; 4: 21) and also as 'children of God' (τέκνα θεοῦ) (Phil. 2: 15). Further, Paul strengthens this feeling of fellowship by the repeated use of the expression 'you all' (πάντες ὑμεῖς) in the beginning of the letter (Phil. 1: 3, 7, 8). The unique feature of this group was that its members shared the same conception of Christ (Phil. 3: 15) and of the Father which is emphasized in the expressions 'my god' (θεός μου) (Phil. 4: 19) and 'our God and Father' (θεὸς καὶ πατὴρ ἡμῶν) (Phil. 4: 20). Just as the citizens of the Roman Empire were registered by the authorities[20] so the Christians were said to have their names written in the 'Book of life' (Phil. 4: 3). A distinguishing quality of this Christian community was its enlargement of the family beyond blood relationship,[21] and the fellowship of this extended family reached into the after-life and was characterized as citizenship in Heaven (Phil. 3: 20).

---

[17] Soldiers in charge were not allowed to marry at that time (See 1.5.1.2, p. 26 n. 125). When they were discharged they earned the right to marry legally ('ius connubium'), which granted citizenship to their children born subsequently, but not to their wives (Balsdon1979, 91). In this respect slaves were privileged since they automatically became Roman citizens by manumission (Balsdon 1979, 86ff).

[18] According to E. Stauffer (1955, 296f n. 518) πολίτευμα (Phil. 3: 20) means the capital or a native city which lists the citizens on a register. Since Philippi was granted the 'ius Italicum' the colony was immediately related to Rome, and similarly, the Philippian church, as a celestial colony, was immediately related to the heavenly capital of Christ.

[19] Gnilka 1980a, 206.

[20] See n. 18 supra. Balsdon 1979, 96.

[21] Paul characterized his relationship to the Christian community as that of brother (ἀδελφοί μου) though no blood relationship existed (Phil. 3: 1).

In contrast to 'the saints' of the celestial colony, people associated with the secular colony are characterized by Paul as 'a crooked and perverse generation' (Phil. 2: 15). To whom he referred in his expression 'enemies to the cross of Christ' (Phil. 3: 18) is not certain, but this latter group were said to worship things earthly (Phil. 3: 19 names banquets and sexual matters in this connection) and, consequently, to them death would mean destruction (ἀπώλεια) (Phil. 3: 19). Whoever Paul referred to in these passages his audience might have assumed that he was referring to their pagan environment.[22]

6.3.1 The Battle for Christianity

The description of the two colonies shows that there existed a deep antagonism in the relationship between them, and we can deduce that the Philippian Christians were regarded with suspicion. In his letter Paul touches upon his conflict with the Roman authorities (Phil. 1: 13) and upon his fears that the Philippians might experience the same treatment (Phil. 1: 30); in this respect his report of 'saints' even in the household of Caesar (Phil. 4: 22), must have been good news to his audience. The exposed position of Philippian Christians within a pagan environment is presented by Paul as a position of strife (ἀγών) (Phil. 1: 30). The military connotations of the word[23] suited the inhabitants of the military colony[24] and fighting was traditionally considered glorious by the Romans.[25] This theme, as used by Paul, not only caught the interest of his audience but it emphasized and illustrated the necessity of unity within the church. The metaphor of war gave those addressed the idea of combatants fighting shoulder to shoulder in massed formation where solidarity is essential for victory. The individual fighter must stand firm and not break the line of battle (στήκετε ἐν ἑνὶ πνεύματι) (Phil. 1: 27); a weak soldier could bring disaster to them all (Phil. 1: 28). Even to a female audience (acquainted with matters of military life through fathers and husbands) Paul's language might have called to mind the well-known battle array which was introduced by Philip II under the name of the 'Macedonian Phalanx'.[26] This serried array was particularly based on unity and collaboration by the soldiers, and it was

---

[22] See n. 6 supra.

[23] It could refer to athletic activities as well (Pfitzner 1967, 1).

[24] Tanner 1978, 380f. The environment of Philippi seems to have been strongly militaristic, according to the surviving epigraphical material (Levick 1967, 161), and the coins have military motifs from Augustus to Gallien (Collart 1937, 232, 236, 238). Cf. 3.2.

[25] Harris 1979, 17. The wreath was an emblem of victory in the Roman army (Baus 1940, 146f), and Paul mentions a crown (στέφανος) as his reward in his struggle for the gospel (Phil. 4: 1).

[26] Diod. Sic.16, 3, 2.

regarded as unbeatable provided that the line of battle remained intact.²⁷

Although Paul's evocation of a battle brought response principally from his male audience, he demanded that women too should participate in it. He referred to his early preaching in Philippi as 'strife' (ἀγών) (Phil. 1: 30) and named the women Euodia and Syntyche as 'fellow-combatants' in the cause of the gospel (ἐν τῷ εὐαγγελίῳ συνήθλησάν μοι) (Phil. 4: 3). They, like bad soldiers, had subsequently broken rank and quarrelled between themselves. He urged them, therefore, to make peace with each other (Phil. 4: 2) and present a united front in their battle for Christianity.

With the exception of a few Macedonian queens in the past,²⁸ the average woman had no active part to play in war in the Roman Empire. However, the everyday hardship of life for women (as described in Chapter 1) might have been interpreted in terms of strife. In particular the pangs of childbirth could easily be associated with this idea, as Euripides' Medea equated the pain of one childbirth with that of three battles.²⁹ Mythically, on the other side, fighting females were well known to those addressed. In Euripides' *Bacchanals* ecstatic women successfully fought the soldiers of King Pentheus, using their thyrsi as spears.³⁰ Further, in the aretalogy from Cyme, Isis proclaims herself as the mistress of war,³¹ and finally Diana, portrayed on the rock carvings as armed with bow and lance,³² would easily be associated with warfare by the inhabitants of a military colony.

6. 4 THE RULER OF THE CELESTIAL COLONY

The strife that was carried on in the celestial colony, however, did not agree with the usual ideas of war. According to Paul the warrior is his own enemy and the battle is fought against the selfishness inherent in himself (Phil. 2: 3-4). Accordingly, warfare meant servitude, and the

---

27 Polyb. 18, 30, 11.
28 Some Macedonian queens appeared as generals; most well-known are Olympias, the mother of Alexander, and her antagonist Eurydice, who was the wife of Alexander's son Arridaios (Kornemann (?), 104f).
29 Eur. Med. 250-251, quoted in p. 29.
30 Eur.Bacch. 761ff. In this respect it is worth noting that Olympias, Alexander's mother who was an ardent adherent of Dionysus (Plut. Vit.Alex.2), is said to have participated in a battle in the guise of a maenad (Ath. 13, 560F).
31 V. 41. Cf. the power inherent in her title of 'Regina' (4.4.2.1)
32 Collart-Ducrey 1975, Nos. 59-79. The goddess was also related to the Amazons who were her fellow-combatants (Callim. Dian. 236-258). Fighting Amazons were a common motif in art (Paus.1, 15, 2 ; 5, 11, 4 ; 5, 25, 11; cf. 2, 32, 9) (Bothmer 1957, 216ff) and in Artemision in Ephesus there were several statues portraying wounded Amazons (Pliny HN 34, 53, 75). Finally, Virgil (Aen. 11, 659ff) mentions the presence of Amazons in Thrace.

victory³³ could be won only through self-sacrifice (Phil. 3: 8). However, this demand for moral action in connection with the worship of a deity was alien to Christians with a pagan background (as was made evident in Chapter 4 and which will be further discussed later) and, consequently, they lacked patterns of identification.³⁴ Paul offered himself and other Christians as model figures for Christian action (Phil. 3: 17), but the ruler of the celestial colony was presented as their principal example of servitude (Phil. 2: 5).

A picture of Christ not only as a model figure for human action of servitude but also illustrating the aspect of omnipotence is presented to the audience in the so-called 'hymn' to Christ' used by Paul in the letter (Phil. 2: 6-11).³⁵ The 'hymn' is careful to clarify the disposition of Christ in a manner which would be comprehensible not only to members from the first days of the church well acquainted with Paul's oral teaching but also to later converts.

As presented by Paul, the 'hymn' portrays the figure of Christ in two different roles–the slave (Phil. 2: 7) and the absolute ruler (Phil. 2: 10-11). To Paul's audience they were seemingly contradictory manifestations,³⁶ but they are, however, essentially connected when illustrating the disposition of Christ. In obedience to the Father, Christ optionally gave up his divine position (Phil. 2: 6) and descended to earth in the guise of a slave and then shared the lot of a slave in being executed on a cross (Phil. 2: 8).³⁷ Because of his self-sacrifice he was exalted by the Father and became absolute ruler of heaven, earth and the underworld (Phil. 2: 10). These roles, taken separately, would be familar to many of Paul's audience from their pagan past, but for the two roles to be combined in one divine figure, as is described in the 'hymn', was hitherto unknown to them.³⁸ However, some matters described in the 'hymn' were familiar

---

33 Although Paul uses the word κερδαίνω, relating to the sphere of commerce (Schlier 1965. 673), the context may give it connotations of warfare.

34 Cf. n. 6 supra.

35 The so-called 'hymn to Christ' (Phil. 2: 6-11) has offered problems to scholars. On the whole, they are of the opinion that Paul used a primitive Christian hymn which he revised to make it correspond to his own theological ideas. P. Gnilka (1980*a*, 131ff) gives an exhaustive report on the problems of the pre-Pauline hymn. H. Riesenfeld (1983, 168), on the other hand, considers Phil. 2: 6-11 to be a piece of rhetoric teaching which lacks poetic qualities and originates from Paul's own pen. Since there is no evidence, however, that Paul's Philippian audience had any knowledge of the pre-Pauline hymn his possible alterations are of no importance to their understanding of its message.

36 On a comparison being made with Alexarchus, the ruler of Uranopolis (see 6.7).

37 M. Hengel (1977) discusses the use of crucifixion as a punishment for various categories of criminals and its connotations among average people in the ancient world.

38 Artemidorus (2, 34) divides the deities into various categories. Some of them can be apprehended only be the intellect while others can be perceived by the senses. He further divides them into aetherial, celestial, terrestrial and chthonic deities. According to this division (which he makes in connection with the interpretation of dreams) the deities of importance to Philippian women are classified in the

to the audience. The power of the Father over the Son was recognizable from the unlimited legal power of the paterfamilias over his son (1.3.1) just as crucifixion was generally known as a common punishment for slaves,[39] and, finally, the honouring of the name of Christ by genuflexion could easily be related to the imperial cult.[40]

6.4.1 Christ as the Model Figure of Servitude

According to the 'hymn' the servitude and humiliation of Christ began with the transformation from his divine state into that of a human being (Phil. 2: 7). The theme of 'a god becoming human' would be familiar to the audience, particularly from Euripides' *Bacchanals* where Dionysus arrives in Thebes in the semblance of a human being[41] in order to be accepted as a god in his place of birth.[42] Even the motif of humiliation is present in the drama. King Pentheus causes Dionysus to be imprisoned,[43] makes fun of his female beauty[44] and threatens to cut off his curls;[45] finally he dishonours the name of Dionysus.[46]

However, humiliation is principally connected with the tasks Hercules was forced to perform in order to satisfy the caprice of King Eurystheus.[47] Judging from the frequency of the episode in art, Hercules' mortification at changing to female dress and female work in becoming Queen Omphale's slave[48] was well known at that time.[49] Women might have viewed this change as a humiliation to them as the

---

following way: Artemis belongs to aetherial deites perceivable by the senses, while her aspect of Hecate and Dionysus are counted among the terrestrial ones; Hecate is perceivable by the senses but Dionysus by the intellect. Persephone, Isis and Hecate (associated with the Underworld) are chthonic but we are not told of the way they are apprehended. We are further told that the aetherial deities are beneficial for influential women, while the terrestrial protect poor people.

[39] Hengel 1977, 51ff.

[40] For instance Dio Cass., 36, 52, 3; 62, 3,4; 68, 9, 6. Genuflexion was also associated with the worship of the gods, particularly of chthonic deities (for instance, Polyb. 15, 29, 8-9). In this respect it may be noted that females are more often portrayed in art in the posture of kneeling than are males (Bolkestein 1929, 35).

[41] Eur.Bacch. 4. Artemidorus (2, 44) tells us that in dreams the deities show themselves in the guise of human beings.

[42] Eur. Bacch. 26ff.

[43] Eur.Bacch. 509ff.

[44] Eur.Bacch. 455f.

[45] Eur. Bacch. 493.

[46] Eur.Bacch. 1079ff.

[47] Apollod.Bibl. 2, 4, 12. In Philippi Hercules was worshipped together with Dionysus and Persephone (see 4.3.1 and 4.3.2.1.1).

[48] Apollod. Bibl. 2, 6, 3; Diod. Sic. 4, 31; Ov. Her. 9, 55ff. Lucian (Hist. conscr. 10) describes Hercules in female dress spinning by the wool basket.

[49] Brommer 1984, 126. Cf. Lucian Hist. conscr. 10. See also 4.3.2.1.1 , p. 101 n. 32.

female role assumed by the hero was part of the punishment inflicted on him. The humiliation of Christ, on the contrary, had another dimension: the crucifixion of Christ in the guise of a slave[50] (necessary for him to become absolute ruler in the after-life) had particular significance for them; it revealed to them the meaning of their own servitude (as is elucidated in Chapter 1) and made it relate to a future blessed existence after death. Consequently, in the view of those Paul adressed the most important aspect of Christ was that of a slave (Phil. 2: 7). In that role Christ became the model for serving Christians whose actions put the interest of others before their own (Phil. 2: 4-5).

However, as already mentioned, the idea of a deity as a prototype for moral action was unknown to the audience.[51] It was the ethical shortcomings of the deities, particularly in Homer,[52] which caused philosophers to criticize the religion of their time.[53] Philosophers of different schools, particularly the Stoics, outlined patterns for human behaviour in imitation of the divine.[54] In this respect human beings were seen as microcosms which were brought into accord with the divine macrocosm by proper action.[55] However, such ethical demands, being anchoraged in the cosmos, were too abstract for ordinary people; to them philosophers became model figures for moral action.[56] Paul follows in this tradition[57] when he exhorts his followers to take him as a model for the Christian life (Phil. 3: 17).[58]

However, the activities of Christ, as described by the 'hymn', involved not only moral action but moral intent, a quality which sprang from his divine nature. According to Paul it was a divine force which worked in adherents of Christ (θεὸς [- -] ὁ ἐνεργῶν ἐν ὑμῖν) and inspired them to moral action (Phil. 2: 13). The idea of divine presence in a human being was not unfamiliar to previous adherents of the Dionysiac cult. In the

---

[50] The humiliation of Christ was expressed both by his assuming the guise of a slave and by the crucifixion (Hengel 1977, 51ff). However, it must not be forgotten that 'slave' was a wide concept; it included persons of widely different social status, from chained captives working in quarries to independent businessmen operating on a large scale (Himmelmann 1971, 43).

[51] This will be further discussed in 6.4.1.1. Cf. also n. 6 supra.

[52] Lucian in one of his dialogues (Men. 3) presented the moral dilemma of human beings in relation to the actions of the gods.

[53] Particularly Xenophanes, who criticized the Homeric gods (Nilsson 1967, 742f).

[54] H. D. Betz (1967) has pointed to the importance of this idea of 'mimesis' to Paul's theology.

[55] Betz 1967, 121ff.

[56] Betz 1967, 110f. Among those model figures of philosophers there is a woman, Hipparchia, belonging to the Cynic school. She is said to have left the parental home and her loom (like the maenads in Euripides' *Bacchanals* [118]) in order to devote herself to philosophy (Diog. Laert. 6, 96ff).

[57] H. D. Betz (1972) sees Paul as being in the tradition of philosophers in their role as model figures.

[58] Betz 1967, 145ff.

Bacchanals Teiresias describes the presence of Dionysus in the ecstatic women in the following expressive way:

> For in his fullness when he floods our frame (ὁ θεὸς εἰς τὸ σῶμ' ἔλθῃ πολύς) he makes his maddened votaries tell the future.[59]

The same idea is found in an account by Callistratus of Skopas' famous statue portraying an ecstatic female follower of Dionysus:

> [- - -] though it had no power to move, it knew how to leap in the Bacchic dance and would respond to the god, when he entered into its inner being (τῷ θεῷ εἰσιόντι τὰ ἔνδον ὑπήχει).[60]

This divine presence in rapturous women, however, had reference only to temporary frenzied experiences resulting in prophecies. Paul's reference to a divine field of force residing in the followers of Christ implied a perpetual communion with God which inspired moral action as exemplified by Christ.

6.4.1.1 Joy in Suffering

According to Paul, adherents of Christ were closely united with his nature (εὑρεθῶ ἐν αὐτῷ) (Phil. 3: 9), a consequence of which was that he provided not only a pattern for moral behaviour but also for suffering (Phil. 3: 10). In times of persecution they were obliged not to withdraw but to share the tribulation which Christ had to undergo during his life upon earth (Phil. 1: 29), even if it would result in death by martyrdom (Phil. 1: 20, 30). On the other hand, sharing the tribulation of Christ implied that his followers were not left alone but could always rely on his spirit for assistance (Phil. 1: 19). Identification with the suffering of Christ, however, was also related to the resurrection and the after-life (Phil. 3: 11). Through carrying the cross of Christ his followers would in a future life be provided with his 'glorious body' (Phil. 3: 21). Consequently, even in the greatest afflictions they were able to feel a permanent joy by contemplating this prospective goal–a joy independent of external conditions (Phil. 4: 4, 6, 11-13). For Paul himself the joy was deeply rooted. Even martyrdom was seen by him as a pouring out of the self to God, an action he likened to the pouring out of wine in cult ceremonies which made libations to the gods (Phil. 2: 17).

However, this picture of suffering was to a great extent unfamiliar to the audience. Tribulation was to them an inescapable constituent element of human life,[61] and it was the lot of human beings to bear it

---

[59] Eur.Bacch. 300f. Transl. A. S. Way. See also 4.3.2.1.2.
[60] Callistr. 3, 10-11. Transl. A. Fairbanks.
[61] Nestle 1946, 440.

without divine assistance.[62] Furthermore, it was considered as a human mark of nobility to be able to endure suffering with dignity and equanimity, a fact which is shown in literature[63] and art, specially in the reliefs on tombstones.[64] Against this background Paul's audience probably found both fresh and surprising the idea that human beings of their own free will should offer themselves to share the tribulation of a deity, and that their doing so was not merely routine ritual but was an action joyously undertaken as part of the Christian way of life (Phil. 2: 17-18).

The idea of suffering and joy in combination, however, was present in the religious referential framework of former followers of Isis. During the celebration of Osiris' revival they used to share in the goddess's grief when she searched for the body of her husband and in her joy when he was found again (4.4.2.3.3). This participation in the tribulation of Isis, however, seems to have been entirely on an emotional level and, as far as we know, it was not expected either to express itself in moral actions or in lasting joy.

Regarding the social background of women, Paul's statement 'for it has been granted to you that for the sake of Christ you should not only believe in him but also suffer for his sake' (Phil. 1: 29) came true particularly for those who were partners in 'mixed marriages'.[65] From the first letter to the Corinthians we know of Paul's teaching on Christian behaviour in such marriages. A Christian wife was not allowed to divorce her husband if he was willing to live with her (1Cor.7: 13), 'for the unbelieving husband is consecrated through his wife' (1Cor.7: 14), and further on, 'otherwise your children would be unclean, but as it is they are holy' (1Cor.7: 14).[66] This implied that Christian wives were expected to remain married and convert their families, and this is confirmed by Paul's question 'Wife, how do you know whether you will save your husband?' (1Cor. 7: 16); only an unbelieving partner could apply for a divorce (1Cor. 7: 15).

As regards religious matters, a wife's changing to or adopting of a new cult might not normally have affected her relationship to her family, although we are told that a wife's attraction to the mystery religions could be criticized by her husband (2.3.3.2).The Christian demand for moral action and its claim to be the only true religion, however, influenced her whole way of life and particularly her role as a priestess of the domestic cult. As stated earlier, she was subordinated to her husband as the high priest of the family and by law she shared in the responsibility for organizing the worship of his family gods (2.3.1); furthermore, it was her duty to initiate the children into the worship of these deities (2.2.1.1). Therefore,there are reasons to assume that a

---

[62] Nestle 1946, 440.
[63] Nestle 1946, 414ff, 427ff.
[64] Nestle 1946, 424f.
[65] The position of these women will be further discussed in 8.3.4.
[66] This crucial passage is discussed by K. Niederwimmer (1975, 101f) and O.L. Yarbrough (1984, 111f).

Christian wife met with difficulties in her refusal to perform these sacred duties. Even in cases where her husband was favourably disposed toward her conversion to Christianity other members of his family could accuse her of neglecting the domestic cult.[67]

6.4.2 Christ–the Absolute Ruler of the Cosmos

The concept of a divine absolute ruler of the heavens, the earth and the underworld was familiar to the audience. In Philippi this idea was specially related to Isis, who was the divine protectress of Colonia Julia Augusta Philippensis (4.4.2.1). According to the aretalogy from Cyme Isis pretended to be the mistress of Fate[68] and of the planetary system.[69] She thus claimed supremacy over the cosmos, since the one who controlled these powers was superior to all other gods and demons.[70]

The appellation of 'absolute ruler' could to an extent be attributed also to Diana-Hecate. According to Hesiod, Zeus had made Hecate participant of the earth, the heavens and the sea (4.2.2.1). As she had only a share in the power it is doubtful, however, whether she can be considered as an absolute ruler, since such omnipotence gives supremacy over the cosmos unchallenged by other deities. Besides these two more or less omnipotent goddesses Christ's power over the heavens and the underworld, taken separately, could be assiociated with several divinities well known to the Philippians.[71]

To begin with Christ's power over the Heaven, it could be related to the same deities who were associated with Mount Olympus, which to the receivers represented Heaven.[72] The *Homeric hymn to Demeter* tells us that, after her adventure in Hades, Persephone was translated to Mount Olympus together with her mother Demeter.[73] Similarly, Dionysus' mother Semele was taken up among the Olympian gods after Dionysus had brought her back from Hades.[74] Finally, Dionysus himself was

---

[67] This must have been considered as a breach of the law (See 2.3.1 and n. 67, p. 43), and rejection of her duties as a priestess of the household could in point of principle render her liable to public prosecution.However, we never hear of such a case in the sources. These matters will be further discussed in 8.3.4.2.3.

[68] Vv. 55 and 56, quoted in 4.4.2.1, p. 119 n. 40.

[69] Vv. 12, 13 and 14. The planets were considered as being closely linked to the fate of human beings (Nilsson 1974, 487ff).

[70] Isis was the mistress of the demons (P Oxy. 11, 1380, 164f).

[71] See n. 38 supra.

[72] Nilsson 1967, 354.

[73] Hymn.Hom.Cer. 483-487.

[74] Paus. 2, 31, 2. See also 4.3.2.3.2.

elevated to Olympus[75] and Hercules was carried away on a cloud to the dwelling of the gods after he had burnt himself at the stake.[76]

Finally, Christ's power over the Underworld which was expressed in the 'hymn' through the one word καταχθόνιος (Phil. 2: 10)[77] could to a great extent be related to the religious environment of Philippi. 'Dis manibus' ('To the infernal ones'), in one case extended to 'Dis inferis manibus' ('To the infernal ones in the Underworld'),[78] is a usual formula on tombstones within the colony but not elsewhere in Macedonia.[79] Further, there is a surviving altar furnished with the inscription ΘΕΩ ΥΠΟΓΑΙΩ ('To the god of the Underworld'),[80] a fact which—along with the above-examined inscription from Doxato (4.3.2.2) and also the story about the rape of Persephone within the colony (3.7.2)— shows the interest of the Philippians in matters referring to the afterlife. Finally, Sarapis, Hercules and Dionysus had a close connection with the Underworld. Like Osiris, Sarapis was a ruler of the Underworld[81] and had the same function of ruling the deceased, while Hercules and Dionysus were only temporarily associated with Hades.[82]

However, the celestial and chthonic power of all these deities[83] was now subordinated to the dominion of Christ who was the absolute ruler of the cosmos (Phil. 2: 10-11). The almighty power of Christ implied superiority over Fate also—a position hitherto attributed only to Isis (4.4.2.1) who was now demoted to the ranks of the other deities subordinated to Christ.

For women, the passing of divine omnipotence from a female goddess to a male god bespoke a withdrawal of support for them in those areas of their lives which related solely to female experience. No male, god or human, had ever suffered the hardship of their lives. However, to Philippian women with a pagan background this concentration of divine power in one omnipotent deity (who, in addition, made ethical demands on his followers) implied a simplification of their religious observances.

---

[75] Hor. Carm. 3, 3, 13; Ep. 2, 1, 5.

[76] Apollod. Bibl. 2, 7, 7 ; Anth. Gr. 9, 468, 469 ; Diod. Sic. 4, 38.

[77] The word καταχθόνιος did not include the dead in the Underworld but only gods and demons (Sasse 1965, 634).

[78] Perdrizet 1900, 313, No. 5.

[79] 'Dii manes', the gods of the Underworld, are mentioned in 6 epitaphs in Philippi ; otherwise they occur seldom in Macedonia (Düll 1977, 147).

[80] The altar, which is undated and has no inventory number, is to be found outside the Archaeological Museum in Philippi.

[81] Bonnet 1953, 651.

[82] Hercules' connection with Hades consisted of his recovery of Cerberus (Hom. Il. 8, 357ff, Od.11, 620ff; Soph.Trach. 5, 1098; Eur.Heracl. 22ff) and Alcestis (Apollod.Bibl. 1, 9, 15; Eur. Alc. 1008ff) from the Underworld. The return of the latter was a motif usual in the sepulchral art in the Roman era, particularly in the area of the river Danube (Brommer 1984, 23), and it is also to be found in the catacomb in the Via Latina in Rome (Bertelli 1965, Pl. 23). Dionysus retrieved his mother Semele from Hades (Diod. Sic. 4, 28 ; Apollod. 3, 5, 3. Paus. 2, 31, 2).

[83] See n. 38 supra.

They were now liberated from the necessity of making offerings to a manifold of deities, and they were also freed from the fear of demons who could bring calamity upon their everyday lives (cf. 2.3.4.2).

In the worship of Christ Philippian women also found a hitherto unknown personal relationship with a deity which affected their earthly lives as well as their lives in the hereafter. In following Christ they shared actively in his servitude and suffering as, by so doing, they could expect to share in his divine nature after death. Such a bond with the Divine, allowing as it did the retention of their own personalities, was unique in their experience. It was to be found neither in the momentary ecstatic union with Dionysus (4.3.2.1.2) nor in the impersonal identification with Diana visible in the Philippian rock carvings (4.2.2.3).[84]

6.5 THE CELESTIAL CITIZENSHIP ULTIMATELY REALIZED

In Paul's letter the conflict between the celestial colony and the Colonia Julia Augusta Philippensis is widened into a question of cosmic dimensions, and victory and defeat are seen from an eschatological point of view. To be defeated implies ultimate destruction (Phil. 1: 28) but to conquer means salvation (Phil. 1: 28) and implies eternal life (Phil. 3: 20-21). To Paul's audience 'salvation' might have involved the reality of deliverance from a restricted earthly existence defined by the female role, as is described in the two first chapters of this book. However, the victory was not won once and for all, but had to be renewed through repeated moral action in imitation of Christ (Phil. 3: 13-14). This implied a perpetual suffering and dying with him as a condition for participation in his exaltation (Phil. 3: 10-11).

Since complete realization of citizenship was expected to take place in the after-life, Paul's comments on this subject were important to his audience. However, he does not treat these matters exhaustively in the letter and he gives two different points in time when citizenship might be achieved. He first states that it will take place at the moment when total fellowship with Christ is attained after he had 'departed' (Phil. 1: 23). Since, however, life itself also brings fellowship with Christ (Phil. 1: 21), the terms 'life' and 'death' present a paradox. Death involves a transition to a fuller form of companionship with Christ and thus becomes a richer life in itself. However, Paul later states that citizenship will not be an accomplished fact until the resurrection of the dead (Phil. 3: 11) and the second coming of Christ (Phil. 3 : 20), which event was expected to take place in the near future (Phil. 4: 5).

---

[84] The desire to retain earthly personality after death for those who worshipped Diana is, however, evident in the grave altar of Aelia Procula in Rome (4.2.2.3.2). It is uncertain whether or not this desire was also present in the cult of the Egyptian gods (4.4.2.3.3).

These two statements are found in different contexts in the letter but both indicate the reasons for moral action. The resurrection (Phil. 3: 11) is mentioned in connection with Paul's attack on the Jews (Phil. 3: 2ff), and the reference to the return of Christ (Phil. 3: 20) follows immediately after the description of the enemies of the cross of Christ and includes a threat of punishment (Phil. 3: 18-19).

However, in the very beginning of the letter Paul hints of the 'Day of Christ', when the moral development of the converts is said to be completed (Phil. 1: 6) and those who are found 'pure and blameless' will be rewarded (Phil. 1: 10); further, on this occasion Paul for his part will present Philippian converts and be recompensed for his sufferings (Phil. 2: 15-16). These latter statements were unaccompanied by threats of punishment: their function was apparently to remind the people of the bliss awaiting them after all their hardships. Further, these statements, positioned at the beginning of the letter, ensured the maximum elation among the receivers in order that they might be prepared for the news of their coming suffering (Phil. 1: 30).

The idea of a 'resurrection' and also of a 'judgement after death'– which could be associated with the Day of Christ (cf. Phil. 1: 10)–were well known to Paul's Philippian audience, particularly in connection with the cult of the Egyptian gods. As is illustrated by the Egyptian 'Papyrus of Ani',[85] which was presumably well-known in the Graeco-Roman world at that time, the followers of Isis had a very detailed picture of the events facing each of them upon entry into the Underworld. The deceased would be judged by Osiris (Sarapis), and after an investigation carried out by 42 assistant judges the heart would be weighed on a balance in the presence of a monster which waited to devour those found guilty. However, in every case the deceased escaped, assisted by the 'negative confession of sin',[86] which was a catalogue of the evil deeds the person in question had not committed.[87] It can be assumed that those listening to Paul were acquainted with his teaching on the last judgement (cf. 2Cor.5: 10) and that those who knew the Egyptian story of Osiris would imagine the trial on the Day of Christ as a similar judgement scene. They could translate the message, illustrated by the above-mentioned papyrus, into the Christian idiom by placing Christ on the judgement seat (2Cor. 5: 10), and the Egyptian catalogue might correspond to the roll of the living where Paul claimed his fellow-workers' names were to be found (Phil. 4: 3). However, the Christian

---

[85] This papyrus, (dated c. 1400 B.C.) is the most exhaustive illustration in the Book of the Dead (Chapt. 125) (Burton 1972, 269), which was still in use in the Roman era (Bonnet 1952, 824). It is, therefore, reasonable to assume that this judgement scene was familiar to followers of Isis, even outside Egypt. In this respect it may be worth noting that Diodorus Siculus (1, 92) mentions some sort of judgement after death in connection with his description of an Egyptian funeral. Although Diodorus' account is thought to lack historical authenticity on this point (Burton 1972, 269f) it still indicates that the idea of a judgement after death in the cult of the Egyptian gods was current in the Graeco-Roman world at that time.

[86] Pap. of Nebseni (Book of the Dead, Chapt. 125). Burton 1972, 269f. See n. 85 supra.

[87] Bonnet 1953, 338ff.

criteria for judgement differed from those applied by the Egyptians since the two peoples operated under different moral codes. The Christian test was positive and judged a person's intention as well as his deeds: the Egyptian test was negative and ignored motivation.

Furthermore, the idea of the deceased being judged after death could also be associated with Hades and Persephone who sat in judgement in the Underworld.[88] According to Lucian, however, only people of an extremely good or extremely bad disposition were so judged. People of an average moral standard, on the other hand, were predestined to an existence in Hades as shadows and were entirely dependent on grave offerings made by their relatives and friends[89]–a fact which may explain the interest in burial funds in Philippi.[90]

However, there were also other ideas of existence in an after-life current within the colony. As we have already seen, the followers of Dionysus saw themselves as participating in the divine festal procession where children also had a place (4.3.2.2). Regarding the cult of Diana, the rock carvings, supported by the inscription from Mesembria, suggest that women expected to dwell in Hades in the guise of the hunting goddess (4.2.2.3.1), and adherents of Isis hoped eventually to associate in some way with Osiris in the Underworld (4.4.2.3.3).

Previous followers of these cults could recognize their earlier beliefs in Paul's brief references to the after-life in his letter. The maenads comprehended Paul's desire 'to depart and be with Christ' (Phil. 1: 23), followers of Diana comprehended the transfiguration of the body into a divine guise (Phil. 3: 21) and those of Isis comprehended the judgement in the Day of Christ (Phil. 1: 10). However, there was a great difference between their conception and Paul's of the qualifications for a blessed after-life. In the cults of Diana and Dionysus existence after death was not conditional on moral worth. Also, the moral code of the cult of Isis differed from that of Christianity in that it had a negative basis. On the other hand, the cults in question shared with Christianity the idea that the deceased survived death in bodily form in some way–as maenads, in the guise of Diana or in association with Osiris. Regarding existence in the after-life we do not know if the followers of the cults of Dionysus and Diana believed in the preservation of earthly identity after death,[91] while the form of the association with Osiris is uncertain.[92]

---

[88] The judgement in the Underworld was a common motif on grave vases in Apulia and on sarcophagii (Andreae 1963, 26ff).

[89] Lucian De Luct. 2-9.

[90] See 4.2.2.2.2 and 4.3.2.2.

[91] Aelia Procula, portrayed with the face of a child and with the adult body of Diana on the Roman grave altar (accounted for in 4.2.2.3.2) may indicate such an idea. Similarly, a sarcophagus in the Ashmolean Museum at Oxford (dated to the 2nd cent. A.D.) shows the bust of the deceased in the centre of the festal Bacchic procession and could be an expression of the same thought (Richmond 1950, 38f). It should be remembered, however, that the ideas expressed in these monuments could have been influenced by Christianity.

[92] Parlasca 1973, 95ff. See 4.4.2 3.3, p. 126 n. 321.

Against this background the future transformation of Christians' earthly bodies into Christ's resplendent body (σύμμορφον τῷ σώματι τῆς δόξης αὐτοῦ) (Phil. 3: 21) was a concept not entirely alien to Paul's audience. To them it implied the taking on of a shape of eternal youth and loveliness, since immortality and beauty were thought to be criteria of divinity.[93] To women in particular it might have seemed attractive to be able to retain youth and beauty in combination with earthly personality and to be equated with the male sex, since the sharing in the form of the body of Christ–in accordance with the 'one-in-Christ' formula in Gal. 3: 28–implied transfiguration into an androgynous form.[94]

Ideas of bisexuality were not entirely unfamiliar to the audience and were particularly associated with the cult of Dionysus. Little girls were associated with the infant god, who is said to have been brought up as a girl*(4.3.2.3.5) and also the adult god had androgynous features; on the vase paintings he is often depicted in female dress at the head of a train of maenads.[95] In addition, Diana had a masculine aspect which showed itself in her dress and her connection with hunting and war (4.2.2.3); on the other hand, it is uncertain whether women's identification with Osiris (Sarapis) after death (4.4.2.3.3) was associated with a participation in male form.[96]

6.6 SUMMARY

The audience who received Paul's letter consisted mainly of Greeks with a pagan religious background. Against their conceptual framework it is reasonable to assume that the concepts of 'celestial citizenship' and 'servitude' were regarded as the main themes of the letter and also as a key to the interpretation of its message. In this respect the slave aspect of Christ, which touched upon the meaning of life and suffering, death and the after-life, presented a prototype for Christian human action.

To a great extent Paul's message agreed with the religious background of his audience, but the reciprocal content of the message was new to them. Pagan worshippers recognized sorrows in the lives of their gods as paralleling their own experiences, but such coincidence did not mean imitation of divine action, and the idea of a god assuming the ills of the world was unprecedented.

---

[93] Otto 1970, 127ff. The beauty of Dionysus is described in the *Bacchanals* (453-459). This idea was of course strengthened by works of art picturing deities exemplifying perfect human beauty. According to Artemidorus (2, 39) a statue representing a god has the same meaning as the god himself.

[94] According to H. D. Betz (1979, 199) the idea of an androgynous deity may hide behind the 'one-in-Christ' formula.

[95] See 4.3.2.3.5, p. 113 n. 243.

[96] See 4.4.2.3.5.3, p. 126 n. 321. For bisexuality with reference to Genius-Juno, see 2.3.1.1 and n. 88, p. 46.

Paul's admonition to bear Christ's suffering was new to his audience: the connection of suffering with resurrection gave human life and tribulation a meaning hitherto unknown. When the imitation of Christ had reference not only to this life but to the hereafter as well, the gap between life and death was bridged, and death was elevated to a new form of fellowship with Christ. Furthermore, the retention of earthly personality after death was promised to Christians with the resurrection, when they were thought to be transfigured into an androgynous form of Christ; to females this implied liberation from the weak characteristics of the female sex. This expectation, in addition to the idea that tribulation had redemptive value, and the fact that the second coming was expected shortly, made Christianity attractive to Philippian women at that time.

A warning, however, partnered this good news: punishment awaited those who were enemies of the cross. Though this warning presumably made reference to the Jewish heretics, it could easily have been thought to include apostate Christians who now bore false witness to the truth of Christianity.

6.7 EXCURSUS: URANOPOLIS-A 'CITY OF HEAVEN'

The concept of 'celestial citizenship' was presumably not unknown to Paul's Philippian auditors. This idea was a common feature of Utopian tales, not only in philosophical literature[97] but also in Hellenistic romances,[98] which latter can be assumed to have been popular among women.[99] The Utopian dreams usually remained on paper,[100] but at least one case is known where a ruler made an effort to carry out his dreams of a heavenly city–and it happened to be in the area of Philippi. The sources give the following information on the undertaking.[101]

Alexarchus, a younger brother of the Macedonian ruler Cassander, founded a town around 316 B.C.[102] on Mount Athos (Map 1),[103] which is situated about 90 km from Philippi as the crow flies. Alexarchus called the town Uranopolis, the 'City of Heaven',[104] and according to Pliny its

---

[97] Such ideas are found specially among the early Stoics (Ferguson 1975, 111f). Cf. Dio Chrys. 30, 26.

[98] For instance, in Iambulos' travel romance, reproduced by Diodorus Siculus, there are the 'Islands of the Sun'. The inhabitants called themselves 'Children of the Sun' (Diod. Sic. 2, 59, 7) and worshipped the ether, the sun and the heavenly bodies (Diod. Sic. 2, 59, 2). (Ferguson 1975, 124ff).

[99] Hägg 1983, 90; 95 f.

[100] Ferguson 1975, 110.

[101] Kern 1938, 124.

[102] Ath. 3, 98D (Ferguson 1975, 108ff).

[103] Strab. 7, fr. 35.

[104] Ferguson 1975, 108.

name still existed in the 1st cent. A.D.[105] Alexarchus associated himself with Helios, the sun-god,[106] and, according to the coins of the town, he called his subjects 'children of Heaven';[107] besides Alexarchus-Helios, Aphrodite Urania was worshipped in the town.[108] This goddess was regarded as 'Nature and the Mother of the Universe' (φύσις καὶ μητὴρ τῶν ὅλων) and she was particularly connected with women.[109] Further, Alexarchus had scholarly ambitions–in an essay he tried to prove that Dionysus was a son of Zeus and Isis.[110] He also tried to create a new language[111] which he presumably intended to introduce into his celestial city, but the result of this effort was slight since this language was considered as incomprehensible.[112]

It would be reasonable to assume that the tradition of this eccentric ruler and his ambitions to found a Heaven on earth on Mount Athos were still known in Philippi at the time of Paul's writing[113] and that the letter evoked surviving anecdotes on the subject. Unfortunately, there is no information in the sources on the position of women in Uranopolis, but Alexarchus' term 'children of Heaven' (οὐρανίδαι) might have included females, as Paul did when he named Christians of both sexes 'children of God' (τέκνα θεοῦ) (Phil. 2: 15; cf. 4: 2). Paul's preaching of citizenship in Heaven must have reminded his audience of the old familiar tale of Uranopolis, but the difference between Alexarchus' earthly kingdom and Christ's heavenly one was immediately apparent: the citizenship of Uranopolis was, as far as we know from the surviving sources, confined to this life only, while the membership of the Kingdom of God was extended to a future existence after death.

---

[105] Pliny HN 4, 10, 37.
[106] Alexarchus transformed himself into the Sun-god (Clem. Al. Protr. 4, 48).
[107] Regling 1923, Pl. IX: 76.
[108] Lederer 1931, 47ff.
[109] She was a protectress of women in cases of partnerships, marriage and childbirth (Artemid. 2, 37).
[110] Plut. Mor. 365E.
[111] Ath. 3, 98E.
[112] Ath. 3, 98E. Weinreich 1933, 108ff.
[113] The name Uranopolis was still alive in the first century A.D. and is mentioned by Pliny (HN 4, 10, 37).

7 LUKE-ACTS AS RECEIVED BY FIRST-CENTURY WOMEN IN PHILIPPI

7.1 INTRODUCTION

As already mentioned, Luke-Acts is the second literary source dealing with the foundation of the Philippian church. Although to a great extent it lacks historical reliability[1] it actually reflects the surviving oral tradition (as mediated to second-generation Philippian Christians[2]) of Paul's first visit to the town and the foundation of the Christian community. However, the whole of Luke's writings can be seen as a 'picture-book' illustrating Christian teaching as practised in his own church. As regards the Philippian community, Luke's description of the early church can be verified to some degree by information given in Polycarp's letter to the Philippian church.[3] To the ears of a contemporary female audience[4] the second part of Luke's double work might have been particularly attractive since it was brought close to the Hellenistic romances of the time[5] by the use of dramatic episodes to elucidate the message.[6] Luke's Gospel, on the other side, must have caught the interest of women since they could recognize matters of their own lives exemplified in the teaching of the Lukan Jesus. In this chapter Luke's double work will be examined as a whole[7] since the contents of the two

---

[1] Cf. 6.1. The historical reliability of Acts has been regarded as a problem for a long time. Nowadays most scholars agree that Luke's theological purpose controlled his selection of facts. (Schneider 1980, 125ff).

[2] Luke belonged to Christians of the second generation, and Luke-Acts is usually dated to about A.D. 80-90 (Schneider 1980, 121).

[3] The dating of Polycarp's letter to the Philippians is crucial. However, one of Polycarp's reasons for writing the letter was Ignatius' passing through the colony on his way to Rome. Since Ignatius was martyred during the reign of Trajan (A.D. 98-117) the letter may be dated to this period (Schoedel 1967, 4).

[4] The Hellenistic romances are suggested to have been popular among women (Hägg 1983, 95ff). In the eyes of Philippian women Luke addressed a predominantly male audience by his use of such phrases as 'men of Athens' (Acts 17: 22) and 'my brothers, my fathers' (Acts 7: 2). None the less, women obviously formed part of his audience as many women are said to have been converted (Acts 5: 14; 8: 12; 17: 4; 17:12).

[5] Schierling 1978, 81ff.

[6] Plümacher 1972, 80ff.

[7] As shown by the prologue in the Gospel of Luke (1: 1-4) and by the dedication in Acts (1: 1) these two writings are closely connected and are to be seen as one work in two parts (Schneider 1980, 80ff).

parts are well integrated in a feminine perspective. The Gospel provided the basis for women's understanding of Acts not only from a religious but also from a social point of view. In it women's roles as followers of Jesus are brought out clearly,[8] and in Acts Luke points to the application of these roles in the service of the second-generation church. Similarly, by the description in the Gospel of the hardship of women's everyday lives, women were prepared to appreciate his presentation of the early church in Acts and, above all, they had every expectation of finding in this part of the work that women were regarded as equally important as men in the eyes of the Christian church.

Luke-Acts (supplemented by Polycarp's letter) will be examined through the eyes of Philippian women of two categories. To begin with I focus on these two audiences as separated by their different religious referential frameworks (7.2). Thereafter, Luke's double work will be scrutinized first from a social point of view (common to all women) (7.3) and then from a religious perspective as it might have been differently perceived by the two audiences (7.4). The Philippian episode in Acts (16: 11-40), being an independent dramatic episode,[9] will be discussed separately under 7.5.

---

[8] In this respect it is worth noting that in the Gospel (8: 2) the women in the circle of Jesus are treated individually and mentioned by name, while in Acts (1: 14) they are, except for Mary (the mother of Jesus), treated collectively. In the Gospel Luke mentions two categories of female followers of Jesus. The first consists of women who had been cured by him of various diseases (Lk. 8: 2). The second is composed of women who were able to support the apostles with their means (Lk. 8: 3). If one looks for social possibilities, the first category were presumably single women who for some reason or other had not married (1.5). Married women can scarcely have had the freedom to wander about with Jesus, since they were confined to their homes (see 1.5.1.1 and also 2.3.1). The second category, as seen by Philippian women, would have been well-off independent widows over fifty, who had fulfilled the requirements of the Augustan marriage laws (see 1.1, p. 9 n. 4).

[9] Plümacher 1972, 95ff.

7.2 LUKE'S PHILIPPIAN AUDIENCES[10]

When Paul's epistle reached the Philippian church about five years after its foundation[11] the reception of the letter's contents was homogenous. Those addressed belonged to one generation only (i.e. they were converted within the same decade) and they still retained their previous pagan way of thinking against which they perceived Paul's message, as has been shown in Chapter 6.

One generation later,[12] however, when Luke's double work appeared in the Philippian community,[13] his message was perceived by two audiences characterized by entirely different religious referential backgrounds. On the one side, there were Christians born into Christianity (there could possibly also have been first-generation Christians still alive retaining a personal memory of Paul) who had received a Christian upbringing and consequently had an entirely Christian referential framework. On the other side, there was another group understanding Christianity against a pagan background. The latter audience consisted of church members who had newly converted to Christianity and included pagan women who had become acquainted with Christian teaching through their Christian sisters' spreading of the joyful message of the gospel.[14]

---

[10] One has to distinguish between three different audiences receiving Luke-Acts. Luke's intention and his intended audience, as described in his works, have been a problem to scholars. The Jews, Christians of a Jewish-orthodox or a Jewish-Hellenistic background or even the Roman authorities have been regarded as Luke's intended audiences. G. Schneider (1980, 139ff) gives a survey of various hypotheses on the subject. Luke's actual audience, that is, church members who listened at least to the Gospel as read out during the service (Acts was not likely to have been included in the canonical scriptures until about A.D.180 [Dibelius 1949, 128 n. 1]) might have differed from his intended audience (whose knowledge of Judaism he assumed) because of the presence of members with an entirely pagan conceptual background–a fact that suggests itself at least for the Philippian church.Finally, because of the efforts of Christians to spread the gospel it is reasonable to assume that the contents of Luke-Acts reached an audience far beyond the churches (Acts 1: 8; cf. 27: 24). This possible audience is likely to have consisted also of pagans with no direct personal knowledge of Judaism (cf. Acts 28: 28).

[11] See 6.1, p. 135 n. 4.

[12] At that time the average life span of one generation is calculated to have been about 35 years (see 1.1, p. 9 n. 2). Consequently, Luke-Acts (c A.D. 80-90) and Polycarp's letter (c.A.D. 98-117) could have been known by a number of Philippian Christian women of the second generation, even though the female mortality rate was high (1.2.3).

[13] See n. 2 supra.

[14] Christian women were obviously present within Luke's actual audience as members of the Philippian church (Phil. 4: 2) (See also 6.2). Pagan Philippian women are likely to have formed part of a wider possible audience (see n. 10 supra) who received his teaching from Christian sisters within their homes or elsewhere in their immediate domestic vicinity (cf. 1.5.1.1).

7.3 LUKE-ACTS AS SEEN BY PHILIPPIAN WOMEN FROM A SOCIAL POINT OF VIEW

In his writings Luke refers to women from every level of society. Although all the women mentioned by him are Jewish (sometimes even designated as 'daughters of Abraham' or 'God-fearers'[15]) his portraying of women from different classes and social positions may have appealed to a wider female audience than those within the Jewish tradition. In this respect it may be suggested that Luke's Philippian audiences, although of different religious persuasions, shared the same experiences of life common to all women under Roman law and male authority (see Chapter 1 and 2).Though the two female figures with direct reference to Philippi (Lydia and the ecstatic girl) are to be found in Acts (16: 14, 16) it would have been particularly the first part of Luke's double work which would have particularly excited his Philippian audiences from a social point of view, as it reflected every aspect of women's everyday lives and referred to problems connected with the hardships of their existence. As mentioned above, however, their interest in Acts would have been strengthened by the work's seeming similarity to the Hellenistic romances. For instance, the rescue of the abandoned Moses by the Egyptian princess (Acts 7: 21), Paul's adventurous sea voyage (Acts 27-28: 13), the exotic appearance of the eunuch of the Ethiopian queen (Acts 8: 27) and the meeting of Paul and Lydia (Acts 16: 14) are all events which could be seen as part of a romance of the time.[16]

In this section I deal first with Luke's portrayal of women of different class and civil status (7.3.1) and then with subjects closely related to the feminine sphere, such as medical matters and those female household duties touched upon by Luke in his double work (7.3.2).

7.3.1 Women of All Classes

Luke-Acts contains a veritable gallery of female portraits, more or less detailed, showing various aspects of female existence. Women at the very top of the social scale are only casually mentioned (the ruling queen of Ethiopia [Acts 8: 27], Berenice, the consort of King Agrippa [Acts 25: 23] and the two distinguished women, Herodias [Lk. 3: 19] and Drusilla [Acts 24: 24]) while lower-class women often are pictured in full. Sappheira, Priscilla and Lydia exemplify women of more modest social positions representing different classes and styles of living. Sappheira represents landowners in the countryside (Acts 5: 1) while Priscilla and Lydia are town-dwellers representing different professions. Priscilla is an artisan and carries on the trade of tent-making (Acts 18: 2-3), and

---

[15] Lk. 13: 16; Acts 16: 14; 17: 4, 12 (Jervell 1984, 148ff).
[16] Schierling 1978, 81ff.

Lydia is a business women (Acts 16: 14).[17] Finally, Dorcas is another town-dweller who is said to perform charitable acts for the church (Acts 9: 36). As regards civil status, Sappheira (Acts 5: 1) and Priscilla (Acts 18: 3) are married women who apparently work with their husbands (cf. 1.5.1.1). Dorcas (Acts 9: 37) and Lydia (Acts 16: 15) are obviously well-off, independent women and both seem to be owners of houses. As seen by a first-century Philippian eye they presumably represented a comparatively privileged group of women–widows who had earned freedom and financial independence by fulfilment of the Augustan matrimonial requirements.[18] At the lowest level of society come maidservants and other poor and humble women. Two of the maidservants seem to have been serving-maids in a household–the girl from the high priest (Luk 22: 56) and Rhoda who belonged to the house of Mary, the mother of John Mark (Acts 12: 13). A third, apparently mentally disordered, was not occupied with domestic duties but worked for her owner in the street by telling fortunes to passers-by (Acts 16: 16).

Besides slave-girls, Luke-Acts calls attention to other categories of pitiable women. Poor widows in particular are in the lime-light;[19] the calamity of losing an only son (Lk. 7: 12), difficulties in the vindication of legal rights (Lk. 18: 2-5), financial exploitation by doctors of the Law (Lk. 20: 46-47), and dependence on the mercy of other people (Acts 6: 1; 9: 39)–all this makes poor widows appear as heroines. This aspect is emphasized in the story of the woman who sacrificed her last coin to the temple (Lk. 21: 2-4). Further, Luke touches on another group of less fortunate women in his full-figure picture of a woman who might have been a concubine or a prostitute (Lk. 7: 37)[20] –a position so deprecated by society (Lk. 7: 39) that estrangment from her family presumably resulted for such a woman. To these pitiable women Luke-Acts brought good news, not only in the demand by Jesus that his followers break with their families (Lk. 12: 52-53; 14: 26; 18: 29-30; 21: 16) but also in its recounting of the Christian fellowship of the early church in Jerusalem (Acts 2: 46; 4: 32). The family group, defined by blood relationship, was to be abandoned in favour of a wider grouping in the fellowship of Christ, which might have been ritually experienced in the 'one-in-Christ' formula (Gal. 3: 28) which is suggested to have been associated with the rite of baptism.[21] In this fellowship even concubines and prostitutes were welcome, as shown by the above-mentioned episode with Jesus and the rejected woman who was accepted by him and made morally equal to married women

---

17 Both these women had opportunities to spread of Christianity through their professions. Trade and immigration were of great importance to the Christian mission (Beskow 1970, 104ff). For women in the purple trade see 1.5.1.1, p. 24 n. 115.

18 See 1.1, p. 9 n. 4.

19 Cf. Apul.Met. 3, 8 and Lucian Dial.Court. 6, quoted in p. 27.

20 There were several reasons for a woman to become a prostitute or a concubine: for instance lack of money for a dowry, ill-health (cf. Lk. 8: 2), and poverty caused by a husband's death or by divorce (see 1.5.1.1 and 1.5.1.3). Jesus' stance against divorce (Lk. 16: 18) implied a guarantee to wives but brought a financial catastrophe to divorced women who were deprived of the opportunity to remarry.

21 Betz 1979, 189f.

(Lk. 7: 47). Furthermore, poor widows also were supported by means of this Christian community (Acts 6: 1) and this too might have occurred in Philippi according to Polycarp's letter, although we are only told of their duty to pray.[22] To all these women belonging to the lowest level of society the Lukan Mary must have been perceived as an eschatological figure bringing revolutionary news to humble and poor sisters. In spite of her lowly position (Lk. 1: 38, 48) she was elected to bring a Saviour into the world (Lk. 1: 35), and with the authority of her divine election she predicted the future abolition of the present oppression by the rich (Lk. 1: 52) and promised the exaltation of the humble (ὕψωσεν ταπεινούς[23]) (Lk. 1: 52). Thus, to pagan Philippian women, Luke's religious message included also a social message based on a new set of values[24]–a message which might have brought them in great numbers into his possible audience.

7.3.2 Female Existence

Whilst those individual female figures from all walks of life who are to be met in Luke-Acts could only be identified by their own counterparts among Luke's audience, his brief references to matters relating to women generally evoked a response from all of their sex, irrespective of their social backgrounds.

As regards the medical aspects of female life, Luke's Gospel immediately caught the interest of women by opening with stories relating to childbirth. Elizabeth is said to have been cured by God of her barreness (Lk. 1: 13)–a condition which was considered a catastrophe for a married woman (Lk. 1: 25)[25]–and Mary to have been forced to give birth to her son out of doors far from home (Lk. 2: 7)–a not infrequent experience for poor Philippian women in the countryside working in the field. In addition, later on in Acts (7: 21) in the episode of the Egyptian princess rescuing the infant Moses, the practice of exposing unwanted children is illustrated–a distressing reality in the lives of many women (1.2.1). Furthermore, besides the calamities relating to childbirth Luke refers to various diseases well known to women–mental disorder (Lk. 8: 2; Acts 16: 18), fever (Lk. 4: 38), haemorrhage (Lk. 8: 43) and curvature of the spine (Lk. 13: 11) (cf. 1.2.3).

---

[22] Polyc. 4, 3.

[23] Although ταπεινός is masculine females could perceive themselves to be included since Mary is presented as one of those ταπεινοί.

[24] Acts of charity in the pagan religion are recorded in 2.3.2.2 and 2.3.4.1. See also Julian Mis. 363A, quoted in p. 194. In this passage the Emperor Julian exhorts pagan husbands to perform the same charitable work in pagan temples as their Christian wives did in the Christian community.

[25] Cf. CIL 6, 1527(=ILS 8393), quoted in p. 30. In this respect, the Lukan Jesus' addressing the women of Jerusalem: 'Blessed are the barren, and the wombs that never bore, and the breasts that never gave suck!' (Lk. 23: 29) could have been consoling to barren wives.

Also, in Luke's Gospel there are several allusions to female domestic duties—the making of clothes (Lk. 5: 36; 12: 27; cf. Acts 9: 39), the grinding of corn (Lk. 17: 36), and the baking of bread (Lk. 13: 21) (cf. 1.5.1.1). There are also passing references to women's fellowship with other females in connection with mourning (Lk. 23: 27) and the laying out of the dead (Lk. 23: 55-56) (cf. 2.3.1.2.2), to the sharing of a sister's joy in pregnancy (Lk. 1: 58) and to the simpler joy of finding a lost silver coin (Lk. 15: 9)—the latter might have alluded to the dowry which it could be a catastrophe for a woman to lose (cf. 1.5.1.1). Finally, women who felt deprived of motherhood and women who had failed to fulfil their role as mothers (1.3.2) could recognize their fate in that of Mary when Jesus broadened the old family structure in favour of a wider, all-embracing Christian family (Lk. 8: 21; 11: 27-28).

7.4 LUKE-ACTS AS RECEIVED BY PHILIPPIAN WOMEN FROM A RELIGIOUS POINT OF VIEW

While the social message of Luke-Acts might on the whole have been viewed similarly by all women of that time, Luke's writings could be variously received according to the religious backgrounds of his audiences. The difference will appear in a comparison being made between two different Philippian audiences: the first one is assumed as consisting of pagan and newly-converted Christian women (7.4.1) and the second one as consisting of second- generation Christians (7.4.2).

7.4.1 A Pagan and Newly-Converted Christian Audience

In his works Luke seldom refers directly to pagan gods,[26] but even if he does not explicitly name the deities familiar to his audience their previous followers could nevertheless adapt the Christian message to fit their pagan conceptual framework. Such an adaptation could easily be made by the followers of Dionysus,[27] but the myth of Isis also had some points of similarity, particularly with the content of Luke's first book. In this respect the narratives about the Lukan Jesus as regards his birth, his teaching and miracles, his death and resurrection, as well as his

---

[26] Of the deities popular with Philippian women only Diana is mentioned by him—though he uses her Greek name of Artemis (Acts 19: 27). This goddess, however, was closely linked to Ephesus as the protectress of the city (Acts 19: 35) and had little significance to worshippers in Philippi (cf. 4.2). Beside Artemis in Ephesus Luke mentions Zeus and Hermes in Lystra (Acts 14: 12) and the unknown god in Athens (Acts 17: 23). In addition there are several references to the worship of idols (Acts 7: 41; 15: 20; 15: 29; 19: 26; 21: 25).

[27] Several scholars have pointed to similarities between the Johannean Jesus and Dionysus, for instance, J. Leipoldt (1931) and H. Noetzel (1960).

relationship to his mother, could be readily understood within a pagan framework.

7.4.1.1 The Lukan Jesus

In the beginning of the Gospel, Elizabeth, Mary and Hannah–three women of interest to followers of Dionysus–are introduced.[28] These women were all connected with the birth of Jesus and could be understood as having had ecstatic experiences–a condition which could be recognized by women who were familiar with Euripides' *Bacchanals*. Mary, like Semele (4.3.2.3.2), is an unmarried young girl who becomes pregnant by divine power and gives birth to a holy child (Lk. 1: 35; 2: 7). When Mary meets Elizabeth, who also is pregnant (Lk. 1: 24), Mary's greeting induces in Elizabeth a state of ecstasy[29] and the latter greets Mary as the mother of the future holy child (Lk. 1 :42); in a similar state of excessive joy, Mary answers Elizabeth with prophecies about her expected child (Lk. 1: 46-55). Similarly, when Hannah sees the infant Jesus in the temple she acquires at divinatory knowledge of his true identity (Lk. 2: 38). Luke's description of these experiences resulting from divine presence might very well have recalled to his audience Euripides' picture of maenads foretelling the future when Dionysus entered their bodies.[30] Further, the presentation of Jesus in the temple could easily be compared with the initiation of the infant Dionysus into the mysteries in the presence of 'mater' and 'pater' (4.3.2.2).

As regards the adult life of Jesus, as decribed in the Gospel, both his teaching and miracles to a degree fitted in with the pagan conceptual framework of the audience. His compassion for children (Lk. 18: 16) was reflected in the Dionysian mysteries into which children could be initiated (4.3.2.2) and Diana (4.2.2.2.1).as well as Isis (4.4.2.3.2) protected children.[31] In addition, the teaching of Jesus on the after-life linked up with the cult of Isis, as deceased Christians would rise after death as 'sons of God' (Lk. 20: 36),[32] even as dead followers of Isis would in some

---

[28] Luke's disposition of his subject-matter was an important instrument to catch and maintain the interest of his female audience. As he begins the Gospel by introducing female figures of interest to women, he places the reports of the early Christian community at the beginning of Acts (2: 45-46; 4: 32).

[29] Elizabeth's expected child is said to have been leaping in her womb for joy (Lk. 1: 41, 44). Similarly, in Semele's womb her expected child joined in her ecstatic dance (Nonnos, Dion. 8, 27ff).

[30] See Eur.Bacch. 300f, quoted in p. 104.

[31] Isis' care for children could be traced in the Jewish history in Acts of the rescuing of the infant Moses by the Egyptian princess (Acts 7: 21)–a story reminiscent of the goddess's saving of the exposed Anubis (4.4.2.3 and 4.4.2.3.2).

[32] That women are included in this phrase may be deduced from the fact that Luke's context is not connected with sex, and also from the fact that the phrase does not segregate the sexes. The latter is shown by a passage in Exodus referring to the song of victory after the crossing of the Sea of Reeds (Ex.15). We know that the choir of the

way identify with Osiris or Horus (4.4.2.3.3). Finally, the miracles of Jesus in the form of healing and raising of the dead (Lk. 7: 13-14) were in harmony with the pagan background of the audience—both Isis (4.4.2.1) and Diana (4.2.2.2.1) had the function of healing in Philippi, and Semele (4.3.2.3.2), Alcestis (4.3.2.3.4) and Persephone (3.7.2) were all well-known mythical figures who were delivered from Hades.

The events relating to Jesus' death and resurrection, as recorded by Luke, could be associated with the mythical stories of Dionysus and particularly with the rituals of the Isiac cult. The mocking of Jesus by Herod in dressing him in a gorgeous robe before his death (Lk. 23: 11) might remind the followers of Dionysus of the humiliation of this deity by King Pentheus in comparing him with a woman.[33] In addition, the events of Jesus' death and resurrection might easily have brought the celebration of Osiris' revival to mind (4.4.2.3.3). Even as Isis and her companions searched for Osiris' body so woman followers of Jesus are said to have looked for his body at the grave (Lk. 24: 1): Isis found and revived Osiris' body, while the Christian women are said to have found the tomb empty and Christ risen from the dead (Lk. 24: 5-7, 22-23). Finally, the account of Christ's ascension to Heaven (Lk. 24: 51) presumably brought to mind the ascensions of Dionysus[34] and Hercules[35] and also the belief that Roman Ceasars united with the Olympians after death.[36]

In the eyes of the Philippian audience the relationship between Jesus and his mother had its mythical counterpart in the circle of the Egyptian gods. Mary, in her role as a suffering mother, might have been exciting to previous followers of Isis. Mary's future affliction through her son was predicted at the infant's presentation in the temple (Lk. 2: 35) and this prophecy was verified when the twelve-year-old Jesus and his parents visited the temple (Lk. 2: 48). Mary's sorrow and disappointment at the behaviour of her son in connection with his breaking the old family structure based on blood relationship (Lk. 8: 19-21; 11: 27-28) corresponded in some degree to the relationship between Isis and her eldest son Horus. The seeming harshness of Jesus towards his mother (Lk. 8: 21) could be related to the episode of the myth of Isis when Horus used violence on his mother because of her mercy for Set, his enemy (4.4.2.3).

Israelites ('sons of Israel') (Ex.15: 1) included women, since we are told that Miriam led all the women in the refrain of the song (Ex.15: 20).
33 Eur.Bacch. 455ff. See also 6.4.1.
34 Hor. Carm. 3, 3, 13; Ep. 2, 1, 15. See also 6.4.2.
35 Apollod. Bibl. 2, 7, 7; Anth. Gr. 9, 468, 469; Diod.Sic. 4, 38. See also 6.4.2.
36 Latte 1960, 317ff.

7.4.1.2 The Spirit and the Early Church in Jerusalem

As Luke's Gospel tells of the earthly life of Jesus, his stories of the Holy Spirit in Acts could be seen as counterparts of myths relating to pagan deities, and would have been particularly familiar to previous followers of Dionysus. In Acts these latter could recognize two ideas which were well known to them from Euripides' *Bacchanals*: the idea of mission[37] and the idea of fire as a manifestation of divine power. The latter is expressed in Luke's version of the events in Jerusalem on the day of Pentecost. The account of the appearance of the Holy Spirit in the form of tongues of fire coming to rest on Christians (Acts 2: 3) corresponded to Euripides' ecstatic women who carried the divine fire on their heads without being burnt.[38] Mary, the mother of Jesus, and some other women are said to have joined the twelve apostles in Jerusalem (Acts 1: 14) and their presence among the men (Acts 2: 1) at the pouring out of the Spirit might have attracted attention to women in a male-dominated society. Moreover, Peter's quotation of prophesying Old Testament ecstatic women ('your daughters shall prophesy' [Acts 2: 17] and 'my maidservants (δούλη) in those days [- - -] they shall prophesy' [Acts 2: 18]) fitted in with the above-mentioned maenads' predicting of the future[39] and could be recognized as a continuation of their activities. In addition, Luke's allusion to wine in connection with his manifestation of divine power (Acts 2: 13) would further facilitate a Dionysian interpretation of events.

Similarly, the picture of the early Christian community in Jerusalem had some characteristics familiar to members of the Dionysiac mysteries; Luke's mention of the joyful meals of the Christians (Acts 2: 46) and their community of property (Acts 2: 44) might have reminded his Philippian audience of the commemoration of the dead and the burial funds (4.3.2.2). Further, the seeming inclusion of children in the promise to their mothers, as assured by Peter (Acts 2: 39), was significant to women. Though he referred to the ten tribes of Israel when including 'all those who are far away',[40] to these women his promise might have encompassed their children, even those who had left the parental home (1.5.1) and infants which had been rejected by their families or left to die (1.2.1). In addition, this fellowship of the Christian community had the features of those Utopian societies dreamed of by philosophers and authors of romances—one of which was close at hand to the audience through Alexarchus' Uranopolis (6.7).Inescapable sufferings connected with human existence could be eliminated, as Peter's shadow (Acts 5: 15) and some garments of Paul had the effect of healing (Acts 19: 12). Death seemed no longer to be the inevitable victor in the battle for human life, for a dead woman of importance to the church was brought back to life (Acts 9: 40). Finally, nobody would die of

---

[37] The motif of mission in the *Bacchanals* will be further discussed in 7.5.1.
[38] Eur.Bacch. 757f.
[39] Eur.Bacch. 300f, quoted in p. 104.
[40] G.Schneider (1980, 278) is of the opinion that Peter included also pagans in his promise.

starvation in this Christian society, since there was common ownership of wordly goods by the members (Acts 2: 45; 4: 32).

From our point of view it is easy to imagine that to this audience, consisting of Philippian women with a superficial knowledge of Christian ideas and with little or no experience of Christian life, the message of Luke-Acts fitted in with the current expectations of a coming prosperous era (presaged in the 'Pax Romana'[41]) which was predicted in the literature of the time[42] and which found its expression in works of art.[43] Against this background it may be suggested that this audience absorbed principally those features of Luke's account attributable to an imaginary state of ideal perfection which was located to this world and where women were equally accepted, irrespective of social position and civil status. This Utopian state (hitherto showing itself only in the Christian communities) would be governed by Christ as the new emperor (cf. Acts 17: 7) who would liberate his followers from the toil of human existence and change their lives into eternal bliss without fear of starvation, disease and death.

7.4.2 A Second-Generation Christian Audience

To an audience consisting of second-generation Philippian Christian women Luke-Acts had an entirely different message, as their religious conceptual framework had already been enlarged by Paul's letter and above all by other teaching and experiences. For my purpose, however, the letter forms a small but safe base for an examination of their reception of this message, although important information is lacking— for instance, Paul's attitude to ecstatic phenomena in Philippi.[44] Two themes of interest for a reception of Luke's work were to be found in the letter—'exaltation through humiliation' as presented in the 'hymn to Christ ' (6.4) and the 'citizenship of Heaven' (6.3).

To the audience the Gospel served principally to illustrate the 'hymn' in its aspects of servitude[45] and divinity.[46] In Stephen's speech in Acts (7: 21) there are no women mentioned in the Jewish salvation history except for the daughter of Pharao, but they played an important role in Christianity as part of the divine action. Christ's assumption of the

---

41 K. Wengst (1986) discusses the significance of the Pax Romana to Jesus and to the early Christians.

42 Among the poets it was principally Virgil who gave expression to such ideas, particularly in his 4th Eclogue.

43 The 'Ara Pacis Augustae' is the best known piece of art symbolizing the idea of a coming glorious age (Rumpf 1964, 482).

44 However, such phenomena can be suggested not to have caused problems in the Philippian church (cf. 1Cor. 14: 23) since the Dionysian cult was strong within the colony (cf. 4.3.2.1) and people were used to ecstatic behaviour.

45 Phil. 2: 7.

46 Phil. 2: 5-6.

condition of a slave[47] was wrought through Mary, who became the instrument for his transformation into human shape (Lk. 1: 35), and the future of the holy child was foretold by Elizabeth (Lk. 1: 42) and in some sense also by Hannah (Lk. 2: 38)–prototypes for women's prophesying role in the early church. The aspect of servitude was also represented by women followers of Jesus. They are not present as apostles in the Gospel, but they had, nevertheless, well-defined positions within the circle of Jesus, and these are demonstrated by Luke in the story of Jesus' visiting of the two sisters Martha and Mary (Lk. 10: 38-42) who represented the role of the server with that of the listener. The latter role seems to have been highly valued by Jesus (Lk. 10: 42), but in the view of Acts the former appears to be more important.[48] However, serving was natural to women since it agreed with their domestic function; therefore Luke might have found it necessary to lay stress on listening–an attribute of importance to women when instructing their children in religious matters (cf. 2.2.1). In the figure of Mary, the mother of Jesus, Luke united the two roles and provided a model figure of Christian life, not only to females but also to males, since Mary's role as a mother is presented in the Gospel as subordinate.[49]

The aspect of Christ as the ruler of cosmos[50] (in the letter connected with the citizenship of Heaven[51]) is apparent in Luke's picture of the early church in Jerusalem (Acts 2: 44-47; 4: 32-35). To the audience, this theocratically-governed community might have appeared as the realization on earth of the celestial citizenship, the fulfilment of which Paul expected only after death. The lives of these early Christians, as described by Luke, were distinguished by characteristics mentioned by Paul in his admonitions to the Philippians: unity (Phil. 2: 2–Acts 4: 32), unselfishness (Phil. 2: 3–Acts 2: 45) and joy (Phil. 4: 4–Acts 2: 46). Although governed by a celestial ruler the community had problems regarding the common ownership of wordly goods, and these problems were mirrored by Luke in the dramatic story of Ananias and Sappheira (Acts 5: 1-10). Their withholding of some money for themselves was punished by the immediate death of the couple; this swift retribution might have acted as a deterrent to rich women (cf. Acts 5: 11), while the church's stewardship of the people's money ensured provision for the poor women of the community. A similar case of misappropriation of money belonging to the Christian church was known to the Philippian audience from their own community; according to Polycarp's letter the

---

[47] Phil. 2: 7.

[48] Only one woman is mentioned in the role of teaching (Priscilla) while there are several in the role of serving (Dorcas, Mary [the mother of John Mark], Lydia and even Priscilla). See further 7.4.2.1.

[49] According to R. E. Brown (1978, 152) Luke's picture of Mary, who is characterized by the attitude of 'keeping these things and pondering them in her heart' (Lk. 2: 19), makes her a model of Christian humility, acceptance and obedience.

[50] Phil. 2: 10.

[51] Phil. 3: 20.

presbyter Valens, presumably in collusion with his wife, had embezzled the means of the church.[52]

However, this ideal Christian community, as described by Luke, was in striking contrast to the existing society and was an object of persecution which also affected women (Acts 8: 3; 9: 2).[53] In this respect, women married to pagan husbands were particularly vulnerable, since conversion to Christianity acted upon their position in relationship to the deities of the household and also upon the religious integrity of the pagan family (2.3.1). Consequently, the demand for Christians to abstain from food sacrificed to idols (Acts 15: 29)—a demand absent in Paul's letter (cf. 1Cor. 8)—could have troubled Philippian Christian wives of 'mixed marriages' since it affected the celebratory meals of the domestic cult (2.3.1.2). In addition, they were further reminded of the danger of persecution when the community received and cared for bishop Ignatius and other Christians passing through the town on their way to martyrdom in Rome.[54] Therefore, Paul's brief allusions to the Christian's sharing in the glorious body of Christ after death[55] might have been full of consolation to those women.[56]

Whereas the first-generation and pagan audience perceived Luke-Acts through the filter of their pagan background, the second-generation Christian audience brought a different perception to bear on the two books. Their outlook had been coloured by their knowledge of Paul's letter and other Christian teaching, and had been further deepened by their experience of Christian life. Consequently, this second audience found Luke's message to contain news of a blessed existence in the after-life rather than a promise of Utopia here and now. To them, Christian life, as seen in the perspective of the 'imitatio Christi', was illustrated in Luke's work by figures enduring various forms of servitude and bondage, and Paul's message that Christian life implied suffering and even martyrdom (6.4.1.1) was thus confirmed.

7.4.2.1 Women's Roles in the Early Church

The roles played by women in the second-generation Christian community were the same as those played by the company surrounding Jesus, as described in the Gospel (8: 2-3). They were charged with acts of charity, of prophecy and of listening (in order to mediate the Good News to their children, to the members of their families and also to pagan

---

[52] Polyc. 11

[53] To the audience it might have been surprising that Paul himself was said to persecute Christian women, but his conversion testified to the absolute power of Christ recorded in the 'hymn' (Phil. 2: 9-11).

[54] Polyc. 1: 1; 9: 1; 13: 2.

[55] Phil. 3: 21.

[56] A wife was by law responsible for her husband's domestic cult (see 2.3.1 and n. 67, p. 43), which is why she was exposed to the risk of public persecution.

sisters)–qualities attributed by Luke to his feminine figures in Acts.[57] Regarding the first of these roles, there were two kinds of charitable work entrusted to women in the early church. The first required them to make their homes available for the meetings of the Christians (cf. Acts 2: 46; 5: 42); Lydia who invited the apostles and the Christian converts to her home (Acts 16: 15, 40), Mary, the mother of John Mark, the home of whom was a meeting-place for Christians (Acts 12: 12), and finally, Priscilla, who took care of Paul (Acts 18: 3; 1Cor. 16: 19), all belong to the first category. The second required them to care for the poor (Acts 2: 42); Dorcas, who devoted herself to caring for poor widows by making clothes for them (Acts 9: 39) is the only example of this category.[58] The second role (that of prophesying) is illustrated by the mention of Philip's four prophesying daughters (Acts 21: 9), and women's ability to tell the future is reflected in the story of the ecstatic girl in Philippi (Acts 16: 16).[59] Finally, women's teaching role (the third one) is exemplified by Priscilla–a role usually connected with the religious education of their children which is verified as regards Philippian women.[60] Priscilla is said to have instructed Apollos 'about the Way' together with her husband (Acts 18: 26), and the fact that the text mentions her before her husband may indicate her leading role in this connection.[61] At this point it may be appropriate to call attention to Luke's effort to convince his intended audiences of the trustworthiness of women. The word of the women who told the apostles that Christ was risen from the dead was distrusted (Lk. 24: 11) but their information was verified by Peter (Lk. 24: 12). In a similar way Rhoda, the maid-servant who recognized Peter's voice, was not believed by the members of the household (Acts. 12: 15) but later they had to admit the accuracy of her claim (Acts 12: 16).

---

[57] As regards females roles in the Philippian church Polycarp's letter (4, 3) mentions only the role of praying attributed to the widows. Such a role of praying is not to be found in Acts.

[58] In Acts this female duty of charity is presented as being privately performed by well-to-do women acting on their own initiative, while offices of charitable work were held by men (Acts 6: 3).

[59] The girl is said to have a πνεῦμα πύθωνα (Acts 16: 16) which to the audience might have alluded to the Pythia, the ecstatic priestess in Delphi (cf. Wikenhauser 1921, 401ff). The Dionysiac oracle on Mount Pangaion had also an ecstatic priestess (4.3.2.1.2).

[60] Polyc.4: 2.

[61] Knopf 1907, 616; Harnack 1931, 54.

7.5 THE PHILIPPIAN EPISODE (ACTS 16: 11-40) AS SEEN BY LUKE'S PHILIPPIAN AUDIENCES

Because of Luke's exhaustive reproduction of the tradition dealing with the foundation of the Christian community, where a woman played a predominant part, there are reasons to assume that to both audiences the Philippian episode was the peak of Luke's double work. It had to do with conditions familiar to them from hearsay, and from his account they could identify the outlines of their town, which was similar in pattern to most other ancient towns.[62] The recognizable points are: one of the town-gates (Acts 16: 13) (Map 3: A, D), the Via Egnatia (Acts 16: 16) (Map 3: B-C), the forum (Acts 16: 19) (Map 3: 15), the prison (Acts 16: 24);[63] and possibly they could also recognize the 'house of Lydia'[64] which is said to have been the meeting-place for the first Christian converts (Acts 16: 40).

However, in view of its religious message Luke's account of Paul's visit to the town was differently received according to the religious framework of the audience. In the following, a reception made possible by a pagan background will first be discussed (7.5.1), and then the episode will be viewed through the eyes of second-generation Philippian Christian women (7.5.2).

7.5.1 A Pagan and Newly-Converted Philippian Audience

To an audience well acquainted with the repertory of the Philippian theatre (cf. 3.4.1.1), and particularly to previous followers of Dionysus, Luke's account of Paul's arrival in the colony and the foundation of the Christian community might have appeared in some way familiar. The fact is that the literary pattern of Luke's account in broad outline corresponded to that of Euripides' *Bacchanals*,[65] and, as regards contents, the following common elements can be extracted:

A prophet with his companions from Asia Minor arrives in a town in order to introduce the cult of a new god, and many women are converted. The god is

---

[62] As to the historical reliability of Acts see n. 1 supra. As regards the Philippian episode, E. Plümacher (1972, 95ff) is of the opinion that Luke had the predominant purpose of showing Paul's heroic role in the progress of Christianity.

[63] There are no surviving traces of this prison in the ancient Philippi. The ruins named the 'Prison of Paul' are from a later period (Elliger 1978, 71).

[64] The surviving remnants from dwelling-houses are presumably too fragmental to have given rise to a tradition of 'Lydia's house' (cf. 3.4.1.1).

[65] The fact that there is a broad correspondence between Euripides' drama and this story as a whole in Acts has never previously been noticed. Only the release of the apostles from the prison through an earthquake has been likened to the *Bacchanals* (Lönborg 1926, 75ff; Rudberg 1926, 29ff; Weinreich 1929, 283ff; Kratz 1979, 375ff).

prophetically announced as a mighty one, but, nevertheless, the prophet and his companions get into conflict with the authorities of the town. They are imprisoned but later delivered by an earthquake. However, the god becomes accepted by the authorities, and the missionaries leave the town in order to go on with their work in another place.

There are several comparable details in this story. Dionysus appears in human form[66] as a prophet accompanied and supported by a group of Lydian women[67]–Paul is guided to Philippi by the Holy Spirit (Acts 16: 9-12) and is supported by Lydia, an immigrant from Lydia in Asia Minor (Acts 16: 14-15).[68] Teiresias proclaims Dionysus as a true god[69]–the ecstatic girl makes known that Paul and his companions are followers of the Most High God (Acts 16: 17). The imprisoned Lydian women praise Dionysus[70] and are told to trust in the god[71]–Paul and his companions sing hymns in the prison (Acts 16: 25), and the gaoler is urged to believe in God (Acts 16: 31). Finally, King Pentheus is conquered by Dionysus[72] – the Roman authorities release the apostles from the prison (Acts 16: 39).

As is previously shown (4.3.2.1.2) there is no reason for questioning that the *Bacchanals* was known in Philippi even at the time of Paul's first visit to the town and his foundation of the church. Consequently, the stories of this latter event, as reported by Luke,[73] could easily have been coloured by this drama, since one of its main themes is 'mission'; the Dionysiac audience could therefore have recognized the same pattern in Acts. Thus, Paul and his companions represented to them a new and mightier Dionysus (also originating from Asia Minor), who displayed his power by driving out that deity from the ecstatic girl (Acts 16: 18).[74] To a Philippian audience this prophesying girl might have linked closely to Dionysian maenads foretelling the future,[75] thus confirming the authenticity of the new god. Further, this new Dionysus demonstrated his power over the underworld by delivering his imprisoned followers by means of an earthquake, and he also controlled the Roman authorities who released the Christians from the gaol (Acts 16: 39).

From a perspective of conversion, the figure of Lydia might have been of importance to Luke's audience, since her trade as a dealer in purple (Acts 16: 14) was entirely connected to the feminine sphere. Purple was

---

[66] Eur.Bacch. 4.
[67] Eur.Bacch.55ff.
[68] Lydia apparently was named after her native country. Slaves in particular were named in that way (Heubeck 1965, 2268).
[69] Eur.Bacch.272ff.
[70] Eur.Bacch.600ff.
[71] Eur.Bacch.604ff.
[72] Eur.Bacch.1030.
[73] A form-critic analysis shows that Luke has put together the story of the events in Philippi from several pieces of different material and has formed them into a united narrative (Haenchen 1965, 502f).
[74] Haenchen 1965, 502.
[75] Eur.Bacch. 300f, quoted in 104.

used in the household for the dyeing of fabrics[76] intended specially for festive dresses,[77] and it was also used as rouge for cheeks and lips.[78] A woman dealer in purple needed to be well dressed herself in order to advertise her goods as her appearance would place her high in the estimation of other women. Consequently, we can suggest that Lydia became an important model of conversion for pagan women who were attracted to Christianity, and to the Christians this prestigious model supported their conversion to the new religion. However, Lydia's opening of her home as a meeting-place for the Christians in Philippi (Acts 16: 40) might have seemed alien to the pagan part of the audience. It would be acceptable as a means of introducing a new deity into the domestic cult (2.3.1) but for strangers to be included in family worship would have been an entirely new idea. The fact that Lydia, who must have been understood to be a widow, urged Paul and his companions to come and stay with her (Acts 16: 15) might have given birth to romantic rumours regarding her real reason for inviting the men to her home.

To sum up, to the pagan section of Luke's female audience the emphasizing of the superiority of Christ over a deity closely linked to women and the conversion of a distinguished Philippian woman were important factors in their decision to adopt Christianity. To the newly-converted Christian women, on the other hand, the friendly treatment of Paul and his companions by the Philippian authorities must have been regarded as evidence of the superiority of Christ in the eyes of the Roman government—a reassuring fact in times of persecution.

7.5.2 A Second-Generation Christian Audience

While Euripides' drama to a great extent formed the referential framework of the first-generation audience for the reception of the Philippian episode Paul's letter had the same function as regards the second-generation audience. To this latter audience who was acquainted with Paul's letter referring to his first visit to the colony[79] Luke's detailed account on the subject (Acts 16: 11-40) might have been considered as a historical document for the foundation of the Philippian church.[80] From a feminine point of view Luke's account was important because it confirmed Philippian women's participation in the foundation of the

---

[76] Strab. 630; Pliny HN 22, 3ff (Reinhold 1970, 48ff).

[77] Verg. Aen. 7, 814; Livy 34, 3; 9, 34, 7.3; Plut. Mor. 527F. A female orant, dressed in a purple tunic, is portrayed in the catacomb of Priscilla in Rome (Bertelli 1965, Pl.16).

[78] Cf. Apul. Met. 8, 27; Jerome, Ep. 127, 3.

[79] Phil. 1: 5; 2: 12; 4: 3, 15-16.

[80] Luke's report of the imprisonment of the apostles and their release through an earthquake (Acts 16: 26) could have been seen as illustrating Paul's mention of tribulation experienced during his stay in Macedonia (Phil.4: 15). Furthermore, the story of Paul's exorcising of the demon from the ecstatic girl (Acts 16: 18) might have reminded the audience of the enemies of the cross of Christ mentioned in Paul's letter (Phil.3: 18). Cf. 6.1, n. 6, p. 135f

church as mentioned by Paul.[81] This participation was illustrated by the story of Lydia (Acts 16: 14-15, 40) who is said to have been attracted to Judaism before she converted to Christianity (Acts 16: 14).[82] Luke's reference to one woman only as a distinguished convert might have suggested that one of the two women (Syntyche and Euodia) mentioned by Paul in the letter had deserted from the church owing to the discord attributed to the two.[83] On the other hand, Lydia's readiness to place her home at the disposal of the apostles and other Christians immediately after her conversion (Acts 16: 15, 40) made her a model for the Philippian woman just as Paul had presented himself and other Christians as exemplars of Christian life.[84]

Finally, besides its historical value to the audience this account might have had a spiritually beneficial effect on them, since Luke presented the teaching which could also be found in Paul's letter in an easily comprehended way by the use of dramatic episodes,[85] for instance, the exorcism of the demon (Acts 16: 18) and the release from the prison through an earthquake (Acts 16: 26), thus illustrating the superiority of Christ as an absolute ruler over pagan deities and Roman authorities.

7.6 SUMMARY

Luke did not directly address women in his works, but, nevertheless, they are present in a remarkable way as he used them in the many aspects of their lives to illustrate his message. Although Luke suggests that his audience had some Jewish conceptual framework, Luke-Acts was attractive to pagan women as well because of its social message and its superficial similarity to the Hellenistic romances. From a religious point of view, on the other hand, the audiences' understanding of Luke-Acts differed according to their religious backgrounds. For pagan and newly-converted women it persuaded principally through the picture of Christ's absolute power and of Christianity as a religion of world-wide geographical and social importance. For Christian women of the second generation, Luke's double work had an edifying effect since it served as a commentary to Paul's letter and provided a collection of examples of Christian teaching. Also, they found their different roles in the church

---

[81] Phil. 4: 2-3.

[82] As regards the presence of Judaism in Philippi the sources do not agree. To the receivers Luke's reference to a προσευχή (Acts 16: 13) corresponded to Paul's attack on the Jews advocating circumcision (Phil.3: 2), and Paul's warning about the Jews was confirmed by Luke's accusation that they incited distinguished women in Antioch in Pisidia to turn against Paul (Acts 13: 50). The archaeological sources, on the other hand, show no traces of Judaism: neither remains of a synagogue nor inscriptions have been found. Therefore, it seems reasonable to assume that there was only a small number of Jews in Philippi (cf. 3.7.1.3 and n. 146, p. 73).

[83] Phil. 4: 2.

[84] Phil. 3: 17.

[85] Plümacher 1972, 95ff.

(as defined in the Gospel) illustrated in Acts through model figures portrayed by Luke, and he also tried to establish women's credibility in order to equate them to men in teaching the gospel.

As regards the Philippian episode we may state that to both audiences the story in Acts of Paul's first visit to Philippi was noteworthy. Women who still retained a pagan conceptual framework received the events in conformity with the pattern of Euripides' *Bacchanals*. To them Christ was a new Dionysus with absolute power over the other deities as well as over the Roman authorities, and Lydia became a typical example of a distinguished convert who was worthy of emulation. To women born into Christianity, on the other hand, this story gave historical evidence of the contribution of their mothers to the foundation of the church in Philippi. In this respect, Lydia embodied an ideal of unselfish Christian action which placed her among the exemplary Christians of Paul's letter.

8 PAGAN PHILIPPIAN WOMEN AND CHRISTIANITY

8.1 INTRODUCTION

As suggested by the title, this final chapter presents the quintessence of the present work and can be seen as a concluding summary to the book. After having read the New Testament texts through the eyes of pagan and converted Philippian women of two generations, I am now–making the most of the facts already given in the previous chapters–going to focus on the problems connected with pagan Philippian women's conversion to Christianity. However, since the texts relating directly to the Philippian church (the letters of Paul and Polycarp, and the Philippian episode in Acts) provide only a few facts dealing with the position of women within the community, they will be supplemented by information on the subject from other letters written by Paul[1] or in the Pauline tradition;[2] I also incorporate information from other scriptures (above all Clement's 1st letter[3]) which also deals with matters related to Philippi. As regards the interpretation of Christianity made by the pagans, Pliny's correspondence with the Emperor Trajan in combination with other pagan sources on the subject will give useful information.

In dealing with the problems of conversion, I shall first of all question the way in which the pagan cults (discussed in Chapter 4) announced themselves to Philippian women (8.2.1) and make a comparison with the

---

[1] In this respect Paul's letters to the Corinthians are most useful. Since the Corinthian church was a Pauline community influenced by Greek culture, the information on women given in these letters may be valid also for the Philippian church. For the practice of Christianity in the household the letter to the Colossians is used, since it contains a Pauline household code (3: 18-4: 1). The authorship of this letter is crucial. E. Schweizer (1982, 23f) holds that it has been written by someone in the 'Pauline school' and he even points to Timothy. J. Gnilka (1980*b*, 20ff) is essentially of the same opinion but does not go so far as Schweizer. According to L. Hartman (1985, 200f) it is reasonable to assume that in the 'Pauline school' there existed copies of letters, written by Paul for different purposes, to be used as patterns by his pupils.

[2] The Pastoral Epistles, from the beginning recognized as the work of Paul (Barrett 1963, 2), are used for the purpose since they are contemporaneous with the second-generation Philippian church (Barrett 1963, 2); even if their receivers are unknown (Barrett 1963, 2), the generally worded directions for Christian women can be considered valid for the Pauline tradition regarding the same area as the Philippian church.

[3] The letter is dated to the end of the 1st cent. A.D. (Vielhauer 1978, 540).

arrival of Christianity (8.2.2). Secondly, the appeal to pagan women of the Christian message, as it was preached by the first (8.2.2.1)–and second-generation Philippian church (8.2.2.2), will be considered. Thirdly, I discuss Philippian women's reaction to Christianity, and instead of enumerating a number of reasons for their conversion I will try to imagine how and to what extent Christianity changed their lives (8.3). Since the conflict, caused by a break with the old religion, would be greater and more easily perceived within a 'mixed marriage' and would be further increased by the demands of an organized and differentiated Christian community, my reconstruction will focus particularly on a married woman of intense religious conviction who converted to the second-generation Philippian church (8.3.4).

8.2 THE APPEAL OF THE PHILIPPIAN PAGAN CULTS AND THE APPEAL OF CHRISTIANITY

For women in antiquity there were two approaches to religion–by birth (2.2.1) and by marriage (2.3.1). They were automatically included in the domestic cult dedicated to the deities of the paternal family, but, in accordance with their religious hunger married women could choose to worship other deities as well (as is shown in Chapter 2), even if their husbands sometimes disapproved of their seemingly excessive religiosity (2.3.3.2). A Philippian woman's worship of a given deity was dependent on her need for divine help for a special purpose, but her choice of the proper cult could be further supported and determined by other factors, as will be shown in the following.

8.2.1 The Appeal of Pagan Philippian Cults

In Philippi the pagan cults announced their presence to women in a very tangible way. On the acropolis the votive reliefs and inscriptions dedicated to Diana testified to her ability of healing (4.2.2.2.1), and sick people waiting for help in the temple of the Egyptian gods were also reminded of Isis as a healing goddess (4.4.2.1). Furthermore, the daily service, the processions and the autumn festival (4.4.2.3.3) announced the existence of this cult which related particularly to the after-life. This aspect was also conspicuous in the rock carvings depicting women in close connection with the hunting goddess (4.2.2.3), and also in carvings showing the phallus (4.3.2), which symbolized the life-force of Dionysus and advertised the presence of mysteries dedicated to this deity (4.3.2.2). Evidence for the existence of a Dionysiac ecstatic cult was further presented by a little building in the area opposite the Via Egnatia (3.4.1.1). As well as these cults, which were of particular importance to Philippian women, there was the official cult where individual women participated through hymn-singing, worship and solemn processions (cf. 2.3.2.1). All these cults demanded many ritual observances, as did the cult of the ancestors which provided public ceremonies at funerals (cf. 2.2.1.2).

From all this we can deduce that the pagan cults announced themselves principally in a passive way by means of buildings, inscriptions and works of art[4] or by worship performed before the public. As well as these clearly visible aspects, the testimonies of Philippian women who recommended the deities they favoured to their sisters in trouble must not be forgotten. The praising of a well-tried god, the recollection of mythical stories appropriate to an individual case,[5] the fellowship of maenads (4.3.2.1.1) and the Isiac ceremony of mourning for Osiris (4.4.2.3.3), were important means of propagating pagan worship.[6] Furthermore, the latter satisfied the longing women had for fellowship outside the home.

8.2.2 The Appeal of Christianity to Pagan Philippian Women

Whilst the family-based recruitement to the ranks of the pagan cults and the rituals associated with the cults made an increase in membership easily observable, Christianity, on the other hand, offered scarcely any discernible signs whatsoever of its presence in the town. The picture of Paul's missionary work in Philippi, reported by Luke (Acts 16: 11-40) to include preaching, exorcism and even a miracle, may reflect a germ of historical truth, but its shaping may be due rather to Luke's representing Paul as a Christian hero[7] than to the way in which Christianity was actually spread throughout the Empire.[8] The ceremony of baptism, at this time seemingly performed outdoors in running water,[9] was the only indication of the existence of Christianity visible to outsiders; the Eucharist was celebrated indoors (cf. Acts 16: 40) by those who, after having been taught of Christian faith, were properly baptized (Acts 2: 41-42). For women in particular, the Christian message spread chiefly by word of mouth privately from one to another (cf. 2.2.1.1) and

---

4   Works of art as a means of teaching children pagan religion is discussed in 2.2.1.2.
5   Such mythological stories are quoted in Chapt. 4.
6   As regards children, the pagan religion learned by listening is discussed in 2.2.1.1.
7   Plümacher 1972, 101; 137. Cf. 6.1 and 7.1.
8   For example, we are never told that the Roman Christian community had a missionary foundation.
9   The prototype for baptism in running water was Jesus' baptism performed by John in the Jordan (Mk. 1: 9). Presumably the eunuch in Acts (8: 26-39) found some running water in the desert for his baptism. Didache (7: 1), dated to the beginning of the 2nd cent. and located to Egypt or Syria (Vielhauer 1978, 737), prescribes that baptism ought to be performed preferably in running water. In Philippi there was running water outside the eastern and western town gate (Map 3).

not through preaching performed in public places;[10] pagan Philippian women would be told of the power of Christ and of the existence of a Christian community by a next-door Christian wife or by some other means of contact with Christian women–for instance, in the market.[11] It goes without saying that Philippian Christian women, as reflected in Paul's letter (Phil. 4: 3), were anxious to bring as many pagan sisters as possible to Christianity before Christ's second coming (Phil. 4: 5; cf. 1: 6, 28). Their missionary work was facilitated by pagan women recognizing features in Christianity similar to those of their pagan cults, and this made the message easier to grasp. Furthermore, Christ might have seemed nearer to them than the pagan deities, since he had once shared their serving lot in his earthly existence as a human being in the guise of a slave.[12] In this respect the Father's action of sacrificing the Son (Phil. 2: 8) was understandable against their knowledge of the legal power of the paterfamilias (1.3.1).

8.2.2.1 The First-Generation Philippian Church

The first period of the Philippian church, characterized by missionary work and hard opposition to Christianity, is mirrored in Paul's letters [13] and also in the Philippian episode in Acts (16: 19-39), although in this case the perspective is that of a later generation. The community seems to have achieved a certain degree of organisation–Paul's letter (Phil. 1: 1) mentions 'bishops' and 'deacons'–which implies more than a few Christians in Philippi (6.2). Furthermore, Paul's addressing of two women, Syntyche and Euodia (Phil. 4: 2),[14] suggests a number of female converts to the Philippian church–women who had either followed the decision of their husbands[15] or who had converted to Christianity of their own will (cf. Acts 16: 15).[16] From Paul's letter we can further deduce that

---

[10] In his correspondance with Emperor Trajan (c. A.D. 111) Pliny (Ep. 10, 96, 9) characterizes Christianity as 'a contagious superstition'. Women seem to have had little opportunity to participate in public meetings; women of the higher classes were occupied inside their homes while poor women had to contribute to the maintenance of the family by working in various trades (1.5.1.1).

[11] Women's occupations outside the household are discussed in 1.5.1.

[12] Phil. 2: 7 and further discussed in 6.4.1. How easily women could identify themselves with this aspect of Christ is reflected in the quotation from the *Martyrs of Lyons* made in p. 196.

[13] Phil. passim, and 1 Thess. 2: 2.

[14] It is possible that these women had reached the position of deacons (Lohfink 1983, 326).

[15] This group of Philippian Christian women is exemplified by the gaoler's wife, who is said to have been converted together with her husband's family (Acts 16: 33).

[16] Lydia is a Philippian model figure for a single woman presiding over her household, and she is said to have made decisions regarding religious matters affecting its members. However, she was not legally entitled to make such decisions, since a women could not found a family (1.3.1, p. 15 n. 51).

a feeling of fear and a presentiment of persecution by the Roman authorities lay heavily on the Philippian church (Phil. 1: 30).

This threatening danger might have accentuated to the receivers (and accordingly also to pagan women who talked to their Christian sisters) the message of the heavenly Kingdom, the citizenship of which would be realized in a short time through a share in the body of Christ.[17] Moreover, it is reasonable to assume that the teaching that Christ had dominion over Heaven and the Underworld, as well as over things earthly,[18] was equally attractive to Christian women and to the pagan Philippian women to whom they talked. It ensured for them and their children more than emotional security against the catastrophes of this life:[19] it offered a blessed existence in the after-life.[20] Finally, the equality of status with men (Gal. 3: 28) that women obtained through baptism,[21] as well as their promised assumption of Christ's glorious body in a future life,[22] might have been a powerful argument for conversion to Christianity.

In addition, against their religious background pagan Philippian women would easily assimilate this joyful news, supplied to them by Christian sisters and confirmed by Paul's message. The tales about Uranopolis, the 'City of Heaven' founded on Mount Athos (6.7), made the idea of a citizenship of Heaven easy to grasp. Further, Dionysus' transferring of Semele from Hades to Olympus (4.3.2.3.2), and also Hercules' rescuing of Alcestis (4.3.2.3.4) supplied the mythical pattern for their understanding of Christ's bringing of Christian women to his heavenly Kingdom.[23] Further, the share in the glorious body of Christ was understandable to them in various ways. The transmutation of worshippers into a deity, uniting as it did male and female into one form, was known to them from their previous cults: the portrayal of Diana in the shape of an armed hunting goddess in male dress, as depicted in the rock carvings (4.2.2.3), and the idea of taking on the being of Osiris in the after-life (4.4.2.3.3) pointed in the same direction. In addition, the epithets attributing androgynistic qualities to Dionysus (4.3.2.3.5), and–above all–the experience women had of having Dionysiac possession within their bodies, as is described by Euripides in the

---

[17] Phil. 4: 5; 3:21. See also 6.5.

[18] Phil. 2: 10-11. The theme is also discussed in 6.4.2.

[19] The high death rates of married women and children are discussed in 1.2.3 and 1.2.2.

[20] The attraction of the mystery religions, similarly promising a happy existence after death, is discussed in 2.3.3.1.

[21] H. D. Betz (1979, 189f) is of the opinion that Gal. 3: 28 is to be seen as a liturgical formula from baptism. The 'one- in- Christ' formula had social and political implications (Meeks 1974, 180f), and in the Christian church the sex distinctions between male and female had lost their significance (Betz 1979, 195). The sexes are named in neuter which indicates that both social and biological distinctions between male and female are involved (Betz 1979, 195).

[22] Phil. 3: 20. Further considered in 6.5.

[23] Phil. 3: 21. See also 6.5.

Bacchanals (4.3.2.1.2), prepared the way for Philippian women's understanding of Paul's promise that they would be refashioned into the form of Christ.[24]

8.2.2.2 The Second-Generation Philippian Church

For this period[25] Polycarp's letter is our only source directly related to the Philippian church;[26] besides this letter, however, Luke-Acts and the Pastoral Epistles[27] will be used for illustrating female roles as they existed in the second-generation Philippian church.[28]

From Polycarp's letter it is clear that Philippian women who converted to Christianity at that time found an organized community with clearly defined female roles. Women of three categories are mentioned: unmarried women, wives and widows. Regarding wives and widows, they were allotted certain tasks in the spreading of the gospel (cf. Phil. 4: 3): the wives were expected to teach their children of Christian faith (Polyc. 4: 2), and the widows to maintain the missionary work through their never-ceasing prayers (Polyc. 4: 3);[29] only the unmarried women had no appointed tasks according to this letter (Polyc. 5: 3).[30] The fact that women had gained such recognition in the Philippian church in the space of only one generation indicates that they

---

[24] This idea was anticipated in the' one-in- Christ' formula (Gal. 3: 28) Cf. n. 21 supra. According to H. D. Betz (1979, 197) the concept of an androgynous Christ-figure may lie in the background.

[25] Female members of the second-generation Philippian church could still have been in existence in the last decade of the 1st cent. and even possibly at the turn of the century, if we suggest about 30-35 years as an average length of life for females (cf.1.1, p. 9 n.2 and also 7.2, p. 157 n. 12).

[26] The letter is nowadays dated to the reign of Trajan (A.D. 98-117) (Schoedel 1967, 4).

[27] See n. 2 supra.

[28] Since Luke himself belonged to second-generation Christians (Vielhauer 1978, 407) his double-work reflects circumstances related to his own time, even if he describes the initial stage of Christianity; it is reasonable to assume not only that the female roles, mentioned in Acts, existed in his own church, but also that he claimed that what he reported was credible (Plümacher 1972, 137ff; van Unnik 1979, 37ff).

[29] There seem to have been two categories of widows in such a group—one supported by her own means or by relatives (see n. 75 infra) and another by the church (1 Tim. 5: 16). To be accepted as a widow of the church a woman had to be not less than sixty years old, faithful in marriage to one man and known for good deeds (1 Tim. 5: 9-10). The meaning of 'faithful in marriage to one man' is obscure (Barrett 1963, 58f). As regards the concept of 'univira' see 1.3.1.

[30] Polycarp mentions unmarried girls as a group but we do not know if they constituted an order similar to that of the widows, who devoted themselves to praying, as apparently was the case in the Smyrnean church (Ign. Smyrn. 13: 1). Neither Schoedel (1967) nor Paulsen (1985) deal with the question.

continued to convert to Christianity in spite of the persecution and martyrdom which still threatened the church.[31]

While the first-generation Philippian community to a great extent focused on Christ's second coming, as is reflected in Paul's letter (Phil. 3: 20-21),the second-generation church also took an interest in earthly matters. Apparently there existed some organized charity work in the first-generation community because of Paul's mentioning 'deacons' in his letter (Phil. 1: 1);[32] in the eschatological perspective, however, it might have been on a small scale and of little significance to individuals as a reason for conversion. At that time the charitable work of the Philippian church was carried out as part of the wider commitment of supporting the Christian community in Jerusalem (Rom. 15: 25-26). This might have discouraged women of 'mixed marriages' from adopting Christianity, since this contributing of money for such a purpose could have resulted in financial difficulties for them. (cf. 8.3.4.1.2).

The growing community of the second-generation Philippian church, on the other hand, was furnished with an established organization for charity inside the community, as is recorded in Polycarp's letter and reflected in Luke-Acts as applying to the church in general. The purely religious reasons for pagan women wishing to convert to Christianity might at that time have been activated by two motives directly associated with their earthly existence.[33] Polycarp (6: 1) urges the presbyter to care for poor widows[34] and children bereft of their parents;[35] in Acts (6: 1) poor widows are presented as being in need of help, and Dorcas is further said to have performed charitable work towards this group of women (Acts 9: 39). Besides needy widows the maintenance of divorced women and unmarried girls must have presented a social problem to the church, even though this is not mentioned by Luke. Since Christianity did not tolerate prostitution (1Cor. 6: 16-18), girls of poor families lost their hitherto usual means of support (1.5.1.3), and, consequently, had to remain in their parental homes beyond the age of marriage as a continuing financial burden on their families;[36] similarly, prostitutes who were converted to Christianity (the Philippian unmarried girls

---

[31] Polyc. 1: 1; 9:1; 13: 2 . See also 7.4.2.1. Furthermore, 1Clement (6: 2) mentions women who were cruelly martyred, and there are references to persecutions and imprisonment of women in Acts (8:3; 9:2). Luke, of course, reflects the circumstances prevailing in his own time (cf. n. 28 supra).

[32] The title διάκονος in the early church attached to members involved in charitable work (Lohmeyer 1953, 326). See also Dibelius 1937, 416f.

[33] For the straitened circumstances of poor women see particularly 1.2.3 and 3.4.1.1.

[34] The problems of poor widows are discussed in 1.5.1.3.

[35] Presumably a number of the orphans consisted of foundlings who were taken care of by the church. The problems of orphans are discussed in 1.2.1 and 1.3.2.2.

[36] Cf. 1 Cor. 7: 25-26. The marriageable age of girls is discussed in 1.2.3, p. 13 n. 30. In a later period, the bishop Ambrose (Virg. 1, 11, 58; 1, 11, 63-56) tells us that girls who wished to remain unmarried got into conflict with their parents (Dassmann 1986, 884). A Christian wife of a 'mixed marriage' was presumably not able to prevent her pagan husband from giving away a daughter in marriage (cf. 1.3.1).

mentioned by Polycarp (5: 3) might partly have belonged to this group) had to look for other means of support, and this was also true for Christian women who had been divorced by pagan husbands (cf. 1Cor. 7: 15) and who lacked sufficient means of support through a dowry (1.5.1.1).Since women had little chance of supporting themselves outside marriage (1.5.1), the church undertook the task of maintaining these groups of women[37]–as may be illustrated in Luke's picture of the fellowship of the ideal Christian community (7.4.1.2)–and presumably entrusted to them some tasks within the church.[38]

The fellowship of the Christian community–ritually expressed by the Eucharist[39] and in Paul's letter theologically strengthened by the idea of the 'citizenship of Heaven' (Phil. 3: 20)–might have been of importance to the spread of Christianity among Philippian women and have presented itself as yet another reason for conversion. The breadth of this fellowship, as exemplified in Luke's account of Jesus' acceptance of the woman who was morally condemned by the Pharisees (Lk. 7: 36-50), must have been very attractive to those lonely and unhappy women with bad experiences of 'broken homes' (1.3.2). Likewise, it offered a haven for those religiously discriminated against for family reasons[40] and for those who were rejected by society.[41] Particularly appealing must have been the fact that low social status seems not to have been an obstacle to those seeking a position in the Christian community.[42] Thus, for this later period of the Philippian church we can assume that not only the news of the joyful message, but also the reports of economic and social advantages offered by the community might have attracted Philippian women to Christianity.

Furthermore, the adoption of Christianity by second-generation woman converts was facilitated by Luke's presentation to them of female model figures for Christian action. To some extent these patterns were

---

[37] This is confirmed by John Chrysostom mentioning specifically widows and virgins as being among the poor who were supported by the Antiochenian church: '[- - -] consider how many widows it succours every day, how many virgins; for indeed the list of them hath already reached unto the number of three thousand'. (Chrys. Hom.in Matth. 66, 3. Transl. G. Prevost & M. B. Riddle). This information is valid for the fourth-century Antiochian church, but the problem might have been common to all Christian communities also in earlier periods.

[38] Lucian (Peregr.12) tells us that old women and orphans came to visit Peregrinus in prison. They might have been engaged in some charitable work in the service of the Christian community.

[39] Acts 2: 42 (Schneider 1980, 286).

[40] For such discrimination against children see 2.2.1.3.

[41] As regards those women see 1.5.1.2 and 1.5.1.3. Their favourable reception in the Christian church may be reflected in Clement's letter. In it a comparison is made between Lot's disloyal wife and Rahab, who was a prostitute.The latter is praised for her faith and she is even entrusted with the gift of prophesy (1Clem. 11-12).

[42] Pliny (Ep. 10, 96, 8) mentions two slave girls who are said to be deaconesses. Priestesses in the pagan cults are discussed in 2.3.2.2 and 2.3.4.2. In the Philippian inscriptions priestesses are mentioned in the imperial cult (3.4.1.3) and in the cult of Diana (4.2.2.2.2).

recognizable to Philippian women from the mythical figures of their previous pagan cults: Isis in her role as mother (4.4.2.3.2) was replaced by Mary (7.4.1.1)–even if Luke (2: 19) presents Mary as a model of Christian discipleship in general[43] rather than as a mother–and the imperative imposed upon the unmarried girls of the community to preserve their chastity (Polyc. 5: 3) was natural for previous worshippers of Diana.[44] In this early period, however, Christianity, still coloured by eschatological expectations,[45] reduced for Philippian women the opportunities they had for identifying themselves with mythical figures which reflected the specifically feminine aspects of the life they encountered in their day-to-day existence. These mythical figures (presented in Chapter 4), and also the figures of deceased female ancestors (cf. 2.2.1.2),[46] previously imitated by Philippian female converts, were principally associated with the roles of childbearing and motherhood. Christ, on the other hand, being the most important figure for converted Philippian women (6.4.1), united the concept of male and female,[47] and, consequently, distanced women from the female role associated with the duty of procreation; similarly, the female model figures, presented by Luke in Acts, were all in some way or other associated with service to the church,[48] and, furthermore, in the Gospel Jesus is said to place low value upon domestic duties (Lk. 10: 41-42). Even if Luke's 'snapshots' of women performing various female tasks (7.3.2) would inevitably catch the interest of female recipients they did not, however, offer full patterns of identification to Christian women for everyday life in their households.

8.3 CHRISTIANITY IN THE LIFE OF A PHILIPPIAN MARRIED WOMAN CONVERTED TO THE SECOND-GENERATION CHURCH

To a Christian woman, conversion to Christianity brought membership of a community whose structure was analogous to that of her own

---

[43] See 7.4.2 , p. 166 n. 49.

[44] See 4.2.2.4 n. 85, p. 94f. Besides converted girls of poor pagan families, otherwise destined to prostitution (1.5.1.3), these group of unmarried Philippian girls, mentioned by Polycarp (5: 3), might have consisted of girls born into Christianity by converted parents who, in the eschatological perspective (1Cor. 7: 25-26), had been hesitating to give their daughters away in marriage. Cf. n. 36 supra.

[45] As to Paul, R. Scroggs (1972, 302) holds the view, that, in the eschatological perspective, the Apostle is asserting the freedom and equality of women.

[46] In a later period they were replaced by female martyrs and saints, offering patterns of identification for Christian women (Lucius 1904, 34ff).

[47] To Philippian women this concept was expressed in the idea of their future share in the body of Christ (Phil. 3: 21). Cf. n. 24 supra.

[48] Also 1Clement (55, 3-6), describing the deeds of Judith and Esther, offers female model figures characterized by a male acting.

household, though its size was immesurably greater and it was governed by God (1Tim. 3: 15). Just as Philippian families were regulated by accepted forms and rules inherited from paternal ancestors (2.3.1), so members of the divine household were governed by rules based on the Commandments.

Following as they did the Christian idea of equality,[49] which saw no intrinsic difference between male and female, slave and freeborn,[50] these new rules, preserved in the so-called household codes, stripped from the head of the Philippian family the power of life and death over his household. Discrimination by means of social status and allotted task continued to exist, and in these areas the sway of the male head remained paramount. Tensions were inevitable as the two sets of rules were frequently in conflict[51]—nowhere more noticeable so than in the case of the first Christian Commandment which prohibited worship of the ancient gods. Women belonging to Christian families opposed the external pagan environment but received support from their immediate kin: their Christian sisters in pagan families, however, were less fortunate as the struggle for them had to be faced within as well as outside their homes.

In discussing this aspect, I shall first give a short survey of congregational Christian worship (8.3.1) (common to all categories of Philippian women), partly by reconstructing the contents of the New Testament text and partly by drawing upon Pliny's letter. Secondly, I shall consider the worship privately performed by a woman of a Christian family (8.3.2) and shall note the strain imposed by that family's relationship to the pagan families in the wider community (8.3.3). Thirdly, the worship privately performed by a Christian wife of a 'mixed marriage' will be considered (8.3.4), and, in addition, some conceivable reasons for conflict within a pagan family (8.3.4.1) will be suggested. Finally, some possible motives for her remaining a Christian will be discussed (8.3.4.2).

---

[49] This idea is expressed in Gal. 3: 28 (Lührmann 1981, 92).

[50] H. D. Betz (1979, 192ff) is of the opinion that this idea of equality on three levels, expressed in Gal. 3: 28, originally brought a politically revolutionary message (cf. n. 21 supra) which had to be internalized to avoid revolutionist movements. This internalization, reviving the ideal of the Roman family of the 'good old days' (1.3.1), is perceptible particularly in the admonitions of obedience to women and slaves in the household codes, for instance, Col. 3: 18 - 4: 5.

[51] As regards the household code addressed to the Colossians, a tension can be noticed in the letter between the new nature, the image of the Creator characterized by 'one in Christ' (Col. 3: 10-11; cf. Gal. 3: 28), and, on the other hand, the actions of subordination 'in Christ' demanded of wives (Col. 3: 18), children (Col. 3: 20) and slaves (Col. 3: 22). By this the author, to whom the subordinated positions of those groups were self-evident, placed the domestic duties in the wider context of the divine intention implied in the creation (cf. Col. 1: 15-20) (Hartman 1986, 167). D. Balch (1981) deals with the subordinated position of women in the domestic code in 1 Peter.

8.3.1 Congregational Christian Worship

Of those activities performed outside the home the ceremony of baptism has already been touched upon (8.2.2). Of public worship the *New Testament* tells us that the Christians met in the house of one of the members (Rom. 16: 5, 23 ; Col. 4: 15; Philem. 1: 2; Acts 16: 40; 2: 46) and greeted each other with a holy kiss (1Cor.16: 20).[52] The ceremony included reading from the Scriptures (2Tim. 3: 15) and also from letters addressed to the community (Col. 4: 16), praying (Acts 1: 14; 2: 42), singing psalms and hymns (Col. 3: 16), speaking in tongues and prophesying (1Cor.12:10; 14: 1) and, finally, partaking of the Eucharist (1Cor. 11: 20; Acts 2: 42).

The information given by Pliny confirms the *New Testament* but adds that the Christians used to gather once a week on a fixed day before daybreak, and he further mentions antiphonal hymn-singing[53] and the members swearing by oath not to perform evil deeds. This last reference probably alludes to their recital of the Commandments.[54] We are further told by Pliny that the Christians came together twice a day–possibly in order to partake of a second meal.[55]

Of these enumerated activities, solitarily performed by members of the community, we do not know how much was entrusted to women. Only praying and prophesying are mentioned by Paul in connection with women, who had to be veiled at such occasions (1Cor. 11: 5).[56] For the Philippian church it may be reasonable to assume that speaking in tongues was highly valued among women because of the strong position of the ecstatic Dionysiac cult in the colony (4.3.2.1.1).

8.3.2 Private Worship inside a Christian Household

According to Paul's teaching, the practice of Christianity in the daily life of a Philippian Christian woman involved her assuming the serving role of Christ, both in her family and in the Christian community.[57] In this

---

[52] The holy kiss might have been a cult act already at that time (Barrett 1968, 396; 398).

[53] Pliny Ep. 10, 96, 7. As to hymn-singing in the pagan official cult see 2.3.2.1.

[54] The Commandments were highly valued in the *New Testament* and in later scriptures (Grant 1947, 1ff). The idea, taken from Hellenistic Judaism by Paul, that the Law of God was essentially the same as the law of nature made possible the use of the Dekalogue in the early church and provided a basis for its understanding by Christians with pagan backgrounds (Grant 1947, 16).

[55] Pliny Ep. 10, 96 7. For common meals in the mystery religions see 2.3.3.2 and 4.3.2.2. Common meals were also a characteristic of the sect of the Therapeutae (Philo, De vit.cont. 64-82).

[56] In the Roman pagan cults males and females had to be veiled when praying and offering sacrifices; the model figures were Aeneas (Verg. Aen. 3, 405) and Numa (Ov. Fast. 3, 363) (v. Severus 1972, 1159).

[57] Phil. 2: 4-5. See also 6.4.1 and 7.4.2.1.

role she perpetuated Christian worship within her own household and propagated the gospel by communicating its message to her pagan sisters in the world outside. This latter cause she strengthened still further by the financial support she gave to missionaries. However, as mentioned above, the female figures presented by Luke in Acts offered her patterns of identification only in the service of the church. As regards further details of private worship inside the home practically nothing is known from this early period,[58] and, consequently, we have to rely on conjectures based on later sources.

8.3.2.1 Praying

It had been suggested that private Christian worship in the home reflected the public service[59] attended by members of the community in that it consisted principally of various kinds of prayers.[60] The Eucharist[61] can be seen as being of particular importance in developing prayers for the blessing of food. To Philippian Christian women with a pagan referential religious framework such a blessing of the food at the beginning of meals was familiar and could be seen as similar to the sacrifice performed by the children of the family to the deities of the hearth (2.2.1.3).[62]

Besides the blessing of the meals, it can be assumed that the Lord's prayer, known to them through Luke's Gospel and presumably also from Paul's teaching,[63] was of importance to Philippian Christian women.[64] According to Luke, Jesus himself taught his followers how to

---

[58] On the whole, the field of private worship for all periods of church history has hitherto been overlooked by scholars (Fischer 1974, 103).

[59] The public service of the early church followed the pattern of the synagogal service, the main part of which consisted of prayer and reading out of the Scriptures (Kalb 1982, 21).

[60] Fischer 1974, 104. For this early period it may be unwise to speculate on Christian customs regarding funerals and baptism of children.

[61] The Eucharist is to be seen as rooted in a Jewish tradition, it being the Berakah of the community for the redemption of Christ (Fischer 1974, 94).

[62] According to John Chrysostom (Expos.in ps. 41, 2), the members of a Christian family ought to sing hymns together after the meals and concludingly say a prayer for the househould (Fischer 1974, 105).

[63] Col. 3: 13. The wording of the exhortation to forgive one another alludes to the Lord's prayer (Gnilka 1980b, 196).

[64] The Lord's prayer became the standard prayer for all Christians (v. Severus 1972, 1173). Didache places the Lord's prayer (Chapt. 8) after the baptism (Chapt.7); from this Jeremias (1962, 6f) concludes that the Lord's prayer was said only by full members of the church. We do not know if there were any precepts regarding private praying at this time in the Philippian church. At a later period it is stated that a Christian ought to say the Lord's prayer three times a day (Did. 8, 3). John Chrysostom (Hom. 26 in Act.) expects Christian families to arise at midnight and pray together (Fischer 1974. 107). According to Tertullian (Ad ux. 2, 5), this

pray (Lk. 11: 2-4), and the Lord's prayer might have been the main daily prayer used alongside other occasional prayers (mentioned by Paul in Phil. 4: 6) the contents of which were determined not only by the hardships and troubles of the day but also by events which offered occasions for rejoicing.[65]

8.3.2.2 Teaching

Together with praying, a Philippian Christian wife was entrusted to teach her children of the Christian faith (Polyc. 4: 2),[66] acting as an intermediary between the Scriptures (which were read out to the community [1Tim. 4: 13]) and her own family. In the roles of learning and teaching Luke provided no less than three model figures: Mary, the mother of Christ (Lk. 2: 19), Mary, the sister of Martha and Lazarus (Lk. 10: 39-42), and, finally, Priscilla (Acts 18: 26). The two Maries personified the virtue of learning by listening, while Priscilla represented a Christian woman in a male role of teaching in the wider context of the church.[67]

As to teaching, it may be noted that, in contrast to pagan religion, Christianity, entirely dependent on oral teaching, lacked works of art (in all aspects) as an important means of communicating and illustrating its message[68]—obviously a pedagogical disadvantage, particularly when dealing with children. Finally, it must be remembered, that children (even at an early age) learned cultic action by participating in the meetings of the community[69] and also by saying prayers together with the members of the family (cf. 2.2.1.3).

---

nocturnal praying was used as an argument against 'mixed marriages' (Fischer 1974, 107).

[65] Daily praying in the domestic cult is discussed in 2.3.1.1, p. 45 n. 75, where two pagan prayers are quoted.

[66] In this respect a Christian nurse might have been an important medium for the spread of Christianity to a pagan family (cf. 2.2.1).

[67] In Corinth Aquila and Priscilla opened their home to the Christian community (1Cor. 16: 19).

[68] In this early period of Christianity Christian homes still retained all kinds of pagan decorations which in some cases could not easily be removed. Pagan motifs, however, could be given a symbolic interpretation to fit the Christian message, for instance the Thracian singer Orpheus was seen as Christ in his role of 'the good shepherd'; such an 'interpretatio Christiana' is evidenced in second-century wall paintings in the catacombs (Pfister 1924, 14f). Pagan wall paintings from the 2nd cent. A.D. can be seen in dwelling-houses inhabited by Christians, for instance, underneath the church of San Giovanni et Paolo in Rome (Henze 1981, 188f).

[69] Pliny (Ep. 10, 96, 2) mentions children among the people accused of being Christians. See also Min. Fel. Oct. 9, quoted in p.190.

8.3.2.3 Charitable Work

In addition to offering daily prayers and teaching children, a Philippian Christian wife was obliged to fulfil some duties of charitable work towards fellow Christians.[70] Accordingly, the role of housewife was widened to serve not only the immediate family, based on blood-relationship, but also brethren and sisters of the Christian community.[71] In the Pastoral Epistles we are told about various kinds of charitable work entrusted to a Christian wife (1Tim. 5: 10); she was expected to take care of children (presumably orphans[72]), to welcome travelling Christians into her home,[73] to help fellow Christians suffering affliction[74] and, finally, she was expected to take care of Christian widowed relatives (1Tim. 5: 16).[75]

The serving roles of Christian women in the larger community of the church are exemplified by Dorcas caring for poor widows (Acts 9:36,39), by Mary, the mother of John Mark, offering lodging to the Christian community in Jerusalem (Acts 12: 12), and, finally, by Lydia showing hospitality to Paul and to Philippian Christian brethren (Acts 16: 15, 40). Mary, the mother of Christ, on the other hand, in the broadened perspective of sharing the lot of the Twelve in Jerusalem together with a few other women, has no serving role but is said to share the same conditions as the men of the community (Acts 1: 14).

However, this spirit of philanthropy, also reflected in Luke's account of the life of the ideal Christian community in Jerusalem,[76] earned for the Christians a reputation for foolishness and credulity, as is shown by the following passage from Lucian:

---

[70] Some of these duties might have been entrusted to deacons (Phil. 1:1). See n. 32 supra. According to Polycarp's letter (6: 1), the presbyter was charged with looking after the sick and the poor. For pagan priestesses in assistance of the poor see 2.3.2.2 and 2.3.4.1.

[71] The nurturing of loving relationships among the members of the Christian community beyond the boundaries of marriage is further reflected in Polycarp's letter (4: 2): Philippian wives are requested to be' tenderly loving their husbands in all truth, and loving all others equally in all chastity' (Transl. K. Lake). The same exhortation is to be found also in 1Clem. 21: 7.

[72] Cf. n. 38 supra.

[73] Polycarp (14:1) recommends a woman to the Philippian community, which presumably implies that hospitality could be expected from the members of the church.

[74] According to Polycarp (1:1; 9:1; 13:2) Philippian Christians welcomed and took care of Ignatius and his fellow prisoners on their way to be martyred in Rome.

[75] According to Barrett (1963, 77f) it is reasonable to assume that widows who had relatives should not burden the resources of the community but be taken care of by their children and grandchildren. As regards the lot of poor pagan widows see 1.5.1.3.

[76] Acts 2:44-46; 4: 32-35. See also 7.4.1.2.

They despise all things and consider them common property, accepting such doctrines by faith alone. So if a cheater who is able to make a profit from the situation comes to them, he quickly becomes rich, laughing at the simple people.[77]

Consequently, the hospitality expected from a Philippian Christian family in imitation of Lydia (Acts 16: 15, 40) could easily be exploited, particularly by such travellers as pretended to be Christians[78] and became financial burdens on households and caused extra work for the women who attended to their needs.

8.3.3 Reasons for Conflict with the Pagan Environment

Besides running the risk of being financially exploited by outsiders, Christian families–and also Christian wives of 'mixed marriages'–were regarded with suspicion for several reasons. While experiences of hostility from other people would strengthen the concord of a Christian family, it would bring disharmony to a pagan household, and the Christian wife in these families would bear the brunt of the discord. In both cases it would be the children who would suffer most from the exceptional circumstance of their Christian upbringing.

8.3.3.1 The Imputed Immorality of Christians

In spite of the fact that Christianity in reality revived the idea of the Roman ideal wife (1.3.1), suspicions of immorality might still have been harboured against a Christian wife. Such rumours could easily grow under the influence of unreliable hersay reporting of the meetings of Christians (attended by both sexes) held early in the morning in private houses (8.3.1) and away from the public gaze.[79] In this respect, the Christian practice of greeting sisters and brethren with a holy kiss (8.3.1)[80] must have contributed greatly to the bad name of the Christians

---

[77] Lucian Peregr.13. Transl. A. M. Harmon.

[78] From the fact that Polycarp (14, 1) vouches for the authencity of a woman who was expected to come to Philippi, we can conclude that the second-generation Philippian church had problems with such travellers.

[79] The meetings of the Christians were not secret since outsiders seem to have had the opportunity to be present (cf. 1Cor. 14: 23) (Barrett 1968, 324f).

[80] S. Benko (1985, 98) is of the opinion that the holy kiss not only symbolized the unity in the church of Christ but was related to the same idea of attaining life which was attributed to the pagan holy marriage. In my opinion, however, the holy kiss may rather be associated with the baptismal formula (Gal. 3: 28) and be seen as prefigurating the future androgynous unity in Christ promised to his followers (Phil. 3: 21). Cf. n. 24 supra.

and have affected particularly the wife of a 'mixed marriage'.[81] The following passage gives us an idea of the general opinion of the Christians in Rome, held by the senatorial class:[82]

On the day appointed they gather at a banquet with all their children, sisters, and mothers, people of either sex and every age. There, after full feasting,[83] when the blood is heated, and drink has inflamed the passions of incestuous lust, a dog which has been tied to a lamp is tempted by a morsel thrown beyond the range of his tether to bound forward with a rush. The tale-telling light is upset and extinguished, and in the shameless dark lustful embraces are indiscriminately exchanged; and all alike, if not in act, yet by complicity, are involved in incest, as anything that occurs by the act of individuals result from the common intention'.[84]

According to this text, which depicts in vivid colours a distorted account of a Christian meeting, children are said to participate in the licentiousness of their parents; it is easy to imagine that such rumours might have caused suffering to Christian children, making them targets for suspicious in the eyes of the pagan parents of their playmates.[85]

8.3.3.2   Fear of the 'Name'

According to Pliny and other sources, Christianity was said to be a kind of superstition.[86] In the minds of Philippian outsiders with some hazy ideas of the contents of Paul's letter and Luke-Acts this superstition might have been to a great extent associated with the name of Christ: pagan husbands reported their Christian wives as praying aloud 'hallowed be thy name' (8.3.2.1),[87] although this prayer actually referred to the name of the Father (Lk. 11: 2); in Paul's letter (Phil. 2: 9-11) the

---

[81] The frequent admonitions in the household code regarding the behaviour of Christian women (e.g. Col. 3: 18) might in part have been rooted in an awareness of their exposed position in the pagan environment.

[82] The contents of this quotation may be compared to the criticism of the mystery religions quoted in 2.3.3.2.

[83] From Pliny (Ep. 10, 96, 7) we can deduce that the Christians were said to eat dangerous and shameful food at their meetings—a fact that he refuted after having tortured two Christian slave girls.

[84] Min. Fel. Oct. 9. Transl. G. H. Rendall. This section is thought to be a quotation from a speech, made about A.D. 150 by M. Cornelius Fronto who was a teacher of Marcus Aurelius, against the Christians; it reflects a common view of the behaviour of the Christians (Frend, 1965, 251f) which may also be valid for the general opinion held by pagans in Philippi about 50 years earlier.

[85] According to the Apostolical Constitutiones (4, 11) (4th cent. A.D.), Christian children were not allowed to play with pagan playmates in order not to learn idleness and vices from them (Dassmann 1986, 882).

[86] Pliny Ep. 10, 96, 9; Tac. Ann. 15, 44, 2-8; Suet. Ner. 16. Cf. the quotations in 2.3.3.2.

[87] The Lord's prayer was regarded with fear and awe also by the Christians (Jeremias 1962, 7); they used to say it three times a day (Did. 8, 3).

name of Christ was further said to dominate the whole cosmos (6.4.2). Such a power, however, implied control over all other divinities and demons—as was demonstrated by Paul exorcising the demon from the Philippian girl (Acts 16: 18)—and, consequently, calling upon the name of Christ could be understood as a means of invoking magic. The speaking in tongues (8.3.1) might have strengthened the suspicion that Christians used magic since this incoherent way of talking could be interpreted as curses controlling divine powers.[88] The name of Christ, however, could be used for healing—Peter healed a lame man (Acts 3: 2-7)—as well as for 'black magic':[89] Paul is said to have blinded the magician Elymas for a time in the name of Christ (Acts 13: 6-12), and also the 'invocation of death' in the story of Ananias and Sappheira [Acts 5: 4-5; 9-10]) gave evidence for such suspicions. Since it was particularly the women who used to devote themselves to magic of various kinds (cf. 2.3.4.2), a Philippian Christian wife could easily be accused of being a sorceress. The making of magic was regarded as illegal according to the law,[90] which is why such an accusation would be disastrous, not only for the wife herself but for the whole family whose activities would be viewed as criminal.

8.3.3.3 Fear of the 'Kingdom'

However, the name of Christ was not only related to magic in the eyes of outsiders, but was also associated with the idea of a new social order. The correspondence between Pliny and the Emperor Trajan makes clear that the mere name of 'Christian' was sufficient for the followers of Christ to be accused of being a danger to society.[91] Their only crime was said to be their refusal to sacrifice to the pagan deities;[92] such a refusal,

---

[88] In writing, such a confusion of seemingly meaningless syllables are known to us through the Greek magical papyri. Paul was aware of the danger that the speaking in tongues could easily be misunderstood by the pagans (1Cor. 14: 23).

[89] Tertullian (Ad ux. 2.5) advised against the marriage of a Christian woman to a pagan husband because of her putting the sign of the cross over her bed and over herself; he could misinterpret this as a form of magic (Dassmann 1986, 874). Later on, Christians had the reputation for disrupting pagan ceremonies by their mere presence, which is said to have caused the persecutions of the Christians under Valerian (Euseb. Hist. Eccl. 7, 10: 3-4) and under Diocletian (Lactant. De mort.persecut. 10) (Benko 1986, 874).

[90] According to Paulus (juridical author living in the 3rd cent. A.D.):'Persons who celebrate, or cause to be celebrated impious or nocturnal rites, so as to enchant, bewitch, or bind anyone, shall be crucified, or thrown to the wild beasts' (Sent. of Paul. 5, 23, 15. Transl. from Benko 1985, 129).

[91] Pliny Ep. 10, 97. The rumour of the Christians' causing of the fire in Rome and their punishing by Nero, as recorded by Tacitus (Ann. 15, 44) and Suetonius (Ner. 16, 2) might have contributed to the bad reputation of the Christians.

[92] According to Pliny (Ep. 10, 96, 5) the Christians could not be forced to invoke the pagan gods or to make sacrifice to them, and Polycarp, refusing to curse Christ

however, implied not only religious but also political and economic consequences for the security of the Empire. It goes without saying that, from a religious point of view, a refusal on a large scale to sacrifice to the official deities would disturb the 'pax deorum' and bring disaster to the Roman people.[93] Politically, the refusal to sacrifice to the emperor could further indicate that Christianity was a revolutionary movement,[94] and, finally, the abandonment by the Christians of the pagan cults obviously caused financial problems to various trades.[95]

Furthermore, a pagan Philippian husband with a Christian wife, subscribing to the idea of Christianity as a threat to society, might well have been frightened by his wife's seeming involvement with revolutionaries. Her daily prayer that 'thy kingdom come' (8.3.2.1) would give credence to his suspicions, and the fears he had would be shared by his relatives and business friends. Similar suspicions would, of course, be directed against Christian families. Consequently, it is easy to imagine friends and neighbours dissociating themselves from members of entirely Christian or 'mixed families' in order not to be suspected of Christian sympathies and involvement in activities dangerous to society.[96]

8.3.4 Private Christian Worship inside a Pagan Household

As mentioned above, there are good reasons to assume that Philippian Christian women were expected to offer up daily prayers in their homes (8.3.2.1) besides teaching their children of the Christian faith (8.3.2.2). While women of Christian families were charged with the carrying out of various works of charity (8.3.2.3), it is unlikely that the wife of a 'mixed marriage' would be expected to open her home to fellow Christians in the service of the church (cf. 6.2). This would have been seen as breaching the unity of a Roman family ruled by the paterfamilias (cf. 1.3.1) and

---

(Act. Mart.Polyc. 9, 3) provides a further example. As regards blasphemy against the deities of the domestic cult, jurisdiction seems to have been handed over to the paterfamilias (cf. n. 122 infra).

[93] Such an idea is expressed by Livy (6, 41) and also by Cicero (Marcell.18).

[94] This suspicion is reflected in Acts (17: 5-7) when Paul is accused by the Thessalonian Jews of 'acting against the decrees of Caesar'. Such ideas of equality, as expressed in Gal. 3: 28, could easily have strengthened the concept of Christianity as a revolutionist movement (cf. n. 21 and 50 supra).

[95] According to Pliny (Ep. 10, 96, 10) the butchers complained of financial difficulties owing to the Christians' refusal to sacrifice. Such economic problems relating to a pagan cult are further illustrated by Luke's report on the upheaval of the Ephesian silversmiths (Acts 19: 23-40).

[96] We are told by Pliny (Ep. 10, 96, 5) that accusations of being a Christian were anonymously made by a placard pointing out many suspected persons by name. Trajan, however, did not accept such information without the name of the accuser (Pliny Ep. 10, 97, 2).

could have provoked greater antipathy towards Christianity on the part of the pagans. In spite of this concession, there were still reasons for a pagan Philippian husband to be disapproving of his wife's commitment to the Christian community.

8.3.4.1 Reasons for Conflict in a 'Mixed Marriage'

Since Christianity claimed to be the only religion of its followers (1Cor. 8: 6) and further denied idolatry (1Cor.10:14), the conversion of a Philippian woman demanded the forswearing of the worship of her previous deities, including those of her husband's household (2.3.1.1). Accordingly, to a wife of a 'mixed marriage' (and also to a widowed or divorced woman with grown-up children who were still pagans[97]) the change of religion would bring in its train conflict of various kinds, particularly if she happened to be a stepmother (cf. 1.3.2.1). In the following some possible charges which could be brought by members of a pagan family against a Christian wife will be considered.

8.3.4.1.1 *Christian Education of Children*

The pressure upon a Christian wife to bring up her children in the faith could easily become a source of discord between the spouses of a 'mixed marriage'. According to Paul's teaching, the children of a Christian wife and a pagan husband were regarded as being sanctified through the parent who was Christian (1Cor. 7: 14),[98] and this might have implied a duty to teach them of the Christian faith. By ancient custom the religious training of children was entrusted particularly to the mother (2.2.1.1), though the children themselves were regarded as belonging to the paternal family (1.3.1). From this it can be seen how sensitive would be the issue, with the mother seeing her duty to her husband being conflict with her duty to her church and with the whole weight of opposition of her husband and his family being directed against her. Although from a later period, a Christian wife's difficulties as regards her pagan husband in giving her son a Christian education may be illustrated by the writings of Augustine:

> Thus did I then believe, as also my mother and the whole house, except my father only; who did not for all this overthrow the power of my mother's piety in me, to the hindrance of my believing in Christ, although himself had not yet believed in him. For she by all means endeavored, that thou, my God, shouldst be my father, rather than he. And herein didst thou assist her to overcome her husband, to whom (though the better of

---

[97] If such a woman had young children they were implied in her household. Cf. n. 16 supra.

[98] The unbelieving party of a marriage was said to be consecrated through the Christian party of either sex (Weiss 1910, 180; Jeremias 1958, 52f; Wendland 1968, 58; Cullman 1948, 55ff).

the two) she continued her service; wherein she principally served thee, who commandedst her so to do.[99]

In addition, a wife's conversion would affect the financial position of the family, since abortion (1.2.3) and exposure of children (1.2.1) in all probability were forbidden to Christians;[100] in this respect, even one more girl, who had to be furnished with a dowry (1.5.1.1), would mean an economic burden on a family of slight economic resources.

8.3.4.1.2 Money Spent on Charity

There was yet another way in which a household's expenditure was adversely affected when a Philippian wife accepted Christianity. Husbands had long criticized their wives for wasting money on sacrifices to the pagan gods and for indulging in all kinds of expensive magic (2.3.3.2); Christianity was to prove itself no more acceptable in this respect than the ancient cults, and Christian women continued their previous pattern of giving by their generosity to their new religion. According to the Emperor Julian, Christian wives were renowned for their readiness to make financial sacrifices for charity in the service of the church. This was in contradistinction to their husbands who continued to adhere to the old pagan religion and whose parsimony did not go unremarked:

> But as it is, every one of you allows his wife to carry everything out of his house to the Galilaeans, and when your wives feed the poor at your expense they inspire a great admiration for godlessness (i.e. Christianity) in those who are in need of such bounty—and of such sort are, I think, the great majority of mankind,—while as for yourselves you think that you are doing nothing out of the way when in the first place you are careless of the honours due to the gods, and not one of those in need goes near the temples—for there is nothing there, I think, to feed them with [- - -][101]

From this text we learn that Christian wives of 'mixed marriages' used to support poor people from the housekeeping money of the family,[102]

---

[99] August. Conf. 1, 11. Transl. W. Watts.

[100] Abortion and exposure of children are not mentioned in the *New Testament*, presumably since a prohibition was self-evident to Christians. On the other hand, Jewish scriptures from the 2nd cent. B.C. (Köster 1980, 269; 282), addressed to pagans such as the *Sibylline Oracles* (3: 765-766), and possibly also the letter of Aristeas (248), condemned these matters. As regards Christianity, abortion and exposure of children are first mentioned in the letter of Barnabas (19:5), in Didache (2:2) and in the epistle to Diognetus (5, 6), all three dating to the 2nd cent. A.D. (Vielhauer 1978, 5; 611; 735).

[101] Julian Mis. 363A. Transl. W.C. Wright. Cf. Ar. Plut. 593-597.

[102] In contrast to other Pauline communities the Philippians were committed to giving Paul financial support (Phil. 4: 14-15), and he praises the Macedonian communities for their readiness to make sacrifices (2Cor. 8: 1-4). Cf. Strab. 297 quoted in p. 55.

even if, as suggested above, they were exempt from the duty of welcoming fellow Christians into their homes (8.3.4). Furthermore, the Emperor's reproaching of pagan husbands for neglecting the needs of the poor underlines the difference between the pagan cults, with their formalized religious observances,[103] and Christianity which expresses itself through acts of mercy towards other people. This difference is probably why Philippian pagan husbands could blame their Christian wives for spending money to support poor fellow Christians.

8.3.4.2 A Christian Wife's Endurance in a Pagan Family

Against this background it is clear that a Philippian Christian wife could become a troublesome embarrassment to a pagan husband. Viewed from the wife's standpoint, however, the position became intolerable as, in many cases, her struggle to uphold and spread the gospel turned her home into a battlefield. It is reasonable to assume, therefore, that many of these women, defeated by the suspicions of outsiders (8.3.3) and by the resistance of the family, either divorced their husbands[104] or were themselves divorced[105] or fell away from Christianity altogether.[106] According to Paul's teaching, however, a Christian wife was expected to remain in her marriage even if her adherence to Christianity brought discord between the spouses:[107]

> If any woman has a husband who is an unbeliever, and he consents to live with her, she should not divorce him (1Cor. 7: 13).

Her pagan husband, on the other hand, could apply for a divorce:

---

[103] The need for ritual observances in Roman religion is portrayed in caricature by Lucretius (5, 1198ff) and Theophrastus (Char. 16). However, to a lesser degree charitable work was performed in the temples (2.3.4.1) and also by priestesses of the official cult (2.3.2.2).

[104] Justin (Apol. 2, 2) mentions a Christian wife who, following the advice of her friends, tried to endure in her marriage with an intemperate pagan husband; at last, however, she could not remain with him any longer and gave him a bill of divorce.

[105] This may be reflected in 1Clem. (6:3): 'Jealousy has estranged wives from husbands, and made of no effect the saying of our father Adam,"this is now bone of my bone and flesh of my flesh". (Transl. K. Lake). As regards pagans, a wife of a marriage 'sine manus' could divorce her husband (See 1.3.2, p. 18 n. 66).

[106] Pliny (Ep. 10, 96, 6) tells us of people who had apostatized from Christianity.

[107] A marriage between Christians was lifelong according to the teaching of Jesus (1 Cor. 7:10), and, consequently, the matter could not be further discussed (Wendland 1968, 57; Niederwimmer 1975, 98ff). In reality, this revived the pagan 'manus marriage' (see 1.3.2, p. 18 n. 66) as regards divorce. In such a marriage a husband could divorce his wife but she could not divorce him (Gardner 1986, 83).

> But if the unbelieving partner desires to separate, let it be so; in such a case the brother or sister is not bound (1Cor. 7: 15).[108]

It is not remarkable, therefore, that Paul, apparently well aware of the difficulties of such a relationship, recommends a widow to choose a Christian when remarrying (1Cor. 7: 39-40).

It is reasonable to assume, however, that many Christian women followed Paul's teaching and succeeded in saving their marriages,[109] and, therefore, it is legitimate to ask how they gained enough strength to remain Christians and even to convert their families (cf. 1Cor.7:16). The remainder of this chapter, will, therefore, be devoted to a consideration of how these women, standing alone as Christians in pagan families, might have succeeded in maintaining their faith.

8.3.4.2.1 Suffering as a Part of Christian Life

Compared with Christian women of other Pauline communities, those belonging to the Philippian church were exceptionally well prepared by Paul's teaching for afflictions to come in their earthly lives. In his letter, suffering is accentuated as a part of Christian life through the imitation of Christ.[110] A Christian woman had to share in Christ's suffering in order to be able to realize citizenship of his Kingdom after death.[111] How strongly this idea affected Christians of the early church is shown in the *Martyrs of Lyons*, where a woman is seen as representing the crucified Lord:

> Blandina was hung on a post and exposed as bait for the wild animals that were let loose on her. She seemed to hang there in the form of a cross, and by her fervent prayer she aroused intense enthusiasm in those who were undergoing their ordeal, for in their torment with their physical eyes they saw in the person of their sister him who was crucified for them, that he might convince all who believe in him that all who suffer for Christ's glory will have eternal fellowship in the living god.[112]

Besides Paul's letter, Luke-Acts prepared Christian women for various kinds of suffering. In Acts, Luke tells of Christian women who were persecuted and even imprisoned,[113] and Philippian women were also reminded of the imprisonment of Paul and his companions in their own town (Acts 16: 23-39). Finally, what might have been of importance to a woman of a 'mixed marriage' was Luke's report in his Gospel (12: 52-53) of distress caused by divisions inside the family:

---

[108] Niederwimmer 1975, 104ff; Yarbrough 1984, 112.
[109] Cf. August. Conf. 1, 11, quoted in p. 193f.
[110] Phil. 2: 5. See also 6.4.1 and 6.4.1.1.
[111] Phil. 3: 10-11. Further discussed in 6.5.
[112] Mart. Lyon. 41. Transl. H. Musurillo. This act is dated to the year A.D. 177 under Marcus Aurelius and Lucius Verus (Musurillo 1979, p. XX).
[113] Acts 8:3; 22: 4. See also 7.4.2. Cf. n. 28 supra.

[- - -] for henceforth in one house there will be five divided, three against two and two against three; they will be divided, father against son and son against father, mother against daughter and daughter against her mother, mother-in-law against her daughter-in-law and daughter-in -law against her mother-in-law.

8.3.4.2.2 *The Transience of Suffering*

As well as the knowledge that hardship and trouble are inescapable concomitants of the Christian life, the eschatological perspective (as expressed in Paul's letter) must have offered consolation to Philippian Christian women—particularly those of 'mixed marriages'. According to Paul, the struggle for Christianity would come to an end when, before long (Phil. 4: 5), Christ would realize his Kingdom (Phil. 3: 20-21); in Acts (14:22) tribulation is said to be the way by which Christians will enter the Kingdom of God.

In addition, the promised citizenship of Heaven (to be marked by Christ's transforming of our vile bodies into his likeness [Phil. 3: 21]) would give reality to the hitherto metaphorical equality of male and female expressed in the 'one- in- Christ' formula (Gal. 3: 28).[114] The idea of equality between the sexes was also to be found in the philosophy of the time;[115] thus the current climate of thought was favourable to the reception of this new concept. Consequently, to a Christian wife, who was acquainted with such ideas, the consciousness of her intrinsic parity of status with the head of her family—a position confirmed by Christianity—might have been a source of great secret joy to her and must have given strength to her ability to endure in a pagan family.[116]

8.3.4.2.3 *Converting the Family*

The expectation of an early realization of the Kingdom of Christ offered yet another motive for a Philippian Christian woman to endure in her marriage. The wording of Paul's exhortation that she participate in the battle for the gospel[117] implied that her share in the missionary work was to operate on two levels. On the one, her financial support was

---

[114] See n. 50 supra.

[115] Particularly the Stoic philosopher Musonius Rufus held the opinion that males and females have the same natural inclination toward virtue and the same capacity for acquiring it (see 1.5.2 n. 151, p. 31).

[116] The message of equality between the sexes, as is expressed in the 'one- in- Christ' formula (Gal. 3: 28) (cf. n. 50 supra) and confirming similar ideas found in philosophical writings (n. 115 supra), could well have contributed to the conversion of women acquainted with these philosophical ideas.

[117] Phil. 1: 27-30. See also 6.3.1.

required for those apostles who worked abroad to spread the gospel,[118] and, on the other, her involvement in the domestic field was demanded (cf. Phil. 1: 6, 27- 28).[119] She was thus expected to convert her husband,[120] and of course also the other members of her family, in order that they might share in the citizenship of Heaven before the coming of Christ (Phil. 3: 20). In the battle for Christianity she was entrusted with bringing them the good news of 'a living God who made the heaven and the earth and the sea and all that is in them' (Acts 14: 15),turning them from the worshipping of dead idols (1Cor. 10: 14; 12: 2; 2Cor. 6: 16).

It is recorded that some women were accused of blasphemy because of their refusal to participate in the official cult,[121] though we never hear of anyone being accused of offending the household gods. The reason for this may be that such conduct would have been considered as a domestic affair to be settled within the confines of the family.[122] Alternatively, a Christian wife could have continued to act as priestess of the household[123] in order to keep the domestic peace while seeking to bring about a gradual conversion of her pagan family. Idols, according to Paul, had a subordinate existence (1Cor. 8: 5-6); sacrificing to them inside the family could be seen as similar to eating sacrificial meat, which was regarded as irrelevant to Christian faith in those cases where it gave no offence to fellow Christians (1Cor. 8: 8-9). By this behaviour she demonstrated her confidence in the superiority of Christ over the idols of the household, the power and influence of whom she completely denied (cf. 1Cor. 8: 5-6).

8.3.4.2.4 Share in the Fellowship of Christian Sisters

The external pressure on Christian households from the pagan environment and the tensions inside 'mixed families' might have brought Philippian Christian women of all categories closer together.[124]

---

[118] The 'partnership in the gospel', attributed to the Philippians (Phil. 1: 5), may allude to financial support of the missionary work (Gnilka 1980a, 45).

[119] As regards missionary work among pagan sisters, see 8.2.2.

[120] Cf. 1Cor. 7: 16. This passage is problematic, but there is reason to believe that Paul's meaning was to exhort Christians to remain married in order to convert their unbelieving spouses (Yarbrough 1984, 112).

[121] For instance, Pliny (Ep. 10, 96, 8) mentions two female slaves.

[122] Tacitus (Ann. 13, 32, 3-5) tells of a woman who was accused of practising a foreign religion. She was handed over to her husband's jurisdiction, and in accordance with ancient tradition he held an inquiry in the presence of the family council.

[123] According to Tertullian (De Idol. 16) a Christian wife was allowed by her church to participate in some family celebrations (ceremonies of the white toga, of espousals, of nuptials, and of name-givings) in spite of the pagan cultic actions on these occasions .

[124] Also female adherents of the pagan cults used to meet outside their homes. Rock carvings on the acropolis (4.2.4) appear to depict pagan Philippian women

As is illustrated by Luke in his Gospel (1: 58; 15: 9), women used to meet and share occasions for rejoicing; similarly, they might have shared their troubles and hardships.[125]

In this respect the wider female fellowship of the Christian community must have been of the utmost importance to women and female slaves living in pagan families. It is tempting to assume that, as well as praying, the widows of the Philippian church, mentioned in Polycarp's letter (4:3), took on the task of guiding the younger Christian wives by drawing upon their matronly authority (1.5.1.1) and experience of life (cf. Tit. 2: 3-5). Even if we have no sources confirming the existence of organized fellowships of Christian sisters in this period of early Christianity, it is safe to say that the opportunity was there for the exchanging of news and the sharing of happiness and sorrow. Paul in his letter (Phil. 4: 4) urged that joy be expressed, and on the occasion of the gratification of a prayer or, say, the conversion of a member of the family the need to share such joy would be particularly great for those women who lacked the support of a Christian family. Above all, however, the rejoicing together with Christian sisters at the prospect of the coming of Christ and their common future sharing in the haevenly Kingdom may well have been the main source of inspiration for Philippian Christian women of all categories in their struggle for the gospel both within and outside their families.

8.4 SUMMARY

From Paul's letter, addressed to the Philippian church, we conclude that Christianity, in its initial stages, attracted many pagan women, and a close investigation shows that a large part of the Christian message was easily accommodated within their existing religious referential framework. Christian women of the first-generation church turned their pagan sisters to Christianity principally by their telling of the joyful message of Christ's dominion over the cosmos and by the promise of a future blessed existence in his bodily likeness–already anticipated in the 'one-in-Christ'-formula which was expected to be speedily realized. As well as bringing these good tidings, the second-generation Philippian church provided financial and social benefits for the poor and deprived among its female converts and thus increased the attraction for Philippian women.

However, conversion could bring suffering of various kinds to a Christian wife and to her children. Wives and offspring of Christian families were principally exposed to external pressure from the pagan environment; for a wife of a 'mixed marriage', on the other hand, most difficulties emanated from a conflict between her loyalty to her husband's household and that to the wider household of the Christian

---

gathered for religious purposes, while inscriptions tell us of a fellowship of women within the Dionysiac ecstatic cult (4.3.2.1.1).

125 Such a case is mentioned by Justin. See n. 104 supra.

community. The two principal areas of discord were the disputes relating to the upbringing of the children and the financial outlay for charitable works. As was the case with women belonging to Christian families, those of 'mixed marriages' were also subjected to suspicions from outsiders that they participated in revolutionary activities and that they indulged in sexual escapades. Such imputations injured their reputations and added to the tensions they experienced in their pagan homes.

Nevertheless, to Philippian Christian women of all categories adherence to Christianity proved a source of overwhelming joy–a joy confirmed and strengthened by Paul's admonition and also by their share in the fellowship of Christian sisters. So great was this ecstasy that it set at naught the sufferings caused by the resistance to Christianity they met inside and outside their families. In the eschatological perspective, their lives and actions in the following of Christ became part of a cosmic drama which would end in eternal bliss; their afflictions, seen in this wide context, became not only acceptable but provided a guarantee of their forthcoming glorious transfiguration from their earthly female existence into the heavenly semblance of the male figure of Christ. Furthermore, in this period the eschatological aspect was further emphasized by the fact that the specifically female roles associated with childbirth and motherhood had no correspondence to the male model figure of Christ or to those women Luke described as being in the service of the church.

9 EPILOGUE

The present investigation is, as far as I know, the first attempt—not only in the field of literary criticism but also in that of New Testament exegesis—to reconstruct empirical receptors from historical sources of a remote past. As previously emphasized (Chapter 5), such a reconstruction is highly dependent on speculative judgement—hence the frequency of such expressions as 'presumably', 'possibly', 'there are reasons to assume', etc., which are to be found throughout this work—and is founded on an amalgamation of facts and possibilities. In this instance, however, even the facts underlying the possibilities are exposed to individualistic treatment, since there are no historical sources in the strict sense which account for the breakthrough of Christianity in Philippi. (Even if we were in possession of reliable sources, however, it is most likely that they would have been silent about the role of Philippian women in the struggle for Christianity, since ancient sources usually are silent about matters relating to the contribution of women in a male orientated world.)

Nevertheless, from the rather sparse material available we are able to glean some important facts, not only about pagan Philippian women who recieved Paul's Christian message, but also about the sender of the message, since an investigation of any communicative act cannot be confined to an examination of the recipients alone.

Surviving archaeological remains indicate that Philippian women showed a great interest in religious matters, and Paul's letter gives evidence that a number of them converted to Christianity at an early stage. Their immediate interest in Christianity can be evinced from the fact that Paul turned to them specifically (as shown in his addressing of Syntyche and Euodia by name [Phil. 4: 2], and by the account of his dialogue with Lydia and other women outside the town gate, as related by Luke [Acts 16: 13-15]) and by the fact (as shown in the present work) that they recognized some important features in the gospel as being similar to features of the pagan cults familiar to them. This recognition facilitated an interpretation of the Christian message for them.[1]

Paul, on his side, was well aware of the problems facing pagan women when converting to Christianity. This awareness is evident in his recommendation that a widow remarry only a Christian (1Cor. 7: 39-40) and also by his answer to the Corinthians regarding the eating of meat sacrificed to idols (1Cor. 8). (It goes without saying that the latter problem had reference specifically to Christian wives of 'mixed

---

1 Such a surviving pagan interpretation, relating to female adherents of the Dionysiac ecstatic cult and visible in the early Philippian Christian art, coloured the understanding of Christianity for at least about three centuries. This Dionysiac influence on the understanding of the Christian message in the Philippian church will be my subject for a coming article.

marriages'.) Paul's interest in women's conversion and in their commitment to the service of the church is further visible in various ways. His direct addressing of the Philippian women Syntyche and Euodia (Phil. 4: 2), his reference to Prisca (1Cor. 16: 19) and Chloe (1Cor. 1: 11) as hostesses in the Corinthian community, and his enumerating of females of various positions in his letters–particularly that to the Romans (16: 1-16)–reveal not only a good relationship between Paul and the women of the church, but also that they willingly supported him in his missionary work.[2] This is also reflected by Luke in his portrayal of women in the service of the Christian community (7.4.2.1).

To sum up, the picture of the Philippian female recipient of the *New Testament*, constructed by a reassembling of the fragmented accounts we have of her, shows that overall her pagan background made possible a fairly wide understanding of Christian teaching. Even those lacking knowledge of Judaism found conversion to the early church well within their powers as their reception of the Christian message accorded in many instances with their experience of the pagan deities. Although being based on degrees of probability and confined to Philippian women, this study (related as it is not only to New Testament exegesis and comparative religion but also facing towards the science of missions) opens the door to a fresh understanding of the *New Testament* for pagan women of every period and cultural background who convert to Christianity. The pagan woman of antiquity can be seen as representative of her pagan sisters throughout time and space.

---

[2] This is shown by H. Cavallin (1982, 19ff).

LIST OF DATES

Aelian (c.A.D. 170-240)
Aeschylus (c.525-456 B.C)
Ambrose (c.A.D. 340-397)
Ammianus Marcellinus (c. A.D. 330-383)
Apollodorus (c.1st cent.A.D.)
Appian (c.2nd cent.A.D.)
Apuleius (2nd Cent. A.D.)
Aristophanes (c.445-386 B.C).-
Aristotle (c. 384-322 B.C.)
Arnobius (c.5th Cent. A.D.)
Artemidorus (c. 2nd cent.A.D.)
Athenaeus (c. 3rd cent.A.D.)
Augustine (A.D. 345-430)

Callimachus (c. 300-240 B.C.)
Callistratus (c.3rd cent. A.D.)
Cato (c. 234-149 B.C.)
Catullus (c.87-54 B.C.)
Celsus (c.2nd cent. A.D.)
Censorinus (3rd cent. A.D.)
Cicero (106-43 B.C.)
Clement of Alexandria (2nd cent. A.D.)
Clement of Rome (1st cent. A.D.)
Columella (1st cent. A.D.)

Demosthenes (384-322 B.C.)
Dio Cassius (A.D. 150-235)
Dio Chrysostom (c. A.D. 40-112)
Diodorus Siculus (1st cent. B.C.)
Diogenes Laertius (3rd cent. A.D.)
Dionysius of Halicarnassus (1st cent. B.C.)

Euripides (c.480-406 B.C.)

Festus (2nd cent. A.D.)
Firmicus Maternus (4th cent. A.D.)

Gellius (2nd cent. A.D.)

Herodotus (c.485-425 B.C.)
Hesiod (c.700 B.C.)
Hesychius (5th-6th cent. A.D.)
Himerius (4th cent. A.D.)
Hippocrates (c.460-370 B.C.)
Homer (9th or 8th cent. B.C.)
Horace (68-8 B.C.)

Ignatius (c.A.D. 35-107)

Isaeus (c.420-350 B.C.)

Jerome (c.A.D. 342-420)
John Chrysostom (c.A.D. 347-407)
Julian (361-63)
Justin (c.A.D. 100-165)
Juvenal (c.A.D. 60-140)

Lactantius (c.A.D. 240-320)
Livy (59 B.C.-A.D. 17)
Lucian (c.120-180 A.D.)
Lucretius (c.94-55 B.C.)

Macrobius (c. A.D. 400)
Martial (c.A.D.40-102)
Menander (c. 342-291 B.C.)
Minucius Felix (2nd or 3rd cent. A.D.)
Musonius Rufus (c.A.D. 30-108)

Nonius (c.4th cent. A.D.)
Nonnos (5th cent. A.D.)

Ovid (c. 43 B.C.-17 A.D.)

Pausanias (2nd cent. A.D.)
Persius (A.D. 34-62)
Petronius (1st cent. A.D.)
Philo (c.25-B.C.-A.D. 40)
Philostratus (the Elder) (3rd cent. A.D.)
Plato (427-347 B.C.)
Plautus (c.250-184 B.C.)
Pliny (the Elder) (A.D. 23-79)
Pliny (the Younger) (c.A.D. 62-114)
Plutarch (c.A.D. 46-120)
Polybius (c.200-120 B.C.)
Polycarp (c.A.D. 69-155)
Propertius (c.50-15 B.C.)
Prudentius (c.A.D. 348-410)

Quintilianus (c.A.D. 35-100)

Seneca (the Elder) (c.55 B.C.-A.D. 40)
Seneca (the Younger) (c.A.D. 4-65)
Sophocles (496-406 B.C.)
Soranus (c.2nd cent. A.D.)
Statius (c.A.D. 45-96)
Strabo (c.63 B.C.-A.D. 19)
Suetonius (c.A.D. 75-150)

Tacitus (c.A.D. 55-120)

Terence (c.195-159 B.C.)
Tertullian (c.A.D. 160-225)
Theocritus (c.3rd cent. B.C.)
Theophrastus (c.370-287 B.C.)
Tibullus (c.55-19 B.C.)

Valerius Maximus (c.1st cent. A.D.)
Virgil (70-19 B.C.)
Vitruv (c.1st cent. B.C.)

Xenophon (c.430-355 B.C.)

LIST OF ABBREVIATIONS

ANRW	Aufstieg und Niedergang der römischen Welt. Geschichte und Kultur Roms im Spiegel der neueren Forschung. Hrsg. H. Temporini-W. Haase. Berlin/New York
BCH	Bulletin de Correspondance Hellénique
CIG	Corpus Inscriptionum Graecarum
CIL	Corpus Inscriptionum Latinarum
DKP	Der Kleine Pauly.Lexikon der Antike. Bd.1-5. Stuttgart, 1964-75
EPRO	Études préliminaires aux religions orientales dans l'Empire romain
FIRA	Fontes Iuris Romani Anteiustiniani
GV	Griechische Versinschriften
IG	Inscriptiones Latinae Selectae
ILLRP	Inscriptiones Latinae Liberae Rei Publicae
ILS	Inscriptiones Latinae Selectae
IPE	Inscriptiones orae septentrionalis Ponti Euxinii
Kaibel	Epigrammata Graeca ex lapidibus conlecta
LAW	Lexikon der Alten Welt. Hrsg. C. Andresen, H. Erbse et al. Zürich/Stuttgart, 1965
LCL	The Loeb Classical Library
OrRR	Die Orientalischen Religionen im Römerreich. Hrsg. M.J. Vermaaseren.(EPRO, Bd. 93) Leiden
GMP	The Greek Magical Papyri
Pleket	Epigraphica II
POxy	The Oxyrhynchus Papyri

RAC	Reallexikon für Antike und Christentum, Hrsg. Th. Klauser. 1950-
RE	Paulys Realencyclopädie der classischen Altertumswissenschaft. Bd.1-72. München 1894-1978
Roscher	W.H. Roscher, Ausführliches Lexikon der griechischen und römischen Mythologie. Bd.I-VII. Leipzig 1884-1921 (1977-8)
Vidman 1969	Sylloge Inscriptionum Religionis Isiacae et Sarapiacae
ThDNT	Theological Dictionary of the New Testament. Vols.I-XIII. Ed. G. Kittel. Engl. Transl. G. W. Bromiley. Grand Rapids, Michigan 1964 (1981)
WGR	Women in Greece and Rome

BIBLIOGRAPHY

Texts and translations

1) ANCIENT TEXTS BELONGING TO THE GREEK AND ROMAN WORLD OUTSIDE CHRISTIAN ORIGINS AND TRADITION

Aelian
> *On the Characteristics of Animals.* (LCL) Vols. I-III. Transl. A. F. Scholfield. Cambridge, Mass./London 1971

Aeschylus
> *The Suppliant Maidens.* (LCL) Vol. I. Transl.H. W. Smyth. Cambridge, Mass./ London 1973

Ammianus Marcellinus
> (LCL) Vols. I-III. Transl. J. C. Rolfe. Cambridge, Mass./London 1972

Apollodorus
> *The Library.* (LCL) Vol. I. Transl. J. G. Frazer. Cambridge, Mass./London 1976

Appian
> *The Civil Wars.* (LCL) Vol. IV. Transl. H. White. Cambridge, Mass./London 1979

Apuleius
> *The Golden Ass.* (LCL) Transl. W. Adlington. Rev. S. Gaselee. Cambridge, Mass./London 1977

Aristophanes
> (LCL) Transl. B. B. Rogers.(*The Acharnians*, Vol.I. *The Frogs*, Vol.II. *The Plutus*, Vol. III). Cambridge, Mass./London 1977-82

Aristotle
> *Histoire des animaux.* Vols. 2-3. Transl. P. Louis (Collection des universités de France). Paris. 1962-3
> *Politics.* (LCL) Vol.XXI. Transl. H. Rackham.
> *Poetics.* (LCL) Vol.XXIII. Transl. W. H. Fyfe. Rev. Ed. (LCL) Cambridge, Mass./ London 1977-1982

Artemidorus
> *The Interpretation of Dreams (Oneirocritica)*. Transl. R. J. White. New Jersey 1975

Athenaeus
> *Deipnosophistai*. (LCL) Vols. I, II, VI. Transl. C. B. Gulick. Cambridge,Mass./London 1959-69

Callimachus
> *Hymns and Epigrams*. (LCL) Transl. A. W. Mair. Rev. Ed. Cambridge, Mass./London 1977

Callistratus
> *Descriptions*. (LCL) Transl. A. Fairbanks. (See Philostratus)

Cato
> *On Agriculture*. (LCL) Transl. W.D. Hooper. Rev. H. B. Ash. Cambridge, Mass./London 1979

Catullus
> (LCL) Transl. F. W. Cornish. Rev. Ed. Cambridge, Mass./London 1976

Celsus
> *De Medicina*. (LCL) Vol.III. Transl. W. G. Spencer. Cambridge, Mass./London 1979

Censorinus
> *De die natali*. Ed. F. Hultsch. Lipsiae 1867

Cicero.
> *De Oratore*. (LCL) Vol.IV. Transl. H. Rackham.
> *Against Verres*. (LCL) Vols.VII-VIII. Transl. L. H. G. Greenwood.
> *Pro Cluentio*. (LCL) Vol.IX. Transl. H. G. Hodge.
> *Pro Sulla*. (LCL) Vol.X. Transl. C. Macdonald.
> *In Vatinium*. (LCL) Vol.XII. Transl. R. Gardner..
> *Pro M. Marcello*. (LCL) Vol.XIV. Transl. N. H. Watts.
> *De Divinatione*. (LCL) Vol.XX. Transl. W. A. Falconer.
> *Letters to Atticus*. (LCL) Vol.III. Transl. E. O. Winstedt. Cambridge, Mass./London 1966-1979

Columella
> *On Agriculture and Trees*. (LCL) Vol.III. Transl. E. S. Forster & E. H. Heffner. Rev. Ed.Cambridge, Mass./London 1979

Corpus Glossariorum Latinorum.
> Vol.III. Ed. G. Goetz. (Teubner) Lipsiae 1892

Demosthenes
> *De Corona*. (LCL) Vol.II. Transl. C. A. & J. H. Vince. Cambridge, Mass./London 1971

Dio Cassius
> *Roman History*. (LCL) Vols.V-VII. Transl. H. B. Foster & E. Cary. Cambridge, Mass./London 1969-1981

Dio Chrysostom
> (LCL) Vol.II. Transl. J. W. Cohoon. Vol.IV. Transl. H. L. Crosby. Cambridge, Mass./London 1946-50

Diodorus of Sicily
> (LCL) Vols.I-V. Transl. C. H. Oldfather. Vol.VII. Transl. C. L. Sherman. Cambridge, Mass./London 1952-1968

Diogenes Laertius
> (LCL) Vol.II. Transl. R. D. Hicks. Cambridge, Mass./London 1970

Dionysius of Halicarnassus
> (LCL) Vols.I-VI. Transl. E. Spelman & E. Cary. Cambridge, Mass./London 1963-1968

Euripides
> *Rhesus.* (LCL) Vol. I. *Bacchanals. Madness of Hercules.* (LCL) Vol.III. *Medea. Alcestis.* (LCL) Vol.IV. Transl. A.S. Way. Cambridge, Mass./London 1979-80

Festus
> *De verborum significatu.* Ed. W. M. Lindsay. (Teubner) Lipsiae 1892

Gellius
> *The Attic Nights.* (LCL) Vols.II-III. Transl. J. C. Rolfe. Cambridge, Mass./London 1978-82

The Greek Anthology.
> (LCL) Vols.II-III. Transl. W. R. Paton. Cambridge, Mass./London 1970-83

Herodotus
> (LCL) Vols.I-III. Transl. A. D. Godley. Cambridge, Mass./London 1971- 81

Hesiod
> (LCL) Transl. H. G. Evelyn-White. Cambridge, Mass./London 1977

Hesychii Alexandrini Lexicon.
> Ed. M. Schmidt. Jena 1867

Himerius
> *Declamationes et orationes.* Ed. A. Colonna. Romae 1951

Hippocrates
> *Aphorisms.* (LCL) Vol.IV. Transl. W. H. S. Jones. Cambridge, Mass./London 1979
> *Über Achtmonatskinder. Über das Siebenmonatskind.* Ed. H. Grensemann (Corpus Medicorum Graecorum, Vol. I, 2, 1). Berlin. 1968
> *Die gynäkologischen Texte des Autors C nach den pseudohippokratischen Schriften De mulieribus I, II und De Sterilibus.* Ed. H. Grensemann. Wiesbaden 1982

Homer
- *The Iliad.* (LCL) Vols.I-II. Transl. A. T. Murray.
- *The Odyssey.* (LCL) Vols.I-II. Transl. A. T. Murray. Cambridge, Mass./London 1971-6

Horace
- *Odes and Epodes.* (LCL) Transl. C.E. Bennett. Rev. Ed.
- *Satires, Epistles and Ars Poetica.* (LCL) Transl. H.R. Fairclough. Rev. Ed. Cambridge, Mass./London 1978

Isaeus
- (LCL) Transl. E. S. Forster. Cambridge, Mass./London 1962

Julian
- *Misopogon.* (LCL) Vol.II. Transl. W. C. Wright. Cambridge Mass./London 1969

Juvenal
- (LCL) Transl. G. G. Ramsay. Rev. Ed. Cambridge, Mass./London 1957

Livy
- (LCL) Vol.III. Transl. B. O. Forster. Vols.IX-XII. Transl. E. T. Sage.
- Vol.XIII. Transl. A. C. Schlesinger. Cambridge, Mass./London 1965-79

Lucian
- *The Cock.* (LCL)Vol.II. Transl. A. M. Harmon.
- *On Funerals.* (LCL) Vol.IV. Transl. H. Harmon.
- *Menippus.* (LCL) Vol.IV. Transl. H. Harmon.
- *The Passing of Peregrinus.* (LCL) Vol.V. Transl. A. M. Harmon.
- *The Dance.* (LCL) Vol.V. Transl. A. M. Harmon.
- *Hermotimus.* (LCL) Vol.VI. Transl. K. Kilburn.
- *Historia.* (LCL) Vol.VI. Transl. K. Kilburn.
- *Dialogues of the Courtesans.* (LCL) Vol.VII. Transl. M. D. Macleod.
- *Amores.* (LCL) Vol.VIII. Transl. M. D. Macleod.
- Cambridge, Mass./London 1953-67

Lucretius
- *De Rerum Natura.* (LCL) Transl. W. H. D. Rouse. Rev. 2nd Ed. Cambridge, Mass./London 1982

Macrobius
- *The Saturnalia.* Translated with an Introduction and Notes by P. V. Davies. New York/London 1969

Martial
- *Epigrams.* (LCL) Vols.I-II. Transl. W. C. A. Ker. Rev. Ed. Cambridge, Mass./London 1978-79

Musonius Rufus
    Entretiens et fragments. Transl. A. Jagu. (Studien und Materialien zur Geschichte der Philosophie, Bd. 5). Hildesheim/NewYork. 1979

Nonius Marcellus
    De compendiosa doctrina. Ed. W.M. Lindsay. Vol.3. (Teubner). Lipsiae 1903

Nonnos.
    Dionysiaca. (LCL) Vols.I-III. Transl. W. H. D. Rouse. Cambridge, Mass./London 1940-2

The Orphic Hymns.
    Text, Transl. and Notes A. N. Athanassakis. (Society of Biblical Literature. Text and Translations 12. Graeco- Roman Religion Series 4). Missoula. Montana 1977

Ovid
    Heroides and Amores. (LCL) Vol.I. Transl. G. Showerman. Rev. Ed.
    Ars Amatoria. Remedia Amoris. (LCL) Vol.II. Transl. J. H. Mozley. Rev. Ed.
    Metamorphoses. (LCL) Vols.III-IV. Transl. F. J. Miller. Rev. Ed.
    Fasti. (LCL) Vol.V. Transl. J. G. Frazer.
    Tristia. (LCL) Vol.VI. Transl. A. L. Wheeler. Cambridge, Mass./London 1967-79

Pausanias
    Description of Greece. (LCL) Vols.I-IV. Transl. W. H. S. Jones. Cambridge, Mass./London 1966-75

Persius
    (LCL) Transl. G. G. Ramsay. (See Juvenal)

Petronius
    Satyricon. (LCL) Transl. M. Heseltine. Cambridge, Mass./London 1913

Philo
    The *Contemplative Life.* (LCL) Vol. IX. Transl. F. H. Colson. Cambridge, Mass./London 1967

Philostratus the Elder and the Younger
    Imagines. (LCL) Transl. A. Fairbanks. Cambridge, Mass./London 1969

Plato
    Symposium. (LCL) Vol.III. Transl. W. R. M. Lamb.
    Republic. (LCL) Vol.V. Transl. P. Shorey. Rev. Ed.
    Laws. (LCL) Vols. X-XI. Transl. R. G. Bury. Cambridge, Mass./London 1967-83

Plautus
    Amphitryon. (LCL) Vol.I.
    Aulularia. (LCL) Vol.I.
    Cistellaria. (LCL) Vol.II.
    Mercator. (LCL) Vol.III.
    Miles gloriosus. (LCL) Vol.III.
    Rudens. (LCL) Vol.IV.
    Transl. P. Nixon. Cambridge, Mass./London 1959-79

Pliny
    Natural History. (LCL) Vols.I-X. Cambridge, Mass./London 1979

Pliny.
    Letters. (LCL) Vols.I-II. Transl. B. Radice. Cambridge, Mass./London 1972-76

Plutarch
    Lives. (LCL)
    (*Numa,* Vol.I. *Cato Major,* Vol.II. *Crassus,* Vol.III. *Alexander,* Vol.VII.
    Cato the Younger, Vol.VIII. *Demetrius,* Vol.IX). Transl. B. Perrin.Cambridge, Mass./London 1958-82
    Moralia (LCL) Vols.I-IX. Cambridge, Mass./London 1968-72

Polybius
    The Histories. (LCL) Vols.III-VI. Transl. W. R. Paton.

Propertius
    (LCL) Transl. H. E. Butler. Cambridge, Mass./London 1976

Quintilian
    The Institutio Oratoria. (LCL) Vols.I,IV. Transl. H. E. Butler. Cambridge Mass./London 1979-80

Scholia in Aristophanem.
    Vol. 2:1. *Aristophanes Vespas.* Ed. W. J. W. Koster. Groningen 1979

Seneca the Elder
    Controversiae. (LCL) Vols.I-II. Transl. M. Winterbottom. Cambridge, Mass./London 1974

Seneca the Younger
    Moral Essays. (LCL) Vols.I-II. Transl. J. W. Basore. Cambridge, Mass./London 1979-85
    Apocolocyntosis. (LCL) Transl. W. H. D. Rouse. (See Petronius).

Servianorum in Vergilii Carmina Commentariorum.
    Vols 1-2. Ed. K.Rand *et al.* (Societatis Philologicae Americanae Cura et Impensis). Lancastriae, Pennsylvaniorum 1947.

Sophocles
> *Trachiniae.* (LCL) Vol.II. Transl. F. Storr. Cambridge, Mass./London 1961.
> *The Fragments of Sophocles.* Ed. A.C. Pearsson. Vol.II. Cambridge 1917.

Soranus
> Corpus Medicorum Graecorum. Vol.IV. Ed. I. Ilberg. (Teubner) Lipsiae 1927
> *Gynecology.* Ed. and transl. O. Temkin *et al.* Baltimore 1956

Statius
> *Silvae.* (LCL) Vol.I. Transl. J. H. Mozley. Cambridge,Mass./London 1982

Strabo
> *The Geography.* (LCL) Vols.II-VI. Transl. H. L. Jones. Cambridge, Mass./London 1967-70

Suetonius
> *The Lives of the Caesars.* (LCL) Vol.I.
> *The Lives of Illustrious men.* (LCL) Vol. II. Transl. J. C. Rolfe. Rev. Ed. Cambridge, Mass./London 1950-1

Tacitus
> *Dialogus.* (LCL) Vol.I. Transl. W. Peterson. Rev. Ed.
> *The Histories.* (LCL) Vol.III. Transl.C. H. Moore.
> *The Annals.* (LCL) Vols.III-V. Transl. J. Jackson.
> Cambridge, Mass./London 1979-81

Terence
> *Hecyra.* (LCL) Vol.II. Transl. J. Sargeaut. Cambridge, Mass./London 1983

Theocritus
> (LCL) The Greek Bucolic Poets. Transl. J. M. Edmonds. Cambridge, Mass./London 1977

Theophrastus
> *The Characters.* (LCL) Transl. J. M. Edmonds. Rev. Ed.
> *Enquiry into Plants.* (LCL) Vols.I-II. Transl. A. Hort. Cambridge, Mass./London 1953-80

Tibullus
> (LCL) Transl. J. P. Postgate. (See Catullus).

Valerius Maximus
> *Factorum et dictorum memorabilium.* Ed. C. Helm. (Teubner) Lipsiae 1865

Virgil
> *Aeneid.* (LCL) Vols.I-II.
> *Georgics.* (LCL) Vol.I. Transl. H. R. Fairclough. Rev. Ed. Cambridge, Mass./London 1965-78

Vitruvius
> *On Architecture.* (LCL) Vol.II. Transl. F. Granger. Cambridge, Mass./London 1970

Women in Greece and Rome.
> Texts, collected and translated by M.R. Lefkowitz & M.B. Fant. Toronto/Sarasota 1977

Xenophon
> *Oeconomicus. Symposium.* (LCL) Vol.IV. Transl. E. C. Marchant & O. J. Todd.
> *Constitution of the Lacedaimonians.* (LCL) Vol.VII. Transl. G. W. Bowersock. Cambridge, Mass./London 1968-84

2) ANCIENT TEXTS BELONGING TO THE WORLD OF CHRISTIAN ORIGINS AND TRADITIONS

St Ambrose
> *Concerning Virgins.* Transl. H. de Romestin. (Nicene and Post-Nicene Fathers of the Christian Church. 2nd Series. Vol.X). Grand Rapids, Michigan 1975

The Apostolical Constitutiones.
> Transl. J. Donaldson.(Ante-Nicene Christian Library. Vol.XVII). Edinburgh 1872

The Epistle of Aristeas.
> The Old Testament Pseudepigraphica. Ed. J. H. Charlesworth. Vol.2. London 1985

Arnobius.
> *Adversus Nationes.* Transl. H. Bryce & H. Campbell. (Ante-Nicene Christian Library. Vol.XIX). Edinburgh 1871

St. Augustine
> *Confessions.* (LCL) Vol.I. Transl. W. Watts. Cambridge, Mass./London 1977

The Epistle of Barnabas.
> (LCL) The Apostolic Fathers.Vol.I. Transl. K. Lake. Cambridge, Mass./London 1977

Clement of Alexandria
> *The Exhortations to the Greeks.*
> (LCL) Transl. G. W. Butterworth. Cambridge, Mass./London 1939

The First Epistle of Clement to the Corinthians.
> (LCL) The Apostolic Fathers, Vol.I. Transl. K. Lake. Cambridge, Mass./London 1977

The Didache.
    (LCL) The Apostolic Fathers, Vol.I. Transl. K. Lake. Cambridge, Mass./London 1977

The Epistle to Diognetus.
    (LCL) The Apostolic Fathers, Vol.II. Transl. K. Lake. Cambridge, Mass./London 1976

Eusebius
    The Ecclesiastical History. (LCL) Vol.II. Transl. J. E. L. Oulton. Cambridge, Mass./London 1980

Firmicus Maternus
    The Error of the Pagan Religion. Transl. C. A. Forbes. (Ancient Christian Writers, No. 37) New York/Paramus, N. J. 1970

The *Holy Bible.* Revised Standard Version. Ed. G. May & B. M. Metzger. New York 1962

Ignatius
    Epistle to the Smyrneans. (LCL) The Apostolic Fathers. Vol.I. Transl. K. Lake. Cambridge, Mass./London 1977

St. Jerome
    Select Letters. (LCL) Transl. F. A. Wright. Cambridge, Mass./London 1953

John Chrysostom
    Homilies on the Gospel of S:t Matthew. Transl. G. Prevost & M. B. Riddle. (A Select Library of the Nicene and Post-Nicene Fathers of the Christian Church. 1st Series. Vol.X). Grand Rapids, Michigan 1975
    Homilies in the Acts of the Apostles. Transl. J. Walker & J. Sheppard & H. Browne. (A Select Library of the Nicene and Post-Nicene Fathers of the Christian Church. First Series. Vol.XI). Grand Rapids, Michigan 1975
    Expositio in psalmos. Ed. J.-P. Migne. Patrologiae...Tom.LV. Paris 1859

Justin
    Apologies. Transl. L. Pautigny. (Textes et documents pour l'étude historique du Christianisme). Paris 1904

Lactantius
    Of the Manners in which the Christians died. Transl. W. Fletcher. (Ante-Nicene Christian Library. Vol.XXII). Edinburgh 1871

Martyrs of Lyons.
    The Acts of the Christian Martyrs. Text and Transl. H. Musurillo. Oxford 1972

The *Martyrdom of Polycarp.*
    (LCL) The Apostolic Fathers. Vol.II. Transl. K. Lake Cambridge, Mass./London 1976

Minucius Felix.
    Octavius. (LCL) Transl. G. H. Rendall. (See Tertullian)
    Novum Testamentum Graece. Ed. Eberhard & Erwin Nestle *et al.* 26. Auflage. Stuttgart 1979

Polycarp
    The Epistle to the Philippians. (LCL) The Apostolic Fathers, Vol.I. Transl. K. Lake. Cambridge, Mass./London 1977

Prudentius
    A Reply to Address of Symmachus. (LCL) Vol.I. Transl. H. J. Thomson. Cambridge, Mass./London 1969

Septuaginta.
    Ed. A. Rahlfs. Vol.1. Stuttgart 1971

The Sibylline Oracles.
    The Old Testament Pseudepigraphica. Ed. J. H. Charlesworth. Vol.1. London 1983

Tertullian
    Apology. (LCL) Transl. T. R. Glover. Cambridge, Mass./London 1984
    On Idolatry. Transl. S. Thelwall. (Ante-Nicene Christian Library. Vol.XI). Edinburgh 1872
    Treatises on Marriage and Remarriage. (To his wife. An exhortation to chastity. Monogamy) Transl. W. P. Le Saint. (Ancient Christian Writers 13). Westminster, Maryland 1951

3) LEGAL TEXTS

Cicero.
>   *De Re Publica. De Legibus.* (LCL) Vol.XVI. Transl. C. W. Keyes. Cambridge, Mass./London 1928

>   *Digesta.* Corpus Iuris Civilis. Ed. P. Krueger & Th. Mommsen. Berolini 1928

>   *Fontes Iuris Romani Anteiustiniani.* Vol.2. Ed. J. Baviera & J. Furlani. Vol.3. Ed. V. Arangio-Ruiz. Firenze 1940-43

>   *Gai Institutiones.* Ed. P. Krueger & G. Studemund. Berolini 1877

>   *Sentences of Paulus.* Corpus Iuris Civilis. Ed. and Transl. S. P. Scott. Cincinnati 1973, I: 326-27

>   *The Twelve Tables.* (LCL) Remains of Old Latins, Vol.III. Transl. E. H Warmington. Rev. Ed. Cambridge, Mass./London 1979

4) INSCRIPTIONS

Corpus Inscriptionum Graecarum. Vols. I-IV. Berlin 1828-77

Corpus Inscriptionum Latinarum. Berlin 1863-

Epigrammata Graeca ex lapidibus conlecta. Ed. G. Kaibel. Berlin 1878

Epigraphica II: Texts on the Social History of the Greek World. Ed. H. Pleket. Leyden 1969

Griechische Versinschriften. Ed. W. Peek. Vol. I. Berlin 1955

Inscriptiones Graecarum. Berlin 1873-

Inscriptiones Latinae Liberae Rei Publicae. Ed. A. Degrassi, Vols.I-II. Florence 1957-63

Inscriptiones Latinae Selectae. Ed. H. Dessau. Vols I-III. Berlin 1892-1916

Inscriptiones orae septentrionalis Ponti Euxinii. Ed. V. Latychew. Petropoli 1890

Sylloge inscriptionum religionis Isiacae et Sarapiacae. Ed. L. Vidman. Berlin 1969

5) PAPYRI

The Papyrus of Ani. The Book of the Dead. (Chapt. 125) Transl. E.A. Wallis Budge. 2nd Ed. London/New York 1928

The Greek Magical Papyri in Translation Including the Demotic Spells. Ed. H. D. Betz. Chicago 1986

The Papyrus of Nebseni. The Book of the Dead (Chapt. 125). Transl. E.A. Wallis Budge. 2nd Ed. London/New York 1928

The Oxyrhynchus Papyri. Vol.XI (Nos.1351-1404). Ed. B. P. Grenfell & A. S. Hunt et al. London 1915

6) ARETALOGIES

For Cyme und Thessaloniki:

Harder, R. *Karpokrates von Chalkis und die memphitische Isispropaganda.* (Abhandlungen der Preussischen Akademie der Wissenschaften. Jahrgang 1943, Phil.-hist. Kl. Nr. 14) Berlin 1944

For Maroneia:

Grandjean, Y. *Une nouvelle arétalogie d'Isis à Maronée.* (EPRO) Leiden 1975

Literature

Aalen, S.
    1984 *Versuch einer Analyse des Diakonia-Begriffes im Neuen Testament.* (The New Testament Age. Essays in Honor of Bo Reicke. Ed. W.C. Weinreich). Mercer

Abrahamsen, V.
    1986 *The Rock Reliefs and the Cult of Diana at Philippi.* Diss. Harvard Univ. (University Microfilms, 1986) Ann Arbor, Mich.1987 *Women at Philippi: The Pagan and Christian Evidence.* (Journal of Feminist Studies in Religion, Vol. 3, No. 2, 17-30)

Altmann, W.
    1905 *Die Römische Grabaltäre der Kaiserzeit.* Berlin

Amundsen, D. W. & Diers, C. J.
    1969 *The Age of Menarche in Classical Greece and Rome.* (Human Biology, 41,127-132)

Andreae, B.
    1963 *Studien zur römischen Grabkunst.* Heidelberg

Areskog, B.
    1982 *Fear of childbirth in pregnant women.* Diss. nr 133. (University of Medical) Linköping

Balch, D. L.
    1981 *Let Wives be submissive: The domestic Code in 1 Peter.* (Society of Biblical Literature, Monograph series, 26). Chico

Balsdon, J. P. V. D.
    1969 *Life and Leisure in Ancient Rome.* New York-St Louis-San Francisco
    1979 *Romans and Aliens.* London

Barrett, C. K.
    1963 *The Pastoral Epistles in the New English Bible.* With Introduction and Commentary. Oxford
    1968 *A Commentary on the First Epistle on the Corinthians.* (Black's New Testament Commentaries) London

Baur, P. V.C.
    1941 *Megarian Bowls in Rebecca Darlington Stoddard Collection of Greek and Italian Vases in Yale University.* (American Journal of Archaeology, 45, 229-248)

Baus, K.
    1940 *Der Kranz in Antike und Christentum.* Bonn
Bayet, J.
    1929 *Un nouvel Hercule funéraire et l' héroisation gréco-romain en Thrace.* (Mélanges d'archéologie et d'histoire. Ecole francaise de Rome. XLVIe année, 1-42)
Benko, S.
    1985 *Pagan Rome and the Early Christians.* London
Bergman, J.
    1968 *Ich bin Isis. Studien zum Memphitischen Hintergrund der griechischen Isisaretalogien.* (Acta Universitatis Upsaliensis. Historia Religionum 3) Diss. Uppsala
    1967 *'I Overcome Fate, Fate Harkens to Me'.* (Fatalistic Beliefs in Religion, Folklore, and Literature. Papers read at the Symposium on Fatalistic Beliefs held at Åbo 1964. Ed. H. Ringgren). Stockholm
    1972 *DECEM ILLIS DIEBUS.* Zum Sinn der Enthaltsamkeit bei den Mysterienweihen im Isisbuch des Apuleius.(Studia Geo Widengren. Vol. 1. 332-346). Leiden
Bergquist, B.
    1973 *Herakles on Thasos.* The Archeological, Literary and Epigraphic evidence for His Sanctuary, Status and Cult Reconsidered. Diss. Uppsala
Bertelli, C.
    1965 *Roma Sotterranea.* Milano
Beskow, P.
    1970 *Mission.* Trade and Emigration in the Second Century. (Svensk Exegetisk Årsbok, Vol. XXV. Ed. H. Riesenfeld, 104-114). Lund
Betz, H. D.
    1967 *Nachfolge und Nachahmung Jesu Christi im Neuen Testament.* (Beiträge zur historischen Theologie 37). Tübingen
    1972 *Der Apostel Paulus und der sokratische Tradition.* Eine exegetische Untersuchung zu seiner "Apologie" 2 Korinther 10-13. (Beiträge zur historischen Theologie 45). Tübingen
    1979 *Galatians.* A Commentary on Paul's Letter to the Churches in Galatia. Philadelphia
Blanck, H.
    1976 *Einführung in das Privatleben der Griechen und Römer.* Darmstadt
Blümner, H.
    1911 *Die römischen Privataltertümer.* (Handbuch der klassischen Altertumswissenschaft, Bd IV:2, 2. 3. Aufl.) München

Bolkestein, H.
   1929 *Theophrastos' Charakter der Deisidaimonia. Eine religionsgeschichtliche Urkunde.* Giessen

Bonner, S. F.
   1977 *Education in Ancient Rome.* From the elder Cato to the younger Pliny. Berkeley and Los Angeles

Bonnet, H.
   1952 (1971) *Reallexikon der Ägyptischen Religionsgeschichte.* Berlin

von Bothmer, D.
   1957 *Amazons in Greek Art.* Oxford

Bradley, K. R.
   1978 *The age at time of sale of female slaves.* (Arethusa, Vol. 11, 243-252)

Bremmer, J.
   1984 *Greek Maenadism Reconsidered.* (Zeitschrift für Papyrologie und Epigraphik, Bd 55, 267-286)

Brommer, F.
   1984 *Herakles II. Die unkanonischen Taten des Helden.* Darmstadt

Brown, R. E.
   1978 *Mary in the Gospel of Luke and the Acts of the Apostles.* (Mary in the New Testament, Ed. R.E. Brown& K.P. Donfried& J. A. Fitzmeyer& J. Reumann, 105-177) Philadelphia-New York / Ramsey / Toronto

Bruck, E. F.
   1954 *Über Römisches Recht im Rahmen der Kulturgeschichte.* Berlin / Göttingen / Heidelberg

Bruhns, E.
   1891 *Die Backchen.* Ausgewählte Tragödien des Euripides. Berlin

Burkert, W.
   1977 *Griechische Religion der archaischen und klassischen Epoche.* (Der Religionen der Menschheit, Bd. 15) Stuttgart / Berlin / Köln / Mainz

Burton, A.
   1972 *Diodorus Siculus 1.* A Commentary. (EPRO) Leiden

Buschor, E.
   1976 *Grab eines attischen Mädchens.* 3. Aufl. München / Zührich

Cagnat, R.
   1914 (1964) *Cours d' épigraphie latine.* Paris. Roma

Cahen, É.
    1930 *Les Hymnes de Callimaque*. Commentaire explicatif et critique. Paris

Carter, I. B.
    1902 (1977) *Epitheta Deorum quae apud poetas latinos leguntur*. (Roscher, Suppl 2, Bd VII) Hildesheim-New York

Cavallin, H. C.
    1982 *Paulus och kvinnan*.(F. Brosché & H. Cavallin, Manssamhällets försvarare–eller skapelsens? Studier och tankar kring frågan om kvinnan hos Paulus och Luther–i gammal och ny gnosticism, 17-108). Uppsala

Clark, G.
    1981 *Roman Women*. (Greece and Rome, Vol. XXVIII, 192-212)

Clauss, M.
    1986 *Heerwesen (Heeresreligion)*. Art in RAC, Lief. 103, 1173-1110

Collart, P.
    1929 *Le sanctuaire des dieux égyptiens à Philippes*. (BCH, Vol. 53, 70-100)
    1933 *Inscriptions de Philippes*. (BCH, Vol. 57, 313-79)
    1935 *Une reféction de la "Via Egnatia" sous Trajan*. (BCH, Vol. 59, 395-415)
    1937 *Philippes*. Ville de Macédoine depuis ses origines jusqu' à la fin de la l' époque romaine. Thèse. Université de Genève, 85, Paris
    1938 *Inscriptions de Philippes*. (BCH, Vol. 72, 409-432)

Collart, P. & Ducrey, P.
    1975 *Philippes I. Les reliefs rupestres*. (BCH, Supplément II) Paris

Cook, A. B.
    1914 (1964) *Zeus*. A study in Ancient Religion.Vol. I. New York

Corbett, J. H.
    1980 *The foster child: a neglected theme in Early Christian life and thought*. (Traditions in Contact and Change. Selected Proceedings of the XIV th Congress of the International Association for the History of Religions, Ed. P. Slater & D. Wiebe, 307-322)

Crook, J. A.
    1967 *Law and Life of Rome*. London

Csillag, P.
    1976 *The Augustan Laws on Family Relations*. Budapest

Cullman, O.
    1948 *Die Tauflehre des Neuen Testament*. Erwachsenen-und Kindertaufe. Zürich

Dassmann, E.
1986 *Haus II (Hausgemeinschaft).* Art. in RAC, Bd. XIII, 801-905

Daux, G.
1962 *Excavation report 1961.* (BCH, Vol. 86, 826)
1965 *Excavation report 1964.* (BCH, Vol. 89, 832)

Dautzenberg, G. & Merklein, H. & Müller, K. (Ed.)
1983 *Die Frau im Urchristentum.* Freiburg im Breisgau

D'Avino, M.
1967 *The Women of Pompeii.* Napoli

Delcourt, M.
1938 *Stérilitées mysterieuses et naissances maléfiques dans l'antiquité classique.* Liège / Paris

Deubner, L.
1966 (1969) *Attische Feste.* 2. Aufl. Hildesheim / New York

Dibelius, M.
1937 *"Bischöfe und "Diakonen" in Philippi.* (Das kirchliche Amt im Neuen Testament. Hrsg. K. Kertelge, 413-417) Darmstadt 1949
(1951)
Die Reden der Apostelgeschichte und die antike Geschichtsschreibung. (Aufsätze zur Apostelgeschichte, 120-162). Göttingen

Dieterich, A.
1905 *Euripides.* Art. in RE, Bd. VI, 1242-1281

Dodds, E. R.
1944 *Euripides Bacchae.* Edited with Introduction and Commentary. Oxford
1951 *The Greeks and the Irrational.* Berkeley / Los Angeles / London

Domaszewski, A.
1895 *Die Religion des römischen Heeres.* (Westdeutsche Zeitschrift für Geschichte und Kunst 14, 1-128)

Drerup, H.
1980 *Totenmaske und Ahnenbild bei den Römern.* (Mitteilungen des Deutschen archaeologischen Instituts, Roemische Abteilung, Vol. 87, 81-129)

Drexler, W.
1890-94 *Isis.* Art. in Roscher II:1, 360-548

Düll, S.
1975 *Götter auf Makedonischen Grabstelen.* (Essays in Memory of Basil Laourdas, 115-135) Thessaloniki
1977 *Die Götterkulte Nord-Makedoniens in römischer Zeit.* München

Dölger, F. J.
    1930 *Zur Frage der religiösen Tätowierung im thrakischen Dionysos-kult. "Bromio signatae mystides" in einer Grabinschrift des dritten Jahrhunderts n. Chr.* (Antike und Christentum, Bd II, 107-116)
    1930 *Antike Parallelen zum leidenden Dinocrates in der Passio Perpetuae.* (Antike und Christentum, Bd II, 1-40)

Egger, R.
    1950 *Der Grabstein von Cekancevo.* (Schriften der Balkankommission, Antiquarische Abteilung, XI, 2. Österreichische Akademie der Wissenschaften, 3-33)

Elliger, W.
    1978 *Paulus in Griechenland.* Stuttgart

Engels, D.
    1980 *The problem of female infanticide in the Greco-Roman world.* (Classical Philology 75, 2, 112-120)

Ernst, J.
    1974 *Die Briefe an die Philipper, an Philemon, an die Kolosser, an die Epheser.* (Regensburger Neues Testament). Regensburg

Excavation reports.
    1922 BCH, Vol. 46, 530
    1935 BCH, Vol. 59, 287

Farnell, R.
    1896 *The Cults of the Greek State.* Vol. II. Oxford

Fehrle, E.
    1910 *Die kultische Keuschheit im Altertum.* Giessen

Ferguson, J.
    1975 *Utopias of the Classical World.* London

Finley, M. I.
    1968 *Aspects of Antiquity.* New York
    1981 *The Elderly in Classical Antiquity.* (Greece and Rome, Vol. XXVIII, 156-171)

Fischer, B.
    1974 *Gemeinschaftsgebet in den christlichen Gemeinden und in der christlichen Familie in der alten Christenheit.* (Liturgisches Jahrbuch, 24, 92-109)

Fowler, R. M.
    1985 *Who is "the Reader" in Reader Response Criticism?* (Semeia 31, 5-23)

Fraser, P. M.
    1972 *Ptolemaic Alexandria.* Vols.I-II. Oxford

Frend, W. C. H.
    1965 *Martyrdom and Persecution in the Early Church. A Study of a Conflict from the Maccabees to Donatus.* Oxford

Frenz, H. G.
    1977 *Untersuchungen zu den frühen römischen Grabreliefs.* Diss. Frankfurt am Main

Frothingham Jr, A. L.
    1905 *De la véritable signification des monuments romaine qu' on appelle "ARCS DE TRIOMPHE".* (Revue Archéologique, 216-230)

Fuhrmann, M.
    1967 *Glossographie II.* Art. in DKP, Bd. 2, 818-821

Gagé, J.
    1969 *Fackel.* Art. in RAC, Bd VII, 154-217

Gardner, J. F.
    1986 *Women in Roman Law and Society.* London / Sidney

Garnsey, P.
    1970 *Social Status and Legal Privilege in the Roman Empire.* Oxford

Georges, K. E.
    1976 *Ausführliches Latein-Deutsches Handwörterbuch.* 14. Aufl. Bd. 1-2. Hannover

Gnilka, J.
    1980a *Der Philipperbrief.* (Herders Theologischer Kommentar zum Neuen Testament. 10:3). 3. Aufl. Freiburg / Basel / Wien
    1980b *Der Kolosserbrief.* (Herders Theologischer Kommentar zum Neuen Testament. 10: 1). Freiburg / Basel / Wien

Goetze, R.
    1974 *Der Tod im Kindesalter: eine medizinhistorische Studie auf der Grundlage von Epitaphen der Anthologia Graeca.* Diss. Erlangen

Golden, M.
    1981 *Demography and the Exposure of Girls at Athens.* (Phoenix. The Journal of Classical Association of Canada, Vol. XXXV, 316-331)

Grandjean, Y.
    1975 *Une nouvelle arétalogie d'Isis à Maronée.* (EPRO) Leiden

Grant, R. M.
    1947 *The Decalogue in Early Christianity.* (Harvard Theological Rewiew, XL, 1-17)

Gren, E.
    1941 *Kleinasien und der Ostbalkan in der wirtschaftlichen Entwicklung der römischen Kaiserzeit.* Diss. Uppsala

Griffiths, J. G.
: 1975 *Apuleius of Madauros. The Isis-Book (Metamorphoses, Book XI)*. Ed. with an Introduction, Translation and Commentary. (EPRO) Leiden

Gruppe, O.
: 1897-1902 (1978) *Orpheus*. Art. in Roscher, Bd. III,1, 1058-1207

Gundel, H.
: 1952 *Pomponius*. Art. in RE, Bd. XXI,2, 2323-2324)

Hack, C.
: 1913 *Zur Geschichte der Säuglingskrankheiten im Altertum*. Diss. Jena

Haenchen, E.
: 1965 (1982) *The Acts of the Apostles. A Commentary*. 14th Edit. Engl. Transl. 1971 Oxford

Hallett, J. P.
: 1984 *Fathers and Daughters in Roman Society*. Women and the Elite Family. Princeton, New Jersey

Hanson, J. A.
: 1959 *Plautus as a Source Book for Roman Religion*. (Transactions and Proceedings or the American Philological Association, Vol. XC, 48-101)

Harder, R.
: 1944 *Karpokrates von Chalkis und die memphitische Isispropaganda*. (Abhandlungen der Preussischen Akademie der Wissenschaften. Jahrgang 1943, Phil.-hist. Kl. Nr. 14)

Harmon, D. P.
: 1978 *The Family Festivals of Rome*. (ANRW, Bd 16:2, 1592-1603) Berlin / New York

von Harnack, A.
: 1931 *ÜBER die beiden Rezensionen der Geschichte der Prisca und des Aquila in Act. Apost. 18, 1-27*. (In Studien zur Geschichtedes Neuen Testaments und der alten Kirche, I. Arbeiten zur Kirchengeschichte 19) Berlin / Leipzig

Harris, W. V.
: 1979 *War and Imperialism in Republican Rome 327-70 B.C.* Oxford

Hartman, L.
: 1985 *Kolosserbrevet*. (Kommentar till Nya Testamentet 12) Uppsala
: 1986 *On Reading Other's Letters*. (Christian and Gentiles. Essays in honor of Krister Stendahl on his 65th Birthday. Ed. G.W. Nickelsburg & G.W. MacRae,SJ, 137-146). Philadelphia

Heckenbach, J.
: 1912 *Hekate*. Art. in RE, Bd. VII, 2769-2782

Hengel, M.
    1971 *Proseuché und synagogé.* Jüdische Gemeinde, Gotteshaus und Gottesdienst in der Diaspora und in Palestina. (Tradition und Glaube. Festschrift für K. G. Kuhn) Göttingen
    1977 *Crucifixion.* In the ancient world and the folly of the message of the cross. Philadelphia

Henrichs, A.
    1978 *Greek Maenadism from Olympias to Messalina.* (Studies in Classical Philology, 82, 121-160)

Henze, A. & Nash, E. & Sichtermann, H.
    1981 *Rom und Latium. Kunstdenkmäler und Museen.* (Reclams Kunstführer Italien. Bd. V). 4. Aufl. Stuttgart

Heubeck, A.
    1965 *Personennamen (A).* Art. in LAW, 2267-2268

Heuzey, L. & Daumet, H.
    1876 *Mission archéologique de Macédoine.* Paris

Heyob, S. K.
    1975 *The Cult of Isis among Women in the Graeco-Roman World.* (EPRO) Leiden

Himmelmann, N.
    1971 *Archäologisches zum Problem der griechischen Sklaverei.* Mainz

Hopkins, K.
    1983 *Death and Renewal.* (Sociological Studies in Roman History 2) Cambridge / London / New York - New Rochelle / Melbourne / Sidney

Horn, H. G.
    1972 *Mysteriensymbolik auf dem Kölner Dionysosmosaik.* Bonn

Hug, A.
    1927 *Lucerna.* Art. in RE, Bd. XIII, 1566-1613

Hunger, H.
    1959 *Lexikon der griechischen und römischen Mythologie.* 5. Aufl. Wien

Hägg, T.
    1983 *The Novel in Antiquity.* Oxford

Iser, W,
    1971 *Indeterminacy and the Reader's Response in Prose Fiction.* (Aspects of Narrative. Selected Papers from the English Institute. Ed. J.H. Miller, 1-45). London
    1974 *The Reading Process.* A Phenomenical Approach. (W. Iser, The Implied Reader, 274-294) London
    1978 *The Act of Reading.* A Theory of Aesthetic Response. London / Henley

Jauss, H. R.
> 1970-71 *Literary History as a challenge to Literary Theory.* (New Literary History, Vol. II, 7-37)
> 1974 *Levels of Identification of Hero and Audience.* (New Literary History, Vol. V, 283-317)

Jeremias, J.
> 1958 *Die Kindertaufe in den ersten vier Jahrhunderten.* Göttingen
> 1962 *Das Vater-Unser im Lichte der neueren Forschung.* Stuttgart.

Jervell, J.
> 1984 *The unknown Paul. Essays on Luke-Acts and Early Christian History.* Minneapolis

Jessen, O.
> 1909-15 (1978) *Semele.* Art. in in Roscher. Bd. IV, 662-676.

Johnson, L. T.
> 1986 *The Writings of the New Testament.* An Interpretation. Philadelphia

Kalb, F.
> 1982 *Grundriss der Liturgik.* Eine Einführung in die Geschichte, Grundsätze und Ordnungen des lutherischen Gottesdienstes. 2. Aufl. München

Kapossy, B.
> 1969 *Brunnenfiguren der hellenistischen und römischen Zeit.* Diss. Zürich

Kazarow, G.
> 1930 *Grabstele von Mesembria.* (Jahreshefte des Österreichischen Archaeologischen Institutes, Bd. XXVI, 111-114)
> 1936 *Thrakische Religion.* Art. in RE, Bd. VI A,1, 472-551

Keller, O.
> 1909-1913 *Die antike Tierwelt.* Vols.1-2. Leipzig (1920 Gesamtregister von E. Staiger)

Kerényi, K.
> 1956 *Die Herkunft der Dionysosreligion nach dem heutigen Stand der Forschung.* (Arbeitsgemeinschaft für Forschung des Landes Nordrhein-Westphalen, Hefte 58, 5-22)

Kern, O.
> 1938 *Die Religion der Griechen.* Vols.III. Berlin

Klein, A. E.
> 1932 *Child Life in Greek Art.* New York

Knaack, G.
> 1903 *Bendis.* Art. in RE, Suppl.Bd. I, 247

Knopf, R.
    1907 *Die Apostelgeschichte,* I, 526-667
Kornemann, E.
    1901 *Collegium.* Art. in RE, Bd. IV, 380- 480
    ? *Grosse Frauen des Altertums.* 4. Aufl. Basel
Kraemer, R. S.
    1983 *Bibliography.* Women in the Religions of the Greco-Roman World. (Religious Studies Review, Vol. 9, 2, 127-139)
Kratz, R.
    1979 *Rettungswunder.* Motiv-, traditions- und formkritische Aufarbeitung einer biblischen Gattung. Frankfurt am Main
Kraus, Th.
    1960 *Hekate.* Studien zu Wesen und Bild der Göttin in Kleinasien und Griechenland. Heidelberg
Krause, C.
    1965a *Naiskosbilder.* Art. in LAW, 2055
    1965b *Römische Stadt* II. Art. in LAW, 2892-2900
Krenkel, W. A.
    1971 *Erotica I.* Der Abortus in der Antike. (Wissenschaftliche Zeitschrift der Universität Rostock, XX. Jahrgang, Heft 6, 443-452)
Kümmel, W. G.
    1970 *The New Testament: The History of the Investigation of Its Problems.* (Engl. Transl. 1972) Nashville / New York.
Köster, H.
    1980 *Einführung in das Neue Testament im Rahmen der Religionsgeschichte und Kulturgeschichte der hellenistischen und römischen Zeit.* Berlin / New York
Laager, J.
    1957 *Geburt und Kindheit des Gottes in der griechischen Mythologie.* Diss. Winterthur
Lampe, P.
    1987 *Die stadtrömischen Christen in den beiden ersten Jahrhunderten.* Untersuchungen zur Sozialgeschichte. (Wissenschaftliche Untersuchungen zum Neuen Testament 18. 2, Reihe). Tübingen
Lanckoronski, L. & M.
    1958 *Mythen und Münzen.* München
Lategan, B. C.
    1984 *Current Issues in the Hermeneutical Debate.* (Neotestamentica 18, 1-17)

Latte, K.
   1960 *Römische Religionsgeschichte.* (Handbuch der Altertumswissenschaft V:4). München

Lazarides, D.
   1973 *Philippoi.* Athen
   1976 *Philippi (Krenides).* Art. in The Princeton Encyclopedia of Classical Sites, 704-5

Lederer, Ph.
   1931 *Symbole der Aphrodite Urania.* (Zeitschrift für Numismatik, Nr. 41, 47-54, Pl.V)

van der Leeuw, G.
   1939 *Virginibus puerisque.* A Study on the Service of Children in Worship. (Mededelingen der Koninklijke Nederlandsche Akademie van Wetenschappen, Afd. Letterkunde. Nieuwe Reeks, Deel 2, Nr. 12, 446-485)

Lefkowitz, M. R. & Fant, M. (Ed.)
   1977 *Women in Greece and Rome.* Toronto / Sarasota

Lefkowitz, M. R.
   1981 *Heroines and Hysterics.* London
   1983 *Wives and husbands.* (Greece and Rome, Vol. XXX, 31-47)
   1986 *Women in Greek Myth.* London

Lemerle, P.
   1935 *Inscriptions latines et greques de Philippes.* (BCH, Vol. 59, 126-164)
   1937 *Nouvelles inscriptions latines de Philippes.* (BCH, Vol. 61, 410-420)

Levick, B.
   1967 *Roman Colonies in Southern Asia Minor.* Oxford

Liddell,H. G. & Scott, R.
   1867-1939 *A Greek-English Lexicon.* New Ed. Rev.H. Stuart Jones- R. McKenzie. Oxford

Lightman, M. & Zeisel, W.
   1977 *Univira: An example of Continuity and Change in Roman Society.* (Church History, Vol. 46, 19-32)

Lohfink G.
   1983 *Weibliche Diakone im Neuen Testament.* (Die Frau im Urchristentum. Ed. G. Dautzenberg & H. Merklein & K. Müller, 320-338) Freiburg / Basel / Wien

Lohmeyer, E.
   1953 *Die Briefe an die Philipper, an die Kolosser und an Philemon.* (Kritisch-exegetischer Kommentar über das Neue Testament 9) 9. Aufl. Göttingen

von Lorentz, F.
   1933 *Mosaik.* Art. in RE, Bd. XVI, 328-343)

Lucius, E.
   1904 *Die Anfänge des Heiligenkults in der christlichen Kirche.*
   (Hrsg. G. Anrich). Tübingen
Luck, G.
   1962 *Hexen und Zauberei in der römischen Dichtung.* Zürich
Lührmann, D.
   1981 *Neutestamentliche Haustafeln und antike Ökonomie.* (New
   Testament Studies, Vol. XXVII, 83-97)
Lönborg, S.
   1926 *En Dionysosmyt i Acta Apostolorum.* (Eranos. Acta
   Philologica Suecana. Vol. XXIV, 73-80)
MacMullen, R.
   1980 *Woman in Public in the Roman Empire.* (Historia, Bd.
   XXIX, 208-218)
Marquardt, J.
   1886 (1980) *Das Privatleben der Römer.* I-II. 2. Aufl. Darmstadt
Meeks, W. A.
   1974 *The Image of the Androgyne: Some Uses of a Symbol in
   Earliest Christianity.* (History of Religions, No.13, 165-208).
   1983 *The First Urban Christians.* The Social World of the Apostle
   Paul. New Haven
Meyer, E.
   1965 *Geten.* Art. in LAW, 1802
Mikalson, J. D.
   1983 *Athenian Popular Religion.* Chapel Hill / London
Mohler, S. L.
   1932 *Feminism in the Corpus Inscriptionum Latinarum.* (The
   Classical Weekly, Vol. XXV, 113-117)
Mommsen, Th.
   1869-82 *Schauspielerinschrift von Philippi.* (Hermes Bd. 3, 465-
   469; Bd. 17, 495-496)
Musurillo, H.
   1972 *The Acts of the Christian Martyrs.* Introduction, Texts and
   Translations. Oxford
Nestle, W.
   1898 *Die Legenden vom Tode des Euripides.* (Philologus, Bd.
   LVII, 134-149)
   1946 *Die Überwindung des Leids in der Antike.* (Griechische
   Weltanschauung in ihrer Bedeutung für die Gegenwart.
   Vorträge und Abhandlungen). Stuttgart

Niederwimmer, K.
   1975 *Askese und Mysterium*. Über Ehe, Ehescheidung und Eheverzicht in den Anfängen des christlichen Glaubens. Göttingen

Nilsson, M. P.
   1906 *Griechische Feste mit Ausschluss der Attischen*. Leipzig
   1954 *Roman and Greek domestic cult*. (Opuscula Romana, Vol. XVIII, 77-85)
   1957 *The Dionysiac Mysteries of the Hellenistic and Roman Age*. Lund
   1967-1976 *Geschichte der griechischen Religion*. Bd. I-II. 3, und 4. Aufl. (Handbuch der Altertumswissenschaft V: 2.1 und V: 2.2). München

Nock, A. D.
   1933 (1972) *Conversion*. London / Oxford / New York

Noetzel, H.
   1960 *Christus und Dionysus*. Bemerkungen zum religionsgeschichtlichen Hintergrund von Johannes 2, 1-11. (Arbeiten zur Theologie, Heft 1). Stuttgart

Noonan (Jr), J. T.
   1969 *Empfängnisverhütung*. Geschichte ihrer Beurteilung in der katholischen Theologie und im kanonischen Recht. Mainz

Norden, E.
   1957 (1984) *P. Vergilius Maro Aeneis Buch VI*. 4. Aufl. Darmstadt

Oehmichen, G.
   1890 *Das Bühnenwesen der Griechen und Römer*. (Handbuch der Altertumswissenschaft V:3,B). München

Ogilvie, R. M.
   1979 *The Romans and their Gods*. (Ancient Culture and Society). London

Orr, D.
   1978 *Roman Domestic Religion: The Evidence of the Household Shrines*. (ANRW, Bd. 16:2, 1556-1591) Berlin / New York

Otto, W. F.
   1933 *Dionysos. Mythos und Kultus*. Frankfurt am Main
   1970 *Die Götter Griechenlands*. Das Bild des Göttlichen im Spiegel des griechischen Geistes. 6. Aufl. Frankfurt am Main

Packer, J. E.
   1971 *The Insulae of Imperial Ostia*. (American Academy in Rome, 65-79)

Paoli, U. E.
   1961 *Das Leben im Alten Rom*. 2. Aufl. Bern / München

Papazouglou, F
: 1982 *Le territoire de la colonie de Philippes.* (BCH, Vol. 106, 89-106)

Parker, R.
: 1983 *Miasma.* Pollution and Purification in early Greek Religion. Oxford

Parlasca, K.
: 1971 *Osiris und Osirisglaube in der Kaiserzeit.* (Les syncrétismes dans les religions greque et romaine. Colloque de Strasbourg 9-11 juin 1971, 95-102) Paris

Patrick, A.
: 1967 *Disease in Antiquity: Ancient Greece and Rome.* (Diseases in Antiquity. Ed. D. Brothwell & A. T. Sandison, 238-246). Springfield, Illinois

Paulsen, H.
: 1985 *Die Briefe des Ignatius von Antiochia und der Brief des Polykarp von Smyrna.* (Handbuch zum Neuen Testament 18). 2. neubearb. Aufl. d. Auslegung von Walther Bauer. Tübingen

Pearce, T. E. V.
: 1974 *The Role of the Wife as CUSTOS in Ancient Rome.* (Eranos, Vol. LXXII, 16-33)

Peiper, A.
: 1951 *Chronik der Kinderheilkunde: Griechen und Römer.* Leipzig

Perdrizet, P.
: 1898 *Voyage dans la Macédoine première (1).* Un tombeau du type "macédonien" au N. O. du Pangée. (BCH, Vol. 22, 335-353)
: 1900 *Inscriptions de Philippes.* (BCH, Vol. 24, 299-323)
: 1910 *Cultes et Mythes du Pangé.* Paris / Nancy

Pfister, K.
: 1924 *Katakombenmalerei.* (Die Kunst des Mittelalters.Hrsg. K. Pfister. Bd. 1). Potsdam

Pfitzner, V. C.
: 1967 *Paul and the Agon Motif.* Traditional Athletic Imaginary in the Pauline Literature. (Supplements to Novum Testamentum, Vol. XVI). Leiden

Pfuhl, E. & Möbius, H.
: 1979 *Die ostgriechischen Grabreliefs.* Bd. I-IV. Mainz am Rhein

Phillips, J. E.
: 1978 *Roman Mothers and the Lives of their Adult Daughters.* (Helios 6, 69-80)

Picard, Ch.
    1922 *Les dieux de la colonie de Philippes vers le Ier siècle de notre ère, d'après les ex-voto rupestres.* (Revue de l'histoire des religions, 117-201)

Plümacher, E.
    1972 *Lukas als hellenistischer Schriftsteller.* Studien zur Apostelgeschichte. Göttingen

Poland, F.
    1909 *Geschichte des griechischen Vereinswesen.* Leipzig

Pomeroy, S. B.
    1976 *The Relationship of the Married Woman to her Blood Relatives in Rome.* (Ancient Society 7, 215-227)

Portefaix, L.
    1981 *Concepts of Ecstasy in Euripides' "Bacchanals" and their Interpretation.* (Religious Ecstasy. Based on Papers read at the Symposium on Religious Ecstasy held at Åbo, Finland, on the 26th–28th of August 1981. Ed. N.G. Holm, 201-210). Stockholm
    1983 *Religio-ecological Aspects of Ancient Greek Religion from the Point of view of Woman: A Tentative Approach.* (Temenos, 144-149)

Préaux, C.
    1978 *Le monde hellénistique.* La Grèce et l'Orient de la mort d'Alexandre à la cõnquete romaine de la Grèce. (323-146 J.-C.). Paris

Preller, L.
    1881 *Römische Mythologie.* 3rd Ed. Berlin

Price, T. H.
    1978 *Kourothrophos. Cults and Representations of the Greek Nursing Deities.* (Studies of the Dutch Archaeological and Historical Society, Vol. VIII) Leiden

Quasten, J.
    1930 *Musik und Gesang in den Kulten der heidnischen Antike und christlichen Frühzeit.* Münster in Westf.

Raditsa, L. F.
    1980 *Augustus' Legislation Concerning Marriage, Procreation, Love Affairs and Adultery.* (ANRW, Bd. 13,2, 278-339)

Radke, G.
    1975 *Voltinia tribus.* Art. in DKP, Bd. 5, 1326

Rapp, A.
    1872 *Die Mänade im griechischen Cultus in der Kunst und Poesie.* (Rheinisches Museum für Philologie, Bd. 27, 1-22)

Redfield, J.
    1982 *Notes on the Greek wedding.* (Arethusa 15, 181-201)

Redford, D. B.
    1967 *The literary motif of the exposed child (cf Ex.II 1-10)*. (Numen, Vol. XIV, 209-228)

Regling, K.
    1923 *Nordgriechische Münzen der Blütezeit*. Berlin

Reinhold, M.
    1970 *History of Purple as a Status Symbole in Antiquity*. (Collection Latomus 16) Bruxelles

Richmond, I. A.
    1950 *Archaeology, and the After-life in Pagan and Christian Imagery*. (Riddell Memorial Lectures, 20th Series) London / New York / Toronto

Riesenfeld, H.
    1983 *Unpoetische Hymnen im Neuen Testament? Zu Phil 2, 1-11.* (Glaube und Gerechtigkeit. In memoriam Rafael Gyllenberg. Ed. J.Kiilunen et al. Schriften der Finnischen Exegetischen Gesellschaft 38, 155-168)

Rix, H.
    1965 *Personennamen*. Art. in LAW, 268-269

Rohde, E.
    1921 *Psyche. Seelencult und Unsterblichkeitsglaube der Griechen*. (Teil. 1-2). 7. und 8. Aufl. Tübingen

Roscher, W. H.
    1886-90 *Hekate*. Art. in Roscher, Bd. I:2,1885-1910.

Rose, H. J.
    1925 *The Bride of Hades*. (Classical Philology, Vol. 20, 238-242)

Rudberg, G.
    1926 *Zu den Bakchen des Euripides*. (Symbolae Osloenses, Fasc.IV)

Rumpf, A.
    1964 *Ara Pacis Augustae*. Art. in DKP, Bd. 1, 482

Rühfel, H.
    1984 *Das Kind in der griechischen Kunst. Von der minoisch-mykenischen Zeit bis zum Hellenismus*. Mainz am Rhein

Salac, A.
    1923 *Inscriptions du Pangée, de la région Drama-Cavalla et de Philippes*. (BCH, Vol. 47, 49-96)

Salditt-Trappmann, R.
    1970 *Tempel der ägyptischen Götter in Griechenland und an der Westküste Kleinasiens*. Leiden

Salskov Roberts, H.
    1977 *En piges chancer i Oldtiden*. (En kvindes chancer i Oldtiden. Opuscula Graecolatina, Museum Tusculanum,Vol. 13, 11-47) Köpenhamn

Salviat, F.
    1958 *Une nouvelle loi Thasienne: institutions judiciaires et fêtes religieuses à la fin du IV siècle av. J.-C.* (BCH, vol 82, 193-267)

Samter, E.
    1901 *Familienfeste der Griechen und Römer*. Berlin

Sasse, H.
    1965 καταχθόνιος. Art. in Th. Dict. N.T., Vol.III, 633-634

Scharffenorth, G. & Thraede, K.
    1977 *"Freunde in Christus werden..."* Die Beziehung von Mann und Frau als Frage an Theologie und Kirche. Gelnhausen / Berlin

Schenk, W.
    1984 *Die Philipperbriefe des Paulus*. Kommentar. Stuttgart / Berlin /Köln / Mainz

Schierling, S. & M.
    1978 *The Influence of the Ancient Romances on Acts of the Apostles*. (The Classical Bulletin, Vol. 54, 81-88)

Schlier, H.
    1965 κερδαίνω. Art. in Th. Dict. N.T., Vol. III, 672-673

Schmaltz, B.
    1983 *Griechische Grabreliefs*. (Erträge der Forschung, Bd. 192). Darmstadt

Schmidt, J.
    1916-24 *Telesphoros I*. Art. in Roscher, Bd. V, 309-326)

Schmidt, R.
    1977 *Die Darstellung von Kinderspielzeug und Kinderspiel in der griechischen Kunst*. Wien

Schneider, G.
    1980 *Die Apostelgeschichte*. Teil I. (Herders Theologischer Kommentar zum Neuen Testament 5). Freiburg / Basel / Wien

Schoedel, W. R.
    1967 *The Apostolic Fathers*. A New Translation and Commentary. (Polycarp, Martyrdom of Polycarp, Fragments of Papias). Vol. 5. London / Camden, N. J. / Toronto

Scholz, U. W.
    1973 *Erinna*. (Antike und Abendland, Bd. XVIII, 15-40)

Schuhmann, E.
    1977 *Hinweise auf Kulthandlungen im Zusammenhang mit plautinischen Frauengestalten*. (Klio, Bd. 59, 137-147)

Schwabacher, W.
    1941 *Hellenistische Reliefkeramik im Kerameikos.* (American Journal of Archaeology, 45, 182-228)

Schweizer, E.
    1982 *The Letter to the Colossians.* London

Schüssler Fiorenza, E.
    1984 *Bread Not Stone. The Challenge of Feminist Biblical Interpretation.* Boston

Scranton, R. L. (Ed.)
    1976-8 *Kenchreai: Eastern Port of Corinth.*
    Vol. 1: Topography and Architecture.(R. Scranton & J. W. Shaw & L. Ibrahim).
    Vol. 2: The Panels of Opus Sectile in Glass. (L. Ibrahim & R. Scranton & R. Brill). Leiden

Scroggs, R.
    1972 *Paul and the Eschatological Women.* (Journal of the American Academy of Religion, Vol. XL, 283-303)

Segal, Ch.
    1978 *The Menace of Dionysos: Sex Roles and Reversals in Euripides' Bacchae.* (Arethusa, Vol. 11, 185-201)

von Severus, E.
    1972 *Gebet I.* Art. in RAC, Bd. VIII, 1134-1258

Seyrig, H.
    1927 *Quatre cultes de Thasos.* (BCH, Vol. 51, 178-233)

Sichtermann, H. & Koch, G.
    1975 *Griechische Mythen auf römischen Sarkophagen.* Tübingen

Simon, D.
    1969 *Ius Italicum.* Art. in DKP, Bd. 3, 14

Simon, M.
    1964 *Remarques sur la catacombe de la Via Latina.* (Mullus. Festschrift Th. Klauser. 327-335). Münster Westfalen

Sittig, E.
    1911 *De Graecorum Nominibus Theophoris.* Diss. Berolinensis. Halis Saxonum

Slater, W. J.
    1974 *Pueri, Turba Minuta.* (Bulletin of the Institute of Classical studies, University of London, Vol. 21, 133-140)

Smith, D. E.
    1977 *The Egyptian Cults at Corinth.* (Harvard Theological Review, Vol. 70, 201-231)

Stauffer, E.
    1955 *New Testament Theology.* 5th Ed. London

Stoll, H. W.
    1884-86 *Ariadne.* Art. in Roscher, Bd. I,1, 540-546.
    1884-86 *Eurydike.* Art. in Roscher, Bd. I,1, 1421-1423
Suleiman, S. R. (Ed.)
    1980 *The Reader in the Text.* Essays on Audience and Interpretation. Princeton
Szepessy, T.
    1972 *The Story of the Girl who Died on the Day of her Wedding.* (Acta Antiqua, Vol. XX, 341-357)
Tanner, R. G.
    1978 *St. Paul's View of Militia and Contemporary Social Values.* (Studia Biblica 1978: III. Papers on Paul and Other New Testament Authors. Ed. E. A. Livingstone, 377-382). Sheffield
Theissen, G.
    1977 *Soziologie der Jesusbewegung.* Ein Beitrag zur Entstehungsgeschichte des Urchristentums. (Theologische Existenz heute 194). München
    1979 *Studien zur Soziologie des Urchristentums.* (Wissenschaftliche Untersuchungen zum Neuen Testament 19) Tübingen
Thraemer, E.
    1886 *Dionysos in der Kunst.* Art. in Roscher, Bd,I,1, 1089-1153
Toynbee, J. M. C.
    1971 *Death and Burial in the Roman World.* London
Treggiari, S.
    1976 *Jobs for Women.* (American Journal of Ancient History, 1, 76-104)
    1979 *Lower Class Women in the Roman Economy.* (Florilegium, Vol. 1, 65-86)
Turcan, R.
    1966 *Les sarcophages romains à représentations dionysiaque.* Essai de chronologie et d'histoire religieuse. Thèse. Paris
van Unnik, W. C.
    1979 *Luke's Second Book and the Rules of Hellenistic Historiography.* (Les Actes des Apôtres. Traditions, rédaction, théologie. Ed. J. Kremer. Bibliotheca Ephemeridum Theologicarum Lovaniensium XLVIII, 37-60). Louvain
Wallace-Hadrill, A.
    1981 *Family and Inheritance in the Augustan Marriage Laws.* (Proceedings of the Cambridge Philosophical Society, No.207, New Series 27, 58-80)
Watts, W. J.
    1973 *Ovid, the Law and Roman Society on Abortion.* (Acta Classica, Vol. XVI, 89-101)

Weiler, I.
   1980 *Zum Schicksal der Witwen und Waisen bei den Völkern der Alten Welt*. Material für eine vergleichende Geschichtswissenschaft. (Saeculum, Bd. 31, 157-193)

Weinreich, O.
   1929 *Gebet und Wunder*. Zwei Abhandlungen zur Religions-und Literaturgeschichte. (Genethliakon Wilhelm Schmid zum 70 Geburtstag). Stuttgart
   1933 *Menekrates Zeus und Salmoneus*. Religionsgeschichtliche Studien zur Psychopatologie des Gottmenschentums in Antike und Neuzeit. (Tübinger Beiträge zur Altertumswissenschaft XVIII). Stuttgart

Weiss, J.
   1910 *Der erste Korintherbrief*. (Kritisch-exegethischer Kommentar über das Neue Testament. 5). 9. Aufl. Göttingen

Wendland, H.-D.
   1968 *Die Briefe an die Korinther*. Übersetzt und erklärt. Göttingen

Wengst, K
   1986 *Pax Romana and the Peace of Jesus Christ*. (Engl. Transl. 1987). London

Vermaseren, M. J.
   1977 *Cybele and Attis*. The Myth and the Cult. London

Vidman, L.
   1981 *Isis und Sarapis*. (OrRR, EPRO, 121-156)

Vielhauer, Ph.
   1978 (1981) *Geschichte der urchristlichen Literatur*. Einleitung in das Neue Testament, die Apokryphen und die Apostolischen Väter. Berlin/New York

Wikenhauser, A.
   1921 *Die Apostelgeschichte und ihr Geschichtswert*. Münster

Wissowa. G.
   1902 *Religion und Kultur der Römer*. (Handbuch der klassischen Altertumswissenschaft IV,5). 2. Aufl. 1912 (1972). München

Witt, R. E.
   1971 *Isis in the Graeco-Roman World*. (Aspects of Greek and Roman Life). London

Vogliano, A. & Cumont, F. & Alexander, Ch.
   1933 *La grande iscrizione bacchica del Metropolitan Museum*. (American Journal of Archaeology, Vol. XXXVII, 215-70)

Vollgraff, W.
   1903 *Inscriptions d'Argos*. (BCH, Vol. 27, 260-279)

Wotschitzky, A.
    1955 *Hochhäuser im antiken Rom.* (Innsbrucker Beiträge zur Kulturwissenschaft, Bd. 3, 151-158)

Wrede, H.
    1971 *Das Mausoleum der Claudia Semne und die bürgerliche Plastik der Kaiserzeit.* (Mitteilungen des Deutschen Archaeologischen Instituts, Roemische Abteilung, Bd. 78. 125-166)

Wüst, E.
    1983 *Pantomimus.* Art. in RE, Bd. XVIII,3, 833-869

Yarbrough, O. L.
    1984 *Not Like The Gentiles.* Marriage Rules in the Letters of Paul. Diss. Atlanta, Georgia

Zahn, Th.
    1906 *Einleitung in das Neue Testament.* Bd. I. 3. Aufl. Leipzig

Ziegler, K.
    1939 *Orpheus.* Art. in RE, Bd. XVIII,1, 1200-1316
    1969 *Matronalia.* Art. in DKP, Bd. 3, 1085

Zingerle, J.
    1928 *Ein Fall von Kindertuberkulose vor 1700 Jahren.* (Zeitschrift für Kinderheilkunde, Bd. 46, 440-444)

AUTHOR INDEX

Aalen	138	Carter	77
Abrahamsen	5, 72, 78, 94	Cavallin	202
Altmann	91	Clark	12, 14, *18*, 22, 42
Amundsen & Diers	13	Clauss	*60*, 73
Andrae	110, 151	Collart	59, *60-73*, 76, 78, 82, 86, 94, 98-100, 104, 105, 114, 115, 118, 140
Areskog	29		
Balch	4, 184		
Balsdon	11, 22, 68, *69*, *139*	Collart & Ducrey	68, 72, 77, *78*, 79, 81-4, 86, 91, 94, *96*, 99, 118, 141
Barrett	*175*, 180, 185, 188, 189		
Baur	107		
Baus	140	Cook	73
Bayet	98	Corbett	21
Benko	189, 191	Crook	26
Bergman	117, 119, 120, 126	Csillag	17, 18
		Cullman	193
Bergquist	98, 101		
Bertelli	110, 148, 171	Dassmann	28, 181, 190, 191
Beskow	159	Dautzenberg	4
Betz	*144*, 152, 159, *179*, 184	Daux	77
		D'Avino	23
Blanck	*64*, 65	Delcourt	10
Blümner	33, *38*, *46*, *47*, *48*, 53, 57	Deubner	97
		Dibelius	*138*, 157, 181
Bolkestein	143	Dieterich	102
Bonner	21, *35*, *36*, 42	Dodds	102, 103
Bonnet	120, 124, 148, *150*	Domaszewski	73
		Drerup	38
Bothmer	141	Drexler	119
Bradley	22	Düll	91, 148
Bremmer	102	Dölger	53, 105, 106
Brommer	21, 143, 148		
Brown	166	Egger	92, *93*
Bruck	43, 98	Elliger	169
Bruhns	102	Engels	11, 12, 13
Burkert	80, 100, 103	Ernst	135
Burton	*117*, 118, *150*		
Buschor	41	Farnell	76
		Fehrle	23
Cagnat	60, 100	Ferguson	153
Cahen	113	Finley	9, 12, 18

Fischer	186		Iser	131, *133*, 136
Fowler	3			
Fraser	121		Jauss	131, *132*, 133
Frend	190		Jeremias	190, 193
Frenz	38		Jervell	158
Frothingham	62		Jessen	109
Fuhrmann	35		Johnson	6, 137
Gagé	89		Kalb	186
Gardner	9, *15*, 21, *22, 23,*		Kapossy	37
	24, 25, *26, 27, 29,*		Kazarow	*76*, 77, 87, *88, 89*
	47, 195		Keller	41
Garnsey	67		Kerényi	98
Gnilka	6, *135*, 136, 139,		Kern	98, 153
	142, 175, 186,		Klein	36, *41*
	198		Knaack	77
Goetze	13		Knopf	168
Golden	12		Kornemann	98, 141
Grandjean	116, *120*, 121		Kraemer	4
Grant	185		Kratz	169
Gren	66, *67*		Kraus	*76, 77, 80*, 82, 88
Griffiths	115, *117*, 121		Krause	62, 86
Gruppe	100, 110, 113		Krenkel	14
Gundel	100		Kümmel	3, 4, 5
			Köster	4, 194
Hack	12			
Haenchen	170		Laager	112
Hallett	18		Lampe	5
Hanson	91		Lanckoronski	37
Harder	117, *118*		Lategan	3, 133, *134*
Harmon	43, 44, *46*, 48		Latte	48, 55, 77, 78,
Harnack	168			97, *99*, 101, 163
Harris	140		Lazarides	59, 61, 63
Hartman	136, 175, 184		Lederer	154
Heckenbach	57, 76		v. d. Leeuw	40, 42, 43
Hengel	142, 143, 144		Lefkowitz	52
Henrichs	102		Leipoldt	161
Henze	187		Lemerle	76, 118
Heubeck	101, 170		Levick	61, *68*, 140
Heuzey	99, 105		Lightman & Zeisel 16, 17, 46, 47	
Heyob	*115*, 116, 126		Lohfink	*138*, 178
Himmelmann	20, 144		Lohmeyer	181
Hopkins	11, 12, 47		v. Lorentz	37
Horn	106		Lucius	183
Hug	99		Luck	57, 58
Hunger	106, 107, 108,		Lührmann	184
	109, 110, 111,		Lönborg	169
	112			
Hägg	153, 155		Mac Mullen	50
			Marquardt	*37*, 40

Meeks	*137*, 179	Quasten	49
Meyer	55		
Mikalson	20	Raditsa	17
Mohler	23, *50*	Radke	84
Mommsen	37	Rapp	103
Musurillo	196	Redfield	86
		Redford	11
Nestle	102, 145, *146*	Regling	154
Niederwimmer	146, 195, 196	Reinhold	171
Nilsson	42-6, 76, 78, 80-2, 88, 91, 97-8, 105-7, 117, 119, 123, 144, 147	Richmond	151
		Riesenfeld	142
		Rix	101
		Rohde	53, 98
Nock	4, 54	Roscher	88
Noetzel	161	Rose	53
Noonan	14	Rudberg	169
Norden	89	Rumpf	165
		Rühfel	41
Oehmichen	86		
Ogilvie	44	Salac	84
Orr	*45*, 46	Salditt-Trappmann	72, *115*
Otto	105, 107, 152	Salskov-Roberts	14
		Salviat	77
Packer	*63*, 64	Samter	57
Paoli	65	Sasse	148
Papazouglou	61	Schenk	135
Parker	33, *57*	Scharffenorth	2
Parlasca	151	Schierling	155, 158
Patrick	14	Schlier	142
Paulsen	180	Schmaltz	86
Pearce	25	Schmidt	*41*, 118
Peiper	10	Schneider	*155*, 157, 164, 182
Perdrizet	73, 76, 82, *84*, 100, *104*, 110, 148		
		Schoedel	155, *180*
		Scholz	31
Pfister	187	Schuhmann	43, 45, 49, 55
Pfitzner	140	Schwabacher	107
Phillips	19	Schweizer	175
Picard	94, 116, 119	Schüssler Fiorenza	3, 4
Pfuhl & Möbius	85, 86	Scranton	115
Plümacher	135, 155, 156, 169, 172, 177, 180	Scroggs	183
		Segal	103
		v.Severus	185, 186
Poland	97	Seyrig	98
Pomeroy	15, *18*	Sichtermann	88
Portefaix	76, 102, 103	Simon, D.	65
Préaux	61	Simon, M.	110
Preller	113	Sittig	109
Price	81	Slater	22
		Smith	115

Stauffer	139
Stoll	107, *108,* 110
Suleiman	131
Szepessy	53
Tanner	140
Theissen	5
Thraede	4
Thraemer	107, 113
Toynbee	13
Treggiari	*24,* 25, *27*
Turcan	105, 108, 109, 112, 113
v. Unnik	180
Vermaseren	52
Vidman	115, 116, 124
Vielhauer	5, 175, 177, 180, 194
Vogliano	103, *106*
Vollgraff	104
Wallace-Hadrill	17
Watts	11, 14
Weiler	18
Weinreich	154, 169
Weiss	193
Wendland	193, 195
Wengst	165
Wikenhauser	132, 168
Wilamovwitz	98
Wissowa	43, 45, 77, *124*
Witt	116
Wotschitsky	63, 64
Wrede	90, 91
Wüst	37
Yarbrough	146, 196, 198
Zahn	137
Ziegler	48, 110, 112
Zingerle	13

GREEK AND LATIN REFERENCES

1) TEXTS OUTSIDE CHRISTIAN ORIGINS AND TRADITION

Ael
NA
10, 23	125

Aesch
Supp
676	77
fr. 31	113

Amm Marc
23, 4	69
27, 4, 8	102

Anth Gr
6, 280	43
7, 710	31
7, 712	31
9, 26	31
9, 46	82
9, 190	31
9, 245	29
9, 468	148, 163
9, 469	148, 163

Apollod
Bibl
1, 3, 2, 2	110
1, 9, 15	148
2, 4, 12	143
2, 6, 3	143
2, 7, 7	148, 163
3, 1, 1	100
3, 4, 3	113
3. 5. 3	148
3, 8, 2	95

App
BCiv
4, 47	124
4, 105-6	71
4, 105	60, 61, 62, 63
4, 106	61
5, 3	60

Apul
Met
3, 8	27, 159
3, 17-18	57
6, 9	28
8, 27	171
11	115, 117
11, 3	122
11, 4	116
11, 5	116, 119
11, 6	119
11, 22	116
11, 24	52

Ar
Ach
241ff	40, 44

Plut
593-97	195

Ran
366	45

Arist
Hist An
588a, 3-10	11
608b, 15	12

Pol
1260a, 9-14	15

Poet
1448a	132
1448b, 2	40
1453b	132

Artem
1, 56   50
1, 74   15
1, 78   19
2, 33   45
2, 34   80, 81, 142
2, 36   82
2, 37   81, 154
2, 39   152
2, 44   143
2, 49   9
3, 36   15
4, 39   102
4, 59   101
4, 78   45

Ath
3, 98D   153
3, 98E   154
13, 555c   23

Callim
Dian
1-40   113
236-58   141

Callistr
3, 10-11   145

Cato
Agr
141, 2   45
143, 1-2   54
143, 2   45

Catull
34, 1ff   42
64, 124ff   108

Celsus
Med
7, 29   13

Censorinus
D N
11, 7   33

Cic
Att
14, 20, 2   14

Clu
9, 27   20
32   14
De orat
3, 23, 87   42
Div
1, 6, 12   55
In Vat
11, 28   88
Leg
2, 21, 52   43
2, 24, 60   48
2, 55   45
3, 19   10
Marcell
18   192
Nat D
3, 5, 12   35
Verr
2, 18, 47   36
4, 35, 77   49

Columella
Rust
11, 1, 19   43
12, 1-8 pref   25
12, 1, 1-3   25
12, 3, 3ff   66
12, 4, 3   42
12, 7-8 pref   16
12, 9-10 pref 17, 25, 126

Corp Gloss Lat
3, 39, 49ff   35

Dem
De Cor
259-60   57
260   57

Dio Cass
36, 52, 3   143
48, 2, 3   60
51, 6   60
51, 25   104
54, 34   104
60, 17, 4   68
62, 3, 4   143
68, 9, 6   143

Dio Chrys		*Bacch*	
30, 26	153	1ff	100
37, 25	69	4	143, 170
		26ff	143
Diod Sic		39	102
1, 23, 1	121	55ff	170
1, 23, 8	109	101-3	103
1, 25, 2-5	118, 119	118	144
1, 25, 6	119, 125	272ff	170
1, 27, 1	122	300f	103, 145, 164,
1, 27, 1-2	121		165, 171
1, 92	150	353	113
2, 59, 2	153	453-9	143, 152
2, 59, 7	153	455f	143, 163
4, 3	101	493	143
4, 3, 3	103	509ff	143
4, 28	148	600ff	170
4, 31	143	604ff	170
4, 38	148, 163	699-703	103
5, 3, 2, 3	112	704-10	103
5, 4, 3-6	112	757f	164
11, 70, 5	59, 60	761ff	141
12, 14, 3-15	20	855	113
12, 68, 1-3	59, 60	1030	170
16, 3, 2	140	1079ff	143
16, 3, 7	60, 62	1236	144
16, 8, 6-7	59, 60, 61	*Heracl*	
25, 2-7	117	22ff	148
		Med	
Diog Laert		238-48	29
6, 96ff	144	250-51	29, 141
10, 4	57	397	44, 45
		Rhes	
Dion Hal		965	104
Ant Rom			
2, 15	10		
2, 22	40	Festus	
2, 25, 2	43	*Gloss Lat*	
2, 26, 4	15	407 s.v. 'Rica'	42
2, 64, 5	56		
9, 51, 6	11		
		Gell	
Eur		*NA*	
Alc		10, 9	69
153-74	111	12, 1, 22-3	20
163-9	53	17, 6, 1	24
280-4	111		
305-7	111	Hdt	
1008ff	110, 148	2, 42	121
		2, 44	98

4, 33	76	*Epod*	
5, 7	70, 76, 98	2, 65f	43
7, 111	73, 104, 99, 100, 104	*Epist*	
		2, 1, 5	148, 163
7, 112	59, 60, 61	2, 1, 62	35
		2, 1, 69ff	35, 42
Hes		2, 2	47
Theog		*Sat*	
411-15	80	2, 5, 12ff	43
411-52	80	2, 6, 77	35
416-20	80	6, 64f	43
429-33	80		
450-2	81, 82, 91	Hsch	
940ff	109	s.v. Ἀδμήτου κόρη	76
947ff	109	s.v. Βενδῖς	76
Cat of wom		s.v. δίλογχον	76
71	89		
		Hymn Hom	
Himer		*Cer*	
6, 2, 3	69	59-61	77
		459-68	112
Hippoc		483-7	147
Aph			
24-8	12	Hymn Orph	
De morb mul		1, 7	80
72, 6-7	14	1, 8	81
Oct.		12, 8	81
450, 20-4	12		
		Isae	
Hom		6, 40-1	47
Il			
6, 130ff	105	Julian	
8, 357ff	148	*Mis*	
21, 483f	77	363A	160, 194-
21, 489-96	94		
Od		Juv	
4, 120-2	95	5, 164	34
6, 102ff	93	6, 184-99	69
6, 149-52	95	6, 434ff	35
10, 235-43	57	6, 535-41	115
11, 620ff	148	6, 602ff	11
17, 36-44	95	6, 652	110
20, 70-2	93	7, 175-7	42
		11, 18	38
Hor			
Carm		Livy	
2, 16, 13ff	42	6, 41	192
3, 3, 13	148, 163	21, 62	64
Carm Saec		34, 3, 9	171
75-6	50	34, 7, 3	171

34, 7, 11-15	16	3, 69	36
37, 3, 6	42	7, 20, 20	64
39, 9	20	8, 3, 13-16	36
39, 9, 5	28	9, 18	64
39, 10	28, 29	10, 68	69
39, 19, 5-6	28, 29	10, 70, 7	82
39, 24	61		
42, 34	19	Mus Ruf	
		III	31, 197
Lucian		IV	31, 197
Amor		XV B, 119	10
42	54, 55		
De Luct		Non	
2-9	29, 151	852	44
11	47		
Dial Meret		Nonnos	
6	25, 27, 122, 159	*Dion*	
Gall		8, 27ff	162
9	18	10, 292f	106
Hermot		27, 341	106
11	18	44, 213	106
Hist conscr		47, 268ff	108
10	143		
Men		Ov	
3	144	*Ars Am*	
Peregr		1, 527ff	108
12	182	*Fast*	
13	189	2, 626	28
Salt		2, 650	42
39	37, 109	3, 363	185
49	37	3, 512	99
51	37	3, 809ff	49
52	110	4, 419ff	112
80	109	6, 305f	43
		Her	
		9, 55	143
Lucr		10	108
5, 1198ff	195	*Met*	
		5, 341ff	112
Macrob		8, 175ff	108
Sat		9, 666-776	119, 121, 123
1, 6, 14	42	10, 1ff	110
1, 15, 22	43	*Rem Am*	
1, 16, 36	33	593-4	97, 104
		Tr	
Mart		2, 533-6	35
1, 35, 1-3	36		
1, 86, 12	64		
1, 117, 7	64		
3, 58, 22	21		

Paus
1, 3, 3	37
1, 15, 2	141
1, 43, 1	89
2, 2, 3	115
2, 31, 2	110, 147, 148
2, 32, 9	141
2, 37, 5	110
5, 11, 4	141
5, 25, 11	141
9, 29, 3	70
10, 28, 3	97

Pers
2, 31-40	20, 34

Petron
Sat
29	44
48, 3	69

Philo
De vit cont
64-82	185

Philostr
Imag
1, 15	34, 108
2, 17	103

Pl
Leg
658D	37
887D	34, 37
887D-E	38

Resp
381D	57
381E	35

Symp
179C-D	112
189D	113

Plaut
Amph
1093f	45

Aul
23-8	40, 44

Cist
660ff	21

Merc
678-80	45

Mil
690ff	55
691f	48
692	49
693f	57

Rud
131ff	56
270ff	56
282	56
283f	56
406	56
1171	34

Pliny
HN
4, 4	100
4, 10, 37	154
7, 16, 72	12
22, 3ff	171
28, 39	34
31	102
33, 84	34
34, 53, 75	141
35, 2, 7-8	38
35, 6	38
36, 29	99

Pliny
Ep
2, 14, 2	69
2, 19, 1	36
3, 19, 4	36
4, 19, 1	21
5, 3, 8	36
5, 19, 3	35
7, 17, 1	36
8, 1	14
8, 1, 2	35
8, 10, 1-2	13
9, 36, 4	35
10, 65	21
10, 96, 2	187
10, 96, 5	191, 192
10, 96, 6	195
10, 96, 7	185, 189
10, 96, 8	182, 198
10, 96, 9	178, 190
10, 96, 10	192
10, 97	191, 192

Plut			Polyb	
Mor			6, 53, 3-6	38, 45, 48
1A-B	26		6, 53, 1-10	39
64F	27, 29		15, 29, 8-9	143
114F-115A	47		18, 30, 11	141
119B	47		31, 26, 3-5	49, 56
133B	27, 29		31, 26, 7-8	49
140D	53		31, 26, 10	49
142D	16		54, 1-3	39
143A-B	28			
144D	26		Prop	
249E-F	102		1, 2, 27-28	42
278E-F	101		2, 1, 9-10	42
351E	121		2, 32, 8ff	77
352C	121		3, 11, 39ff	114
356A	124		4, 3, 51	47
356A-361D	121		4, 11	16
358B	125			
361D	125		Quint	
361E	124		*Inst*	
364E	115, 121		2, 10, 5	20
365E	154		1, 1, 7	21
407C	53		1, 8, 5ff	69
497E	10f		1, 9, 2	35
527F	171		10, 1, 67-68	35
557D	106			
609B	47		Schol. Serv. Aen	
679D	44		1, 730	42
704B	42		2, 351	46
753D	26		11, 543	42
Vit Alex				
2	101, 141		*Schol in Vesp*	
41, 5	27		804	81
Vit Ant				
4, 2	27		Sen	
Vit Cat Mai			*Controv*	
20	16, 21		2, 1, 17	38
Vit Cat Min			9, 5	20
1	21		9, 6	20
Vit Crass			10, 4, 17	11
8	104			
8, 3	73		Sen	
Vit Demetr			*Ad Marc*	
24, 1	27		2, 3ff	47
Vit Num			3, 1ff	47
9-11	56		*Apocol*	
10, 2	23		13, 4	125
12	11, 12		*De ir*	
			1, 15, 2	10

Soph		Tac	
Trach		*Ann*	
1098	148	2, 86	40
fr		3, 76	40
583	13, 29	12, 8	78
		13, 32, 3-5	198
Sor		15, 44, 2-8	191
Gyn		15, 44	192
1, 5, 25	13	*Dial*	
1, 8, 33	13	28, 4-5	16, 18, 20
1, 10, 38	10	28, 4	19, 21
1, 10, 39	10	28, 5	28
1, 14, 46	13	29, 1-3	17, 35
2, 6, 10	10	*Hist*	
2, 10, 16	12	4, 53	40
2, 12, 19	19	5, 5	11
2, 21, 47	19		
2, 21, 48	12	Ter	
		Hec	
Stat		220	28
Silv		623	28
3, 5, 64ff	42		
		Theoc	
Strab		*Id*	
239	77	2	57
297	9, 101, 112, 194	2, 10ff	57
319	89	15	49
630	171		
824	11	Theophr	
frs		*Char*	
7, 34	61	16	44, 45, 195
7, 35	153	16, 14	57
7, 41	60	*Hist Pl*	
		2, 2, 7	61
Suet		6, 6, 4	61
Aug			
64, 2-3	21	Tib	
Calig		2, 1, 21-4	21
16	42		
Claud		Val Max	
27	10	5, 6, 8	34
Ner			
6	57	Verg	
16	190	*Aen*	
16, 2	191	1, 496-504	95
Vesp		3, 405	185
2, 1	21	4, 511	76, 77
Gram		6, 426-9	53
7, 21	11	6, 637-8	89
		6, 796ff	114

7, 803-7	95		Clem. Alex.	
7, 812-17	95		*Protr*	
7, 814	171		4, 48	154
8, 685ff	114			
11, 659ff	141		Clem. Rom.	
G			1, 6, 2	181
2, 128	20		1, 6, 3	195
4, 453ff	110		1, 11-12	182
			1, 21, 7	188
Vitr			1, 47, 1	136
De Arch			1, 55, 3-6	183
8, 16	102			
			Did	
Xen			2, 2	194
Lac			7	186
1, 3	12		7, 1	177
Oec			8	186
7, 7-8	43		8, 3	190
7, 35-36	25			
Symp			Diog	
9, 2-7	108		5, 6	194

2) EARLY CHRISTIAN TEXTS–CHURCH-FATHERS

			Eus	
			Hist Eccl	
			7, 10, 3-4	191
			Firm Mat	
Ambr			*Err prof rel*	
Virg			2, 1-3	124
1, 11, 58	181		2, 9	125
1, 11, 63-65	181			
			Ign	
Apost Constit			*Sm*	
4, 11	190		13, 1	180
Arist			Jerome	
248	194		*Ep*	
			14, 3	21
Arnob			54, 15	20
Adv Nat			127, 3	171
2, 67	42			
			J Chrys	
Aug			*Hom in Mt*	
Conf			66, 3	182
1, 11	194, 196		*Hom in Acts*	
			26	187
Barn			*Hom in Ps*	
19, 5	194		41, 2	186

Just
Apol
2, 2   195, 199

Lactant
De mort. persecut.
10   191

Mart Lyon
41   196

Mart Polyc
9, 3   192

Min Fel
Oct
9   187, 190
23, 1   124
24, 1   35

Polyc
Phil
1, 1   167, 181, 188
4, 2   168, 180, 187, 188
4, 3   138, 160, 168, 180, 197
5, 3   183
6, 1   180, 183, 188
9, 1   167, 181, 188
11   167
13, 2   167, 181, 188
14, 1   188, 189

Prudent
c Symm
1, 215-44   36
1, 629ff   125
1, 197-214   41

Sib Or
3, 765-6   194

Tertull
Ad ux
2, 5   187, 191
Apol
15, 1-3   37
De exhort cast
13   47

De idol
16   198
De monog
17   87

3) LEGAL TEXTS

Cic
Leg
2, 21, 52   43
3, 19   10

Dig
23, 2, 44   26
25, 4, 1   14
32, 49, 4   26
35, 2, 9, 1   14
48, 19, 38, 5   14

FIRA
Vol.2, XV   12
Vol.2, 321   12
Vol.3, 19   11, 12

Gai
Instit
1, 55   10

Paul
Sent
5, 23, 15   191

XII Tabl
4   10
4, 3   25
10, 1   64
10, 4   47

4) INSCRIPTIONS

CIL
2, 1743   24
3, 651   65
3, 664   132
3, 686, B1233   105
3, 6113   37
6, 1527   18, 30, 39, 160
6, 9846   24

6, 9848	24	
6, 10 230	39	
6, 37 965, 8-31	27	
8, 12 881	30	
8, 22 770	46	
9, 3429, 7-11	42, 51	
10, 1951	30	
11, 6426	126	
14, 2804	51	

Kaibel
314   13

IG
2 (2), 7873   20
10, 2, 1, 539   91
12, 8, 356   98
12 Suppl 14, 3   101

ILLRP
973   25

ILS
1259, 13-37   50, 52
5213   19

IPE
519   53

Pleket
8, 22-31   51
20   24

5) PAPYRI

POxy
1380, 164f   146
1380, 190-220   121
1380, 214-1   121

Pap Ani   150

Pap Nebseni   150

GMP
4, 1390-1495   80
4, 2708-84   53, 80

6) ARETALOGIES

Cyme
10   120
12-14   147
17-20   120
27   120
30   120
41   141
55-56   118, 147

Maroneia   120

Thess   120

7) BIBLICAL TEXTS

OLD TESTAMENT

Ex
15: 1   162f
15: 20   162f

NEW TESTAMENT
(Selected passages)

Mk
1: 9   177

Lk
1: 1-4   155
1: 13   160
1: 24   162
1: 25   160
1: 35   160, 162, 166
1: 38   160
1: 41   162
1: 42   162, 166
1: 44   162
1: 46-55 162
1: 48   160
1: 53   160
1: 58   161, 199
2: 7   160, 162
2: 19   183, 187, 166
2: 35   163
2: 38   162, 166

2: 48	163
3: 19	158
4: 38	160
5: 36	161
7: 12	159
7: 13-14	163
7: 36-50	182
7: 37	159
7: 39	159
7: 47	160
8: 2	160, 156, 159
8: 3	156
8: 19-21	163
8: 43	160
10: 38-42	166
10: 39-42	187
10: 41-42	183
11: 2-4	187
11: 27-28	161, 163
12: 52-53	159, 196
13: 11	160
13: 16	158
13: 21	161
14: 26	159
15: 9	161, 199
16: 18	159
17: 36	161
18: 2-5	159
18: 16	162
18: 29-30	159
20: 36	163
20: 46-47	159
21: 2-4	159
21: 16	159
22: 56	159
23: 11	163
23: 27	161
23: 29	160
23: 55-56	161
24: 1	163
24: 5-7	163
24: 22-23	163
24: 11	169
24: 12	169
24: 51	163

Acts
1: 1	155
1: 8	157
1: 14	156, 164, 185, 188
2: 1	164
2: 3	164
2: 13	164
2: 17	164
2: 18	164
2: 39	164
2: 41-42	177
2: 42	168, 185, 182
2: 44	164
2: 44-46	164-165
3: 2-7	191
4: 32	165
5: 1	158
5: 1-10	166
5: 4-5	191
5: 9-10	191
5: 11	166
5: 14	155
5: 15	164
5: 42	168
6: 1	159, 160, 181
6: 3	168
7: 2	155
7: 21	158, 160, 162, 166
8: 3	167, 181
8: 12	155
8: 26-39	177
8: 27	158
8: 28-30	35
9: 2	167, 181
9: 36	159, 188
9: 37	159
9: 39	159, 181, 188
9: 40	164
12: 12	168, 188
12: 13	159
12: 15	168
12: 16	168
13: 6-12	191
13: 50	172
14: 15	198
14: 22	197
15: 29	167
16: 9-12	170
16: 11-40	5, 7, 135, 169-72
16: 13	73
16: 13-15	201

16: 14	158, 159, 171, 172	8: 6	193
		8: 8-9	198
16: 15, 40	138, 168, 171, 172, 188, 189	10: 14	193, 198
		11: 5	185
16: 16	158, 159, 168, 169	11: 20	185
		12: 2	198
16: 16-18	137	12: 10	185
16: 17	170	14: 1	185
16: 18	160, 170, 172, 191	14: 23	189
		16: 19	168, 187, 202
16: 19	169	16: 20	185
16: 23-39	196		
16: 24	169	2 Cor	
16: 25	170	5: 10	150
16: 26	172	6: 16	198
16: 31	170	8: 1-4	194
16: 33	178		
16: 39	170	Gal	
17: 4	155, 158	3: 28	152, 159, 179, 184, 189, 197
17: 5-7	192		
17: 7	165		
17: 22	155	Phil	
18: 3	158, 159, 168	1: 1	136, 137, 138, 139, 178, 181
18: 26	168, 186		
19: 12	164	1: 3	139
19: 23-40	192	1: 5	139, 197
19: 27	161	1: 6	150, 178, 198
19: 35	161	1: 7	139
24: 24	158	1: 8	139
25: 23	158	1: 10	150, 151
27: 24	157	1: 13	139, 140
27-28: 13	158	1: 19	145
28: 28	157	1: 20	145
		1: 21	149
Rom		1: 23	149
15: 25	181	1: 27-30	140-1
16: 5	185	1: 28	149
16: 23	185	2: 1	139
		2: 2	166
1 Cor		2: 2-5	138
1: 11	202	2: 5	142, 166, 196
6: 16-18	181	2: 6-11	142-8
7: 10	195	2: 13	144
7: 13	146, 196	2: 15	139, 154
7: 14	146, 193	2: 15-16	150
7: 15	146, 182, 196	2: 17	145
7: 16	146, 196, 198	2: 25	137
7: 25-26	181	3: 1	139
7: 39-40	196-201	3: 2	135, 136
8: 5-6	198	3: 2ff	150

259

3: 8	142	2 Tim	
3: 9	145	3: 15	185
3: 10-11	149		
3: 13-14	149	Tit	
3: 15	139	2: 3-5	199
3: 17	142, 144		
3: 18	140, 172	Philm	
3: 19	135, 140	1: 2	185
3: 20	139		
3: 20-21	149-152		
4: 2	137, 138, 141, 178, 202		
4: 3	139, 151		
4: 4	145, 167, 199		
4: 5	149 178, 197		
4: 6	145, 187		
4: 11-13	145		
4: 14-15	194		
4: 14-16	138		
4: 15	172		
4: 15-16	138		
4: 18	137		
4: 19	139		
4: 20	139		
4: 21-22	139		
4: 22	139, 140		

Col
1: 15-20	184
3: 10-11	184
3: 13	186
3: 16	185
3: 18	189
3: 18-4: 1	175
3: 18-4: 5	184
3: 20	184
3: 22	184
4: 15	185
4: 16	185

1 Thess
2: 2	135, 178

1 Tim
3: 15	184
4: 13	187
5: 9-10	180
5: 10	188
5: 16	180, 188